Hands-On GUI Application Development in Go

Build responsive, cross-platform, graphical applications with the Go programming language

Andrew Williams

Packt>

BIRMINGHAM - MUMBAI

Hands-On GUI Application Development in Go

Copyright © 2019 Packt Publishing

All rights reserved. No part of this book may be reproduced, stored in a retrieval system, or transmitted in any form or by any means, without the prior written permission of the publisher, except in the case of brief quotations embedded in critical articles or reviews.

Every effort has been made in the preparation of this book to ensure the accuracy of the information presented. However, the information contained in this book is sold without warranty, either express or implied. Neither the author, nor Packt Publishing or its dealers and distributors, will be held liable for any damages caused or alleged to have been caused directly or indirectly by this book.

Packt Publishing has endeavored to provide trademark information about all of the companies and products mentioned in this book by the appropriate use of capitals. However, Packt Publishing cannot guarantee the accuracy of this information.

Commissioning Editor: Aaron Lazar
Acquisition Editor: Shahnish Khan
Content Development Editor: Anugraha Arunagiri
Technical Editor: Divya Vadhyar
Copy Editor: Safis Editing
Project Coordinator: Ulhas Kambali
Proofreader: Safis Editing
Indexer: Rekha Nair
Graphics: Tom Scaria
Production Coordinator: Pratik Shirodkar

First published: February 2019

Production reference: 1220219

Published by Packt Publishing Ltd.
Livery Place
35 Livery Street
Birmingham
B3 2PB, UK.

ISBN 978-1-78913-841-2

www.packtpub.com

Mapt

`mapt.io`

Mapt is an online digital library that gives you full access to over 5,000 books and videos, as well as industry leading tools to help you plan your personal development and advance your career. For more information, please visit our website.

Why subscribe?

- Spend less time learning and more time coding with practical eBooks and Videos from over 4,000 industry professionals

- Improve your learning with Skill Plans built especially for you

- Get a free eBook or video every month

- Mapt is fully searchable

- Copy and paste, print, and bookmark content

Packt.com

Did you know that Packt offers eBook versions of every book published, with PDF and ePub files available? You can upgrade to the eBook version at `www.packt.com` and as a print book customer, you are entitled to a discount on the eBook copy. Get in touch with us at `customercare@packtpub.com` for more details.

At `www.packt.com`, you can also read a collection of free technical articles, sign up for a range of free newsletters, and receive exclusive discounts and offers on Packt books and eBooks.

Contributors

About the author

Andrew Williams has over 15 years of commercial software development experience across a variety of programming languages, including Java, C, Objective-C, and Go. He has been a core developer in large open source projects such as Enlightenment, EFL, and Maven, as well as maintaining various community websites and tutorials. Since 2007, Andrew has been working as CTO with many early-stage and growing software start-ups. After 6 years spent expanding an award-winning mobile app development company, he is now applying the lessons he has learned to cross-platform desktop applications using Go. Andrew is passionate about building tools and services that make software development simpler and improve productivity, as well as making it easier to become a great software engineer.

> *I extend my eternal thanks to my wife, Michelle, for believing in me and encouraging me to write this book. My thanks also go to my friends and family for always providing support and inspiration. Thanks to my great reviewer, Al, for the care and time he devoted to polishing this book. Thanks also to the tech community in Edinburgh for championing learning and innovation. Lastly, this book would not have been possible without the supportive team at Packt.*

About the reviewer

Alastair Roy Poole is a programmer and writer from Aberdeen, Scotland. He has a passion for writing low-level implementations of popular technologies, as well as creating simple solutions to complicated problems.

He has been working with free and open source software since the mid-1990s, and many of his projects have been distributed worldwide as an author of both applications and libraries. He specializes in C, Perl, and, increasingly, in Go (among other technologies).

Alastair has a strong aversion to reliance on cloud-based technologies and severe reservations about the corporate-led direction of most open source technologies today. He has great admiration for projects with strong leadership, especially the OpenBSD project.

> *I would like to thank my family for their continued support throughout my life. Most specifically, I must mention my partner-in-crime, Anastasija, for pushing me and keeping me motivated in my work and making me happy too.*

Packt is searching for authors like you

If you're interested in becoming an author for Packt, please visit `authors.packtpub.com` and apply today. We have worked with thousands of developers and tech professionals, just like you, to help them share their insight with the global tech community. You can make a general application, apply for a specific hot topic that we are recruiting an author for, or submit your own idea.

Table of Contents

Preface	1

Section 1: Section 1: Graphical User Interface Development

Chapter 1: The Benefits of Native Graphical Applications	11
Return of the graphical application	11
Personal computers	13
From desktop to internet	15
Smart phones, apps, and customer retention	17
Native performance	18
Integrated user experience	19
Reliability and offline functionality	19
Maintainability and testing	20
Summary	21
Chapter 2: Graphical User Interface Challenges	23
Standard look and feel or app theme	23
GUIs and visual hierarchy	28
Multiple documents	28
Accessory windows	30
Visual hierarchy	32
Mobile standards	34
Concurrency and multi-threading	36
Switching threads	36
Avoiding complexity	37
Web services and cloud integration	38
Communications	39
Data parsing	40
Standard components	40
Developing for multiple platforms	41
Cross-platform APIs	41
Icons and design	42
Testing	43
Packaging and distribution	44
Summary	45
Chapter 3: Go to the Rescue!	47
Introduction	48
Cross-platform for any application	51
Cross-compiling	53

Table of Contents

Standard library	55
Concurrency in language design	**55**
Goroutines	56
Channels	57
The sync package	62
Web services included as standard	**64**
Choosing your look and feel	**67**
Summary	**68**

Section 2: Section 2: Toolkits Using Existing Widgets

Chapter 4: Walk - Building Graphical Windows Applications	**71**
Background and aims	**71**
Get started with walk	**72**
Setup	72
Code	73
Build	74
Run	75
Benefits of a declarative API	**76**
Compared with the native API	76
Using both APIs for flexibility	78
Building a user interface	**80**
Style	81
Layout	82
Toolbar and menu	86
Communicating with the GUI	89
View model	90
Detail view	91
List view	92
Background processing	93
Walk in a cross-platform application	**95**
Summary	**97**
Chapter 5: andlabs UI - Cross-platform Native UIs	**99**
Background and history	**99**
Getting started with andlabs UI	**100**
Prerequisites	100
Microsoft windows	101
macOS	101
Linux	101
Setup	102
Rebuilding the UI library (workaround)	102
Code	103
Build	105
Run	106
Generic API for multiple platforms	**106**

[ii]

Controls	107
Box	107
Containers	108
Widgets	109
Menu	110
Area and drawing	111
Building a user interface	114
Style	114
Layout	116
Main email window	117
Email compose dialog	119
Toolbar and menu	122
Communicating with the GUI	124
Background processing	129
Example	129
Challenges with multiple native GUIs	130
Consistent style	130
Brand styles	130
User experience	131
Testing	133
Cross-compilation	133
Building for Linux on macOS or windows	135
macOS	135
Windows	136
Building for windows on Linux or macOS	136
Building for macOS on Linux or Windows	137
A better solution	137
Summary	138
Chapter 6: Go-GTK - Multiple Platforms with GTK	139
GTK+ background	140
Getting started with Go-GTK	141
Prerequisites	141
Installing GTK+	142
macOS	142
Windows	142
Linux	142
Install Go-GTK	142
Build	143
Run	144
Signals and namespaces	145
Signals	145
Passing data	146
Namespaces	147
Sample application	148
Layout	149
Compose layout	152
Signaling	154

[iii]

Table of Contents

Thread handling	155
Cross compilation	156
Theming	156
Summary	161
Chapter 7: Go-Qt - Multiple Platforms with Qt	163
Qt background	164
Getting started with therecipe/qt	165
Prerequisites	166
Preparing CGo	166
Installing Qt	166
macOS	166
Windows	167
Linux	167
License / Qt account	167
Installing qt (the bindings)	168
Build	169
Run	170
Object model and event handling	171
Inheritance	171
Memory management	171
Signals and slots	172
Sample application	173
Layout	173
The compose layout	176
Signalling	178
Thread handling	179
Cross-compilation	180
Theming	180
Summary	181

Section 3: Section 3: Modern Graphical Toolkits

Chapter 8: Shiny - Experimental Go GUI API	185
Background and the vision for Shiny	186
Design and supported platforms	186
Architecture	186
Lower layer	187
Higher layer	188
Supported platforms	188
Drivers currently included	189
Getting started with Shiny	189
Setup	190
Example	190
Cross-compiling	192
Cross-compiling for macOS	193
Widgets and material design	194

Table of Contents

Design	194
Icons	196
Themes	197
Widgets	198
Getting started continued	199
Code	199
Supporting code	200
Build and Run	202
Building a user interface	203
Design	204
Layout	205
Navigation	208
File list	209
Image view	212
Communicating with the GUI	215
Background processing	219
Summary	223
Chapter 9: nk - Nuklear for Go	225
Background and design of Nuklear	225
Rendering and platform support	227
Rendering modules	227
Supported platforms	228
Getting started with nk	228
Prerequisites	228
Linux	229
macOS and Windows	229
Android	230
Setup	231
Example	232
Code	233
Build and run	236
Cross-compiling	237
Widgets, layout, and skinning	238
Widgets	238
Layout	240
NkLayoutRow	240
NkLayoutRowTemplate	241
NkLayoutSpace	241
Drawing	242
Command queue	242
Draw functions	242
Skinning	243
Layout	245
Main email window	246
Email compose dialog	248

[v]

Table of Contents

    Toolbar and menu — 250
    Communicating with the GUI — 252
    Background processing — 255
  Summary — 255

Chapter 10: Fyne - Material Design-Based GUI — 257
  Background and vision for Fyne — 257
  Getting started with Fyne — 258
    Prerequisites — 258
      Linux — 258
      macOS — 259
    Setup — 259
    Example — 260
    Code — 261
    Build and run — 262
    Cross compiling — 262
  Rendering and vector graphics — 263
    Vector graphics — 263
    Drivers — 265
    Supported platforms — 266
  Canvas, widgets, and layouts — 267
    Canvas (drawing) — 267
    Layout — 268
    Widgets — 269
    Themes — 270
      Packaged themes — 271
  Building a user interface — 272
    Layout — 272
      Main email window — 272
      Compose dialog — 275
    Toolbar and menu — 277
    Communicating with the GUI — 279
      Loading emails — 279
      Sending email — 280
    Background processing — 281
  Building an image viewer — 282
    Layout — 282
    Navigation — 285
    File listing — 286
    Image view — 287
    Communicating with the GUI — 289
    Background processing — 293
  Summary — 296

Table of Contents

Section 4: Section 4: Growing and Distributing Your Application

Chapter 11: Navigation and Multiple Windows — 299
Planning application layout — 300
Standard layouts — 300
Device form factors — 303
Responsive or adaptive design — 303
Custom layouts — 305
Navigating your application — 306
Progressive disclosure — 307
Example 1 – Microsoft Edge — 307
Example 2 – Skyscanner flight search — 308
Menus and toolbars — 309
Toolbar — 309
Menu — 310
Multiple windows — 312
Window types and keeping things clean — 312
Standard dialogs — 313
Modal windows — 314
Window hints — 314
Sizes — 315
Other hints — 315
Notifications and task status — 316
Minor alerts — 316
Background progress — 317
Platform-specific considerations — 318
Window grouping — 319
Application instances — 319
Extra features — 321
Summary — 322

Chapter 12: Concurrency, Networking, and Cloud Services — 323
Concurrency, threads, and GUI updates — 323
Managing long-running processes — 324
Signaling shutdown — 324
Checking completion — 326
Communicating through channels — 328
Graphical updates from goroutines — 330
Network resources and caching — 333
Loading remote resources — 333
Images — 333
JSON — 335
Caching resource data — 336
Connecting to cloud services — 338
Encoding — 338

[vii]

JSON	339
XML	340
Authentication – OAuth 2.0	342
First request	342
Storing tokens	344
Posting data	347
GUI integration	349
Incoming messages	349
Activity notifications	349
Spinner	350
Status panel	350
Consistent user experience when offline	**351**
Caching responses	351
Queuing actions	352
Starting offline	353
Summary	**354**
Chapter 13: Best Practices in Go GUI Development	**355**
Separation of concerns	**356**
Suggested application structure	356
Test-driving UI development	**358**
Designed to be testable	358
Example application test	359
Continuous integration for GUIs	**361**
Approaches to GUI test automation	361
Avoiding external dependencies	362
Managing platform specifics	**364**
Summary	**366**
Chapter 14: Distributing Your Application	**369**
Metadata and icons	**370**
Application icon	370
Describing your app	371
Bundling assets	**371**
go-bindata	371
packr	372
rsrc	374
fyne bundle	374
Building a release	**375**
Preparing	376
Compiler installation	376
Building	377
Packaging	378
Linux	379
Create metadata files	379
Packaging release	380
macOS	382

Table of Contents

Creating metadata files	382
Packaging release	383
Windows	384
Creating metadata files	385
Packaging release	385
Cross-platform packaging tools	387
fyne package	387
Distributing to platform marketplaces	**389**
Mac App Store	389
Packaging	389
Uploading	390
Reviewing	390
Microsoft Store	391
Packaging	391
Uploading	392
Reviewing	392
Linux package manager	392
Debian (.deb)	393
Packaging	393
Distribution	394
Red Hat (.rpm)	394
Packaging	394
Distribution	395
Tarball (.tar.gz)	395
Arch Linux	395
Gentoo Linux	396
Others	396
Containers	396
Summary	**397**
Appendix A: Installation Details	**399**
Installing Go	**399**
Microsoft Windows	399
Git	399
Go	400
Environment	401
Apple macOS	401
Linux	402
Setting up Cgo	**402**
Microsoft Windows	402
Apple macOS	404
Linux	404
Appendix B: Cross Compiler Setup	**405**
Cross compiling for macOS with CGo	**405**
To macOS from Linux or Windows	405
Cross compiling for Windows with CGo	**406**
To Windows from macOS	407
To Windows from Linux	407

Cross compiling for Linux with CGo — 407
- To Linux from macOS — 408
- To Linux from Windows — 408

Appendix C: Comparison of GUI Toolkits — 409

Appendix D: Connecting GoMail to a Real Email Server — 413
Download Gmail credentials — 413
Creating a server provider — 414
- Downloading inbox messages — 414
- Sending messages — 417
- Listening for new messages — 417
Updating an example to use Gmail — 419

Other Books You May Enjoy — 421

Index — 425

Preface

Since the 1.0 release of the Go programming language in 2012, developers have enjoyed the increased productivity brought by the easy-to-read, quick-to-learn, cross-platform design of Go. Web apps and system utilities around the world are being built with Go to rapidly deliver reliable performance. Learning the language is easy, due to its centralized documentation and great programming environment support. Creating **Graphical User Interfaces** (**GUIs**) with Go, however, is still very new and there is not yet a standardized UI toolkit.

This definitive guide to programming GUIs with Go explores the most popular GUI packages available. It compares the vision behind each toolkit to help you pick the right approach for your project. Each toolkit is described in detail, outlining how to build beautiful, performant applications that users will love. Code samples and screenshots will aid any level of Go developer to create applications using these emerging technologies.

Who this book is for

This book is written for Go developers who are interested in building native graphical applications for desktop computers and beyond. Some knowledge of building Go applications (command line based or web apps) is assumed, but not essential. The first section of this book looks at the history of the GUI, its importance to the evolution of modern personal computers, and how it can pose additional challenges to software developers.

Developers of GUI applications that are interested in trying Go may also find this book useful. `Section 2`, *Toolkits Using Existing Widgets* and `Section 3`, *Modern Graphical Toolkits*, explore the various frameworks available to the Go language and demonstrate how applications can be rapidly developed from basic principles.

Additionally, an experienced Go developer may find the final section useful. The chapters of `section 4`, *Growing and Distributing Your Application* covers how to design and build complex graphical interfaces that fit user expectations. It looks at the different approaches possible to support multiple operating system standards and how to integrate the GUI well with network resources and cloud services. The final chapters cover best practices in GUI applications with Go, and look at how to package and distribute your software through the various distribution channels available.

Preface

What this book covers

Section 1: *Graphical User Interface Development*

Chapter 1, *The Benefits of Native Graphical Applications*, contains a re-introduction to the GUI and its role in the modern software ecosystem. It discusses the benefits of coding a native GUI for a responsive user experience and platform integration. By the end of the chapter, you will be comfortable deciding which of your projects would benefit from a native graphical interface.

Chapter 2, *Graphical User Interface Challenges*, shows how GUIs present various challenges to the designer and developer beyond that of a web app or systems application. This chapter will explore the details of the most common challenges, including look and feel, performance, platform integration, and distribution. On completion of this chapter, you will be familiar with the additional complications of building a graphical desktop application, and know what to consider when designing a GUI.

Chapter 3, *Go to the Rescue!*, shows how the design of the Go language is well suited to solving the challenges described in the previous chapter. It will demonstrate how the Go language, despite not having a standard user interface API, has all the required constructs to ease development of graphical applications. At the end of this chapter, you will be ready to progress to the detailed toolkit API descriptions that follow in Section 2, *Toolkits Using Existing GUIs*.

Section 2: *Toolkits Using Existing GUIs*

Chapter 4, *Walk - Building Graphical Windows Applications*, discusses Walk, which is a *Windows Application Library Kit* for the Go programming language. This chapter covers API design, common usage patterns, and how to use the library as part of a multi-platform strategy. You will learn how to build a simple Windows application using the Walk toolkit through examples and illustrations.

Chapter 5, *andlabs UI – Cross-Platform Native UIs*, explores Andlabs UI, which is a popular GUI toolkit that uses the existing graphical technologies on each of the platforms it supports. This chapter discusses the benefits of such an approach and shows how the API is designed. You will learn how to build a simple application using the andlabs UI toolkit through examples and illustrations.

Chapter 6, *Go-GTK – Multiple Platforms with GTK*, here, Go-GTK examines the Go language bindings for GTK+, a multi-platform toolkit for creating GUIs. GTK+ supports many platforms and comes preinstalled on many environments. In this chapter, we look at the details of the GTK+ toolkit, the platforms it supports, and how to make use of it in your application. You will learn how to build a simple application using the Go-GTK API through examples and illustrations.

Chapter 7, *Go-Qt – Multiple Platforms with QT*, explains that Go-Qt allows you to write Qt-based graphical applications in Go. Qt is a cross-platform application framework that is used for developing applications that can be run on various software and hardware platforms. In this chapter, we look at the details of the Qt framework, the platforms it supports, and how to make use of it in your application. You will learn how to build a simple application using the Go-Qt API through examples and illustrations.

Section 3: *Modern Graphical Toolkits*

Chapter 8, *Shiny – Go's Experimental API*, looks at the Shiny project, an experimental GUI library written in pure Go, and is designed to create portable apps that have a consistent look across multiple platforms. This chapter explores how to write portable cross-platform applications with Shiny. You will learn how to build a simple cross-platform graphical application using the Shiny APIs through examples and illustrations.

Chapter 9, *nk – Nuklear for Go*, explains that Nuklear is a lightweight widget library that focuses purely on the graphical interface (rather than window management and platform integration) to create an easy-to-use API. The graphical interface, originally designed for embedded applications, renders identically across all supported platforms. Its implementation has no dependencies and achieves this by avoiding a standard render context and operating system drivers. You will learn how to set up a render context and use this toolkit to create an example application.

Chapter 10, *Fyne – Material Design-Based GUI*, explores the Fyne project, designed to be an easy to use UI toolkit and app API written in Go that follows the Material Design principles. It uses OpenGL backend to provide cross-platform graphics that look identical on any supported platform. This chapter explores how to write beautiful applications for multiple platforms with Fyne. You will learn how to build a simple multi-platform graphical application using the Fyne toolkit through examples and illustrations.

Preface

Section 4: *Growing and Distributing your Application*

Chapter 11, *Navigation and Multiple Windows*, covers the workflows and growing complexity of expanding a graphical application. As well as planning and presenting a clear navigation and workflow, it also covers how to manage multiple windows, dialogs, and application instances. It also explores the differences between how desktop operating systems consider application life cycles, and how this may impact your application design. After completing this chapter, you will be confident in how to adapt your application design as you expand its functionality.

Chapter 12, *Concurrency, Networking, and Cloud Services*, explains how more advanced aspects of large application programming fit within a graphical Go application. We cover concurrency and networking, looking at how to work with goroutines and long-running threads, remote resources, and how to handle the user impact of unreliable network conditions. Additionally, you will learn how to connect with and utilize cloud services to provide a rich user experience, both online and offline.

Chapter 13, *Best Practices in Go GUI Development*, illustrates that the Go language comes with a well-understood set of best practices, covering features such as style, documentation, and code structure. In this chapter, you will learn how to apply these to the development of graphical applications, and which additional practices are recommended. You will learn how the toolkits described in the previous chapters agree on topics such as binary packaging and managing platform specific code.

Chapter 14, *Distributing your Application*, shows how distribution of applications for multiple platforms is a challenge, but it's important that your users have a seamless experience. In this final chapter, you will learn how to package your application and its assets for consistent distribution across the operating systems you target. We will explore the various options for app-store or marketplace deployment, along with how to deliver direct downloads. At the end of this chapter, you should have the knowledge to design, build, and distribute your graphical application using the Go language.

To get the most out of this book

A basic knowledge of the Go language is assumed throughout this book. If you are not yet familiar with its basic concepts, consider running through the online tutorial before you begin reading (`tour.golang.org`).

Preface

To benefit the most from later chapters, it would be ideal if you have in mind a particular application you are working on or would like to build. Applying the frameworks and tools used in this book to a particular project will aid your understanding of the various concepts. Additionally, this will deliver the benefit of you completing your project and preparing it for distribution.

Download the example code files

You can download the example code files for this book from your account at `www.packt.com`. If you purchased this book elsewhere, you can visit `www.packt.com/support` and register to have the files emailed directly to you.

You can download the code files by following these steps:

1. Log in or register at `www.packt.com`.
2. Select the **SUPPORT** tab.
3. Click on **Code Downloads & Errata**.
4. Enter the name of the book in the **Search** box and follow the onscreen instructions.

Once the file is downloaded, please make sure that you unzip or extract the folder using the latest version of:

- WinRAR/7-Zip for Windows
- Zipeg/iZip/UnRarX for Mac
- 7-Zip/PeaZip for Linux

The code bundle for the book is also hosted on GitHub at `https://github.com/PacktPublishing/Hands-On-GUI-Application-Development-in-Go/`. In case there's an update to the code, it will be updated on the existing GitHub repository.

We also have other code bundles from our rich catalog of books and videos available at `https://github.com/PacktPublishing/`. Check them out!

Conventions used

There are a number of text conventions used throughout this book.

Preface

`CodeInText`: Indicates code words in text, database table names, folder names, filenames, file extensions, pathnames, dummy URLs, user input, and Twitter handles. Here is an example: "Mount the downloaded `WebStorm-10*.dmg` disk image file as another disk in your system."

A block of code is set as follows:

```
html, body, #map {
  height: 100%;
  margin: 0;
  padding: 0
}
```

When we wish to draw your attention to a particular part of a code block, the relevant lines or items are set in bold:

```
[default]
exten => s,1,Dial(Zap/1|30)
exten => s,2,Voicemail(u100)
exten => s,102,Voicemail(b100)
exten => i,1,Voicemail(s0)
```

Any command-line input or output is written as follows:

```
$ mkdir css
$ cd css
```

Bold: Indicates a new term, an important word, or words that you see onscreen. For example, words in menus or dialog boxes appear in the text like this. Here is an example: "Select **System info** from the **Administration** panel."

> Warnings or important notes appear like this.

> Tips and tricks appear like this.

Get in touch

Feedback from our readers is always welcome.

General feedback: If you have questions about any aspect of this book, mention the book title in the subject of your message and email us at `customercare@packtpub.com`.

Errata: Although we have taken every care to ensure the accuracy of our content, mistakes do happen. If you have found a mistake in this book, we would be grateful if you would report this to us. Please visit `www.packt.com/submit-errata`, selecting your book, clicking on the Errata Submission Form link, and entering the details.

Piracy: If you come across any illegal copies of our works in any form on the Internet, we would be grateful if you would provide us with the location address or website name. Please contact us at `copyright@packt.com` with a link to the material.

If you are interested in becoming an author: If there is a topic that you have expertise in and you are interested in either writing or contributing to a book, please visit `authors.packtpub.com`.

Reviews

Please leave a review. Once you have read and used this book, why not leave a review on the site that you purchased it from? Potential readers can then see and use your unbiased opinion to make purchase decisions, we at Packt can understand what you think about our products, and our authors can see your feedback on their book. Thank you!

For more information about Packt, please visit `packt.com`.

Section 1: Graphical User Interface Development

For many years, **graphical user interfaces (GUIs)** have been the standard way for the average computer user to engage with a software product. They provide an intuitive user experience for potentially complex workflows within the familiar context of a desktop environment. Having evolved over more than 40 years, the traditional graphical application is being challenged by the ubiquity of web-based software and the emergence of mobile applications on modern smartphones and handheld computers. Despite these new trends, there are still many reasons why building a native graphical application for desktop (and laptop) computers could be the right strategy for your product.

In this introductory section, we will look at the history of the desktop GUI and how it has developed alongside technological innovation. We will discuss why, despite new alternative approaches, native graphical applications are still a great way to provide an intuitive user experience and a reliable software product. Building anything of quality takes effort, and software is no exception. We will explore the challenges that teams are likely to face when designing and building a native graphical application that aims to support multiple operating systems. Having reviewed the importance of the GUI and the challenges it can pose, we examine the Go programming language and demonstrate that its design fits very well with the creation of modern native graphical applications for multiple platforms.

The following chapters will be covered in this section:

- `Chapter 1`, *The Benefits of Native Graphical Applications*
- `Chapter 2`, *Graphical User Interface Challenges*
- `Chapter 3`, *Go to the Rescue!*

The Benefits of Native Graphical Applications

Since they first appeared in the 1970s, it has been clear that graphical interfaces make it easier to work with software applications. In the early days, they were typically presented through **Windows, Icons, Menus and Pointer** (**WIMP**) interfaces. While these varied in design across platforms and over time, the interactions have been relatively consistent.

Recent changes in software development have increased the understanding of user experience, which focuses on creating applications that are intuitive for even the least experienced computer user. This, combined with the mobile-driven move towards a post-WIMP approach to computer interaction, prompts the question: what's next for desktop computer software?

This chapter will cover the following topics:

- The history of **Graphical User Interfaces** (**GUIs**) through desktop, web, and mobile
- The importance of a well-integrated and responsive application interface
- User expectations of both online and offline native applications
- The developer benefits of building native graphical applications

Return of the graphical application

"The best way to predict the future is to invent it."
- Alan Kay, PARC

The Benefits of Native Graphical Applications

It was 1973 and **Palo Alto Research Center (Xerox PARC)** had just completed the Alto computer, the first commercial example of a computer GUI. While the screen orientation and lack of colors make it a little peculiar to the modern eye, it's clearly recognizable as a graphical interface, with a mouse and keyboard for interaction. While it took another seven years to be generally available to the public, in 1981, as the Xerox Star, it was clear that this was the beginning of something big:

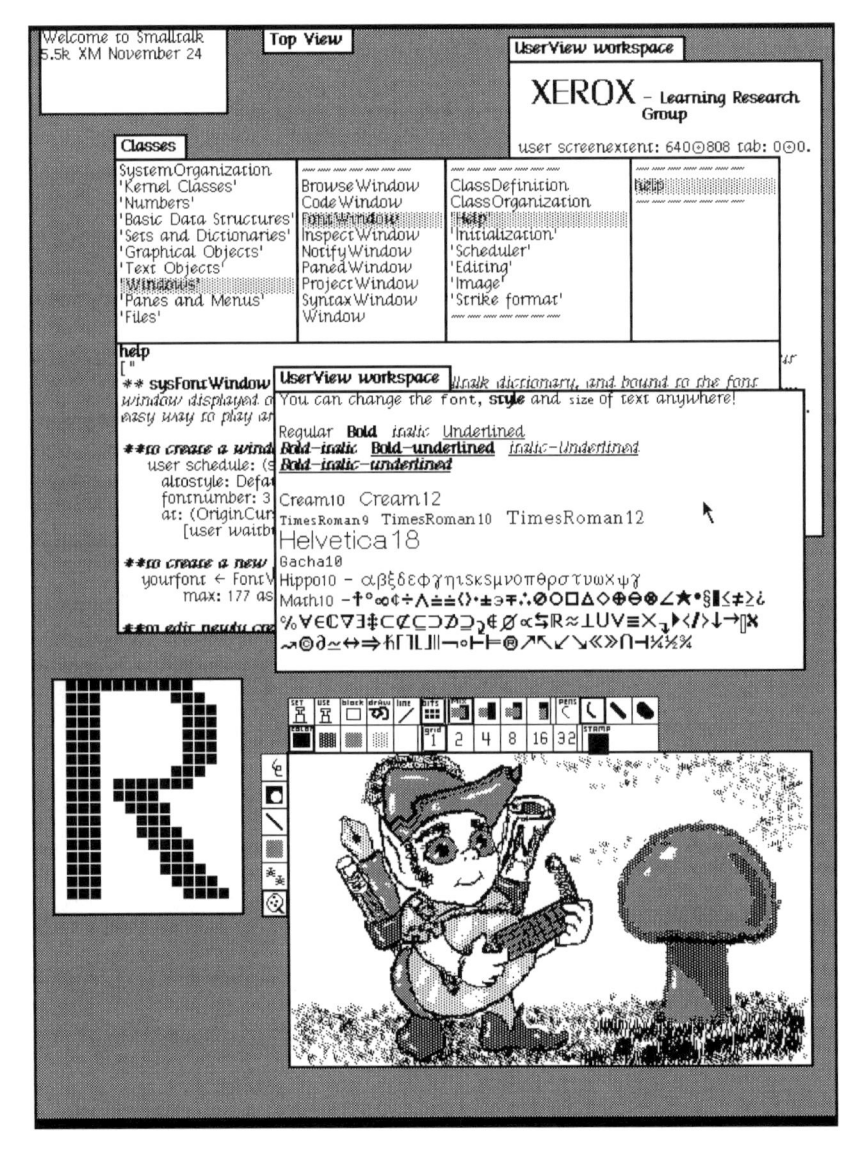

Dynabook environment desktop (1976: Smalltalk-76 running on Alto). Copyright SUMIM.ST, licensed CC BY-SA 4.0.

This was a huge leap forward for the usability of computers—a welcome change from the standard interaction of text-mode computer screens. Not only does a graphical interface allow for more advanced functionality, it's also much easier to learn for a novice looking to get started. While the command-line interface remains popular with programmers and other experts, it's fair to say that, without the GUI, personal computers wouldn't have reached the popularity we all know:

```
BBC Computer 32K
Acorn DFS
BASIC
>_
```

A traditional text mode (command-line) interface typical well into 1980's

Personal computers

Over the 10 years that followed the Xerox Star public release, many graphical platforms emerged, including Microsoft Windows, Apple Macintosh, X11 (started at MIT for UNIX computers), and DRI's GEM (primarily for Atari ST). Though the background of each of these is different, they shared a common ambition to provide a desktop environment that enabled a computer user to interact with multiple graphical applications at the same time.

The Benefits of Native Graphical Applications

This was one of the defining characteristics of the emerging **Personal Computer** (PC) market and it led to a whole new world of computer software:

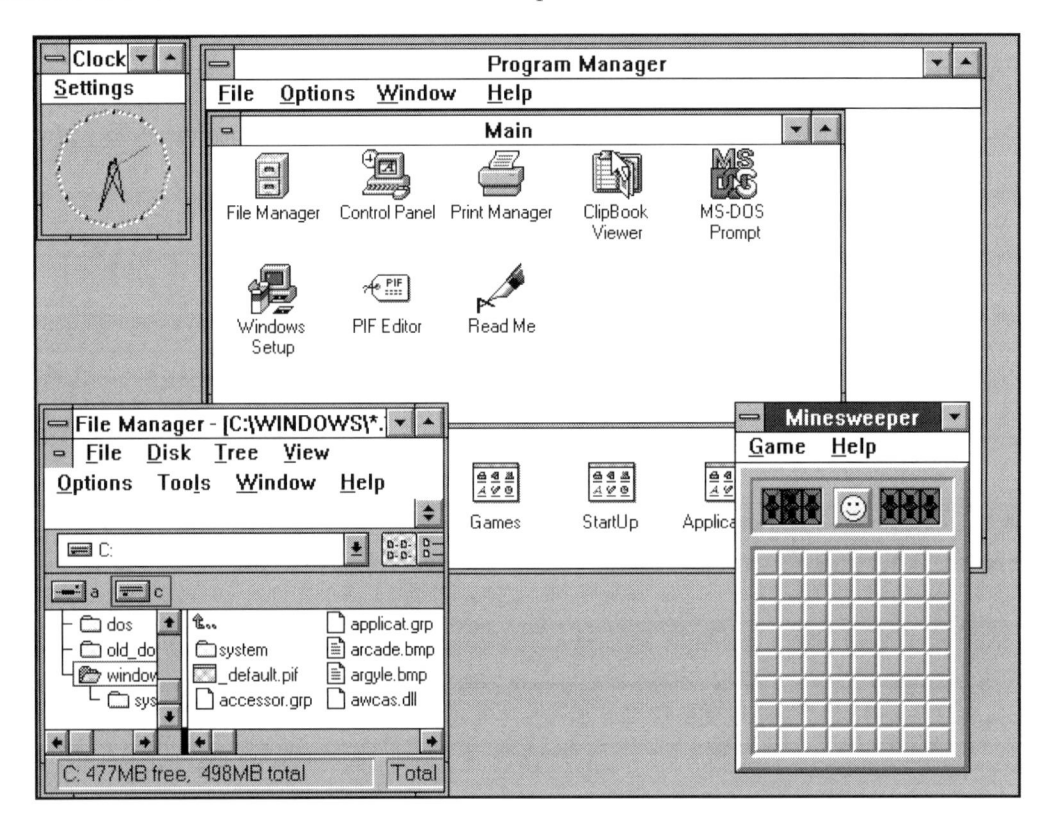

Microsoft Windows for Workgroups 3.11. Used with permission from Microsoft.

As PCs became more powerful, advancements in hardware supported more sophisticated software applications. Higher resolution screens allowed the display of more information and removable storage devices (such as floppy disks, CDs, and then USB sticks) enabled transferring larger datasets between applications. What used to commonly be simple interfaces with a few options became more sophisticated and more complicated.

[14]

The default graphical interface elements and layouts needed to be extended to keep up. Menus got larger, toolbars were introduced to highlight common tasks, and built-in help systems became necessary to help users achieve their tasks. We also see platforms start to take on their own identity, leading to additional hurdles when learning new software. It was common for an average off-the-shelf software product to come with an instruction manual longer than this book, explaining how to interact with its various features.

From desktop to internet

In the mid-1990s, the World Wide Web (which would come to be our global communications platform) was getting started and the PC market started to see various web browsers arrive. These were initially distributed as software packages (on floppy disks) and then later as part of the desktop environment (pre-installed on new computers). Mosaic, Netscape Navigator, and Internet Explorer arrived in quick succession to give early adopters access to the emerging information channel. In those days, it was largely academic texts and reference materials; you needed to know where to look to find things and, similarly to early computer use, it wasn't particularly intuitive.

What became clear, however, was that this new medium was starting to facilitate the future of communications and information exchange. People began to see that being the main technology within that space would be critical; and so began the *browser wars*. As web browsers vied for the top spot, the technology became embedded in the desktop platforms as a way to quickly deliver well-presented content. Initially, those bulky user manuals were moved to HTML (the language of web pages) and bundled with the software download, and then more functionality of each application moved online. As an internet connection became commonplace in most homes, we saw the rise of full web-based applications.

A web application is one that requires no software installation beyond the internet browser already on your computer. They always deliver up-to-date information direct from the source. This is usually customized based on your location, preferences, or even browsing history on the web application or those of partner companies. Additionally, a web application can be improved at any time by the company providing it; often, following experiments where the company sees which version of an application has a better user experience. The following illustration shows a possible architecture for an application delivered over the web.

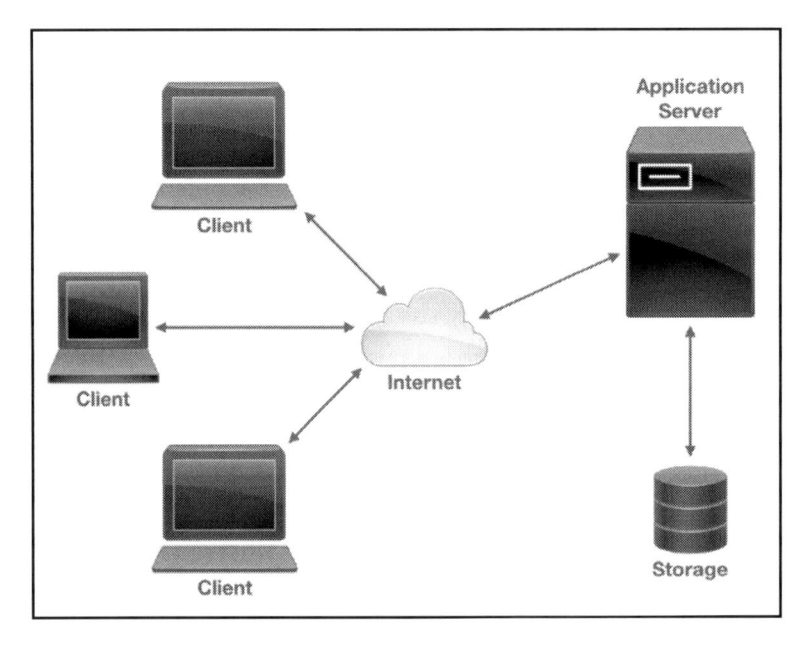

A simple web application architecture

As the technologies behind web-based applications developed, they became viable alternatives to desktop software. Software companies began to realize that it is a lot easier to deliver your product directly through a website rather than the traditional download model. Not only that, but it also meant that one product would work on almost any computer. Attempts in the past to make a write-once-run-anywhere platform (such as Python and Java) had great success at the time, but after the web technologies reached a certain level of complexity, it became clear that the performance penalties and distribution overheads required by the cross-platform interpreters made web applications far more attractive where possible.

Smart phones, apps, and customer retention

For a long while, it looked like websites were the future for delivering software products, which was until the entry of smart phones. Once mobile phone technology developed to the point that you could access websites in the palm of your hand, the requirements for web-based applications changed once again. Now, developers needed to consider how smaller screens could present meaningful content. How could a touchscreen-based user interface operate where a mouse and keyboard used to be assumed? And how could people engage in a meaningful way when they had only five minutes while waiting for their coffee order?

Delivering a single application, available through desktop browsers and mobile phones, across a plethora of different operating systems and devices, has clear advantages for developers, but there are also challenges. The internet is a very large place and your product can easily get lost in the noise; how do you attract new users and how do you ensure that your existing customers keep coming back? One major response to this was the introduction of *native apps* (applications designed and built for specific platforms) for mobile devices. The iPhone launched with web-based applications only, but within eight months, Apple delivered the capability for developers to build native applications. These applications provided a more meaningful engagement with users; they were designed for the device they ran on, they could be found easily through a marketplace or *app store*, and once installed, remained a constant reminder on the device's home screen.

And so we enter a time where our target audience has become accustomed to software designed specifically for their device. A polished user experience is a must-have if companies expect to engage and retain their customers. Waiting for pages to load or dealing with intermittent errors are niggles that users are no longer willing to put up with. This higher bar for software delivery is now a well understood phenomenon, but the improvement in quality for software delivered through mobile devices hasn't yet been reflected on the desktop. Until recently, the browser was still king; long lists of website bookmarks are used in place of expecting applications delivered through a store and installed onto the computer. This, however, is changing and we're going to explore how to deliver a quality user experience through beautiful desktop applications.

Native performance

"Users really respond to speed."
- Marissa Mayer, Google VP

One of the main reasons that businesses often opt for a website-based approach is to avoid having to build many products for the platforms they wish to support. We're seeing a similar approach to mobile application development: as more platforms enter the market, developing native apps becomes an overhead that many businesses can't afford. They opt for the web-based approach or *hybrid app,* where the user believes they're installing a native app that's really just a website packaged into a download. While this can be good enough for simple applications with basic data processing, it is often not going to meet user expectations. Additionally, the interaction paradigms for a web browser are usually different to that of the system applications around it. If the user expects an application to behave in a certain way, then an embedded web browser could prove to be a confusing experience.

The biggest challenge in delivering a large application through web technologies (through a browser or downloaded application) is achieving good performance. As a browser is designed primarily for information exchange, it isn't well suited to large data processing or complicated graphical representations. When delivered through a web browser, much of this can be performed by a remote server that has the capacity to run complex calculations and return the summary to the user. Unfortunately, when you're running a local application, this cannot be relied upon and users expect immediate results in their application (remember, this is not a browser window with lots of open tabs to browse while waiting). Additionally, recall one of the benefits of web-based delivery—the chance to update the software continually without distribution issues? While that may be great for development, it's possible that your customers don't want the interface to be changing all of the time; they want to be in control of when (and if) to update their systems.

In applications where there's a lot of computation to run or complicated graphics to display, most web apps will struggle to run as fast as a user expects. Native applications, which are compiled for the computer they're used on (and will have been downloaded in advance, so no waiting), are currently the best way to get high performance. There are various virtualization technologies that aim to provide near-native performance with a single application (for example, Java), but this is not always appropriate or sufficient, and often suffers side effects such as long start up times or huge downloads. As you've chosen to read this book, you'll probably already be aware of another approach: a language that allows you to write a single application but have it compile to a high performance native application for any platforms you wish to support.

Integrated user experience

A consistent user experience is of paramount importance if users are expected to pick up software and be able to use it quickly. When programmed to match system design and layout, as well as use standard components, it is easier for a new user to understand how the application will likely work without the need for one of those weighty user manuals. The graphical user interfaces for most popular operating systems have been very carefully designed so that applications written for them will feel *natural*. The user should inherently recognize the design language and know how to accomplish most of the main tasks right away. Carefully designed platforms such as macOS or Windows 10 provide a toolkit that ensures applications built using it will be immediately familiar to users. This includes peripheral items such as how you choose a file to open, what should happen if you copy and paste a complex file type, and how the application should respond if an item is dragged onto its window. Very few of these features are available to, or correctly utilized by, web-based or command-line applications.

An additional consideration for professional application producers would be assistive technologies. GUIs built using the platform standard toolkits work with provided (or complementary) accessibility enhancers such as screen readers or braille devices. Both web pages and text-based applications typically have to work much harder to support these technologies. Remember that each platform your web page or hybrid application will load on could have very different standard behaviors for assistive technologies. Building a graphical application using the tools of your target platform typically benefits your users, whether they use the interface you designed directly or through accessibility options.

Reliability and offline functionality

One benefit of great applications is their ability to work online and offline, even to deal with an internet connection that's unreliable. For example, blog applications that allow authoring but don't need the internet until you publish, or document editors that download all of your work and share any changes you make with a central location any time you're online, have significant benefits over any web app with an always-online approach. Desktop computers and even newer smart phones have significant processing power and storage, and as application developers, we should make the most of the resources available. User experience is not limited to design and system integration, but also the responsiveness and workflow of an application. If we can hide the complexities of a process or technology from end users, we may find them coming back to the application frequently—even if their internet connection is currently unavailable.

The Benefits of Native Graphical Applications

While caching (keeping downloaded content around for offline work) is a relatively easy problem to solve, synchronization (combining all changes made from various locations) is not. Thankfully, native applications have tools available to assist with this complicated task, whether through a platform toolkit (such as Apple's CloudKit for iCloud) or by use of third-party technology (such as Dropbox's API or Firebase's offline capabilities for iOS and Android). Due to the incredible rise in popularity of mobile apps most development is focused there, but many of these technologies apply just as well to native applications on the desktop.

Web technologies continue to make strides in providing increased reliability and offline capabilities, but they are a long way from meeting the standards expected of native graphical applications.

Maintainability and testing

"Chance favors only the prepared mind"
- Louis Pasteur

To support the fast pace of software development, evolution in technology, and user demand for more features, it is imperative that our software be well-organized and highly maintainable. Any one on your team, or yourself at some point in the future, should be able to easily understand how the code works and quickly make the required change or addition. Supporting this sort of future development requires a well-organized project and an investment of time to maintain standards.

Native applications are typically written using a single language: that of the platform they are built for. This constraint means that an entire application can follow standard layout, naming, and semantic conventions, making it easier to work on any portion of the software. Modularity and code reuse are far easier to accomplish, and so duplication or incomplete changes are less likely to be a problem within the project. Test Driven Development, by now a well-utilized methodology, doesn't require a single language within the code base to work well, but the tooling required to make it possible does vary by language and having only one setup to support per project is beneficial.

One of the reasons that the other forms of graphical applications (mainly web-based) use multiple languages is also why they are harder to test: their interface is presented using a web browser (or embedded HTML renderer), which can vary hugely from one platform to another. Irrespective of the age of the hardware or the type of device it's being used on, people will expect your application to load fast and look right. This means a lot of variation to deal with and a lot of testing for each change. Compare this to a native graphical application, where the target devices are known and fully supported by the toolkit used for developing. Testing is easier and faster, and so changes can be made rapidly and with confidence. Native graphical applications truly are the best way to make beautiful, responsive applications that will spark joy in your target audience.

Summary

With the first graphical user interfaces in the early 1970s, computers became more accessible, and ever since developers and designers have been finding ways to improve user experience. As technologies evolved, the focus moved from desktop applications to web-based software and mobile apps. Through each change in development, we see the need to make applications responsive, reliable, and engaging. In this chapter, we explored the history of the GUI and how native applications continue to provide the best user experience.

By creating quality graphical applications using native technologies, developers are able to provide better reliability and a more responsive user interface. Ensuring that applications integrate seamlessly with the operating system, as well as working well online and offline, will provide a consistent workflow that will keep your users happy. We also saw that the structure and format of a native application can benefit software developers and support processes that ensure a higher quality product.

In the next chapter, we'll discover how some of these benefits are created within graphical applications and the challenges they can pose. We'll compare various approaches to these complexities and outline some of the decisions that will need to be made when designing a modern, native graphical user interface.

2
Graphical User Interface Challenges

In the previous chapter, we explored the history of graphical user interfaces, looking at how they evolved and why they can provide a better user experience than contemporary alternatives. Unfortunately, despite all the benefits of graphical applications for end users, they can pose many challenges to the team designing and building them. In this chapter, we look at the sorts of issues that a team may face at various stages of creating an average-complexity graphical application.

This chapter will cover the following topics:

- Choosing a look and feel to match the operating system or product brand
- Different approaches to application layout and multiple windows
- The challenges of concurrency and cloud service integration
- Overheads introduced when developing a graphical application for multiple platforms

Standard look and feel or app theme

When designing your graphical application, it's likely that an early question will be around the visual identity; should the application fit within the operating system's look and feel or should it have a brand of its own? Do you want to work on a complete theme for the user interface that the user will identify with, or do you wish to make use of the well-crafted and commonly understood interface elements of the user's operating system?

Graphical User Interface Challenges

As with most questions that we will encounter throughout this chapter, there is no right or wrong answer, and whichever path you choose will have positive and negative side effects. Going with completely standard components will likely result in faster development and be easier for users to understand, but how do you differentiate your app from others? If you design the complete application interface from scratch, then you will develop a good brand identity for the software that users will recognize, but it may take them longer to learn and it could look out of place on the platform you are targeting.

Different design approaches typically suit different types of applications. Games clearly rely on heavily customized graphical interfaces and rarely use standard components but their users, the gamer community, understand the standard interactions of the genre so don't need the common visual cues that using the operating system's default elements provides. Utility apps (those that you load to do a quick task alongside your current work) will benefit from blending in so that very little thought is needed to operate them and no identity needs to be associated with the experience:

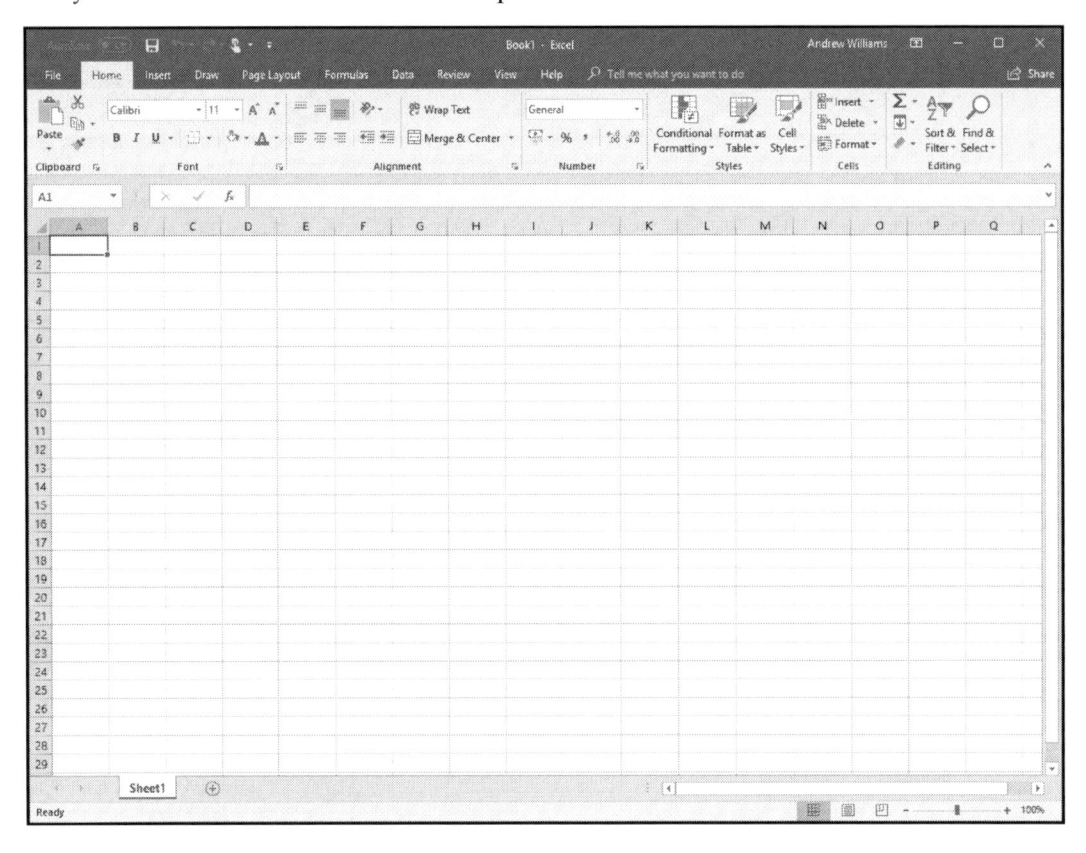

Microsoft Excel uses a blend of system components and brand identity. Used with permission from Microsoft.

Assuming that you have decided whether your visual design will fit with a standardized look or require a more bespoke approach, you need to consider the platforms you will deploy to. Is this an application designed for a single operating system or for many? If your software will only work on Windows, then using the standard look and feel could clearly be the way to go, but what if you are looking for a cross-platform distribution? macOS looks very different to Windows, which in turn is not the same as an average Linux desktop. Which do you target? Or, do you opt for the same interface design on all platforms?

The complexity of cross-platform GUI design is not a new problem, but it is one that requires some thought as you design the application experience. If you have a standardized interface design that works for your brand or application, will it apply equally well across different operating systems? Alternatively, if you aim to use standard components on each platform, how will you ensure a consistent user experience and how much more time will be put into support materials or your help desk?

When Java Swing was the standard for cross-platform graphical applications, their approach was unique: allow the developer to code against a standard API for building the GUI, but provide the ability for it to have different presentation modes, to look consistent across platforms, or to blend in with the system it is running on. This meant that the same application could be configured to look the same across all operating systems or to fit within the current desktop environment. Unfortunately, this method has its limitations, due to the way that it ends up providing a lowest-common-denominator set of functionality. Advanced integrations in one area would not be usable in a cross-platform app unless it were a feature of all supported operating systems.

Graphical User Interface Challenges

Additionally, the user interface design can age badly on an operating system that changes look drastically from one release to another (such as Microsoft Windows moving from Vista to 7 to 10, each of which had quite distinctive looks):

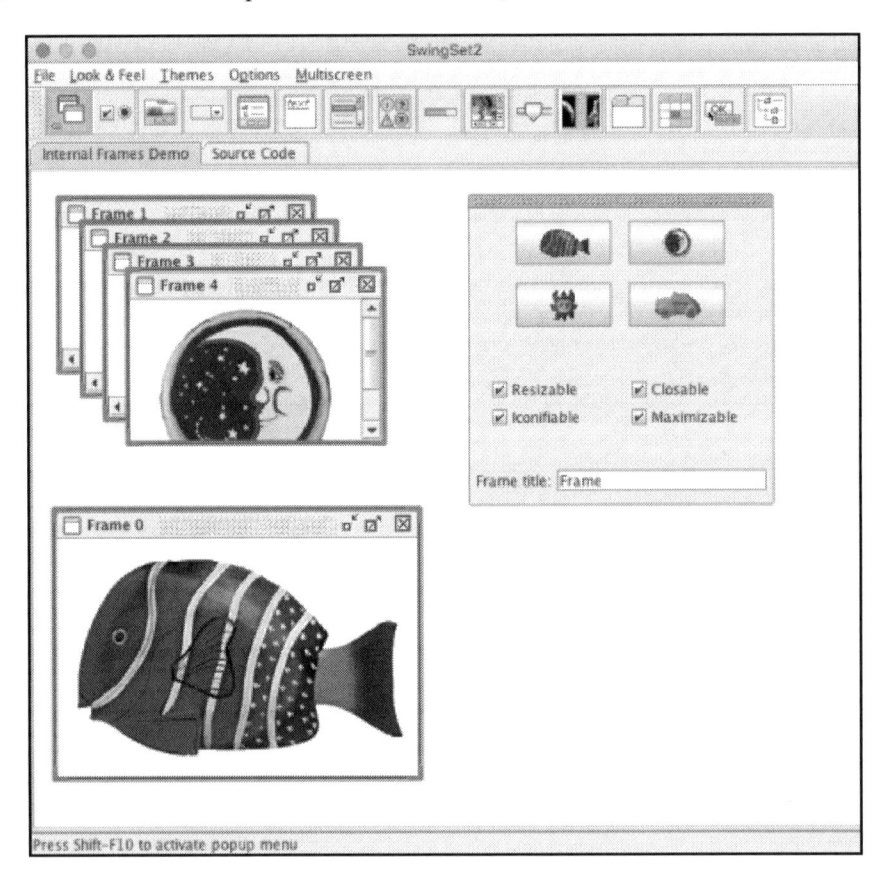

Chapter 2

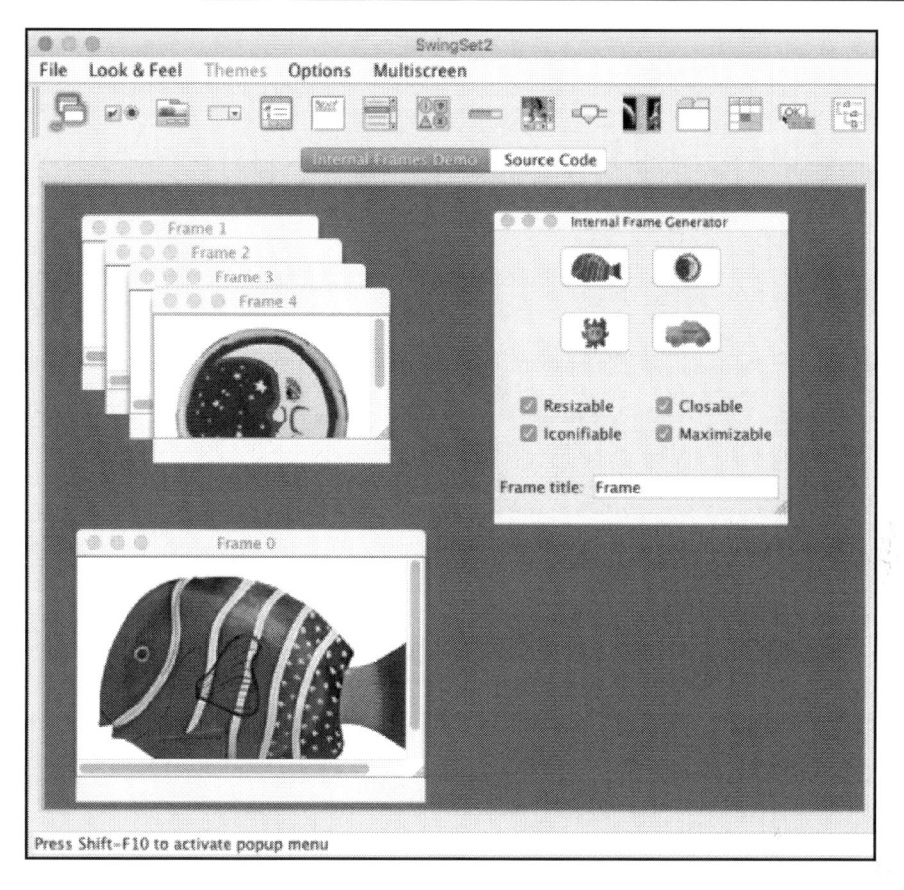

Java Swing demo – cross-platform look (metal) on the top. macOS system look on the bottom

Over time, the number of ways to build graphical applications has increased, with many options available for most programming languages. Some are designed to use the system style, some prefer their own graphical style, and others leave that to developer or user preference. And so you must choose: do you want your app to blend in to a standard operating system look, or are you aiming for a brand identity or design that looks the same on each system you will deliver to? We will explore both options in `Section 2`, *Toolkits Using Existing Widgets* and `Section 3`, *Modern Graphical Toolkits* of this book.

GUIs and visual hierarchy

The graphical language and common visual layouts of software have evolved a lot over the recent history of consumer software products and continues to evolve. Each operating system and graphical toolkit focuses on usability while attempting to have a unique look. These principles have driven each platform in slightly different directions, which impacts the software we write and the content we present.

Multiple documents

Let's first look at the ways that applications can handle multiple concurrent documents. These interfaces all aim to present a way to work with many documents at the same time. Whether it's a word processor, an image editor, or a web browser, there are many ways to approach this. An operating system typically has a default behavior that application developers are encouraged to use (sometimes by promoting enhanced usability with the latest changes, and other times by adding or removing APIs within their respective toolkits). These interface preferences can change over time, but can also become standardized around certain categories of application. For example, earlier in their history, Microsoft promoted the Windows **multiple document interface** (**MDI**) layout, which remains popular with text editors and **integrated development environments** (**IDEs**):

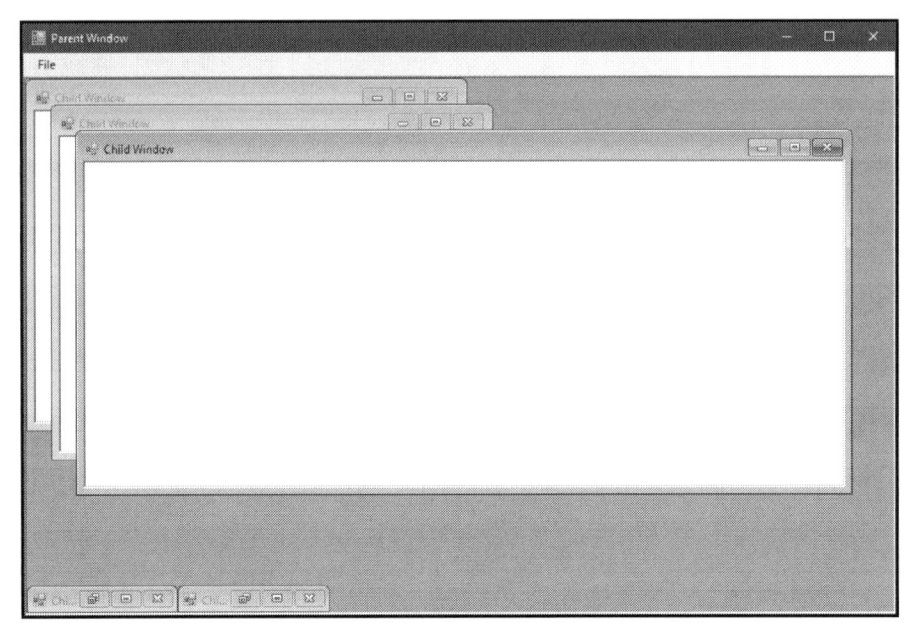

An example application using the Microsoft Windows MDI layout

Developers of native macOS applications are encouraged to use a new window for each document, but to group them under the same application, so the user only sees one icon that groups them:

Multiple documents in macOS load as windows of a single application

Graphical User Interface Challenges

The Chrome web browser decided to integrate their tabbed display into the window header bar, a space that normally shows just the title of the application or loaded document:

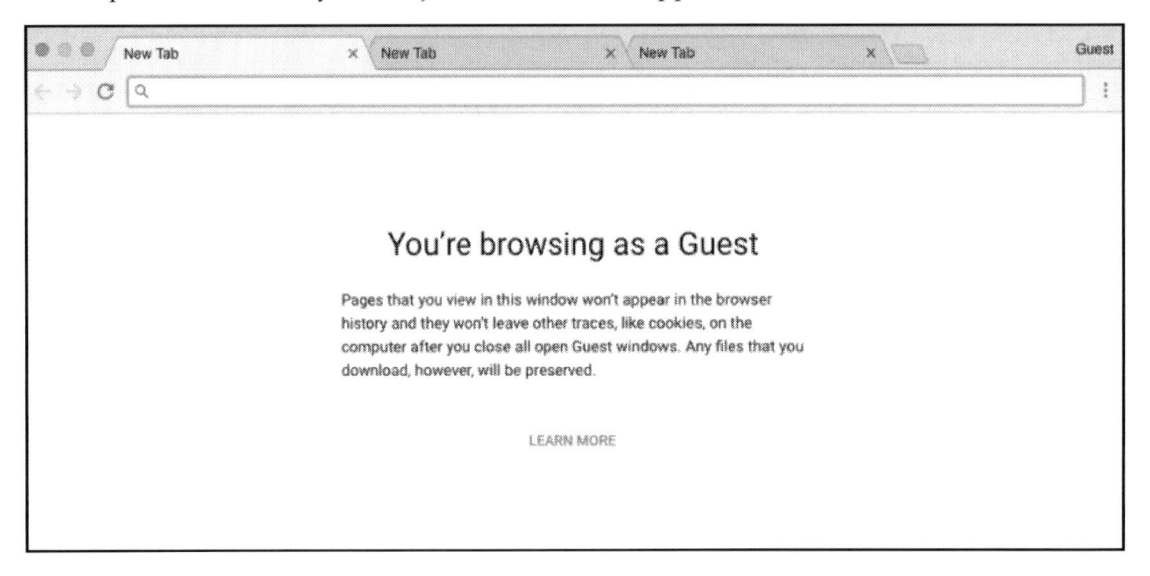

This Chrome screenshot shows their distinct look for the tabbed display of loaded web pages

With all these possible approaches, which is right for your application? If you have to deal with multiple documents, it's worth looking at applications that manage similar file types, or comparing how various applications in the same environment handle window management.

Accessory windows

There is also a notable variance in the positioning of toolboxes and the grouping of features that relate to common areas of functionality. Over the years, there have been many iterations such as drawers (which slide out from the window) and pop-out dialog windows (still used where context is important but the tools are used less often), but the always-visible toolbar or accessory window remains the most popular.

Chapter 2

For example, applications designed for Linux and Unix desktops are typically presented using separate windows for each of the supporting tool panels:

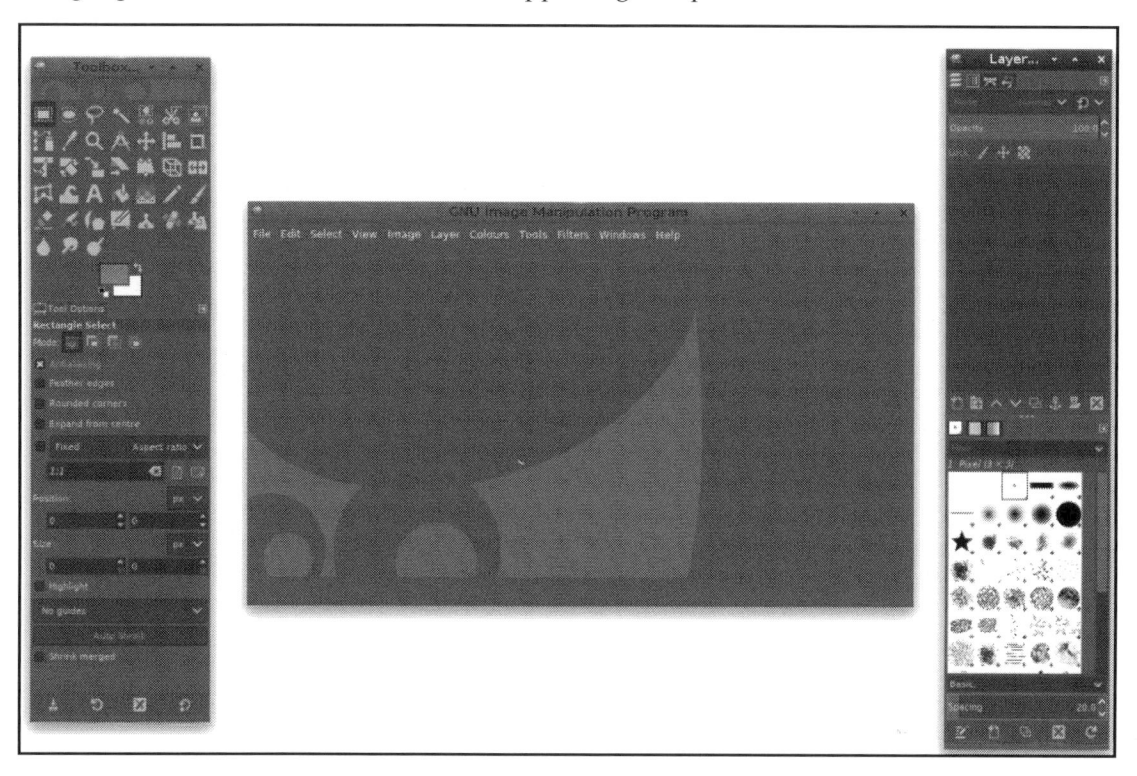

Multiple windows were commonly used in Gimp, the popular open source image manipulation program

Graphical User Interface Challenges

Compare this with Windows software, which commonly uses a combined layout where controls are positioned around the borders of the document window:

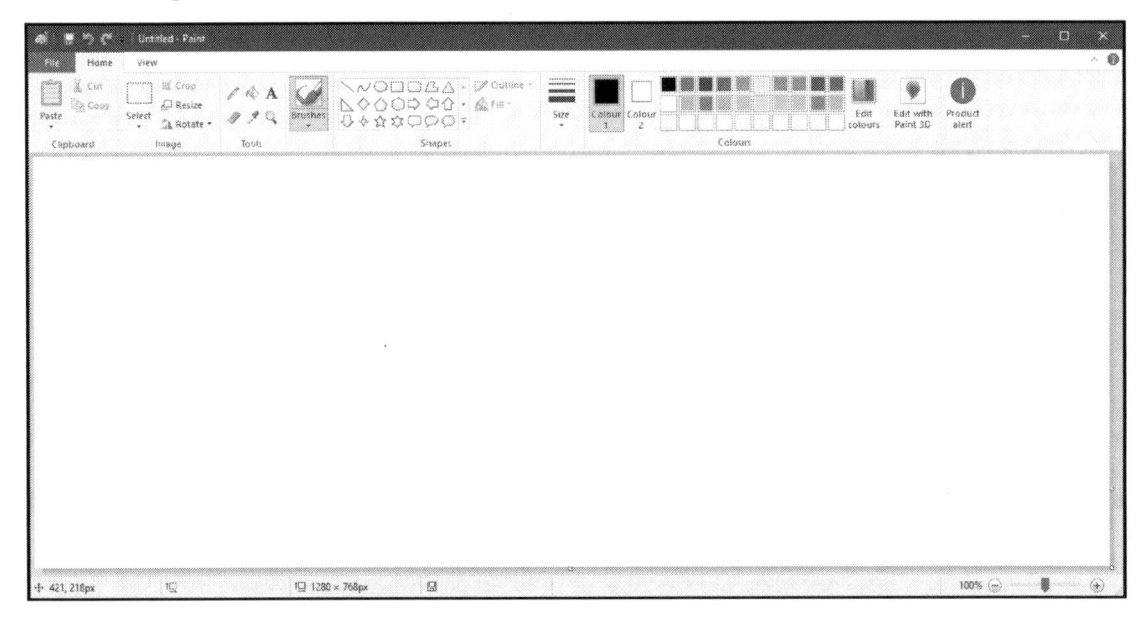

In Microsoft Paint, however, the tools are grouped at the top of the document. Used with permission from Microsoft.

Both of these approaches, within a single platform, provide a consistent user experience, but for a graphical application that targets multiple operating systems, it is important to consider which approach suits best. Does your software particularly suit one approach or the other? Maybe it will be easier for people to use your application if its graphical design adapts the layout to match the conventions of the platform it is running on.

Visual hierarchy

The evolution of web-based applications followed a different path. Historically, this medium has been used for presenting large amounts of textual information and academic documents. This was usually formatted as hyperlinked content and often included a list of popular links in a navigation area that would help people to find important content. While it was common for each site to have a very individual look (distinct colors and typesetting have had their trends along the way), this grouping of content was largely consistent across the internet. It was a big shift from the desktop software at that time, but once a user had learned the way to interact with one website, they could relatively easily find their way around most of them.

In terms of applications that were delivered through a website, this had a large benefit: the standardized layout or visual hierarchy meant that a new, distinct design would still be usable by most internet-savvy computer users. This was in addition to the fact that they would look the same on any operating system or web browser. This consistency for the user made it easier for designers to apply rich visuals or branding to a web application without reducing the user experience. As the evolving **Cascading Style Sheets** (**CSS**) open standard gained popularity, it became easier to share subsets of these designs and to separate the layout details from the visual styling and brand. As a result, there emerged common code for structuring websites and applications, similar to the desktop toolkits that developers were familiar with. But combined with consistency across any internet-connected computer, this standard approach started to make desktop applications seem confusing to learn in comparison:

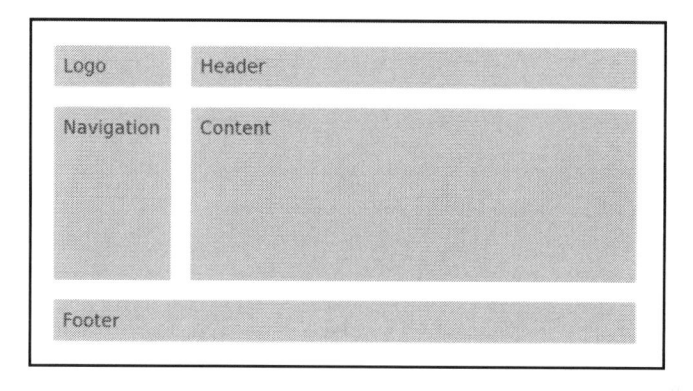

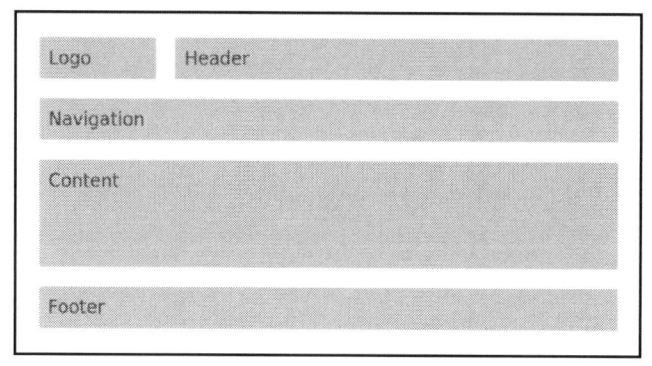

Standard web page layouts—on the top. the navigation is a side bar. and in the next image. it is a shorter inline area

Graphical User Interface Challenges

Mobile standards

Mobile applications pose a different design challenge: how to make a great user experience on a far smaller screen when the main input device is a touch screen where your fingers may obscure content. The companies behind the major mobile operating systems (Apple, Google, and Microsoft) spent many years developing a visual language and standard interactions that provided a smooth flow through increasingly complicated applications. As previously with web applications, it was important that native mobile applications behave in a consistent manner for users to quickly learn and feel comfortable with these new platforms. iOS, Android, and Windows Phone provide standard APIs that developers can use to create applications that fit with the platform standards. Within each platform, there are enough customization options to support brand identity through use of color, icons, or the content of each screen within the app. While the specific design aesthetic of mobile platforms has changed over the years, it is clear that the carefully designed layout and workflow aspects remain consistent throughout. Users can comfortably pick up the latest iPhone, appreciate its new design, and still be completely familiar with how the applications will work:

A standard iOS layout: navigation at the top and actions at the bottom

A similar iOS layout 4 years earlier

There is clearly a lot more to designing an application GUI than designing a workflow and picking a color scheme. Will your application take inspiration from modern application UX, or is it aimed at users who are more familiar with the classic look of desktop applications established over many years? Will you be sticking to a single platform and its standard look and feel, or are you interested in launching your software across multiple operating systems? Before we look at the different toolkits available, take some time to consider these options and identify which is likely the right strategy for your application.

Concurrency and multi-threading

A GUI must remain responsive to user input at all times. While this is largely an aesthetic consideration, it is also possible that the operating system may monitor applications and force unresponsive user interfaces to quit. Effective event handling is what makes this possible, and this is the core paradigm for a GUI. The event handler is responsible for responding to user events (such as mouse click, finger tap, and keyboard entry), system events (such as file changes, network availability, and application state), and also for updating the user interface (such as rendering content, changing interface state, and more). Anything that stops this work from occurring could cause the application to stop responding. In most graphical toolkits, there is a single thread (a task that manages a set of concurrent operations) that is responsible for the event handling and graphical updates. In some systems, this is the main thread (where an application launches from), and in others it is a separate thread or process. It is important to know the semantics of the system you are using, as it is commonly required that only the graphical or event handling thread can make changes to the user interface.

Switching threads

The ways that different toolkits and languages handle multithreading and graphical updates vary substantially. The following illustrations aim to highlight the complexity of this problem, in case you are not familiar with these constraints. The specifics sometimes vary based on language or version, but the concepts are usually consistent, otherwise software developed using the APIs would be very difficult to manage.

For our first example, consider an application written in Java. Its convention is that the graphics and user interaction are handled by a single event dispatch thread. Therefore, any change you wish to make to the user interface needs to be pushed to this thread using `SwingUtilities.invokeLater()`:

```java
SwingUtilities.invokeLater(new Runnable() {
    public void run() {
        button.SetText("Updated!");
    }
});
```

The approach for working with Apple's operating systems is slightly different. Applications built with AppKit or UIKit (which are used for desktop and mobile applications respectively) start the user interface event handling on the main thread. This means that after the interface is configured, all processing must be handled on a background thread and changes to the user interface must be executed on the main thread. The objective-C block construct (for encapsulating a single behavior) makes this a little easier, but the code is still non-trivial:

```
dispatch_async(dispatch_get_main_queue(), ^{
    [button setTitle:@"Updated!" forState:UIControlStateNormal];
});
```

Applications using GTK (which supports building apps for various different platforms) have a similar restriction. For those, the graphical updates must be processed on whichever thread you invoked `gtk_init()` and `gtk_main()`. For such applications, the thread handling provided by `GLib` will help to manage multithreading in your application, but you have to set this up in the interface initialization code:

```
...
gtk_init(&argc, &argv);
...
gdk_threads_enter();
gtk_main();
gdk_threads_leave();
...
```

Then, you can use the gdk thread helpers to manage background updates as follows:

```
gdk_threads_enter();
gtk_button_set_label(GTK_BUTTON(label), "Updated!");
gdk_threads_leave();
```

Avoiding complexity

Graphical toolkits do a lot to help application developers avoid the complications of concurrency where possible. For example, a button's click handler will typically run on the thread that controls graphical updates; this means that simple cases of user feedback or displaying data as a result of a user action can be done without worrying about multi-threading complexity. A simple callback function for an Android application may be as simple as the following code:

```
button.setOnClickListener(new View.OnClickListener() {
    public void onClick(View v) {
        button.SetText("Updated!");
```

```
        }
    });
```

However, even a modest application is unlikely to avoid these complications for long. Consider a simple RSS newsfeed application; all it does is set up a GUI, load the contents of a newsfeed from a set URL, and display the results in a list in the user interface. To remain responsive, the graphical interface must be presented when the application loads, before requesting the contents of the news feed. As the feed downloads, it can be parsed and the items displayed. However, because this is executing as a background process, it is not allowed to simply make changes to the interface, such as adding list items. Instead, it must identify the items to be added and pass this information back to the main (or event dispatch) thread to show the updates to the user. Such code can be difficult to read and will often lead to debugging complexity, as concurrent software may not always behave in the same way. In the next chapter, we will look at how Go's design for handling concurrency can simplify this for us.

Web services and cloud integration

Web services and online functionality is a core part of most applications today. Whether you are working with data downloaded from a central source, collaborating on documents stored online, or just looking to share your creation, this will probably be done via the internet. The core of most graphical toolkits and APIs are focused solely on the widgets—the presentation of the interface to the user. While this is due to various different reasons (and is evolving and expanding over time), it mostly reflects the period when they were created. Programming languages such as C and C++ underpin many of the native graphical toolkits (especially those targeting multiple platforms), and they pre-date cloud services and web-based APIs as we know them today. Powerful web services and standardized protocols for communications vastly improve the speed of development for web-based applications. Conversely, they can make it harder for native graphical applications on the desktop where support is lacking from the core language or standard libraries.

Communications

Assuming that your chosen language either has good support for connecting to HTTP web services, or that a suitable library has been identified, then making a data transfer from your required service is not going to be a problem. However, what happens if the connection fails? While native GUI applications typically sit on a desktop or laptop computer where permanent network connections are common, it is not wise to rely on this. With increased remote working, coffee shop meetings, and higher levels of mobility (enabled by Wi-Fi and cellular networks), any modern application needs to handle unexpected network conditions.

When developing a web-based application, it may not be necessary to be as diligent as the user is probably already online. It's also possible that a failure of the internet connection could represent a fatal situation for the software, so in some situations an error displayed to the user asking them to try again later may be acceptable. However, user expectations of native graphical applications are far higher than this. Smart phones and the software they come with are expected to gracefully handle such failure conditions caused by frequent changes in network condition or availability. So, what can we do to match this higher expectation in these situations? This probably takes some planning; the error message of *Try again later* must be a last resort.

How much of your application actually requires an internet connection all the time (or at a specific point in the workflow)? Are there elements that can be accessed occasionally and stored locally (cached)? And is it OK for outgoing communications to happen at a later time, rather than immediately on user action? It's helpful to be creative when thinking about a network connection and when it's really needed. Not too long ago, a chat client (such as IRC, ICQ, MSN, and others) would need to be online all the time, and if the connection stopped responding, you'd have to wait until it reconnected. More recently, expectations have shifted and new chat services (such as Slack and Skype) will allow you to type into chats or channels even when offline, and messages will be delivered as soon as they can.

Graphical User Interface Challenges

One additional challenge in a web-based connected world is authentication. Old password- and application secret-based authentication worked easily within most programming languages, but they had security issues. The most recent standard to be adopted is OAuth2, which aims to ensure that the user knows what they are allowing when applications connect to a secured service. The workflow is designed to work well in a web browser, but from within a native application, will it be a reasonable user experience to switch to a web browser when asking for permission? Will you improve the flow slightly by embedding a web view within your application? Unfortunately, it's been noted that this is also open to potential security attacks, and there is now a document focusing on the best practices for OAuth2 integration into native applications (IETF RFC 8252). Adapting applications to implement these recommendations will become a requirement over time.

Data parsing

Having established a connection to a remote server (or loaded the data from a local cache), the next challenge is likely to be parsing the response. Complicated string processing (which is what most HTTP-based APIs require due to their human readable design) is not a strength of many older programming languages that are common for native application development. Numerous libraries have been developed that will help with this task and are often shared freely (using an open source software license), but if the programming language does not have great string handling, it may still be a non-trivial task.

Extensible Markup Language (XML) and **JavaScript Object Notation (JSON)** are the main formats for transferring data over the internet, both reinforced by the great support they have in all languages aimed at web development (it should be no surprise that JSON usage is trivial in JavaScript applications). As the name implies, they are designed to transmit object-oriented, or structured, data, and there should be sufficient metadata within the content to allow objects to be recreated in the client software without complex un-marshaling code.

Standard components

One huge advance in cloud service integration with web development is the addition of **Asynchronous JavaScript and XML (AJAX)** functionality. Due to the ubiquitous support for JavaScript, XML, and HTML in all modern browsers, a web developer can configure parts of their user interface to refresh as a result of a web service request. Such an update does not require data parsing or merging information; the data from the server can literally be the replacement state for the user interface (in HTML or JavaScript format normally), and this directly replaces the old content.

Unfortunately, most native application toolkits do not have built-in components for displaying the results of a web service function call. Over time, however, popular services will often release libraries that assist with these features. If the company behind a web service does not create a supporting library or component, it is often the case that one may have been created independently and shared online. Languages that have good support for external modules, or provide a suitable package manager, often benefit the most from these sorts of contributions.

Developing for multiple platforms

Beyond the challenges described earlier in this chapter, graphical applications face additional complications when targeting multi-platform distributions. Dependency and package management are out of scope for this section as they affect system and web applications in broadly the same way, although system applications rarely have to handle packaged resources (such as images and design elements) and web applications are unlikely to publish binary packages. Outlined in this section are the main challenges that are unique to, or harder for, GUI-based applications planning a cross-platform strategy. While each of these can be overcome, they typically introduce additional development overheads that should be taken into consideration when designing your application.

Cross-platform APIs

When designing for multiple platforms the first consideration is probably the look and feel (see the *Standard look and feel or app theme* at the beginning of this chapter). However, it is also very important to consider whether your interface design will be easy to understand for your users (should it match the desktop widgets?). For a high-quality graphical application, it's important to consider how it will interact with the rest of the user's environment. For example, if your workflow included opening a web page outside the current interface, the expectation would probably be that it should open in the default web browser, which maybe configured by the operating system. Does the toolkit you selected handle opening web pages or other types of document specified by a URL? Will you instead need to write some code for each platform you wish to support to make the right thing happen?

Graphical User Interface Challenges

To learn from the recent developments in mobile applications, we should look at the `Share` functionality. On Android, and more recently on iOS, an application can initiate a share action, and the platform toolkit will show an appropriate visual choice of ways to share that type of content. The user will then make their selection, and the application registered to handle that type of share will receive the content and request any further information required. How can native application developers of cross-platform applications provide similar functionality? If that is important to your application, then you could look for a language or toolkit that aims to provide this feature, but you may be left to try and implement it directly within your own code or to work with an external, web-based service to provide a similar experience.

Icons and design

Most graphical environments (such as desktop, mobile, and more) have a default set of icons—those that are used to show file types, navigation arrows, and standard toolbars to help users recognize common actions. If your application is providing more than just the simplest of functionality, there will probably be a need to add some graphical elements to the design— most likely icons or symbols to help your users along. Will your additional icons match those provided by the environment the application is running in? If you are supporting just one platform, this is probably not an issue, but when you are aiming for a cross-platform solution, this could be much harder:

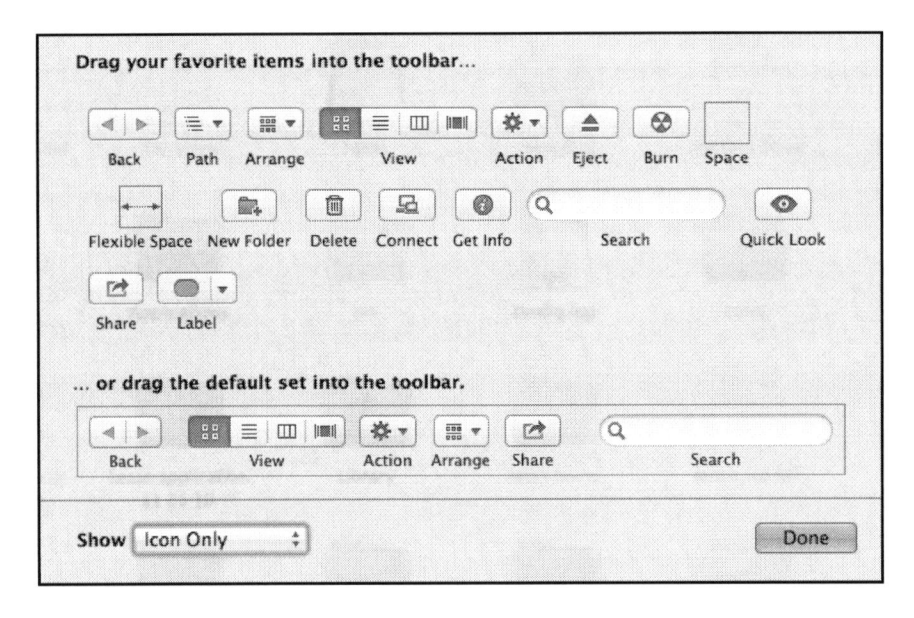

The default style for macOS toolbar icons

Chapter 2

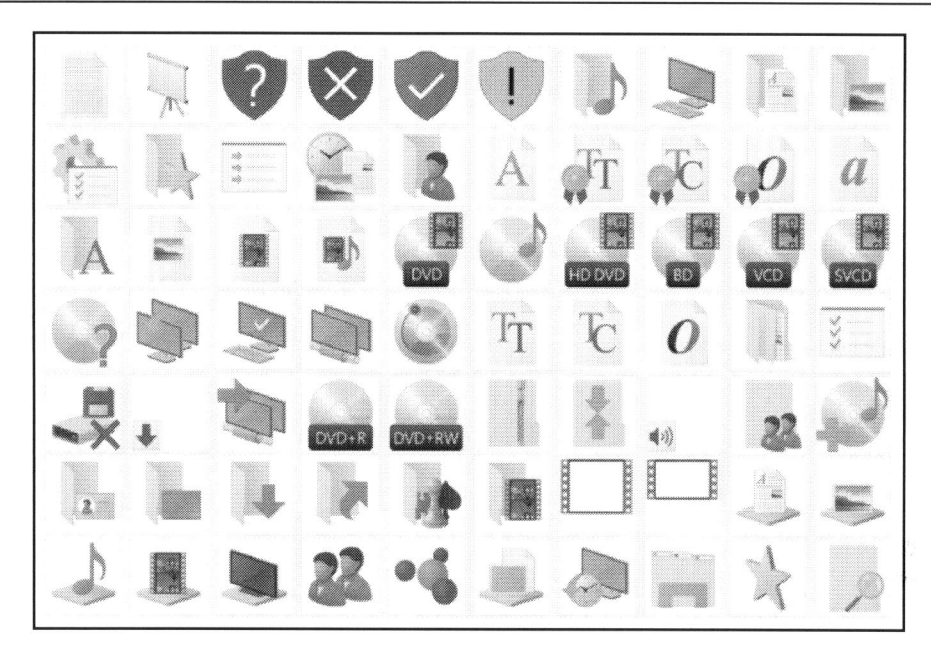

Windows uses a very different style to macOS

Think about this challenge when designing your application GUI: do you need additional icons or graphical elements? Doing so may be different to the system style, but it may match your user's expectations.

Testing

The only way to ensure a good-quality application is to test it on each platform that you aim to support. This is the same for system applications (which could aim to work on Linux and Mac, for example) and for web applications (each web browser could behave slightly differently). However, the variance in graphical desktop environments can be substantial, potentially leading to many different versions of your user interface. Additionally, setting up each of these platforms probably requires more computers, or some complicated multiple-boot setups. Virtualization offers a good solution here: where possible, you could create virtual environments to mimic each of the operating system installations you need to test on.

If you are including Linux or similar open source operating systems, remember that users are free to choose different desktop environments, each of which have a different look and default behavior. For example, if you are supporting Ubuntu Linux, you probably need to test the default environment (Unity) but also the very common *Gnome* alternative. There are many different desktop environments for Linux to consider, including KDE and Xfce, which are also very popular, each with a different look and feel and often with different workflows to consider.

Even if you intend to focus support on just Windows and macOS, you will still need to consider what versions you will support. The look and feel, and even default interactions, can change from one major release to another, so will you aim to adapt to these nuances or instead just provide a great experience for the latest version of these systems? Be sure to record which operating systems and versions (and even desktop configurations if you are going to target Linux) you will support and set up a test environment for each of these, if possible. It will help in the long run!

Packaging and distribution

Packaging a native graphical application for multiple platforms can introduce additional challenges. A native GUI will typically have to adapt to the current platform and it will need to include package metadata to integrate as expected on a user's desktop. Most graphical apps also require many assets to be embedded into the release package. Additionally, the semantics of installing an application vary from one operating system to another. macOS, for example, expects that applications are packaged as a *bundle* that can be dragged (or moved) from the `Downloads` folder into the `Applications` folder. Windows users will expect a single executable file that will run once downloaded, or an installer that can set up the components required. The platforms you aim to distribute on may impact your application capabilities or the resources it can be packaged with, and we want to do this using a single code base for ease of maintenance.

In recent years, we have seen many platforms create *app stores* or similar, where users can browse the applications available for their computer. This provides some free marketing and a new channel for downloads, but adds additional overheads for the developer. Screenshots and other metadata about your application will be required as a minimum, and to stand out, you may even need to create a video of your software in action. Stores such as these make installation trivial for the user but often place additional constraints on the developer. Be sure to research these distribution methods if you intend to use them for your application.

Summary

In this chapter, we discussed various additional complications that developers of native graphical applications are likely to face, especially if looking to build for multiple operating systems. Addressing the challenges around graphical presentation (visual hierarchy, system look or application design, and custom graphical elements) will take some planning and investigation—not just to design the ideal application, but also to choose the constraints or overheads that you will work with.

The remaining technical challenges—concurrency, web integration, packaging, and distribution—will vary based on the implementation language. As outlined previously, many graphical toolkits are created using languages that did not originally provide support for these considerations. Some provide low-level support that the developer must build upon for their application to meet the expected level of functionality for a modern GUI-based application. Thankfully, Go provides elegant solutions to many of these challenges. Although the language was not designed with GUIs built into the standard library, we will look at why Go is a great match for this kind of application in the next chapter.

3
Go to the Rescue!

Having read the previous chapter on the challenges of building native graphical applications, you may be wondering whether it's worth all the effort. Hopefully, you are confident that your users will appreciate the quality user experience you are designing, and your team will be keen to see the benefits of taking this route over a web app or other approach. Thankfully, the team at Google that designed the Go programming language understood these challenges and decided that something should be done to aid developers in their quest!

In this chapter, we will take a detailed look at the Go language and see how its design can solve (or help with) the various challenges discussed in Chapter 2, *Graphical User Interface Challenges*. In particular, we will look at the following topics:

- A cross-platform approach for any applications
- How the concurrency model helps create reliable applications
- Built-in support for working with web services
- Choosing the look and feel of your GUI and managing the GUI code

By the end of this chapter, you will be familiar with how the Go language can support GUI application design, and be ready to start working on real examples using the various frameworks available to Go developers.

Introduction

Go is a language that (like C, C++, Lisp, and many others) compiles to a native binary on every platform it supports. This is important for graphical applications as it's the best way to create the most responsive and smoothest user interfaces on mainstream computer hardware. At the time of writing, the platforms that Go runs on includes Windows, macOS, Linux, Solaris, and other popular Unix-based operating systems (which is essentially all desktop personal computers). What stands out about Go compared to other modern languages is that its source code will compile, without any alterations or special adaptation, to native code on every platform that it supports. The language also comprises a large library of APIs that fully support every one of its supported operating systems. This is a huge advantage for developers who want to write an efficient application for multiple operating systems without maintaining slightly different versions for each platform. Go is also a *typed* language, which means that every variable, constant, function parameter, and return type must have a single, defined type. Unlike some older typed languages, Go is often able to infer a type, which helps avoid the duplication of information in the source code. These features help to create a language that's great for development—so let's look at some real code and how this is built and run. We'll work with a simple *hello world* example, which we will write into a file named `main.go`:

```
package main

import "fmt"

func main() {
    fmt.Println("Hello World!")
}
```

This example shows the most basic Go program. The first line indicates the package name (here, `main` means that the file describes an executable command). Then, we have the import block where you reference any standard library packages or external code. Finally, there is a `main()` method, which is the start of any Go program—and this method simply prints *Hello World!* to the command line using the `fmt` package. This method doesn't mention a return type (which would be placed after `main()`)—that means there is no return type, such as `void` in C or Java programs. We run this application using the `go run main.go` command, as follows:

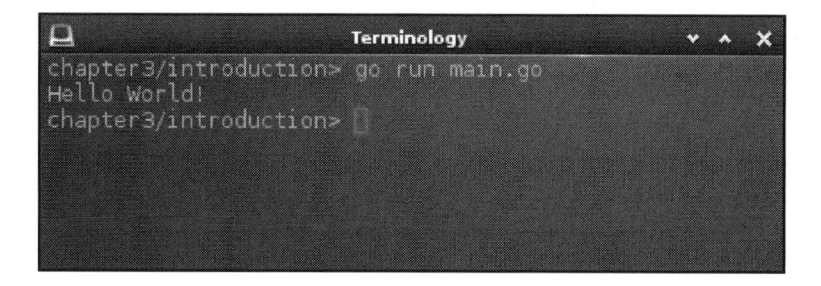

Running main.go outputs the message before exiting

Alongside each Go file will usually be a test file that runs unit tests against the main code. Let's demonstrate that with another trivial example. Enter the following code into `main_test.go`:

```
package main

import "testing"

func TestLogic(t *testing.T) {
    if true == false {
        t.Error("It's illogical")
    }
}
```

Before we run this code, you should notice two important differences compared to a regular Go file. First, the import list includes `"testing"`—this is required for writing any test method. Second, the method name starts with `Test` this time, and includes a single parameter of the `*testing.T` type. Any method that conforms to those conditions and is in a file that has a name ending in `_test.go` will be considered a unit test. Now let's run the tests using the built-in test runner:

Running Go tests in verbose mode

In this command, the `-v` parameter requests verbose output, which is seen as the tests run, and the resulting `command-line-arguments` indicates that the tests were run on the files specified in our parameter list, rather than a full package. Alternatively, typing `go test` would output less information and would run all the tests in the current package.

In addition to these basic commands, Go comes with many tools that help developers to write and maintain high-quality code. The three that are most commonly used are as follows:

- `gofmt`: This ensures that source code is formatted according to the Go specification, and can rewrite your files if requested (by passing `-w`).
- `godoc`: This runs a local documentation server to check how your API will look to other developers.
- `go vet`: This examines the code for common programming mistakes that a compiler won't detect.

You may have noticed that these commands simply run without needing to compile – but how can that be, if Go is a compiled language? That is because the `run` command is actually a shortcut to build the application and then run it. This makes running the latest version of an application much quicker than the usual approach of compiling and then running, without losing any of the benefits of being a native binary. In this mode, the built application is discarded when the run finishes. If you want to build and then run many times, you can use the `build` command, as shown here:

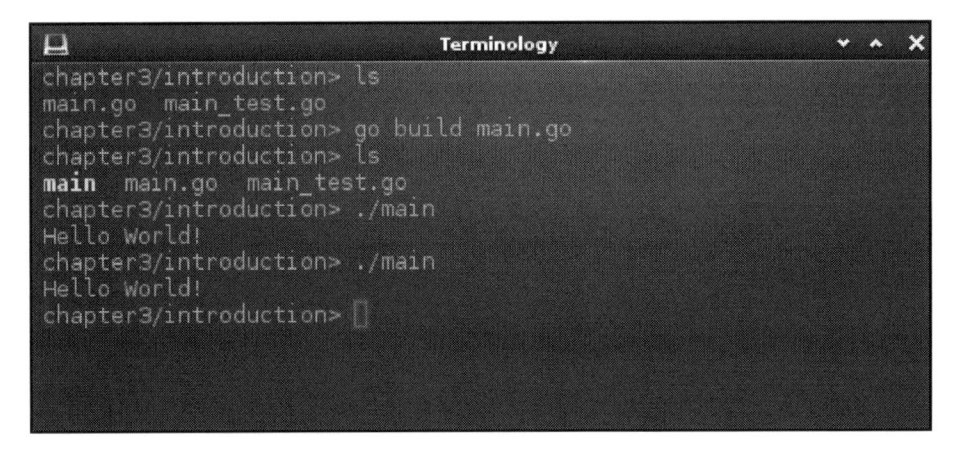

```
chapter3/introduction> ls
main.go    main_test.go
chapter3/introduction> go build main.go
chapter3/introduction> ls
main       main.go    main_test.go
chapter3/introduction> ./main
Hello World!
chapter3/introduction> ./main
Hello World!
chapter3/introduction>
```

Building a binary to run many times

As you can see, the compiler has created an executable file that has the same name as the file we entered the code into. This file is the native application built from our source code and it can be run like any other application. Note that this is a native application and so it's not portable the way that a Java application is. It will run on the computer we built it on and others like it, but an application built on a Windows computer will not run on macOS directly. The source code is compatible with both platforms, but the binary application is not.

It should be noted at this point that the Go language also provides *garbage collection*, which contributes to the ease of development. This means that when objects we created are no longer needed, the system will ensure the memory they occupy is freed up. Compared to C and other (older) compiled languages where this isn't provided, we have less code to write, and a much lower risk of our application leaking memory. Now that we know the language, let's explore the compiler features that support the cross-platform approach and see how to build these examples for different operating systems.

Cross-platform for any application

In the introduction, we saw that a file with a name ending in `_test.go` would automatically be run as part of the test phase. Go uses this naming convention for additional compiler features to provide the ability to include code for a specific platform or computer architecture. For example, a file named `main_windows.go` will only be included in the compilation if you are building for Microsoft Windows, and the `main_darwin.go` file would only be compiled for macOS (darwin is the name of the underlying operating system). Similarly, the computer architecture can be used to conditionally include source code, and so a file named `main_arm.go` would only be part of the build for a 32-bit ARM-based processor.

Go also supports the conditional compilation of arbitrary files through the use of build constraints (also known as build tags). These operate at a file level to determine whether a file should be included in the build. To use this functionality, a comment is placed at the top of the file before the package declaration (with an important blank line afterward):

```
// +build linux,!386

package myapp
```

Basic build tags match the platform and architecture strings used for the file naming described previously, with the addition that they can be combined and negated (using the ! character). Therefore, the preceding example will be included when compiling for Linux on a non-32-bit processor (!386). This functionality can be further extended by the use of custom tags that can be passed to the compiler. In this way, an application that has advanced features only for a Macintosh could update the file to read the following:

```
// +build darwin,coolstuff

package myapp
```

This means that, when compiling for a macOS computer, you could invoke the compiler with an extra parameter to enable this `coolstuff` functionality as follows: `go build -tags coolstuff main.go`.

This level of conditional compilation means that the code is not cluttered or confusing to read—each file either is, or isn't, included when building. Often, a file that contains conditional code will be paired with another that contains the alternative implementation, such as `// +build !darwin !coolstuff` to provide a fallback of the preceding extra functionality (this would be compiled if not on macOS or not passing the `coolstuff` tag). For more information about the way that build constraints are calculated, please read the documentation: https://golang.org/pkg/go/build/.

One additional compiler feature that is very useful in native app development (but should be used with caution) is the ability to call C code directly from Go, this is known as **Cgo**. The following example illustrates a small Cgo program that, through importing the `"C"` package, is able to call C code. It also defines a small inline function that can be helpful in keeping your Go code neat if you have multiple C calls to make in a method:

```
package main

/*
#include <stdio.h>
#include <stdlib.h>

void print_hello(const char *name) {
    printf("Hello %s!\n", name);
}
*/
import "C"
import "unsafe"

func main() {
    cName := C.CString("World")
    C.print_hello(cName)
```

```
    C.free(unsafe.Pointer(cName))
}
```

When this is run like a normal Go program, this will print out the message exactly as you would expect:

Running C code from a go file.

As you can see, the inline C method is part of a comment, along with the required imports, which is read by Cgo when placed immediately before `import "C"`. Notice also that a Go string cannot be passed directly to C code, but must be converted to a `CString` through the `"C"` package. It's also possible to call Go functions from the C code that is included in the compilation. A full explanation of Cgo is outside the scope of this book, but more information can be found in the documentation at https://golang.org/cmd/cgo/. While this is very powerful functionality, it can quickly lead to platform-specific code, so it's unwise to use this unless absolutely necessary.

Cross-compiling

The compiler features that we've explored so far have been built only for the current platform. This means that when developing on Linux, the compiler will create (and run, if requested) a native Linux binary (known technically as ELF). If executed on macOS, the result will be a native binary for darwin (a Mach-O executable), and on Windows it would be a native binary for the Windows platform (PE32+). If developers wish to target many different platforms, one option is to have a different computer for each build, but this is expensive and time-consuming. It's far more convenient to create native binary applications for various platforms from the developer's computer—this is called **cross-compiling**.

Go to the Rescue!

Cross-compiling with the Go toolchain is simple. All you need to know is the operating system and architecture you wish to compile for. To run a build for a different platform, we simply set the GOOS and GOARCH environment variables (for the operating system and architecture, respectively) and invoke "go build". In this example, we illustrate the principle by compiling the introductory example for different platforms and check the resulting application using the Unix file command. As you can see from the first invocation, this illustration is executed from a 64-bit Linux computer and we then build for 32-bit Linux, Windows, and macOS, respectively:

```
chapter3/introduction> go build main.go
chapter3/introduction> file main
main: ELF 64-bit LSB executable, x86-64, version 1 (SYSV), statically linked, th debug_info, not stripped
chapter3/introduction> GOARCH=386 go build main.go
chapter3/introduction> file main
main: ELF 32-bit LSB executable, Intel 80386, version 1 (SYSV), statically linked, with debug_info, not stripped
chapter3/introduction> GOOS=windows go build main.go
chapter3/introduction> file main.exe
main.exe: PE32+ executable (console) x86-64 (stripped to external PDB), for MS indows
chapter3/introduction> GOOS=darwin go build main.go
chapter3/introduction> file main
main: Mach-O 64-bit x86_64 executable, flags:<NOUNDEFS>
chapter3/introduction>
```

Building for different platforms on one computer

And so you see how simple it is to build a Go application for any platform. With this knowledge, we can create a graphical application on the developer's preferred platform and cross-compile it for many of the most popular operating systems, without any custom code or build configurations.

[54]

Standard library

The standard library of a programming language is the set of APIs and features that are provided by the language runtime. C, for example, has a very small standard library—as a low-level language, the number of features that it supports for every operating system is limited. Java, on the other hand, historically known for being heavy on memory and startup time, provides a massive standard library—including the Swing GUI described in `Chapter 2`, *Graphical User Interface Challenges*.

The size of the standard library is usually part of the trade-off when choosing a programming language. For performant native applications that start quickly, the number of built-in APIs is often small. When building with a higher-level language, developers typically expect a lot of supporting features and API packages—and this will usually come with a penalty in startup time or performance. The Go language attempts to provide a full standard library without any of the runtime penalties. This is managed through its cross-platform compilation and static linking, which includes all of the utilized features in the native binary being built. This means that the files are probably larger than programs compiled from C code and they may take longer to compile—but these one-time costs (building and downloading) enable the high performance of Go apps across all platforms.

The standard library included with Go includes powerful features across many areas, including cryptography, image manipulation, text handling (including Unicode), networking, HTML templating, and web service integration. You can read the full documentation at `https://golang.org/pkg/#stdlib`.

Concurrency in language design

In most mainstream programming languages, concurrency and multithreading can add complexity and make code harder to read. The designers of Go decided that concurrency should be built in from the beginning, making it easy to manage many threads of execution while still avoiding the difficulty of shared memory management. Go does not expose traditional *threads*, but instead introduces the concept of **goroutines**—these are akin to lightweight threads, but it's possible to have several thousand at the same time. Shared memory is normally the main communication mechanism for concurrent applications, but in Go communication is used to share instead—this built-in feature is called **channels**. In addition to these language features, Go has a `sync` package within the standard library that provides tools for further concurrency management.

Goroutines

First, let's examine the most basic Go concurrency feature: the goroutine. Any normal function, when called, will execute the code inside and exit when `return` is encountered, or the function exits—at which point it will return control to the function that invoked it. A goroutine is one that starts execution, but immediately returns control to the function calling it—essentially creating a background process for each invocation. Any function can be called as a goroutine simply by prefixing `go` to the invocation, as follows:

```
package main

import (
    "fmt"
    "time"
)

func tick(message string) {
    for i := 0; i < 5; i++ {
        time.Sleep(10 * time.Millisecond)
        fmt.Println(message)
    }
}

func main() {
    go tick("goroutine")
    tick("function")
}
```

This code sample defines a `tick(string)` method that will output the requested message every 10 milliseconds. The `main()` function calls this code in two different ways: first, it is invoked as a goroutine, and then as a normal function call. If this were invoked as two function calls, one after the other, we would see a lot of copies of `"goroutine"` output to the command line, followed by `"function"` many times. Instead, however, the goroutine executes concurrently with the following code, and so we see this output instead:

```
chapter3/goroutine> go run goroutine.go
goroutine
function
function
goroutine
goroutine
function
function
goroutine
goroutine
function
chapter3/goroutine>
```

Concurrent output with a goroutine

What you see may be slightly different, as the order appears a little random. What you should see is that each pair of output lines say either "goroutine" or "function" with a small time gap between them. The order of each pair will depend on the scheduler, but what you can clearly see is that two invocations of the tick function were running at the same time (that is, concurrently). Goroutines are not limited to such trivial examples but as they occupy the same address space (like a normal function call), they have access to shared areas of memory. When multiple threads can write to the same area of memory, synchronization is typically required to ensure correct operation. To provide better semantics for communicating in this way, the Go language has a feature named **channels**.

Channels

The philosophy for sharing data with Go is *Don't communicate by sharing memory; instead, share memory by communicating*. Channels are the language construct that support this approach – they allow the sharing of data by communicating between goroutines correctly, rather than sharing common data. This is the main way that Go avoids race conditions (that is, one thread writing data while others read the same data). Channels are used for all sorts of patterns in Go – they can communicate the result of a goroutine (or pass data between routines), provide updates when data changes, or even signal that processes should finish.

Go to the Rescue!

Channels, just like all variables and constants in Go, require a type. The type of a channel determines the data that can be communicated through it. The type could be `bool` if you want to send information that is just `true/false`, or it could be a custom `struct` data type if you wish to communicate more information, such as a data-changed notification. In this example of channels, we are using a simple string channel that is read from a number of times while a goroutine continues to write into it:

```go
package main

import "fmt"

func say(words string, to chan string) {
    fmt.Println("Speaking:", words)
    to <- words
}

func talk(to chan string) {
    say("Hello", to)
    say("Everyone", to)
    say("My name is...", to)
    fmt.Println("Never mind")
}

func listen(to chan string) {
    heard := <-to
    fmt.Println("I heard:", heard)}

func main() {
    chat := make(chan string)

    go talk(chat)

    listen(chat)
    listen(chat)
    fmt.Println("Bye")
}
```

Running this sample will demonstrate that each time the channel is written to (in `say`), it must wait until the channel is read (in `listen`) before it can be written to again. You can also see that the `talk` goroutine never completed the message because we didn't read all of the data it was waiting to write:

Communicating through a simple channel

By default, writing to a channel will block until some code is ready to read from the other end, and likewise, reading will block until data is written to the channel, at which point the program flow will continue. This behavior can be altered by using a buffered channel – if a channel has a buffer size of 5, it could be written to 5 times before blocking; similarly, reading from that channel would potentially return 5 values before blocking (reading a channel will always block when no data is available). If we updated the preceding example to create a buffered channel of size 3 (by using `make(chan string, 3)`), we would see that the full message is written and the `talk` method completes:

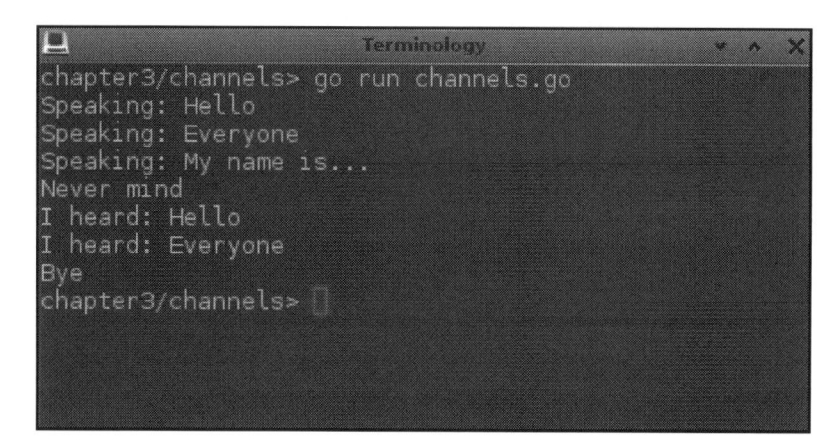

Adding buffering to the channel

Go to the Rescue!

This trivial example indicates how you can safely communicate between goroutines, but let's look at some more practical examples by including some additional features. For example, a configuration struct could be communicated through a channel each time it changes, so that the application can respond accordingly:

```
go func() {
    for {
        config := <-configManager
        myWidget.applyConfiguration(config) }
}()
```

To be able to manage concurrency and communication between multiple goroutines, the language has an enhancement for the `select` keyword, which provides the ability to wait on multiple channels. This means that you don't have to have a goroutine for each blocking channel. The following example illustrates how a background function can work on some complex calculations (in this case, `square`) that are fed back to the main function, and also wait on a signal to finish processing:

```
package main

import "fmt"

func square(c, quit chan int) {
    sq := 2
    for {
        select {
        case c <- sq:
            sq*=sq
        case <-quit:
            fmt.Println("quitting")
            return
        }
    }
}

func main() {
    c := make(chan int)
    quit := make(chan int)
    go square(c, quit)

    func() {
        for i := 0; i < 5; i++ {
            fmt.Println("Square", <-c)
        }
        quit <- 1
    }()
}
```

Running this example will output the calculations returned until the process is signaled to stop:

Reading from the calculation channel until quit is signaled

And finally, the channels in Go can be closed by the writer; this means that the function reading from a channel may stop getting new values. To avoid this deadlock situation, a reader of a channel can detect whether the channel has been closed. The syntax to check for the status of a channel is to read an optional second parameter, `val, ok := <-ch`, where `val` is the value read and `ok` indicates that the channel isn't closed. In addition to this, a new `range` keyword has been added, which will iterate through the values of a channel until it closes. The following example includes a `download()` function that simulates downloading data and updating its percentage to completion. The process reaches a logical conclusion and so the `main` function can complete. You can see how this could be used to ensure a progress bar stays up to date while other parts of the program keep running:

```go
package main

import "fmt"

func download(file string, c chan int) {
    fmt.Println("Downloading", file)

    c <- 10
    c <- 40
    c <- 65
    c <- 100

    close(c)
}
```

```go
func main() {
    c := make(chan int)
    go download("myfile.jpg", c)

    for i := range c {
        fmt.Printf("Progress %d%%...\n", i)
    }
    fmt.Println("Download complete")
}
```

Running this example will show how a simulated download progresses and returns once the process is complete. The simple `range` keyword is used to avoid handling the channel-close condition directly:

Iterating on a channel range

Sometimes, you need to go beyond the concurrency primitives and handle special cases. This is what the standard library `sync` package provides.

The sync package

The sync package of Go's standard library provides additional synchronization features that aren't included in the language itself. Its additions to concurrency management include Mutex, WaitGroup, and Once, which we'll look at briefly.

`Mutex` is used when you want to ensure mutual exclusion—that is, if you only want one goroutine to access a piece of data at a time (to avoid potential conflicts). The key methods are `Lock()` and `Unlock()`, which surround the section of code that should never be executed concurrently. If a second goroutine attempts to enter the section, it will block until the lock is released:

```
var vals map[string]string
var lock sync.Mutex

func Get(key string) string {
    lock.Lock()
    defer lock.Unlock()
    return vals[key]
}

func Set(key, value string) {
    lock.Lock()
    vals[key] = value
    lock.Unlock()
}
```

In the preceding example, we have a map, `vals`, that we want to share and so must ensure thread-safety. We add `sync.Mutex` to guard the access and ensure that the lock is obtained before using the map. Note that in the `Get` method, we use the `defer` keyword to ensure the code is called as the method exits—this avoids needing to access the map, storing the value, and unlocking before then returning (making the code neater).

`WaitGroup` is helpful if you want to create a number of background activities and then wait until they all complete. For example, this code snippet creates a download method that takes an additional parameter for the group it's part of. Each download instance increments the group counter (`Add(1)`) at the start of the download and clears it (`Done()`) at the end. The calling function sets up a wait group and then calls `Wait()`, which will return once all downloads are complete:

```
func Download(url string, group *sync.WaitGroup) {
    group.Add(1)
    http.Get(url)
    group.Done()
}

func main() {
    ...
    var group sync.WaitGroup
    go download("http://example.com/image1.png", group)
    go download("http://example.com/image2.png", group)
```

Go to the Rescue!

```
        group.Wait()
        fmt.Println("Done")
        ...
}
```

The last example, Once, is rather self-explanatory—it allows code to be executed once only. Invoking its Do(func()) method will cause the passed function to never be called more than once. This is helpful if you're trying to implement a lazy-loading singleton pattern, such as the following code:

```
var instance *myStruct
var once sync.Once

func GetInstance() *myStruct {
    once.Do(func() {
        instance = &myStruct{}
    })

    return instance
}
```

The full documentation is available at https://golang.org/pkg/sync/; however, it's recommended to use the channel constructs when possible, instead of most of these features.

Web services included as standard

As a modern programming language, Go comes with extensive support for HTTP clients, servers, and standard encoding handlers, including JSON and XML. Combined with the built-in string and map features, this removes many of the hurdles of working with web services. In addition to this, the format for structs in Go allows for additional tags that can provide metadata to its fields. Both the encoding/json and encoding/xml packages make use of this to understand how to correctly encode and decode instances of these structs. The following example demonstrates these features by connecting to a web service, accessing a JSON response, and decoding it into a struct that is then used like any other:

```
package main

import "encoding/json"
import "fmt"
import "io/ioutil"
import "net/http"

type Person struct {
```

```go
        Title       string `json:"title,omitempty"`
        Firstname string `json:"firstname"`
        Surname   string `json:"surname"`

        Username string `json:"username"`
        Password string `json:"-"`
}

func readFromURL(url string) ([]byte, error) {
    var body []byte
    resp, err := http.Get(url)
    if err != nil {
        return body, err
    }

    defer resp.Body.Close()
    return ioutil.ReadAll(resp.Body)
}

func main() {
    person := &Person{
        "",
        "John",
        "Doe",
        "someuser",
        "somepassword",
    }
    fmt.Println("Struct:", person)

    data, _ := json.MarshalIndent(person, "", "  ")
    fmt.Println("JSON:", string(data))

    fmt.Println("Downloading...")
    data, _ = readFromURL("http://echo.jsontest.com/title/Sir/" +
        "firstname/Anthony/surname/Other/username/anon123/")
    fmt.Println("Download:", string(data))

    person = &Person{}
    json.Unmarshal(data, person)
    fmt.Println("Decoded:", person)
}
```

Go to the Rescue!

In the preceding example code you can see the usage of struct tags prefixed with "`json:`". These provide hints to the "`encoding/json`" package that manages the encoding and decoding of theses objects. We can run this example and see the output of converting a struct into JSON and back again:

```
chapter3/webservice> go run webservice.go
Struct: &{ John Doe someuser somepassword}
JSON: {
  "firstname": "John",
  "surname": "Doe",
  "username": "someuser"
}
Downloading...
Download: {
   "username": "anon123",
   "title": "Sir",
   "surname": "Other",
   "firstname": "Anthony"
}

Decoded: &{Sir Anthony Other anon123 }
chapter3/webservice>
```

Encoding and decoding JSON for an HTTP request

Notice that zero value fields marked with `omitempty` were not included in the JSON output, and equally the password field that was marked as "`-`" (meaning do not include) was ignored when encoding the data. After downloading the data from a test web service, it was marshaled directly into an instance of the `Person` struct, leaving missing fields with their zero value. This was all possible using built-in features of the language and standard library. It's very straightforward, thanks to Go's readiness for working with web services.

Choosing your look and feel

As discussed in `Chapter 2`, *Graphical User Interface Challenges*, there are many approaches to graphical applications, leaving developers to choose between native versus hybrid (packaged web apps) and designers to pick from system look and feel, a multi-platform widget set, or even a custom design. The choice you make will probably be impacted by the needs of your application and the platforms you aim to target—is performance important and do you aim for a cross-platform deployment? Go doesn't have a standard graphical toolkit, and this omission has led developers to think it's not a language to be used for coding GUI applications. However, as we've seen in this chapter, it's a great fit for graphical application development. This leads to the question: which toolkits are available to build GUI apps in Go?

Simply put: a lot. You can see a list of the major, currently-maintained toolkits online at `https://awesome-go.com/#gui`—there is probably an option that suits most use cases. As we are looking to build high-performance applications that look great, we'll skip the items that rely on bundling web content to create hybrid applications. That still leaves a large list! There are some that give direct access to system components for a truly native experience, and some that provide abstracted APIs for the same platform look and feel. Others provide their own rendering of the user interface, which is consistent on all platforms they support (similar to Java Swing's *Metal* look and feel).

As well as a great language for GUI development, Go presents us with the opportunity to choose the right GUI toolkit for our application. `Section 2`, *Toolkits Using Existing Widgets* (Chapters `4`, `5`, `6` and `7`), and `Section 3`, *Modern Graphical Toolkits* (Chapters `8`, `9` and `10`), introduces developers to each of the main options, and shows how to start building beautiful graphical applications with each of them. `Section 2`, *Toolkits Using Existing Widgets*, is focused on building applications that match the operating system's look and feel, and `Section 3`, *Modern Graphical Toolkits*, is for applications that are going for a more modern look that aims to be consistent across multiple platforms.

Summary

In this chapter, we looked at how the Go language is very well-suited to developing graphical applications. Its design for handling concurrency makes the types of multithreading needed by GUIs easy to manage. Channels, the main thread-communication feature, are a little hard to learn, but through some basic examples, we saw how common concurrency issues could easily be avoided. The write-once-compile-anywhere ethos of Go means that developers can easily compile the same code and deliver native apps across most common platforms from a single codebase using the provided tools. As a modern language, it's designed to operate in a connected world and its support for network communications and web services is excellent – we ran examples that illustrated how objects can be easily transformed to and from common web formats.

Having explored the many ways that Go suits graphical application development, we also reflected on the many toolkits available to choose from. Despite not having a standard user interface, there are many possibilities for building great-looking graphical apps with Go. In Chapter 4, *Walk - Building Graphical Windows Applications,* Chapter 5, *andlabs UI - Cross-platform Native UIs,* Chapter 6, *Go-GTK - Multiple Platforms with GTK,* Chapter 7, *Go-Qt - Multiple Platforms with Qt* Chapter 8, *Shiny - Experimental Go GUI API* Chapter 9, *nk - Nuklear for Go,* and Chapter 10, *Fyne - Material Design based GUI,* we'll look at the different toolkits available and how to start building your first Go-based GUI. We start by exploring how to build traditional user interfaces, beginning with apps for Microsoft Windows in Chapter 4, *Walk - Building Graphical Windows Applications.*

Section 2: Toolkits Using Existing Widgets

Let's look first at graphical app toolkits for Go that use existing widgets. These toolkits help you build applications that will match the operating system's look and feel, which is a great choice if you want to build an app that's immediately familiar to your users. This approach may have a downside, however, in the amount of testing and potential customization required for each platform you aim to support. The APIs we explore have different levels of abstraction and platform integration, so depending on your application's requirements, the effort required may vary.

This section covers three different approaches to creating GUIs that match the operating system. Firstly, we'll look at Walk, which is a Go API that's specifically for creating Windows applications. This is the most direct way to create the app you wish for the Microsoft Windows desktop, but it's not obviously portable to other platforms. After that, we'll switch to andlabs/ui, which is an abstraction for Windows, macOS, Linux, and other widget sets. The application built in that chapter will use native platform widgets while being portable to many platforms. After then, we'll look at themeable widget sets, which behave the same way across multiple platforms and load themes that match the native user interface. In this category, we'll set up applications using Go bindings for the GTK+ and Qt toolkits.

Section 2: Toolkits Using Existing Widgets

The following chapters will be covered in this section:

- `Chapter 4`, *Walk – Building Graphical Windows Applications*
- `Chapter 5`, *andlabs UI – Cross-Platform Native UIs*
- `Chapter 6`, *Go-GTK – Multiple Platforms with GTK*
- `Chapter 7`, *Go-Qt – Multiple Platforms with Qt*

So let's dive right in and build our first application for Windows using the Walk API. If you are developing for a different operating system, then this chapter may be less relevant, so you can jump to `Chapter 5`, *andlabs UI - Cross-Platform Native UIs*, where we move on to andlabs UI.

4
Walk - Building Graphical Windows Applications

Walk is a Windows GUI toolkit for the Go programming language—its purpose is to enable us to build native desktop GUI applications for Windows using Go. It's built on top of the win package by the same authors, which is a direct Go binding of the Windows API. The main API is designed to make working with the **Windows API (WinAPI)** both easier and more in keeping with Go design principles.

In this chapter, we will cover the following topics:

- Background and aims
- Get started with Walk
- Benefits of a declarative API
- Building a user interface
- Walk in a cross-platform application

Let's get started exploring the background of the Walk project and its solution for Go apps developed for the Windows platform.

Background and aims

The Walk project is one of the oldest GUI toolkits for Go, having been started in September of 2010. The name stands for **Windows Application Library Kit**, which reflects its purpose to support building GUI apps for the Microsoft platform. Its project home is on GitHub, where you can check out the latest developments and discussions: `https://github.com/lxn/walk`.

The project API was inspired by the Qt Widgets module for the Qt framework (which will be covered in `Chapter 7`, *Go-Qt - Multiple Platforms with QT*). Qt Widgets is a selection of standard user interface features for creating graphical applications with a familiar look and feel. By matching the Qt design closely, it's possible to use some of the Qt tools, such as UI designer, when preparing a Walk-based user interface for your application. Walk currently supports the most commonly-utilized widgets, which means it may not be suitable for every application. At the time of writing, the **Multi Document Interface** (**MDI**) and dockable tool windows described in `Chapter 2`, *Graphical User Interface Challenges* are not supported—though the author notes that it is an open source project and contributions are welcome.

Walk offers a great API for building applications for the Windows desktop. Although it doesn't provide the choice of themes or presentation styles that some toolkits offer, applications that use it look exactly like other Windows apps. One of the project aims is for it to work without any additional dependencies or complicated setup, which means that it's a great place to get started—as you'll see in the next section.

Get started with walk

Now that we've learned a bit about the Walk library, let's see it in action. The steps that follow aim to create a trivial application using the Walk API, which will verify everything is working. If you have any problems with these steps, consider looking at the `Appendix`, *Installation Details,* and work through the *Microsoft Windows* section within *Installing Go.*

Setup

Before we can start writing a GUI with Walk, we need to install the library—this means that Go will be able to compile the code we write, and also that any development environments installed will be able to offer suggestions when writing the code. Simply execute `go get github.com/lxn/walk` from the Command Prompt. This command will download and install the Walk library to `%GOPATH%/src` so it can be used in your applications. If you have not set the `GOPATH` environment variable manually, don't worry, as the Go installer will have set up a default for you (normally `%HOMEDRIVE%%HOMEPATH%/go`).

Code

Now let's write some code! First of all, create a new directory to put this code into—due to the way that Walk binaries are created (see the following code), we need to build at a directory level, rather with than single files, so it's good to have a clean workspace. Copy the following code into a file named `hello.go`:

```go
package main

import (
    "github.com/lxn/walk"
    . "github.com/lxn/walk/declarative"
)

func main() {
    MainWindow{
        Title: "Hello",
        Layout: VBox{},
        Children: []Widget{
            Label{Text: "Hello World!"},
            PushButton{
                Text: "Quit",
                OnClicked: func() {
                    walk.App().Exit(0)
                },
            },
        },
    }.Run()
}
```

In the preceding code, you can see two different imports for Walk—we will talk about that more later. Inside the `main()` function, we set up a simple window with two items in a `VBox` layout: one `Label`, and one `PushButton` that will exit the app when clicked. Next, we need to create an additional file, named `hello.exe.manifest`, with the following contents (this manifest file is needed in the build process):

```xml
<?xml version="1.0" encoding="UTF-8" standalone="yes"?>
<assembly xmlns="urn:schemas-microsoft-com:asm.v1" manifestVersion="1.0" xmlns:asmv3="urn:schemas-microsoft-com:asm.v3">
    <assemblyIdentity version="1.0.0.0" processorArchitecture="*" name="HelloWorld" type="win32"/>
    <dependency>
        <dependentAssembly>
            <assemblyIdentity type="win32" name="Microsoft.Windows.Common-Controls" version="6.0.0.0" processorArchitecture="*" publicKeyToken="6595b64144ccf1df" language="*"/>
```

```
            </dependentAssembly>
        </dependency>
        <asmv3:application>
            <asmv3:windowsSettings
    xmlns="http://schemas.microsoft.com/SMI/2005/WindowsSettings">
                <dpiAware>true</dpiAware>
            </asmv3:windowsSettings>
        </asmv3:application>
</assembly>
```

This manifest file is required to tell Windows runtime that we are using the Common Controls framework version 6.0.0.0 (or newer), which is required by the Walk APIs.

Build

Once you have saved the two files, you can build the application. Due to the nature of a Walk application (specifically, the Windows APIs that are described in the manifest file), there is an additional step to prepare the directory. The walk applications require a manifest file that will be embedded in the executable we are building. To do this, we need to download the rsrc tool from `github.com/akavel/rsrc`, which will embed the required metadata. We then run the `rsrc.exe` command with the `-manifest` parameter to generate the embedded file, as follows:

```
chapter4\hello>go get github.com/akavel/rsrc

chapter4\hello>rsrc.exe -manifest hello.exe.manifest

chapter4\hello>dir /b
hello.exe.manifest
hello.go
rsrc.syso

chapter4\hello>
```

The rsrc tool generates the .syso file to embed

That step will create a `.syso` file, which will automatically get included in the next step. Now we can actually run the go build. On the command line, we add an extra `ldflag` parameter, set to `"-H windowsgui"`, which tells the compiler to output a GUI app, rather than a command-line app. While it would work OK without this parameter, your application would show a command-line window behind it when launched from a regular icon-click:

```
chapter4\hello>go build -ldflags="-H windowsgui"

chapter4\hello>dir /b
hello.exe
hello.exe.manifest
hello.go
rsrc.syso

chapter4\hello>
```

Running go build again will embed the `.syso` file

Run

The hello world app that was built in the last step can be executed in two ways: either by running it from the command line, or by clicking the icon from the file manager:

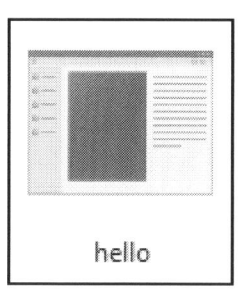

The hello app icon

You should see an icon like the preceding one in your file manager in the current directory. Alternatively, return to the command prompt and simply enter the `hello.exe` command from the project directory. Using either method, you should now see this app running on your desktop (you may need to hunt as it's a very small window):

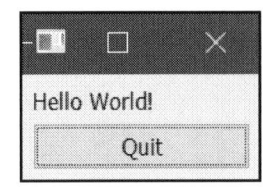

A Walk-based Hello World

Benefits of a declarative API

As illustrated in the code example, the Walk API is split in to two notable packages: `github.com/lxn/walk` and `github.com/lxn/walk/declarative`. The declarative API is the preferred approach for developing application GUIs using Walk, as it offers a better abstraction to work with and is more idiomatic. The implementation of the declarative API also provides various standard metrics and default values that help to create a standard user interface with minimal code. The package is typically imported using the `.` prefix, so that GUI code can avoid repeatedly using the `declarative.` prefix.

Compared with the native API

Using the native API, (Go bindings of the native winAPI) is possible, but in most cases this is more verbose, as you are working directly with a low-level API. Coding in this way can't make use of standard metrics or configurations that are handled by the higher-level declarative API, designed to better suit a modern programming language. To illustrate the difference, here is what the preceding example would look like if we only used the native API:

```
package main

import (
   "log"

   "github.com/lxn/walk"
)
```

```go
var marginSize = 9

func buildWindow() (*walk.MainWindow, error) {
   win, err := walk.NewMainWindowWithName("Hello")
   if err != nil {
      return nil, err
   }
   layout := walk.NewVBoxLayout()
   layout.SetMargins(walk.Margins{marginSize, marginSize, marginSize, marginSize})
   layout.SetSpacing(marginSize)
   win.SetLayout(layout)

   label, err := walk.NewLabel(win)
   if err != nil {
      return win, err
   }
   label.SetText("Hello World!")

   button, err := walk.NewPushButton(win)
   if err != nil {
      return win, err
   }
   button.SetText("Quit")
   button.Clicked().Attach(func() {
      walk.App().Exit(0)
   })

   return win, nil
}

func main() {
   win, err := buildWindow()
   if err != nil {
      log.Fatalln(err)
   }

   win.SetVisible(true)
   win.Run()
}
```

This code can be compiled in the same way as the previous example, and when run, it will look exactly the same. Clearly, this is a lot more code to obtain the same result and it is a lot harder to read with no particular gain. The error handling that clutters this alternative example is handled implicitly when using the declarative API. Putting aside the differences in the Go syntax, it should be clear that the native API calls used in this example are directly manipulating widgets from the WinAPI. In fact, each of the objects created (through `NewLabel()`, `NewPushButton()`, and `NewMainWindowWithName()`) is a lightweight wrapper for Go the bindings of the WinAPI (provided by `github.com/lxn/win`).

There are many times where usage of this native API can be useful; most commonly, when you need control of fine details or are dealing with changes to existing widgets, for example within event-handling code. The declarative API is designed for easy definition of an application user interface, but it isn't normally enough to manage the workflow of a complex GUI. Therefore, it's common to use both of these APIs together—using the power of each at the right time.

Using both APIs for flexibility

It's important to understand the difference between the declarative and native APIs, as any application will probably require the use of both. Using the declarative syntax is great for a concise description of the user interface, but runtime manipulation of the graphical elements will require a reference to one of the native widgets that this code wraps. To make this connection, each of the declarative types has an `AssignTo` field, which is typically passed a pointer to a `var`, which itself is a pointer to an object that represents a native type. This means that, during the user-interface-construction phase, the declarative API parser can create native widgets and set the pointer within your code for later use. Let's look at this feature in action:

```
package main

import (
   "fmt"

   "github.com/lxn/walk"
   . "github.com/lxn/walk/declarative"
)

func main() {
   var message *walk.Label
   var userName *walk.TextEdit
```

```
MainWindow{
    Title: "Hello",
    Layout: VBox{},
    Children: []Widget{
        Label{
            AssignTo: &message,
            Text: "Hello World!",
        },
        TextEdit{
            AssignTo: &userName,
            OnTextChanged: func() {
                welcome := fmt.Sprintf("Hello %s!", userName.Text())
                message.SetText(welcome)
            },
        },
        PushButton{
            Text: "Quit",
            OnClicked: func() {
                walk.App().Exit(0)
            },
        },
    },
}.Run()
}
```

The preceding code can be compiled exactly as the previous *hello world* examples (don't forget to include and process a manifest if you have created a new project for this sample). When running this example, you should see the following interface with an additional text input field. When you type into the input box, the welcome message will change, for example `John Doe` was entered for this screenshot:

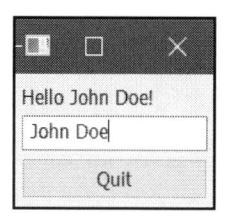

The hello world with name entry

You will notice that the `message` and `userName` variables are not initialized directly by the application code, but by the time the function assigned to `OnTextChanged` is called, they hold valid references to instantiated widgets. Using this approach, we can get the type of access that the native API wrappers provide while also writing an easy-to-read UI definition provided by the declarative API.

Building a user interface

Armed with the knowledge of how the Walk API is designed and utilized, let's move on to a real-world example. In this book, we will be building the same user interface for each toolkit explored (in Chapters 4, 5, 6, 7, 8, 9, and 10), which will be a simple email application named GoMail. Due to the close relationship between Walk and Qt widgets, we can quickly get started designing the user interface using the UI Builder included in Qt Creator (documentation is available at `http://doc.qt.io/qtcreator/creator-using-qt-designer.html`).

The basic application will be formed of two windows: the main email browser and a secondary window for composing new emails. The main window will contain a list or tree view that shows the emails we have received, a larger panel to display the content of the currently-selected email, and a menu and toolbar for accessing the various features of our email application:

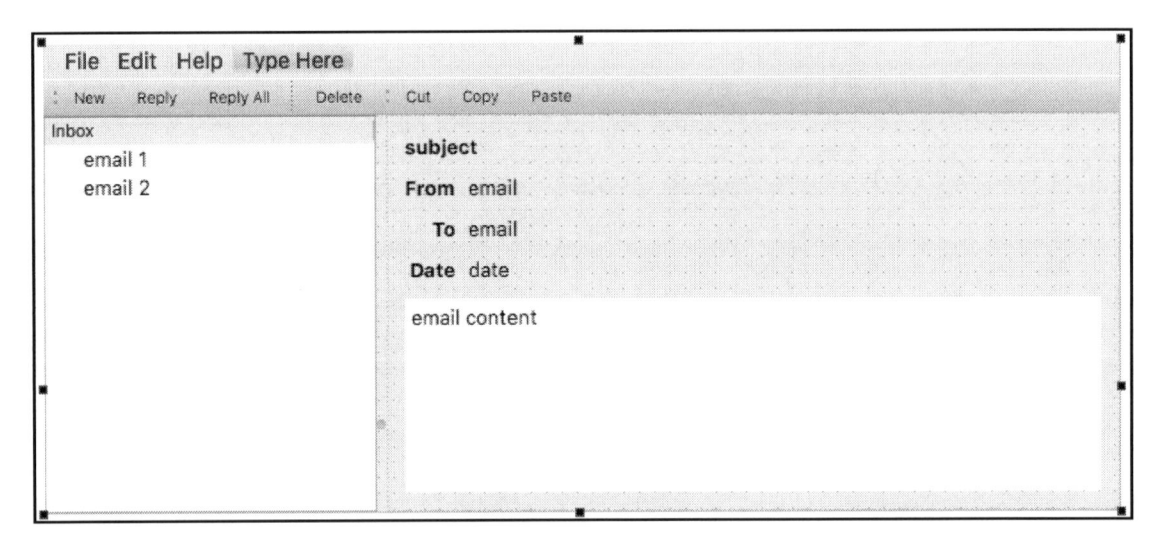

The main email window within Qt Designer

To compose new emails, we will show a secondary window that will ask for the various details for the email being sent. Opening a new window will allow the user to continue reading emails while they compose new emails to be sent. The compose window will also have buttons to send or discard the email being written:

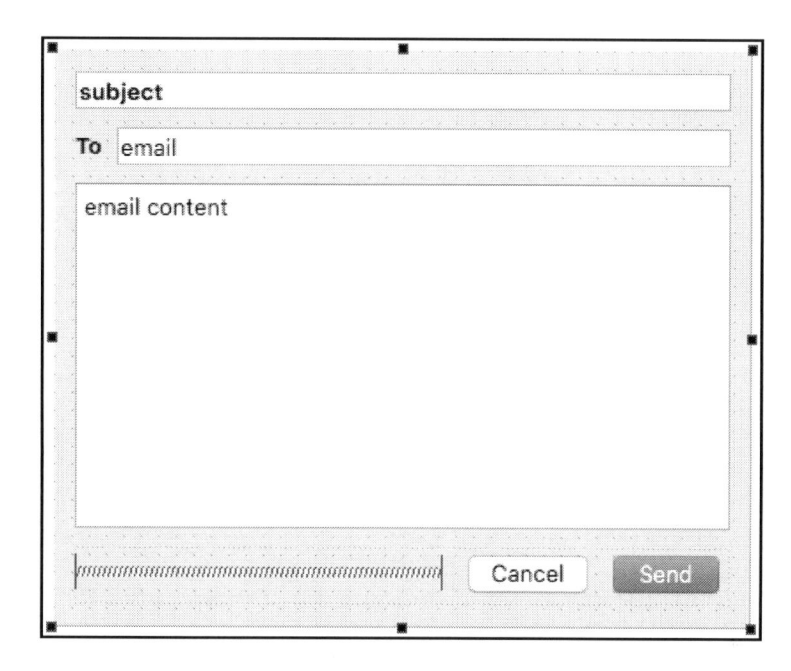

The additional compose window being designed

Style

Applications built using Walk are composed of native Windows components, and, as such, the style is set by the implementation provided by Microsoft (this is provided by Common Controls, part of `ComCtl32.dll`). The version required by Walk (version 6.0) adds support for visual styles; this is the system that provides the ability for applications to use the correct visual style for the version of the Windows desktop that is currently running.

This functionality is available as far back as Windows XP, but comes as standard from Vista onward:

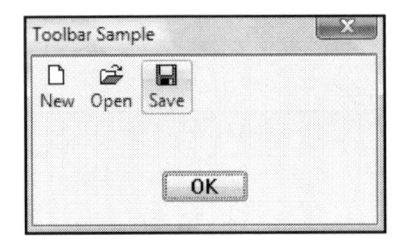

Windows 7 default theme (Aero –used with permission from Microsoft)

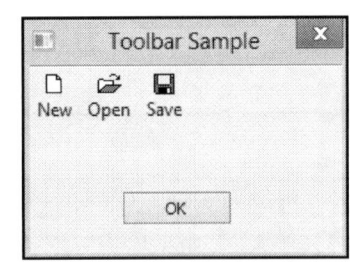

Windows 8 default theme (called Windows used with permission from Microsoft)

The preceding images show how a simple application will adapt to the theme on different versions of Windows. These illustrations are using the default theme, but the user may apply additional customizations on their desktop, which will also apply to any applications built with Walk.

Layout

Walk layouts (like those Qt Widget layouts they were inspired by) are based on a limited number of grid-based variants. The list of implemented layouts includes the following:

- GridLayout: Items are laid out in a regular grid
- VBoxLayout: Items are placed in a single column
- HBoxLayout: Items are aligned in a single row

If you have explored the Qt UI Builder or are familiar with Qt, you may be expecting a fourth layout, FormLayout, which is not currently present in Walk. This can be simulated, however, using a two-column GridLayout and applying alignment properties as required.

Chapter 4

In addition to the standard layouts, there are various widgets (some of which are invisible in the final interface) that help group UI elements and provide a more satisfying layout. The most commonly used of these are as follows:

- `Splitter`: Places a draggable split bar between two child widgets
- `Spacer`: Used to create visual padding so items can shrink instead of filling space
- `Separator`: Provides a visual separation between widgets, such as in a toolbar or menu
- `ScrollView`: A standard widget for providing scrollable content
- `GroupBox`: A visual widget container with a border and optional title
- `Composite`: A widget container used to logically group items

Let's get started implementing our email app user interface by creating some Go code using the declarative API. We start with a `MainWindow` that has a suitable `MinSize` set and an `HSplitter` that will hold our content. `TreeView` is used for listing emails on the left of the splitter (as the first item in the `Children` list), and on the right (item two in the list) is a `Composite` set to use a `Grid` layout—the closest we have to the form layout designed. Within the group, we add many instances of the child `Label` where we will show email details (that will be updated in *Communicating with the GUI* section):

```
MainWindow{
    Title:   "GoMail",
    Layout:  HBox{},
    MinSize: Size{600, 400},
    Children: []Widget{
        HSplitter{
            Children: []Widget{
                TreeView{},
                Composite{
                    Layout: Grid{Columns: 3},
                    Children: []Widget{
                        Label{
                            Text:       "subject",
                            Font:       Font{Bold: true},
                            ColumnSpan: 3,
                        },
                        Label{
                            Text: "From",
                            Font: Font{Bold: true},
                        },
                        Label{
                            Text:       "email",
                            ColumnSpan: 2,
                        },
```

```
                    Label{
                        Text: "To",
                        Font: Font{Bold: true},
                    },
                    Label{
                        Text:       "email",
                        ColumnSpan: 2,
                    },
                    Label{
                        Text: "Date",
                        Font: Font{Bold: true},
                    },
                    Label{
                        Text:       "email",
                        ColumnSpan: 2,
                    },
                    TextEdit{
                        Text:       "email content",
                        ReadOnly:   true,
                        ColumnSpan: 3,
                    },
                },
            },
        },
    },
  },
}
```

The preceding code can be run by replacing the `MainWindow` in the previous *hello world* example, recompiling, and then running the example again. If you set up a new project, remember to include the manifest file and run `rsrc` again! When run, it should look like the following screenshot, taken on Windows 10:

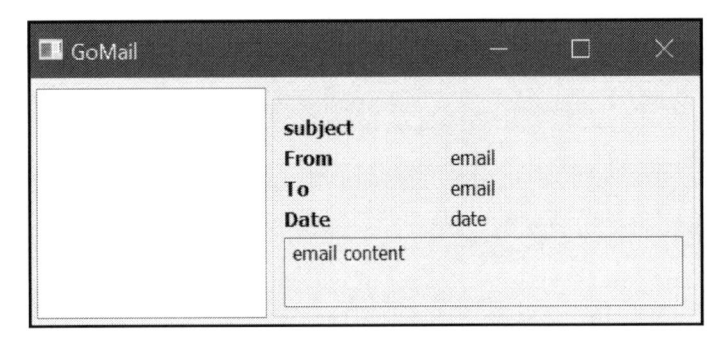

The basic email interface using Walk's declarative API

Next, we will make a `Dialog` with a similar layout that replaces the instances of `Label` with `LineEdit` or `TextEdit` for entering details of a new email. Last, we add another `Composite` with an `HBox` layout that contains the instances of `PushButton` for `Cancel` and `Send`, along with an `HSpacer` to complete the layout:

```
Dialog{
    Title:    "New GoMail",
    Layout:   Grid{Columns: 3},
    MinSize: Size{400, 320},
    Children: []Widget{
        Composite{
            Layout: Grid{Columns: 3},
            Children: []Widget{
                LineEdit{
                    Text:       "subject",
                    Font:       Font{Bold: true},
                    ColumnSpan: 3,
                },
                Label{
                    Text: "To",
                    Font: Font{Bold: true},
                },
                LineEdit{
                    Text:       "email",
                    ColumnSpan: 2,
                },
                TextEdit{
                    Text:       "email content",
                    ColumnSpan: 3,
                },
                Composite{
                    Layout:     HBox{},
                    ColumnSpan: 3,
                    Children: []Widget{
                        HSpacer{},
                        PushButton{Text: "Cancel"},
                        PushButton{Text: "Send"},
                    },
                },
            },
        },
    },
}
```

If you want to test this code, the easiest approach is to replace `Dialog` with `MainWindow` and run it like the main layout (don't forget to change it back before moving on).

Once we have some event-handling, this will open like a dialog box, which is why it's not a `MainWindow` in the preceding listing. Running the code should produce the following screenshot:

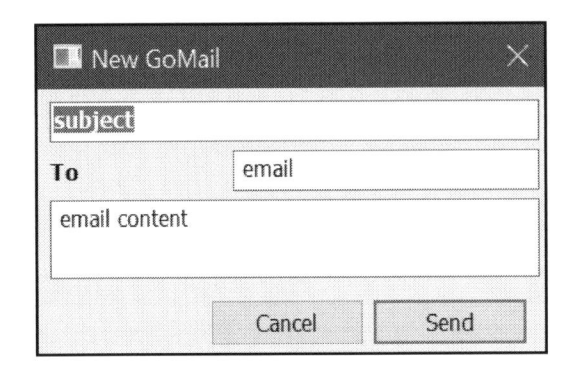

The compose email view using Walk's declarative API

That's all that's required to complete the layout code of the main interface features. Next, let's add the menu, toolbar, and set up actions for the buttons we have defined.

Toolbar and menu

Adding menus and toolbars with the declarative API is very straightforward. The `MainWindow` struct has the `Menu` field (which is a slice of `MenuItem`) and the `ToolBar` field (which takes a `ToolBar` struct that contains an `Items` field for the `MenuItem` list). Each item in the list is either an `Action`, a `Separator`, or another `Menu` that mirrors the designs we created earlier.

Each `Action` in the declarative API expects a `Text` string that is used for the display in menus. Toolbars also use this content for tooltips, and for display if the style is set to `ToolBarButtonTextOnly`. An `Image` field allows you to set an icon for the toolbars if you want to reference installed images or icons distributed with your app. Most important is the `OnTriggered` field, which should be set to a `func()` that will be executed when the button or menu item is clicked.

The following code is used set up the menu on the `MainWindow` we created in the *Layout* section:

```
MenuItems: []MenuItem{
    Menu{
        Text: "File",
        Items: []MenuItem{
```

```
            Action{
                Text: "New",
            },
            Action{
                Text: "Reply",
            },
            Action{
                Text: "Reply All",
            },
            Separator{},
            Action{
                Text: "Delete",
            },
            Separator{},
            Action{
                Text: "Quit",
            },
        },
    },
    Menu{
        Text:  "Edit",
        Items: []MenuItem{
            Action{
                Text: "Cut",
            },
            Action{
                Text: "Copy",
            },
            Action{
                Text: "Paste",
            },
        },
    },
    Menu{
        Text: "Help",
    },
},
```

The code for the toolbar is almost identical and so the details have been omitted, but you can add it to the `MainWindow` using the `ToolBar` field, as follows:

```
ToolBar: ToolBar{
    Items: []MenuItem{
        Action{
            Text: "New",
        },

// full listing omitted but is available in the book's example code
```

```
        },
        ButtonStyle: ToolBarButtonTextOnly,
    },
```

The result of the code added should be a window like that in the following screenshot:

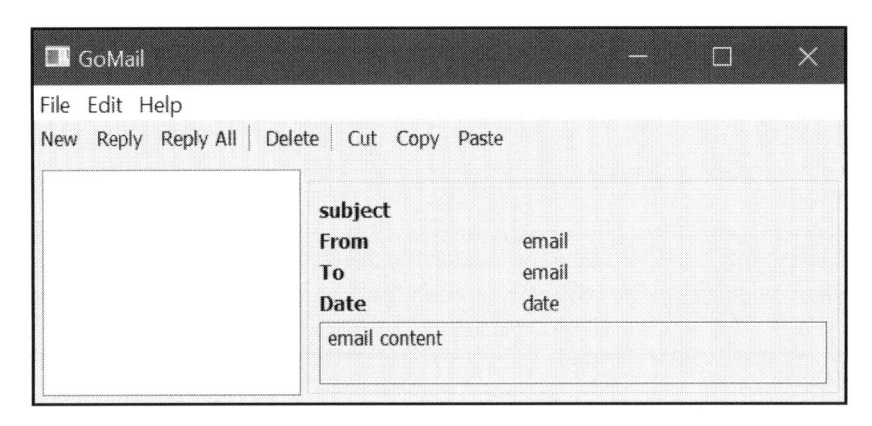

The main email interface with the menu and toolbar added

Don't worry if the code for the new button didn't work for you—the completed application source code is available to download at `https://github.com/PacktPublishing/Hands-On-GUI-Application-Development-in-Go`. Before the user interface code is completed, we should add some code that will help us to navigate the app. The simplest is the quit item from the file menu. Just add the following code to the preceding `Quit` action:

```
OnTriggered: func() {
    walk.App().Exit(0)
},
```

The opening of our compose dialog is a little more complicated because a dialog needs to know which parent it's loading from. To do this, create a local variable, called `window`, of the `*walk.MainWindow` type and assign it to the `MainWindow` declarative API using the following line:

```
AssignTo:    &window,
```

This can then be referenced in your New action handler, where NewCompose is a function that creates the email compose window:

```
OnTriggered: func() {
    NewCompose().Run(window)
},
```

Finally, we should set up default behavior for the buttons on our compose dialog. To do this, we need to declare two *walk.PushButton variables that are assigned to the Cancel and Send buttons, respectively. By then passing these to the dialog definition using the CancelButton and DefaultButton fields, we get the appropriate behavior:

```
DefaultButton: &send,
CancelButton:  &cancel,
```

Now, let's set the cancel button to close the dialog—you will need to create a walk.Dialog variable to AssignTo the declarative API as with the main window. With these steps complete, either clicking the **cancel** button or pressing the *Esc* key should dismiss the compose window:

```
OnClicked: func() {
    dialog.Cancel()
},
```

Communicating with the GUI

To populate the user interface, we need to define a data model and load some test data. Within the code for this book, there is a client package that contains a data model and some test data to simulate an email server. We will use that package by importing it into the Go files for this project using the github.com/PacktPublishing/Hands-On-GUI-Application-Development-in-Go/client package. We won't cover the details of the package in this chapter, but we will reference its defined client.EmailServer and client.EmailMessage types. The email message definition is as follows—the field names will be useful when loading email details in the UI:

```
type EmailMessage struct {
    Subject, Content string
    To, From         Email
    Date             time.Time
}
```

Walk - Building Graphical Windows Applications

View model

To communicate with the Walk user interface, we need to define another data model. This view model is designed to communicate information in a way that the declarative API understands. We will create a type named `EmailClientModel`, which will handle translating data from our client code to our user interface definition. Create a new file, `model.go`, where you can start to define these models. The first section of the code allows an email server to be set causing the email list to update accordingly.

For brevity, the trivial methods for `walk.TreeModel` have been left out—you can find them in the full code listing for this book:

```
type EmailClientModel struct {
   Server *client.EmailServer

   root walk.TreeItem

   itemsResetPublisher  walk.TreeItemEventPublisher
   itemChangedPublisher walk.TreeItemEventPublisher
}

// TreeModel methods omitted - see full code listing

func (e *EmailClientModel) SetServer(s *client.EmailServer) {
   e.Server = s

   e.root = NewInboxList(s.ListMessages())
   e.itemsResetPublisher.Publish(e.root)
}

func NewEmailClientModel() *EmailClientModel{
   return &EmailClientModel{}
}
```

The email list for this model needs to represent our email list as items in a tree, rather than a simple list as returned by the client code. To support this we need another type, `EmailModel`, that implements the `walk.TreeItem` interface. Here, again, we have omitted the trivial details—each email item will never contain child elements and so we can ignore this complexity:

```
type EmailModel struct {
   email  *client.EmailMessage
   parent walk.TreeItem
}

// TreeItem functions omitted - see full code listing
```

We want to group our emails under an `Inbox` heading, so we need to build the root node and then populate the email list within it. For this, we define one more type, `InboxList`, which also implements `walk.TreeItem`, but this time it will allow access to the child list (emails) it holds. We will also need to write a method for building the inbox list from a list of messages (which we would be provided by the client code). See how the final method in this code snippet creates instances of `EmailModel` for each message and adds them to the inbox list:

```
type InboxList struct {
    emails []walk.TreeItem
}

func (i *InboxList) Text() string {
    return "Inbox"
}

func NewInboxList(l []*client.EmailMessage) *InboxList {
    list := &InboxList{}

    for _, item := range l {
        list.emails = append(list.emails, &EmailModel{item, list})
    }

    return list
}
```

Detail view

Now that we have a data model built, let's display the data that's loaded. Starting with the email detail view, we will make use of Walk's declarative API, `DataBinder`. This allows us to avoid having to manually set the data on each label every time a new message is loaded. To work correctly, we also need to create a `walk.DataBinder` to assign to—this will handle the actual bindings:

```
emailDetail *walk.DataBinder
```

Then we can update the `Composite` widget that displays the email information to use this data binding. Let's also set the default content through the `DataSource` field. This information will come from the model, which we will initialize shortly:

```
DataBinder: DataBinder{
    AssignTo: &emailDetail,
    DataSource: model.Server.CurrentMessage(),
},
```

Then, each item simply has its static `Text` field changed to an appropriate `Bind()` call; the parameter will be the name of the field on an `client.EmailMessage` type described in the *View model* section:

```
Text:      Bind("Subject"),
```

For the `Date` field, we can't directly bind a `time.Time` type, so use the `DateString()` helper instead:

```
Text:      Bind("DateString"),
```

And finally, let's create a helper method that will allow us to update the email message that is currently bound:

```
func (g *GoMailUIBrowse) SetMessage(email *client.EmailMessage) {
    g.emailDetail.SetDataSource(email)
    g.emailDetail.Reset()
}
```

List view

Most of the work for our email list was done in the preceding model code—now we need to connect it to the user interface. The following code sets up a `walk.TreeView` class that we use to keep track of the current item and assigns it to the declarative `TreeView`. After that, the model is set and then we pass a function that will be informed when the current item changes:

```
emailList *walk.TreeView

TreeView{
    AssignTo: &g.emailList,
    Model: model,
    OnCurrentItemChanged: func() {
        item := g.emailList.CurrentItem()

        if email, ok := item.(*EmailModel); ok {
            g.SetMessage(email.email)
        }
    },
},
```

With all that in place, the application will load the email details from the current email message using `model.Server.CurrentMessage()` via the default `DataSource` of the `DataBinder`. When the main list is clicked, the function passed to `OnCurrentItemChanged` checks that the item is an `EmailModel` and, if so, updates the detail view. Finally, we need to set up the model that will be used in the preceding code, as follows:

```
model := NewEmailClientModel()
model.SetServer(client.NewTestServer())
```

This model is used to set the list content and also to set the default content of the detail view. When built and run, the application should now look like a complete, albeit basic, email client:

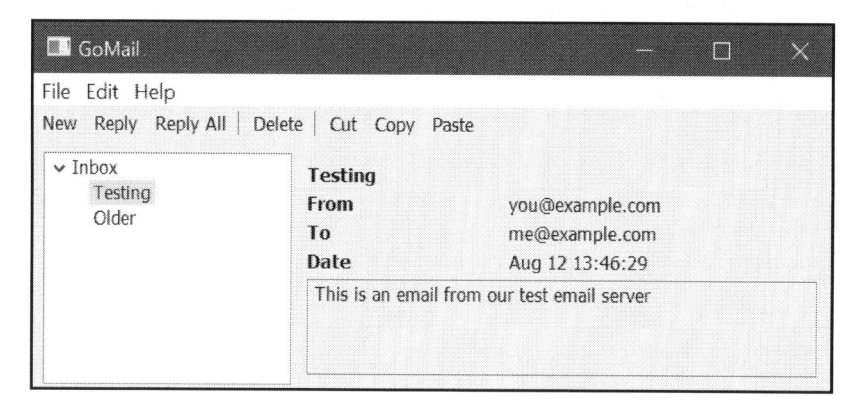

Our email interface with some test data loaded

Background processing

All user interface code with Walk must run on the main thread; this is a constraint of the winAPI that handles the widgets. This means that any work in the background must change threads before running any UI code. This is done using the `Synchronize()` function on `walk.Window`. It takes a single function as a parameter and ensures that the code it contains will be run appropriately.

[93]

Walk - Building Graphical Windows Applications

To handle the updating when an incoming email arrives, we create a new function, `incomingEmail()`, that will update our email list model. This function will cause an email to be added to the model, which will happen on the main thread so that the user interface can be updated to reflect the new data:

```
func (g *GoMailUIBrowse) incomingEmail(email *client.EmailMessage, model *EmailClientModel) {
   g.window.Synchronize(func() {
      model.AddEmail(email)
   })
}
```

To support this change, we need to update `EmailClientModel` to add this new `AddEmail()` function. The function will add an item to the list and publish the data-reset event:

```
func (e *EmailClientModel) AddEmail(email *client.EmailMessage) {
   e.root.Add(email)
   e.itemsResetPublisher.Publish(e.root)
}
```

This, in turn, needs an `Add()` function in the `InboxList` type that we created to provide data to the model:

```
func (i *InboxList) Add(email *client.EmailMessage) {
   i.emails = append(i.emails, &EmailModel{email, i})
}
```

Finally, we need to listen to the `Incoming()` server channel, which will deliver each new email to our application. As this channel read will block until an email is received, this must run in a separate goroutine—hence the background processing. When an email arrives, we simply call the function we just created, passing the new `email` and a reference to the `model` which we should refresh:

```
server := client.NewTestServer()
model.SetServer(server)

go func() {
   incoming := server.Incoming()
   for email = range incoming {
      g.incomingEmail(email, model)
   }
}()
```

With this code in place, you will see the email list update when a new email arrives. The email can then be clicked to see the details.

Walk in a cross-platform application

Walk is clearly a library aimed at creating graphical user interfaces for the Microsoft Windows platform—but this doesn't mean that building your application with Walk limits you to Windows only. Using the techniques explored in Chapter 3, *Go to the Rescue!*, we can set the code for Windows to be conditionally included when building for the platform, and introduce other files that could provide a user interface for other platforms.

The first step is to update the files we have built so far to only build on Windows. We do this using the build constraints comment format (you could also use file naming for this step if you wish):

```
// +build windows

package main

...
```

We then introduce a new file that will handle the fallback case when we're on a different platform. For this simple project we will call it nonwindows.go as the content will run for any computer not running Windows. In this file, we place a small amount of code that will print a failure message and quit if the application is launched on any unsupported platform. Note that the build constraint here is set to compile on any non-Windows platform; this too would be updated to match any fallback cases your project may have:

```
// +build !windows

package main

import "log"

func NewMailUIBrowse() {
    log.Fatalln("GoMail with Walk only works on windows")
}
```

Walk - Building Graphical Windows Applications

Note the `NewMailUIBrowse()` function name—this is our generic method name for loading and running the main GoMail browse interface. You probably need to update the name of the method that was previously used to run the application. Most likely, you used `main()`, but we will need to provide a new `main.go` with that method. This new file is the only file in the project with no build constraints. It will compile for any platform and, when running, it will execute whichever `NewMailUIBrowse()` method was compiled in for the target platform:

```
package main

func main() {
    NewMailUIBrowse()
}
```

If we switch to another operating system, say macOS, and compile the code now, there should be no compile errors. Running the application will yield a simple error message and it will immediately quit. Clearly this code could do something more meaningful than just exiting with an error message:

```
[chapter4/gomail> go env GOOS
darwin
[chapter4/gomail> go build
[chapter4/gomail> ./gomail
2018/08/13 18:06:17 GoMail with Walk only works on windows
[chapter4/gomail>
```

And so you see how we can use Walk to develop a Windows-specific user interface. As part of a multi-platform strategy, this could help ensure greater platform integration for your audience on Windows, or you may wish to provide certain sections of your application with platform-specific implementations. Whatever the reason, you can see how easy it is to include multiple platform-specific alternatives within a cross-platform application build with Go.

Summary

In this chapter, we started the exploration of GUI toolkits by first looking at the Walk API for Windows' graphical application development. We looked at how to get a Go-based Windows application running, and learned how the Walk project is structured into separate declarative and native APIs. We also saw how each of these APIs provides different benefits and how they are best combined to create a simple application.

As the Walk design was heavily inspired by the Qt project (which we will return to in `Chapter 7`, *Go-Qt - Multiple Platforms with Qt*), we were able to use the interface-designer features of Qt Creator to mock up a basic email application that we then built out using the declarative API. This email application is a design that can be reused for each of the toolkit-exploration chapters. To support the example applications, we imported another package that is provided in this book's source code, which provides some data models and test data. By combining our UI code, the email client library, and the data binding capabilities of the Walk toolkit, we were able to create a simple email application that would run natively on the Windows platform using the system-provided widgets. Through some small alterations, it was shown that this could be part of a wider cross-platform strategy where each platform's graphical presentation is provided by different toolkits.

In the next chapter, we will move our focus to code that provides a native look and feel across multiple platforms. We will be looking specifically at andlabs UI—a GUI toolkit that aims to provide a look and feel that matches the current operating system. If used on Windows, this will be similar to Walk, but it also adapts to different desktop platforms while only needing to write the user-interface code once.

5
andlabs UI - Cross-platform Native UIs

Like the Walk API we explored in the previous chapter, andlabs UI aims to create a Go API on top of operating system native widgets, but, unlike Walk, andlabs UI project supports multiple operating systems with a single API. This means that graphical applications created using the API can be compiled and run on Windows, macOS, and Linux using the same source code.

In this chapter, we will explore cross-platform native applications that match the operating system's look and feel. In particular, we will cover the following topics:

- Background and history
- Getting started with andlabs UI
- Generic API for multiple platforms
- Building a user interface
- Challenges with multiple native GUIs

Before we get started with the benefits and complexities of a cross-platform API using native widget toolkits, let's look more at the background of the project.

Background and history

The andlabs UI project was created to provide a simple-to-use way to create native graphical applications using Go. The API is minimal as it aims to provide only what is necessary to create GUI programs. The core is a C library, which hides the platform-specific APIs, allowing the main library to manage the idiomatic considerations for a Go GUI API. Recently, the C library (libui) was moved to a separate project, which is included in the Go project for developers' convenience.

There is a demonstration of the widgets available included in the project—when run on a Linux computer, it will look like the following screenshot:

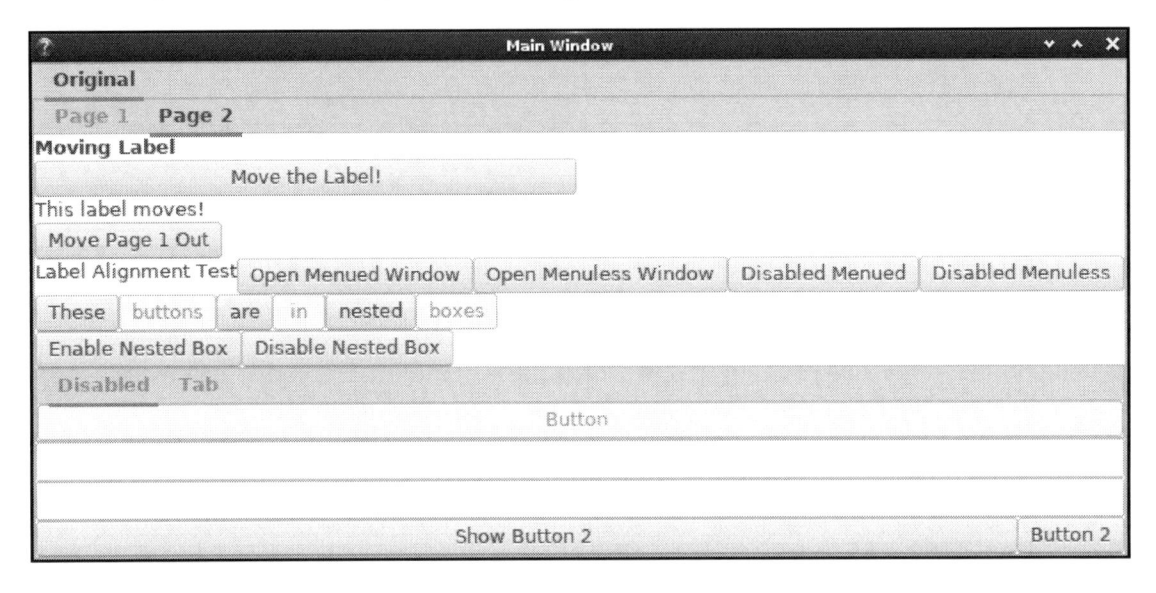

The widget demo from andlabs UI

As a platform-native implementation, the widgets in andlabs UI will look different on each operating system. On Windows and macOS, the library uses the native widget set, and on Linux it uses the GTK+ library. This approach creates applications that are consistent with other software on the current computer and so should be simple for users to understand. This approach is powerful and has substantial benefits, but can add complications for application developers. We will explore the benefits and challenges of such an approach within this chapter, but first let's get running with a simple *hello world* application.

Getting started with andlabs UI

Andlabs UI is easy to get started with on most platforms, but the details vary from system to system. Due to the nature of linking to many different operating systems' native widget toolkits, there can be some hidden complexities, especially when developing Linux-based applications. Before we can build our first andlabs-based application GUI, there is some setup required. We need to prepare the current development environment to work with native widgets.

Prerequisites

As an API that utilizes the native widgets for each platform, the prerequisites vary for Windows, macOS, and Linux. Any packages that need to be installed in this section will be required by any users of the applications that you develop as well. It's also necessary to have CGo running (the ability for Go code to call C functions is illustrated in Chapter 3, *Go to the Rescue!*), which may require the installation of additional build tools.

Microsoft windows

The native widgets used on Windows are the Common Controls—the same used by the Walk library that we explored in detail in the Chapter 4, *Walk - Building Graphical Windows Applications*. As they are native to the operating system, no installation is required when using Windows Vista or later. If you want to support earlier versions (back to Windows XP), it's possible if you install at least version 6.0 of ComCtl32.dll.

Andlabs UI, like many of the other toolkits featured in this book, requires the presence of CGo to utilize native libraries. On a full development system, it's likely that this is already set up. If you're unsure, or would like a reminder of how to set up the Cgo dependencies, please check *Setting up CGo* section from the Appendix, *Installation Details*.

macOS

When developing for macOS, the native widgets are used directly. As these are provided by the operating system for every recent version of macOS, no additional libraries are required.

CGo support is required for andlabs UI and this requires XCode command-line tools to be installed. If you have not already set this up please check the *Setting up CGo* section from the Appendix, *Installation Details*.

Linux

On Linux, andlabs UI uses the GTK+ widget library (which we will explore in detail in Chapter 6, *Go-GTK - Multiple Platforms with GTK*) and so the library must be installed on your computer. If you have the Gnome desktop installed, or other applications that use GTK+ (such as Gimp), the library will already be installed. If not, you will need to install this dependency using your system's package manager.

While this is a simple task, the package name varies across systems—it will probably be called `gtk3-devel`, `libgtk-3-dev`, or `gtk3`. Install this in the usual manner and you'll be ready to set up andlabs UI library.

To enable CGo, required by andlabs UI, on Linux you must have a compiler (gcc or clang) installed. This is often already installed on a development Linux installation, but if you're unsure, you can follow the *Setting up CGo* section from the `Appendix`, *Installation Details*.

Setup

The setup of andlabs UI is very simple—it only requires you to get the library using Go tools. You only need to execute `go get github.com/andlabs/ui`. This works exactly the same on Windows, macOS, and Linux, assuming that you have Go installed and running (if not, check out *Installing Go* section in the `Appendix`, *Installation Details*). If you encounter an error, first check that your Go installation is up to date—these issues often get fixed quickly—and that you have set up CGo as described.

Rebuilding the UI library (workaround)

The libui library that andlabs UI is built upon is packaged with the main library, but sometimes this gets out of date or is not compiled for the exact configuration of your computer. If you see an error when this happens, such as `relocation R_X86_64_32S against '.rodata' can not be used when making a shared object`, these instructions will help. If you see no error when installing, please skip these tips!

The following commands will rebuild the libui file for your computer. It assumes a Linux bash shell, as this situation is most likely to occur on a Linux computer. This is not going to be needed for anyone using the applications you build—just for setting up your development environment. The libui project is downloaded from Github and built using standard cmake tools. Be sure to specify the `-DBUILD_SHARED_LIBS=OFF` parameter, as we must build a static library to embed in the Go library:

```
$> cd `go env GOPATH`/src/github.com/andlabs
$> git clone git@github.com:andlabs/libui.git -q
$> cd libui/
$> git checkout alpha3.5 -q
$> mkdir build
$> cd build/
$> cmake -DBUILD_SHARED_LIBS=OFF .. >> build.log
$> make >> build.log
/home/andy/Code/Go/src/github.com/andlabs/libui/unix/alloc.c: In function 'unini
tComplain':
/home/andy/Code/Go/src/github.com/andlabs/libui/unix/alloc.c:27:26: warning: zer
o-length gnu_printf format string [-Wformat-zero-length]
   *str = g_strdup_printf("");
                          ^~
/home/andy/Code/Go/src/github.com/andlabs/libui/unix/image.c: In function 'uiIma
geAppend':
/home/andy/Code/Go/src/github.com/andlabs/libui/unix/image.c:56:13: warning: sug
gest braces around empty body in an 'if' statement [-Wempty-body]
   /* TODO */;
              ^
$> cp out/libui.a ../../ui/libui_`go env GOOS`_`go env GOARCH`.a
$>
```

Rebuilding libui if the packaged version doesn't work

The commands are designed to work without any environment configuration, but you will need cmake installed—your system's package manager will be able to install it if you find it isn't installed. Once the build is complete, the resulting library, `out/libui.a`, should be moved into the UI project and renamed appropriately.

Code

Now that the library is installed, it's time to write some code. The following sample is andlabs UI equivalent of the *hello world* example we used in the Chapter 4, *Walk - Building Graphical Windows Applications*. Start by entering the following code into a new file, named `hello.go`:

```
package main

import "github.com/andlabs/ui"

func main() {
        err := ui.Main(func() {
                window := ui.NewWindow("Hello", 100, 50, false)
```

[103]

```
            window.SetMargined(true)
            window.OnClosing(func(*ui.Window) bool {
                    ui.Quit()
                    return true
            })

            button := ui.NewButton("Quit")
            button.OnClicked(func(*ui.Button) {
                    ui.Quit()
            })
            box := ui.NewVerticalBox()
            box.Append(ui.NewLabel("Hello World!"), false)
            box.Append(button, false)

            window.SetChild(box)
            window.Show()
        })
        if err != nil {
                panic(err)
        }
}
```

This code is pretty straightforward, but there are a few things that we should cover, so let's step through it. As usual, for a simple graphical Go app, we are using the `main` package and importing the toolkit library, before defining the `main()` function. We then call the main entry point for an andlabs UI application, `ui.Main()`, which takes a single function that will build and show the app's GUI. If an error occurred, we cause the binary to panic, as the interface couldn't be loaded.

In our user interface code, we first set up a window with `ui.NewWindow()`, with a title and a default size, and the final parameter indicates whether the window should have a menu bar. We turn on the default margin (padding) and assign a closing function to exit the app by calling `ui.Quit()`. Next, a new button is created with `ui.NewButton()`, labelled `Quit`, that also exits the application when clicked. These components are laid out using a container with `ui.NewVerticalBox()`. A `Hello World!` label and the `Quit` button are both added. The `Append()` method of `ui.Box` takes a Boolean parameter, `stretchy`—if this is set to `true`, the component will expand to fill the available space. Last, we set the content of the window with `SetChild()` and show it using `Show()`.

Build

Building this sample app is trivial. For example, in the following screenshot, we are running a Terminal on a Linux computer and simply execute `go build hello.go`. This creates an executable file that can be run directly without needing the Go tools installed:

Building for the current Linux environment

Building on a Windows computer (as long as gcc is in the command-line path—see *Prerequisites* section mentioned earlier) is just as simple as on Linux or macOS:

Building the hello world app on Windows

In these examples, we are building the applications on the platform they will run. Cross-compilation, one of the strengths of the Go toolchain, is more complicated with andlabs UI.

andlabs UI - Cross-platform Native UIs

Run

The application can be run from the command line (`./hello` on Linux or macOS, and `hello.exe` on Windows) or simply by double-clicking the file icon from your system's file browser. Either way, the result should be the appearance of a familiar *hello world* window. This will look very similar across multiple operating systems, but the look and feel will vary:

On Windows this is the same as Walk:

Andlabs UI hello world on Linux:

Hello world running on macOS:

Generic API for multiple platforms

The andlabs UI project provides a generic API that wraps operating-system-native widgets on Windows, Linux, and macOS. Due to this approach, it's largely limited to the *lowest common denominator* level of functionality, but considering how similar these toolkits are, the resulting API is surprisingly rich.

All widgets inherit from the `ui.Control` interface, which defines the `Show()`, `Hide()`, `Enable()`, and `Disable()` methods that all controls must implement (with obvious expected behavior). Additionally, it defines the `LibuiControl()` and `Handle()` methods, which provide a pointer to the low-level libui and operating-system widgets, respectively. The use of those methods is generally not recommended and so not covered in this chapter.

When compared to the Qt inspired Walk API of the `Chapter 4`, *Walk - Building Graphical Windows Applications*, the layout capabilities of andlabs UI appear limited with fewer controls managing the GUI visual flow. Native controls (while broadly similar) are programmed differently and not necessarily compatible with the same high-level layout definitions. What you will see in the following section is that containers are typically set up to expect one child, which is laid out using a `ui.Box` control. Many widgets, which could be considered containers in other toolkits, are managed as a single control in andlabs UI (such as `ui.RadioButtons`) so that the operating-system-specific implementation can be handled internally.

Controls

All the widgets defined in andlabs UI implement the `Control` interface and, as such, can be shown, hidden, enabled, or disabled and set as the content of a window through `SetChild()` (with the obvious exception of `ui.Window`). A window may not be the child of any other `ui.Control`, for obvious reasons. The definition of `show()` and `hide()` for a window will be set by the operating system or widget toolkit, as will the manner of disabling the window content.

Box

It is probable that any window will have its content set to a Box—this is because it's the only control that provides a way to group multiple controls together. It's a control with no visible container, which is the basic layout mechanism within andlabs UI. You can create a new box using `ui.NewHorizontalBox()` or `ui.NewVerticalBox()`, which lays out its child controls horizontally or vertically in a linear arrangement. In a horizontal arrangement, the child items will all have the same height (which will match the height required for the tallest child), and in a vertical (stacked) configuration, they will all have the same width.

The method of adding child controls to a box is to call the `Append()` function, which takes a `ui.Control` child parameter and a `bool` stretchy parameter. The **child** will be added to the list of the components, and the **stretchy** parameter determines how the available space should be filled. When the stretchy parameter is `true`, the item will expand to fill extra space; if it's `false`, the minimum size will be observed. If multiple components have stretchy switched on, the spare space will be divided equally between them.

It's often going to provide a better visual flow for your user interface if widgets are separated by some space. There is a suitable method provided, `SetPadded()`, which will set a standard space between child widgets in the box. This size is set by the widget toolkit's standard metrics, and will vary from platform to platform. The padding applied in this way is placed between the child components—for outer (surrounding) space, you should set a margin. The margin is available in controls which embed a child control—dubbed `containers` in this chapter.

Containers

Containers, or controls that allow us to embed another control, are typically identified by the existence of a `SetChild()` or `SetMargined()` function in their type definition. As these controls embed one another, a margin around the content is often desirable—this is the outer equivalent of the padding in `ui.Box`. This can be turned on using `SetMargined(true)`, and the system-defined margin size will be introduced around the child control.

The following containers are defined as part of andlabs UI:

- `Window` controls describe an application window and are the main entry point for an andlabs UI graphical application. The main content is set using `SetChild()`. Margins should probably be switched on if it's a simple content window, or left off if you are adding further container controls.
- `Group` defines a frame around a child widget (assigned with `SetChild()`) with a title (passed to `ui.NewGroup()`). The appearance of the group control will vary across systems; on some it may be a box around the child, and on others it may be invisible. As with the window controls, you should consider the child content before deciding whether the margins should be enabled.

- `Tab` is slightly different from the others, as it may contain multiple child controls—but only one is visible at a time. As there are multiple child controls, the method to add the child is `Append(string, Control)`—the first parameter is the title to be displayed on the tab and the second is the child for this new tab. To accommodate multiple child controls, the margin control is adapted also—you will need to call `SetMargined(int, bool)` where the first parameter is the tab index, and the latter is the usual parameter to turn margins on or off.

That's all of the controls that manage others, let's look at the details of the main widgets that an andlabs UI application is constructed from.

Widgets

The remaining widgets will be familiar to to any developer of desktop graphical applications, or indeed anyone who uses them. Provided here is a quick overview for the features or limitations of each:

- `Button`: A standard `pushbutton` with a label, and an `onClicked` callback
    - `Checkbox`: A toggled entry that is either checked or unchecked; an `onToggled` callback will trigger on change
- `Combobox`: A widget that provides a list of strings to select from
- `DateTimePicker`: A field for entering date and/or time—the configuration is set by different constructor functions
- `Entry`: A single-line text-entry widget, which can be read-only; it supports an `onChanged` handler for change events
- `Label`: A simple read-only text component for annotating the user interface
- `ProgressBar`: A horizontal bar to indicate progress; values range from 0 to 100
- `RadioButtons`: A control for presenting a list of options, such as check boxes, but where only one can be selected
- `Separator`: A horizontal or vertical line to visually separate other controls
- `Slider`: A horizontal bar for selecting between the set min and max integer values by moving an indicator
- `Spinbox`: An entry box for selecting an integer between the min and max values with the up and down buttons

A noticeable omission on this list is menu or toolbar widgets; they are not included in andlabs UI toolkit at the time of writing. Next, we'll look at a potential workaround for menus (which unfortunately will not work for a toolbar) by accessing the underlying libui.

Menu

At the time of writing, andlabs UI doesn't expose a menu API (despite `ui.NewWindow()` taking a `hasMenubar` parameter). There is a project underway to properly expose menu functionality to the Go API, but for now it's only available if you work with the underlying libui C code. The menu defined in the C library can be accessed from a Go project by adding a little CGo code, such as the following:

```
/*
void onMenuNewClicked(uiMenuItem *item, uiWindow *w, void *data) {
    void menuNewClicked(void);
    menuNewClicked();
}

int onQuit(void *data) {
    return 1;
}

void loadMenu() {
    uiMenu *menu;
    uiMenuItem *item;

    menu = uiNewMenu("File");
    item = uiMenuAppendItem(menu, "New");
    uiMenuItemOnClicked(item, onMenuNewClicked, NULL);
    uiMenuAppendSeparator(menu);
    item = uiMenuAppendQuitItem(menu);
    uiOnShouldQuit(onQuit, NULL);

    menu = uiNewMenu("Help");
    item = uiMenuAppendItem(menu, "About");
}
*/
import "C"
```

The code snippet sets up a click handler for a **New** menu item, and a quit handler for the **Quit** menu item (which is a special item due to macOS handling a quit menu item differently). Then we have a `loadMenu()` function, which sets up a **File** menu to which the child items are added, with a separator, and a currently-empty **Help** menu.

To compile this code correctly will require the `cfuncs.go` file knowing where the header file and C library are stored. Before running this code make sure that the `CFLAGS` and `LDFLAGS` show the correct locations. While the code to build a menu is not very complicated, the CGo configuration and linking is rather complex, and as such, may not be recommended:

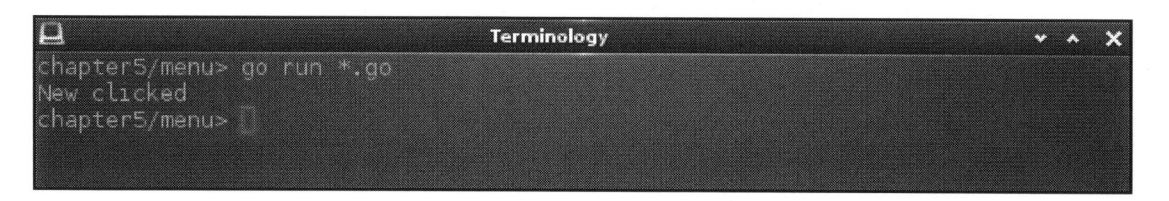

Launching the menu example

The result should look similar to this screenshot, which was taken on a Linux computer:

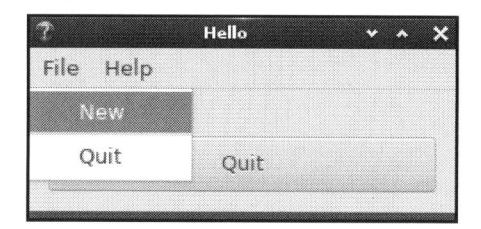

The andlabs libui menu

There is a complete menu project in the code repository for this book. Unfortunately, it isn't a cross-platform project and may not execute correctly on every operating system or version of Go.

Area and drawing

The `ui.Area` widget presents a canvas-like control—a surface that can be drawn on using Path and other drawing primitives. At the time of writing, these APIs are all part of the `ui` package, but it may soon move to `ui/draw` in an effort to separate them from the main controls API. An area can either be the size of the space it occupies or it can be larger, in which case it will be embedded in a scrollable control. The desired behavior is chosen based on whether `ui.NewArea(handler)` or `ui.NewScrollingArea(handler, width, height)` is called (where width and height are the desired content size).

andlabs UI - Cross-platform Native UIs

The logic behind an area is `ui.AreaHandler`, the first parameter to either of the area constructor functions. Its `Draw(*ui.Area, *ui.AreaDrawParams)` function is invoked by the toolkit whenever the area needs to be redrawn, the first parameter being the area it's registered on and the second providing context, such as the clipping rectangle to be filled. As well as drawing the content of an area, the handler is responsible for handling the mouse and key events, with `MouseEvent(*ui.Area, *ui.AreaMouseEvent)` being called whenever a mouse event occurs and `KeyEvent(*ui.Area, *ui.AreaKeyEvent)` for any keyboard events.

To look more closely at the drawing capabilities, let's run a little code. In this example, we are creating a new `ui.AreaHandler` type (named `areaHandler`) that implements all the required functions from the interface. The only method of interest is the `Draw()` call, which is included here:

```
func (areaHandler) Draw(a *ui.Area, dp *ui.AreaDrawParams) {
    p := ui.NewPath(ui.Winding)
    p.NewFigure(10, 10)
    p.LineTo(dp.ClipWidth - 10, 10)
    p.LineTo(dp.ClipWidth - 10, dp.ClipHeight - 10)
    p.LineTo(10, dp.ClipHeight - 10)
    p.CloseFigure()
    p.End()

    dp.Context.Fill(p, &ui.Brush{Type:ui.Solid, R:.75, G:.25, B:0, A:1})
    dp.Context.Stroke(p, &ui.Brush{Type:ui.Solid, R:.25, G:.25, B:.75, A:.5},
        &ui.StrokeParams{Thickness: 4, Dashes: []float64{10, 6}, Cap:ui.RoundCap})
    p.Free()
}
```

This code is split into two parts: first we set up a `ui.Path` and then we use the path to draw. The path (named p) is set to be 10 pixels inside the clip area that is being drawn—this is done so the canvas background is demonstrated (the drawing area is cleared before every `Draw()` call). Next, we use this path to `Fill()` and `Stroke()` within the draw context (`dp.Context`). The call to `Fill()` specifies a Brush that is a solid orange color of full opacity (A in the preceding code stands for alpha). Then, we call `Stroke()` using the same path (this will draw a line around the filled box). We are asking for a four-pixel-wide dashed line with round caps—this time with a semi-transparent blue color.

To draw this to screen, we need to configure a window to have a `ui.Area` control that expands to fill the window, as follows:

```
func main() {
    err := ui.Main(func() {
        window := ui.NewWindow("Draw", 200, 150, false)
        window.SetMargined(false)
        window.OnClosing(func(*ui.Window) bool {
            ui.Quit()
            return true
        })

        handler := new(areaHandler)
        box := ui.NewVerticalBox()
        box.Append(ui.NewArea(handler), true)

        window.SetChild(box)
        window.Show()
    })
    if err != nil {
        panic(err)
    }
}
```

If you put all this together (or run the `chapter5/draw` example), you should see something like the following screenshot:

Andlabs UI draw functions

Notice how the transparent blue is outlining the orange—filled rectangle, and also displaying the rectangle and the background from beneath. If we reversed the order of the `Fill()` and `Stroke()` calls, the orange rectangle would completely cover half of the dashed outline.

Building a user interface

Now that we've looked at the API capabilities of andlabs UI, let's look at building a graphical application of some complexity. For this section, we will follow the design of the "GoMail" application introduced in the `Chapter 4`, *Walk - Building Graphical Windows Applications*. The design presented was created using the Qt Creator tool which, while being a good fit for developing applications with the Walk library, is not a direct fit for all GUI toolkits. The multiple-platform approach of andlabs UI to use the native widgets means that some components are not available, but some can be created by combining simple widgets to form more complex components.

With that in mind, let's have a quick look at how the different platforms' styling capabilities may affect the application we are building. After exploring styles, we will start implementing the basic layout of our application and add the controls and features to demonstrate the user interface capabilities.

Style

The styling of an andlabs-UI-based application is platform-specific and is normally set by the operating system. Some support user-based customization, which can subtly or vastly affect the look and feel of your application—so it's important to consider the possible variations during your application design and testing.

When run on Microsoft Windows, the toolkit in use is Common Controls (discussed in the `Chapter 4`, *Walk - Building Graphical Windows Applications*). Essentially, the controls will look somewhat different across versions of Windows, which helps the applications blend in with the evolving desktop's look and feel. Most user-customization options within Windows are focused on the newer ("Universal") applications, but may show some color changes within applications built using Common Controls (and therefore with andlabs UI). Be sure to consider which versions of Windows you intend to support when testing your application layout and design.

Apple also evolves their macOS widget toolkit look and feel over time, though most recent versions (since OS X 10.5—released in 2007) remain largely consistent in the layout and sizing of components. Applications running on andlabs UI in the macOS environment should remain fairly consistent across all supported versions—unless users enable the new `dark mode` in macOS Mojave (released in late 2018). Following this new user-configuration option, the user interface may be presented in a light (default) or dark mode to match the user's preference. Application designers should consider this and ensure their content presents well in both configurations.

The widgets used within andlabs UI adapt correctly to this new style, but custom content may not. There is currently no API to detect which color mode is being used and so the easiest approach is to either limit your interface to standard controls or to pick a color scheme that will look suitable in either mode:

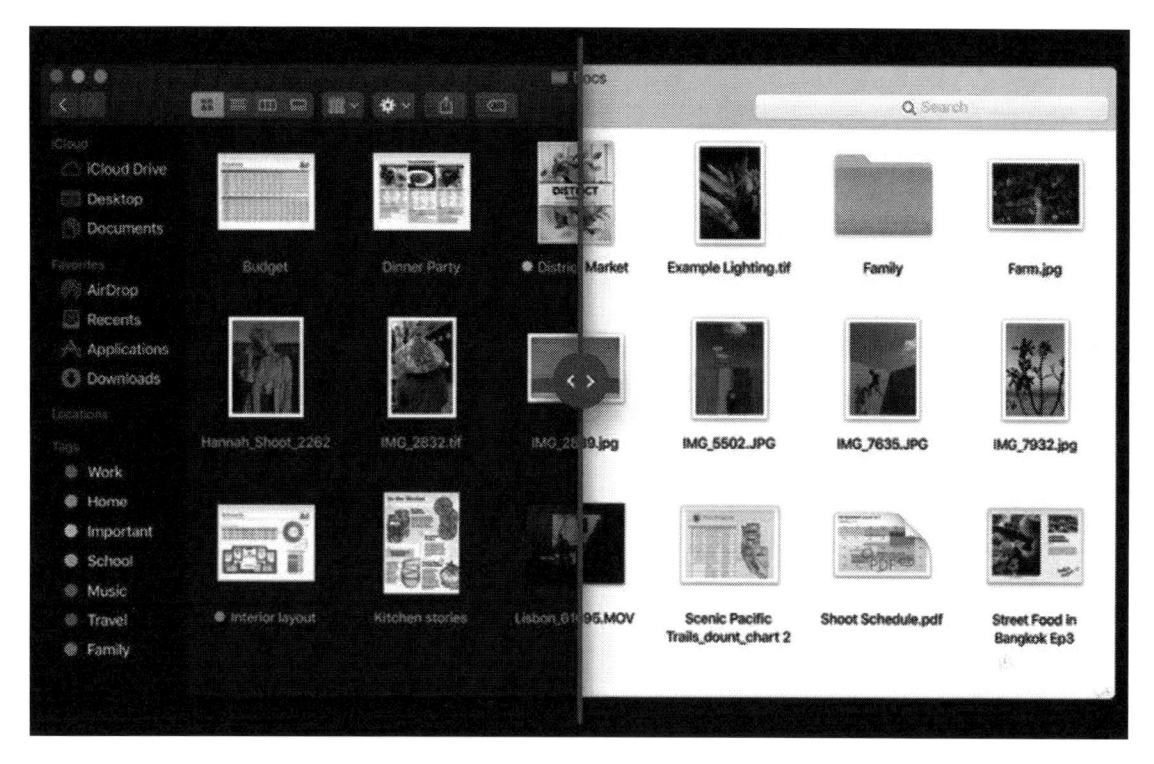

Side- by-side comparison of macOS light and dark modes (copyright IDG UK via MacWorld)

In Linux, andlabs UI toolkit is built upon the GTK+ widget set, which is designed to allow theming and style adjustments. While these types of themes can't substantially change the layout of components, they can significantly impact the sizing, padding, and colouring that a theme provides, and so affect the flow and sizing of an application's user interface. This can present a challenge for software developers who want to support the inherent flexibility in their programs. There are over a thousand GTK+ themes, and many can be found on the Gnome Look website: `https://www.gnome-look.org/browse/cat/135/ord/top/`. GTK+ Theming is explored further in `Chapter 6`, *Go-GTK - Multiple Platforms with GTK*. where we take a deeper look at the GTK+ toolkit.

These two screenshots compare a popular light and dark theme—clearly they can change more than simply the color scheme:

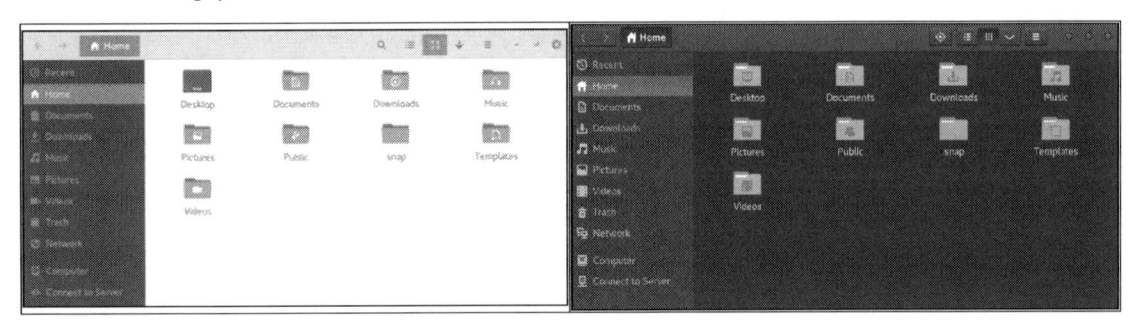

GTK+ SuperFlat and Vertex themes compared

Each of these platform themes and configuration options can have an impact on the look and feel of the resulting application. If you're planning to support these visual styles, the best strategy is to avoid custom controls, and draw features and let the native controls adapt appropriately. If your application requires custom content or rendering, it will be important to choose a color palette that works well across many different themes or styles.

Layout

Layouts in andlabs UI are composed of horizontal and vertical boxes, each of which contain a list of child elements, which may be stretched or static. Horizontal boxes are laid out on a single row, and every control within has the same height (that is, matching the height of the tallest element). In a vertical box, the controls are laid out in a single column and every element is the same width (being that of the widest item). If the container is larger than the minimum required to fit the items, any extra space is shared between any element that was appended as *stretchy*—if none stretch, the items will remain left- or top-aligned.

To provide a visual separation between groups of elements, we can use the `ui.Separator` control, which draws a thin line horizontally or vertically—remember to mark it as not stretchy within the box layout. If you wish to introduce space within your layout without the visual line, you can create a blank label (using `ui.Label("")`) and set its stretchy parameter to `true` when appended to a box.

Chapter 5

Main email window

The main layout box of our email client, `content`, is a horizontal box created with `ui.NewHorizontalBox()`, which contains the email list on the left (the first item to be appended), a vertical `ui.Separator`, and the detail view on the right (as it was the list item to be appended). The email list is composed of a `ui.Group` named `inbox`, which includes the `Inbox` title; note that our title label is followed by a series of spaces—this helps to create a more spacious layout in our application. Within this, we have a vertical `ui.Box`, which has a `ui.Label` for each of our emails.

As there is no grid layout available, the `detail` view is composed of various boxes. You can see that the `meta` box is a horizontal layout of two child instances of a vertical `ui.Box`: the first containing a vertical box of labels, the second being the list of values that will be filled later—the padding will provide a suitable gap between them.

As with the *hello world* example, we create a window with the `GoMail` title, a requested size, and set `false` for the `hasMenu` parameter. At the end of the sample, we set the content of the window and `Show()` it:

```
window := ui.NewWindow("GoMail", 600, 400, false)
window.SetMargined(true)
window.OnClosing(func(*ui.Window) bool {
    ui.Quit()
    return true
})

list := ui.NewVerticalBox()
list.Append(ui.NewLabel("email1"), false)
list.Append(ui.NewLabel("email2"), false)
inbox := ui.NewGroup("Inbox")
inbox.SetChild(list)

subject := ui.NewLabel("subject")
content := ui.NewLabel("content")
labels := ui.NewVerticalBox()
labels.Append(ui.NewLabel("From "), false)
labels.Append(ui.NewLabel("To "), false)
labels.Append(ui.NewLabel("Date "), false)

values := ui.NewVerticalBox()
from := ui.NewLabel("email")
values.Append(from, false)
to := ui.NewLabel("email")
values.Append(to, false)
date := ui.NewLabel("date")
```

```
values.Append(date, false)

meta := ui.NewHorizontalBox()
meta.SetPadded(true)
meta.Append(labels, false)
meta.Append(values, true)

detail := ui.NewVerticalBox()
detail.SetPadded(true)
detail.Append(subject, false)
detail.Append(meta, false)
detail.Append(ui.NewHorizontalSeparator(), false)
detail.Append(content, true)

content := ui.NewHorizontalBox()
content.SetPadded(true)
content.Append(inbox, false)
content.Append(ui.NewVerticalSeparator(), false)
content.Append(detail, true)

window.SetChild(content)
window.Show()
```

By dropping that code into the same `main()` wrapper that we used in the *hello world* application, we can run this user interface to see how the layout works. You should see something like the following screenshot:

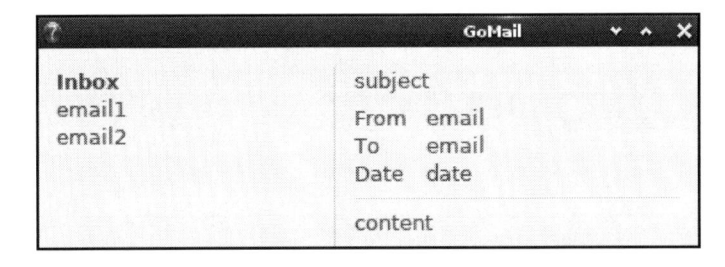

The main email browser layout

As you can see, we weren't able to use the splitter from the Walk example, but have simulated that look using `ui.Separator`. Whilst the code is the same, they can behave differently across different operating systems, like the following expanded vertical `ui.Box` on macOS:

On macOS, the layout is different but will improve as we add content

The tree, or list, component on the left is a simple collection of labels at this stage, as there is no standard list component provided. Lastly, we have not rendered the labels in bold. This is possible, but only by using the draw API, which significantly complicates the code. Additionally, the use of drawing can cause parts of the user interface to vary from the loaded platform theme; for this purpose, we have stuck with the standard `ui.Label` component. In the preceding screenshot, you can see how different platforms have very different layouts at this stage—this will even out as we add more content.

Email compose dialog

The layout of our compose dialog window is slightly more basic: a vertical box named `layout` manages the stack of controls into which the input elements are appended. We need to create another box, in horizontal arrangement, to place the **To** label before the input field; make sure to turn the padding on to provide some spacing. Each of the text input boxes is created using `ui.NewEntry()`, which creates a simple one-line input field. Unfortunately, at the time of writing, there was no multi-line input field—a constraint that does not have an obvious workaround at this stage. The next release of the UI library will have a new `ui.MultilineEntry`, which will provide this functionality.

The last of the compose layout is the second horizontal box, `buttonBox`, which uses the familiar empty label trick to cause the **Cancel** and **Send** buttons to be right-aligned within the available space:

```
window := ui.NewWindow("New GoMail", 400, 320, false)
window.SetMargined(true)
window.OnClosing(func(*ui.Window) bool {
    return true
})

subject := ui.NewEntry()
```

```
subject.SetText("subject")

toBox := ui.NewHorizontalBox()
toBox.setPadded(true)
toBox.Append(ui.NewLabel("To"), false)
to := ui.NewEntry()
to.SetText("email")
toBox.Append(to, true)

content := ui.NewEntry()
content.SetText("email content")

buttonBox := ui.NewHorizontalBox()
buttonBox.SetPadded(true)
buttonBox.Append(ui.NewLabel(""), true)
buttonBox.Append(ui.NewButton("Cancel"), false)
buttonBox.Append(ui.NewButton("Send"), false)

layout := ui.NewVerticalBox()
layout.SetPadded(true)
layout.Append(subject, false)
layout.Append(toBox, false)
layout.Append(content, true)
layout.Append(buttonBox, false)

window.SetChild(layout)
window.Show()
```

As you can see in the preceding code, it uses the same `ui.NewWindow()` as the main email browser code—this is because andlabs UI doesn't differentiate between types of windows. Various dialog windows do exist but they are predefined for specific purposes, and so for our custom dialog, we will use a normal window. Therefore, you can test this code easily by using the same `main()` method as the previous code examples. Once run, you should see something similar to these screenshots:

The email compose window:

Email compose on macOS:

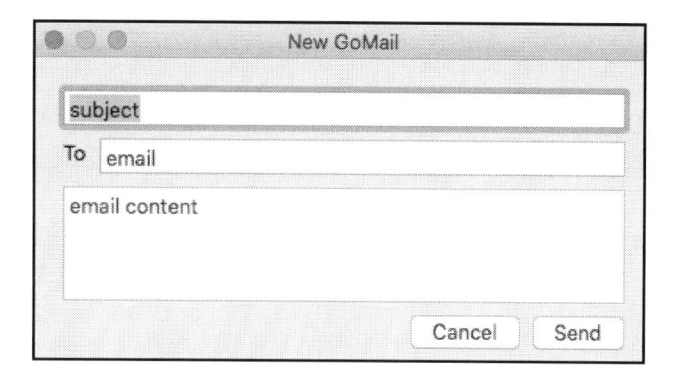

Loaded on a Windows computer:

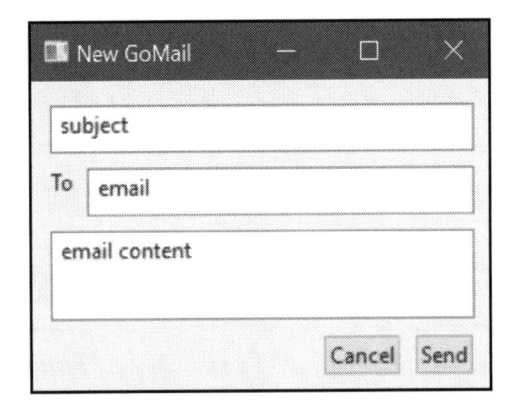

Toolbar and menu

Unfortunately there is currently no API support for menu or toolbar features in andlabs UI. Instead, we will simulate a toolbar by using a horizontal box, buttons, and a separator, which should provide the desired effect. As the separator can be very thin, we are padding it with an extra space on either side:

```
toolbar := ui.NewHorizontalBox()
toolbar.Append(ui.NewButton("New"), false)
toolbar.Append(ui.NewButton("Reply"), false)
toolbar.Append(ui.NewButton("Reply All"), false)

toolbar.Append(ui.NewLabel(" "), false)
toolbar.Append(ui.NewVerticalSeparator(), false)
toolbar.Append(ui.NewLabel(" "), false)
toolbar.Append(ui.NewButton("Delete"), false)
toolbar.Append(ui.NewLabel(" "), false)
toolbar.Append(ui.NewVerticalSeparator(), false)
toolbar.Append(ui.NewLabel(" "), false)

toolbar.Append(ui.NewButton("Cut"), false)
toolbar.Append(ui.NewButton("Copy"), false)
toolbar.Append(ui.NewButton("Paste"), false)
```

As you can see, we have specified that no buttons, separators, or spacers should expand, so the buttons will be left-aligned on the bar. This behavior could be changed if you'd prefer the buttons to spread out, by passing `true` for the `stretchy` parameter, for example, when appending the empty `ui.Label` controls.

We need to add this to the window—a new vertical box, called layout, is added and the previous content is packed underneath the toolbar. To provide some separation between this toolbar and the main content, we've called `SetPadded(true)`. Notice that the toolbar and space don't stretch (vertically), but the content layout does:

```
layout := ui.NewVerticalBox()
layout.SetPadding(true)
layout.Append(buildToolbar(), false)
layout.Append(content, true)

window.SetChild(layout)
```

By combining this code with the main layout described, you should get an application that's approaching the look of the email user interface that we designed in `Chapter 4`, *Walk - Building Graphical Windows Applications*:

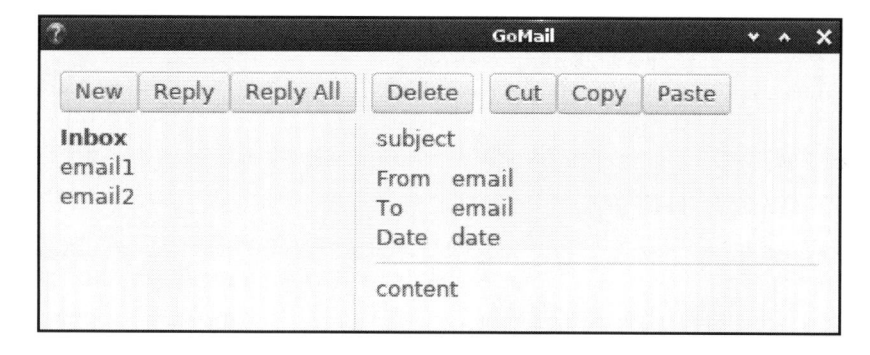

A box of buttons is added to simulate a toolbar

Notice how the look can vary between different operating systems—the following is running on Microsoft Windows:

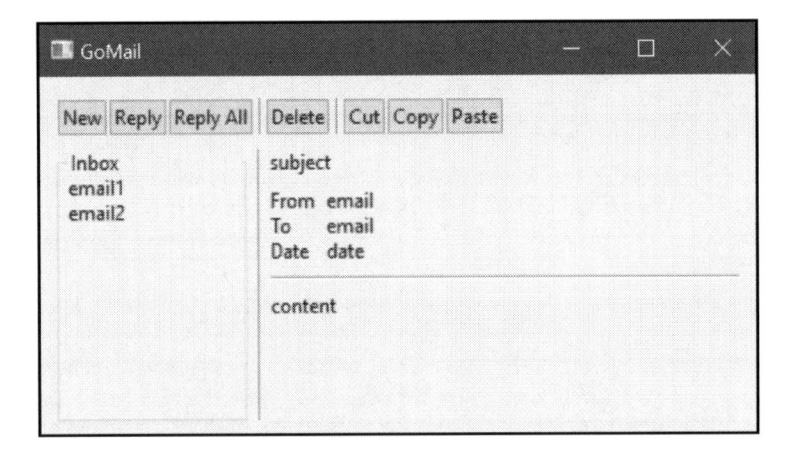

The addition of our toolbar box on Windows

Communicating with the GUI

Now that the basic layout is coded, we will add functionality to present some data from a mock email server. As with the Walk example, we will load the model definitions and a test email server from the `github.com/PacktPublishing/Hands-On-GUI-Application-Development-in-Go/client` package.

First of all, let's write the code to load content from our model into the user interface. We will create a `SetEmail(EmailMessage)` function that sets the content of an email into the user interface. To help with converting from `client.Email` and `time.Time` to `string`, we will use the helper `ToEmailString()` and `DateString()` functions. This function will be called during interface load and also whenever we change the selected email:

```
func (m *mainUI) setEmail(e *client.EmailMessage) {
    m.subject.SetText(e.Subject)
    m.to.SetText(e.ToEmailString())
    m.from.SetText(e.FromEmailString())
    m.date.SetText(e.DateString())
    m.content.SetText(e.Content)
}
```

Next, we should update the email list. Instead of two dummy emails in the list, we create a new method that will iterate over all emails and add an item for each. To be able to set the email content when clicked, we have to move from `ui.Label` to `ui.Button` (no other andlabs UI standard controls have an `OnClicked` callback). As you can see, we set a new function for each button added, which sets the displayed email by calling the `setEmail()` function. The `captured` variable is required to avoid the for loop's re-definition of `email` in each iteration:

```
func (m *mainUI) listEmails(list []*client.EmailMessage) {
    for _, email := range list {
        item := ui.NewButton(email.Subject)
        captured := email
        item.OnClicked(func(*ui.Button) {
            m.SetEmail(captured)
        })
        m.list.Append(item, false)
    }
}
```

To invoke these new functions on load, we need to update the `main()` method. First, a new server is created with `client.NewTestServer()`, and then the functions we wrote are invoked with the appropriate information from the server:

```
func main() {
    server := client.NewTestServer()
    err := ui.Main(func() {
        main := new(mainUI)
        window := main.buildUI()

        main.listEmails(server.ListMessages())
        main.setEmail(server.CurrentMessage())
        window.Show()
    })
    if err != nil {
        panic(err)
    }
}
```

The last step for the main view is to open the compose window when the user clicks on the **New** button. This is easily accomplished with another `OnClicked` handler, which builds and shows the secondary `ui.Window`:

```
compose := ui.NewButton("New")
compose.OnClicked(func(*ui.Button) {
    compose := &composeUI{}
    compose.buildUI().Show()
})
```

Before we can send an email, we need to construct one from the controls in the compose user interface. This new `CreateMessage()` function simply gathers the information entered by the user and encapsulates it in a new `client.EmailMessage` that's ready for sending:

```
func (c *composeUI) createMessage() *client.EmailMessage {
    email := &client.EmailMessage{}

    email.Subject = c.subject.Text()
    email.To = client.Email(c.to.Text())
    email.Content = c.content.Text()
    email.Date = time.Now()

    return email
}
```

Lastly, we want the **Cancel** and **Send** buttons to function as expected. Both should close the compose window, but the **Send** button should first attempt to send the email. We add simple `OnClicked` handlers for these buttons, attached to the buttons which are appended to the `buttonBox` already created in the UI code:

```
cancel := ui.NewButton("Cancel")
cancel.OnClicked(func(*ui.Button) {
    window.Hide()
})
buttonBox.Append(cancel, false)
send := ui.NewButton("Send")
send.OnClicked(func(*ui.Button) {
    email := c.createMessage()
    c.server.Send(email)

    window.Hide()
})
buttonBox.Append(send, false)
```

Once all of this code is put together, you can run it, and should see an application that looks something like these screenshots:

- The GoMail interface with test data loaded running on Linux:

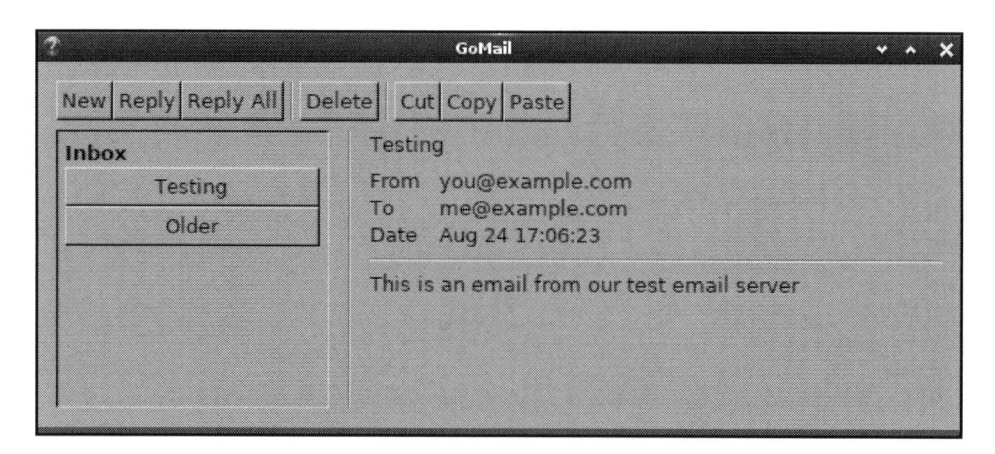

- The same interface with a different theme (Minwaita):

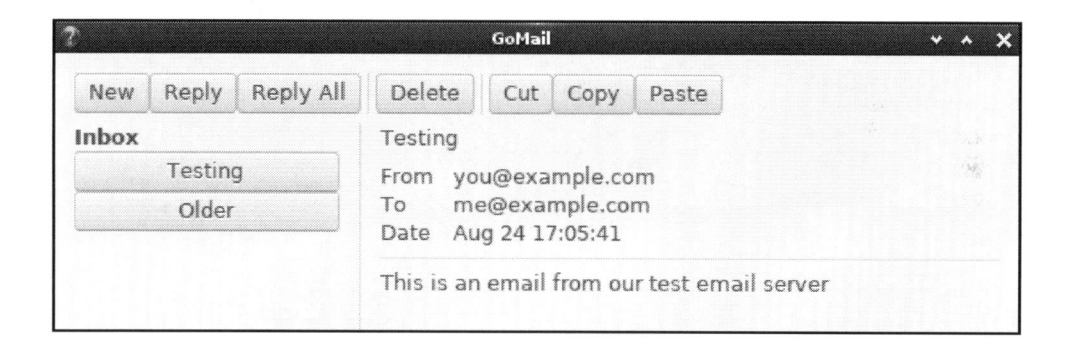

- The completed GoMail interface running on macOS:

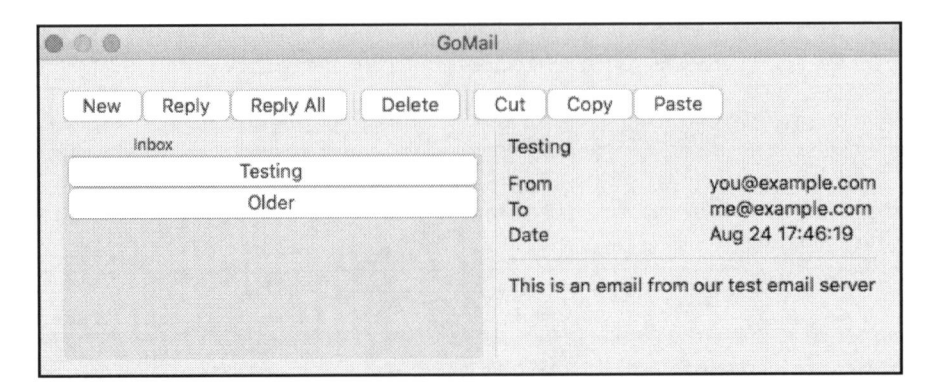

- Running on macOS dark mode:

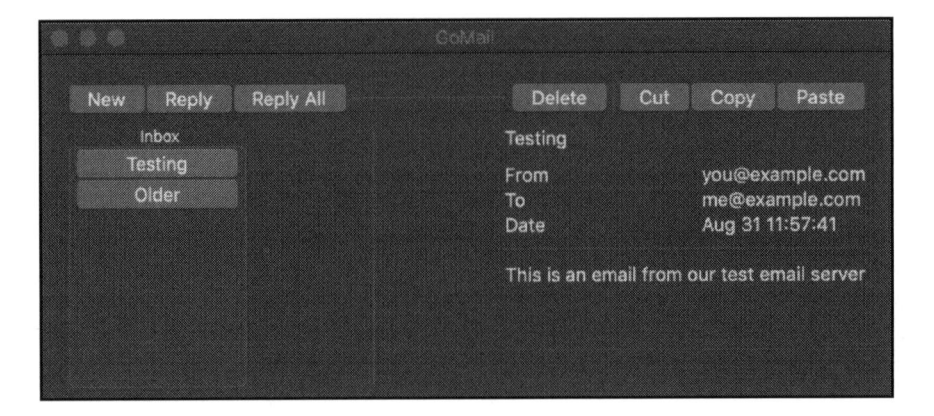

- The GoMail interface running on windows 10:

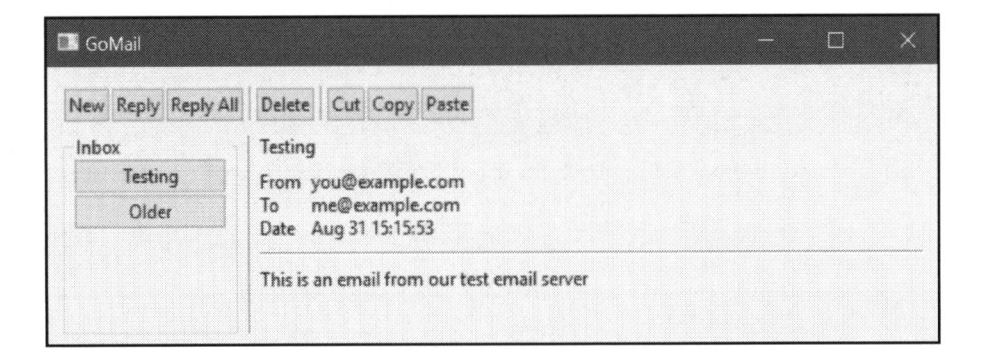

Background processing

As you may have realized from the first line of andlabs UI code (`ui.Main(func() { ... })`), multithreading is something that needs to be considered when building using this API. This is due to the fact that most of the toolkits it integrates with will require graphical updates to all execute on the same thread (often, the main application thread). The andlabs UI aims to hide this complexity by managing the threads internally and provides helper methods to manage this.

As a result of this design, any user interface updates outside of the `ui.Main()` setup (or callbacks on controls created there) must be passed to the `ui.QueueMain()` method in the form of a function, as with the initial setup. This allows andlabs UI code to process the updates on the appropriate thread for the current framework. The following code illustrates how a label's text could be changed as the result of some background processing:

```
ui.QueueMain(func () {
    label.SetText("background")
})
```

Callbacks such as `OnClicked()` and `OnClosing()` also take a `func()` parameter, just as the `ui.QueueMain()` function does. This code will automatically be executed on the correct thread, so there is no additional complexity to worry about.

Example

To look at the impact of background threads, we will add another feature to the GoMail application—updating the user interface when a new email arrives. To enable this, we must listen to the `Incoming` channel that our `client.EmailServer` type defines.

First, we create a function that will handle incoming email. This is simply a wrapper to a new method, `appendEmail(*client.EmailMessage)`, that handles adding new items to the email list. But it must create a wrapping `func()` and pass it to `ui.QueueMain` so that the code executes on the correct thread:

```
func (m *mainUI) incomingEmail(email *client.EmailMessage) {
    ui.QueueMain(func() {
        m.appendEmail(email)
    })
}
```

andlabs UI - Cross-platform Native UIs

Then we add a little more code to our `main()` method to listen for incoming emails from `client.EmailServer`. The following code requests the incoming channel from the server model and then loops over any emails that are communicated through the channel, triggering our handler for any that arrive:

```
go func() {
    incoming := server.Incoming()
    for email := range incoming {
        main.incomingEmail(email)
    }
}()
```

With these updates running, the same client will trigger a new email to appear after 10 seconds. With Go, the concurrency is simple to handle, and the preceding code shows how andlabs UI allows us to benefit from that in the handling of our user interface.

Challenges with multiple native GUIs

In this chapter, we've seen how a single code base can create applications that work with native widget toolkits across multiple platforms. This is a very powerful approach to quickly develop graphical apps that are consistent with the platform style to provide a familiar user experience. However, this approach also has challenges you may need to overcome for your project.

Consistent style

While it may not be obvious that a consistent style is important when choosing to adapt to the native toolkit, there are many parameters involved in style and application design. Does your design team or product specialist have defined standards or approaches to user experience that they wish to apply across all applications and platforms? Are there brand guidelines that you should be including in your interface design?

Brand styles

As andlabs UI is a toolkit that aims to provide an abstraction to standard widgets (and therefore using the current platform's look and feel), customization options are limited. The only facility to introduce custom elements is the `ui.Area` widget and the draw features we explored. This enables a company font or logo to be drawn (support for loading images is said to be coming in a later version) at a certain location in the interface.

Chapter 5

If you are looking for further abilities to customize or theme the applications you are building, then andlabs UI may not be the right solution for your project. It's probably better to explore GTK+ or Qt (which we cover in `Chapter 6`, *Go-GTK - Multiple Platforms with GTK*, and `Chapter 7`, *Go-Qt - Multiple Platforms with QT*) or skip to Part 3 (`Chapter 8`, *Shiny - Experimental Go GUI API*, `Chapter 9`, *nk - Nuklear for Go* and `Chapter 10`, *Fyne - Material Design based GUI*) and read about other approaches to graphical application design.

User experience

Using a single API does not guarantee consistency across multiple operating systems. The toolkits used may have different layout defaults, with different padding or alignment, for example. The andlabs UI (and the underlying andlabs libui) API is designed to provide an application that's as close to the OS defaults as possible. If you have specific requirements that should be met regarding the user interface appearance (other than the style), such as layout or alignment, you may need to write special code. Using Go's approach to build tags and load different code for different operating systems, you can adapt your code to behave slightly differently on different platforms.

If we look at the previous *hello world* example, we can update the code to adjust the quit button's layout on different platforms. Here, we will load a right-aligned button for macOS, but leave it as full width for other systems.

The code to create the **Quit** button is removed from `hello.go` and replaced with a line that calls into a new `layoutQuit()` function:

```
button := layoutQuit()
```

In a new file, called `custom_other.go`, we move the previous button definition into a new `layoutQuit()` function. Additionally, a conditional build comment is added at the top to ensure that this file is not included for macOS (darwin). Note that the text has also changed to **Exit**, to illustrate how platforms can be adapted:

```
// +build !darwin

package main

import "github.com/andlabs/ui"

func layoutQuit() ui.Control {
   button := ui.NewButton("Exit")
   button.OnClicked(func(*ui.Button)
   {
      ui.Quit()
   })
```

andlabs UI - Cross-platform Native UIs

```
        return button
}
```

That's all pretty straightforward; then we add another file, named `custom_darwin.go`, where we define the alternative behavior. In this file, we don't need the build definition, as the filename provides that for us. In this implementation, we create a horizontal `ui.Box` with the **Quit** button padded to the right using an empty, stretchy `ui.Label`, as follows:

```
package main

import "github.com/andlabs/ui"

func layoutQuit() ui.Control {
    button := ui.NewButton("Quit")
    button.OnClicked(func(*ui.Button) {
        ui.Quit()
    })

    box := ui.NewHorizontalBox()
    box.Append(ui.NewLabel(""), true)
    box.Append(button, false)

    return box
}
```

Using this approach, it's possible to adapt your user interface to appear slightly differently on specific platforms. This is a useful approach if you need to have different widget layouts on different systems:

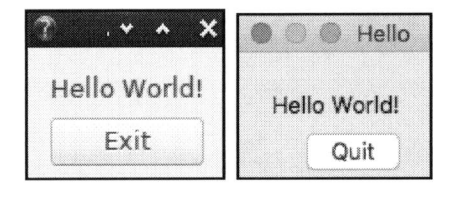

The updated hello app (left) and layout for macOS (right)

Testing

Due to various aspects of multiple-platform abstraction (including the variation in style), it can take a long time to test an andlabs UI application. As well as developing an application that, by design, looks and works slightly differently across Windows, macOS, and Linux, the application may be subject to additional user customization. All three of those platforms offer some user options to change the user interface—Windows allows color adjustments, macOS similarly has highlight colors and recently added a dark mode, and GTK+ (the Linux implementation) offers full theme support.

Part of testing an application built in this way is to decide which platforms and variations you will support. Should your Windows users all be on the latest version of Windows, or will you ensure the application works with older widget styles? On macOS, are you checking that your interface reads well in dark and light modes? With Linux, are you supporting (and therefore testing) a variety of different themes?

It's highly recommended that you have a configured test environment for every variation of a system that can impact how your application looks. Thankfully, this is made easier with virtual machines—you no longer need to have rows of computers or complex multi-boot configurations. If you can load and set up each of these configurations in separate virtual machine images, it should be possible to test all of these potential variations. Note that macOS licensing requires that it's run on a Macintosh computer—even if within a virtualized environment.

Of course, the impact of this cross-platform approach may be wider-reaching—operating systems have many non-visible differences as well. It's important to load and fully run through your application to check all features, simply looking at the user interface isn't enough to satisfy a solid test strategy.

Cross-compilation

Due to the way that libui builds against native widget APIs, the cross-complication is more complicated than a simple Go application. As well as the developer tools that are required for building an application with andlabs UI for the current computer, you will need to have access to the widget library definitions to successfully cross-compile. In some instances, that means a simple library installation, in other cases it may be necessary to install the operating system's **Software Development Kit** (**SDK**). Let's look at the details for each target platform.

andlabs UI - Cross-platform Native UIs

As with normal Go cross-compilation, we start by setting the environment variable, `GOOS` (and optionally `GOARCH`), to define the target platform of our build. To work with libui, we need to turn CGo back on (this is disabled when cross-compiling by default) using `CGO_ENABLED=1`. Simply executing the build with this setup would likely fail due to a missing library or SDK, as shown here:

Building on macOS for Linux fails

A Linux computer failing to compile for macOS

Let's look into how cross-compilation can be enabled for various configurations.

Building for Linux on macOS or windows

To be able to cross-compile for Linux, the main requirement is the GTK+ library, which provides the widgets for andlabs UI on Linux. Installing this is a little more difficult as the operating systems don't come with a standard package manager, but if you follow the steps described here it should be possible. The process also involves installing the cross-compiling toolchain, much like other examples in this section. The details for setting up cross-compilation can be found in *Cross compiling for Linux with CGo* section given in the `Appendix`, *Cross-Compiler Setup*. The main steps are outlined here for quick reference.

macOS

To cross-compile with macOS, we need to install a package manager. The easiest and most complete is Homebrew—you can install it from `https://brew.sh/`. The recommended toolchain for Linux compilation is `musl-cross`, which is in the `FiloSottile/musl-cross/musl-cross` package. With Homebrew installed, execute the following commands in your Terminal window:

1. `brew install gtk+3`
2. `export HOMEBREW_BUILD_FROM_SOURCE=1`
3. `brew install FiloSottile/musl-cross/musl-cross`

Once that is completed, you should be able to build for Linux by setting the `GOOS=linux`, `GOARCH=amd64`, `CGO_ENABLED=1`, and `CC=x86_64-linux-musl-gcc` environment variables with `CXX=x86_64-linux-musl-g++`. You can then build as normal, resulting in a Linux executable instead of macOS:

```
[chapter5/hello> export GOOS=linux
[chapter5/hello> export GOARCH=amd64
[chapter5/hello> export CGO_ENABLED=1
[chapter5/hello> export CC=x86_64-linux-musl-gcc
[chapter5/hello> export CXX=x86_64-linux-musl-g++
[chapter5/hello> go build hello.go
chapter5/hello>
```

Building a Linux executable from macOS

Windows

Cross-compiling with Windows is a little more complicated as there is no standard package manager. The recommended approach is to install Cygwin (from `cygwin.com/install.html`). Then install the gtk3 and linux-gcc (cross compiler) packages. From there, follow the preceding instructions for macOS, but use `CC=linux-gcc` and `CXX=linux-g++`.

Building for windows on Linux or macOS

Building for Windows from another platform requires an installation of mingw (similar to what we installed on Windows to support CGo). The details for setting up cross-compilation can be found in the *Cross compiling for Windows with CGo* section of an `Appendix`, *Cross-Compiler Setup*.

The main steps are outlined here for quick reference:

Using your package manager (Homebrew on macOS and various on Linux), install the mingw package, which is usually named `mingw-w64-clang or w64-mingw`. If you cannot find this package, it can be installed directly using the instructions at https://github.com/tpoechtrager/wclang.

Once installed, we need to set up the appropriate build flags—specifically `CC=x86_64-w64-mingw32-clang` (for the C toolchain) and `CXX=x86_64-w64-mingw32-g++` (for C++ requirements). Assuming you also have set `CGO_ENABLED=1` and `GOOS=windows`, you can build the Windows binary. Looking at the resulting `hello.exe` file, you can see it's an MS Windows binary:

```
chapter5/hello> export GOOS=windows
chapter5/hello> export CGO_ENABLED=1
chapter5/hello> export CC=x86_64-w64-mingw32-clang
chapter5/hello> export CXX=x86_64-w64-mingw32-g++
chapter5/hello> go build hello.go
chapter5/hello> file hello.exe
hello.exe: PE32+ executable (console) x86-64, for MS Windows
chapter5/hello>
```

Using mingw (x86_64-w64-mingw32-clang), we built a Windows-native UI application on Linux

When building from macOS, you can use Homebrew to install the mingw-w64 package.

[136]

Building for macOS on Linux or Windows

Cross-compiling for mac requires that the macOS SDK is available to link against. When building from a Linux or Windows computer, we must download and install the SDK and also update our build toolchain to use it. The easiest way to do this is with the *osxcross* tool. The details for this setup can be found in the *Cross compiling for macOS with CGo* section of an `Appendix`, *Cross-Compiler Setup*. The main steps are outlined here for quick reference using a Linux terminal—the Windows setup is similar once you have installed the cygwin or mingw terminals.

First, we need to download the macOS SDK, which is bundled with Xcode. Download `XCode.dmg` from the Apple download site at `https://developer.apple.com/download/more/?name=Xcode%207.3` (7.3.1 is recommended for osxcross). Next, install the osxcross tools from `github.com/tpoechtrager/osxcross` (full installation details are available at that URL or in the Appendix). Completing the installation will have extracted the macOS SDK and created the compilation toolchain that will build against these installed APIs.

And now we are ready to build. As well as the previous environment variables, we add `CC=o32-clang`, after which our build command should succeed. Here you can see that our Linux computer managed to create a macOS 64-bit Mach-O executable file named `hello`:

```
chapter5/hello> export GOOS=darwin
chapter5/hello> export CGO_ENABLED=1
chapter5/hello> export CC=o32-clang
chapter5/hello> go build hello.go
chapter5/hello> file hello
hello: Mach-O 64-bit x86_64 executable, flags:<NOUNDEFS|DYLDLINK|TWOLEVEL>
chapter5/hello>
```

Using osxcross (o32-clang), we built a macOS-native UI application on Linux.

The process for Windows is similar and full details can be found in the *Cross compiling for macOS with CGo* section of an `Appendix`, *Cross-Compiler Setup*.

A better solution

These steps are complicated and potentially fragile. Due to these challenges, a new project was created to assist in the cross compilation of andlabs UI applications. You can find out more and compare the process with those detailed here by visiting the project homepage at `https://github.com/magJ/go-ui-crossbuild/`.

Summary

In this chapter, we explored andlabs UI toolkit, which provides a single API to build graphical Go applications using the native widgets of the running operating system. We stepped through getting set up to build an andlabs UI application on macOS, Windows, and Linux, and showed how a simple *hello world* application could be run on each system from a single Go source file. We then looked in detail at the widget API for building applications and the drawing APIs for custom rendering.

With this knowledge, we revisited the GoMail application from `Chapter 4`, *Walk - Building Graphical Windows Applications*, and built the user interface again using andlabs UI library. While there were some limitations with the current version, we were able to simulate some of the missing widgets to almost completely recreate the application. The benefit, of course, is that we could then run the GUI on Windows, Linux, and macOS from the same source code.

Testing an application built with a library where the user interface varies, and ensuring it looks as consistent as possible, may be difficult depending on your app design. Additionally, the simple cross-compilation that Go provides is significantly harder with andlabs UI due to the way it implements using operating-system-specific widget APIs. We explored how to work within these constraints and build applications for different platforms.

In the next two chapters, investigate existing cross-platform widget libraries that have been made available through Go APIs. GTK+ (which we saw being used by andlabs UI for Linux) and QT both present a standard widget set, which will seem familiar to users of existing desktop applications. We'll start by exploring GTK+ in detail in the next chapter.

6
Go-GTK - Multiple Platforms with GTK

We've explored toolkits that connect directly to an operating system's native widget set (Walk for Windows only and andlabs UI for Windows, macOS, and Linux) in Chapter 4, *Walk - Building Graphical Windows Applications*, and Chapter 5, *andlabs UI - Cross-platform Native UIs*. In this chapter and the next (Chapter 7, *Go-Qt - Multiple Platforms with Qt*), we'll look at widget toolkits that were designed to look similar to traditional native widgets while being built for multi-platform distribution. In each chapter, we'll work with a popular Go binding that provides access to most of the functionality of the underlying API.

In this chapter, we'll explore Go-GTK, the most popular Go binding to the GTK+ widget library. We'll cover the following:

- GTK+ background
- Getting started with Go-GTK
- Signals and namespaces
- Sample application
- Theming

By the end of this chapter, you'll be familiar with GTK+ and the Go-GTK library, having explored a few example applications. We will build a new version of the GoMail application and compare the results with our previous versions built with Walk and andlabs UI.

GTK+ background

GTK+, or the **GNU Image Manipulation Program** (**GIMP**) Toolkit (a popular cross-platform image editor), is a cross-platform API for creating graphical applications. The project aims to provide a complete set of GUI widgets, supporting small graphical utilities up to large application suites:

GIMP, which uses GTK+, shown on Windows Vista; copyright the GTK+ team

Since its creation, the toolkit's adoption has rapidly expanded, supported by its open source license, which supports its use in commercial and freely available applications alike. While version 1.0 (released in 1998) was primarily to support the functions of the GIMP application, by 1.2 (released less than a year later) the toolkit was aiming at a broader audience. In 2002, version 2.0 was released, which saw GTK+ become the official tookit for the Gnome Linux desktop. This fully featured release greatly expanded adoption, to become one of the most popular widget sets available for cross-platform development—and minor releases of the 2.x version are still very popular in 2018. In 2011, 3.0 was released with many changes included, the most visual of which was a new theme engine based on **Cascading Style Sheets** (**CSS**), which is familiar to most web developers. Though CSS is easier to create themes for, there have been criticisms of the new approach, and many distributors continue to deliver version 2.24 despite it being more than seven years old.

One of the benefits of Go is that it offers a single API for applications that behave consistently across multiple platforms. GTK+ (and Qt, covered in the following chapter) is an API that has a similar approach to enabling GUI application development. By combining the two through a binding to the Go language, we can create applications that can (depending on a user's theme settings) look and behave the same across all supported operating systems (Windows, macOS, Linux, and many Unix distributions). The Go bindings that we're working with in this chapter were created by Yasuhiro Matsumoto and the project has a long list of maintainers. It focuses on GTK2 support and aims to offer bindings for the complete API, but currently many features aren't available. As you will see in this chapter, the bindings currently available support the needs of most applications and so the partial completion of their goal won't impact most developer's use of this API.

Getting started with Go-GTK

Getting up and running with Go-GTK involves installing the GTK+ library on your system (if it's not already installed), setting up CGo, and downloading the Go bindings. Users of applications built using Go-GTK will need the GTK+ library installed on their computer and so the *Installing GTK+* section may need to be included in your documentation.

Prerequisites

Compiling against the GTK+ library will require CGo to be set up; if this isn't already done, you can work through the `Appendix`, *Installation Details*.

Installing GTK+

Using a package manager to install the GTK+ library is the easiest way to get it set up, as it'll also configure your development environment.

macOS

The recommended approach with macOS is to install it using Homebrew. If you haven't previously set up Homebrew, you can simply follow the instructions at `https://brew.sh`. Once Homebrew is installed, you can simply open a Terminal and run `brew install gtk+`.

Windows

Windows doesn't come with a standard package manager for things such as GTK+, but the `MSYS` project aims to solve this problem. Using the `MSYS Mingw-w64` terminal (installed previously if you followed the CGo setup instructions), we can install the additional libraries. By issuing the following commands, the correct libraries should be up and running:

```
pacman -S mingw-w64-x86_64-gtk2
```

This installs the GTK+ library and all of its dependencies. The examples in this chapter will need to run from the MSYS terminal, even once built.

Linux

On a Linux installation, there's a good chance that you already have GTK+ 2 installed, as so many applications use this widget set. If not (or if you are not sure), then your system's package manager will manage the installation; simply look for a package named `gtk2` or `gtk`. You may need to install an additional `gtk2-dev` or `gtk-dev` package if your distribution splits development headers from the runtime library.

Install Go-GTK

Once Go is working and the GTK+ dependency is installed, you can simply `go get github.com/mattn/go-gtk` and then `go get github.com/mattn/go-pointer`, on which the `go-gtk` project depends. With that installed, we're ready to build a test application.

Build

A basic hello world application with Go-GTK is similar to the previous one we looked at: we create a window, add a vertical box, and append a label and a button. The following code sample should be straightforward, but we'll look in more detail at some of the specifics:

```
package main

import "github.com/mattn/go-gtk/gtk"

func main() {
    gtk.Init(nil)
    window := gtk.NewWindow(gtk.WINDOW_TOPLEVEL)
    window.SetTitle("Hello")

    quit := gtk.NewButton()
    quit.SetLabel("Quit")
    quit.Clicked(func() {
        gtk.MainQuit()
    })

    vbox := gtk.NewVBox(false, 3)
    vbox.Add(gtk.NewLabel("Hello World!"))
    vbox.Add(quit)

    window.Add(vbox)
    window.SetBorderWidth(3)
    window.ShowAll()
    gtk.Main()
}
```

Firstly, we import the `github.com/mattn/go-gtk/gtk` package for the main GTK namespace. The Go-GTK project is split into various namespaces, which we will explore further later in this chapter. Next, the window is created with `gtk.NewWindow()`—note that the parameter to this function is the window type, not its title (which is set next with `SetTitle()`). The Quit button is created with `gtk.NewButton()` and the text is set with `SetLabel()`, and then we add the code to quit using the `Clicked()` function, passing an anonymous function.

The layout is managed by a vertical box that's created with `gtk.NewVBox(bool, int)`. The parameters to this message are firstly a *homogeneous* `bool` flag (determining whether all child components should be the same size), and secondly an `int` value for *spacing* (this specifies the amount of padding to place between each child element).

Lastly, the content is set on the window using `Add()` and we set a padding consistent with the spacing in the VBox using `SetBorderWidth(3)`. Calling `ShowAll()` sets the window and its contents to be shown (as widgets are hidden by default), and the call to `gtk.Main()` runs the application to render and respond to user input.

You can build this using the standard `go build hello.go` command, which should create a runnable file for your operating system:

Building the hello world example with Go-GTK

Run

You can run the built file from the command line by double-clicking the file icon, or even using the Go tools (with `go run hello.go`). No matter how it's launched, you should see something like this screenshot appear:

Go-GTK hello world:

Go-GTK on macOS:

Go-GTK default Windows look:

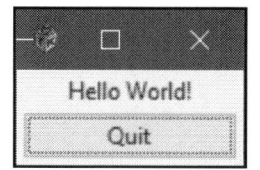

You can see that, just like with andlabs UI, we were able to run this single file on many operating systems. The difference here is that the applications look almost identical. That's the benefit of using a toolkit like GTK+ and why you may consider Go-GTK for your next application.

Before we look at a more complete application user interface, we should investigate some of the details of the Go-GTK API.

Signals and namespaces

GTK+ is an event-driven toolkit; that means that nothing happens unless an event is emitted and a callback is registered to receive it. The events in GTK+ are implemented through signals, and registering a callback for a signal is called connecting. Signals include most events involved in the GUI behavior and communication, including button click events or the window life cycle.

Signals

Did you notice that, in our hello world example, the Quit button would exit the application, but that closing the window did not? That's because we didn't connect any callback to the window destroy signal. We can fix this by adding the following lines to handle this case:

```
window.Connect("destroy", func() {
    gtk.MainQuit()
})
```

This code connects the provided anonymous function to the `destroy` signal of `window`. When the signal is emitted, the function is called and the application will now exit correctly. As the `gtk.MainQuit()` function takes 0 parameters, we could write the same more concisely as follows:

```
window.Connect("destroy", gtk.MainQuit)
```

But hold on a moment, how come the button click worked? That's because we used the `Clicked()` function on the `button` component. This is a convenience function that sets up the signal connection for you (and keeps the code a little neater!). If you look at the source code for the `Button.Clicked()` function, you will see what happens:

```
func (v *Button) Clicked(onclick interface{}, datas ...interface{}) int {
    return v.Connect("clicked", onclick, datas...)
}
```

And so, you can see it is not always essential to *wire* these connections manually as `Go-GTK` provides many convenience methods like this one.

Passing data

The previous examples all use a function with no parameters. While this is often enough, it can be helpful to pass additional information into your signal handling functions. This can be done easily as the connect functionality (mirrored by the `Clicked()` convenience function) allows for additional parameters to be sent. After the function reference, you can pass additional data parameters, which will be available to the function that executes the callback.

We can demonstrate that by creating a new button and passing this button along with the function to the signal connection:

```
button := gtk.NewButton()
button.SetLabel(label)
button.Clicked(clicked, button)
```

In the callback function, we update the function signature to accept a `*glib.CallbackContext` parameter. This parameter contains the data that was specified when the signal was connected. The data can be accessed using the context's `Data()` function call.

It's convenient to convert the type of the data returned, but remember to be careful when asserting the new type, as an incorrect type will cause your program to crash:

```
func clicked(ctx *glib.CallbackContext) {
   button := ctx.Data().(*gtk.Button)
   log.Println("Button clicked was:", button.GetLabel())
}
```

Bringing this together in a simple example where we create three buttons with the same callback function, we can see how this data parameter allows us to avoid unnecessary functions being created:

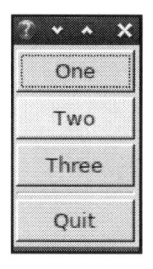

Multiple buttons: The clicked function handling multiple buttons' click callbacks

As you may have noticed, the previous code snippet mentioned a new package, `glib`. Let's look at the different packages that the Go-GTK project consists of and when you might want to use them.

Namespaces

The Go-GTK project contains a number of namespaces used to organize the code and make it easier for developers to find what they're looking for. These sub-projects or packages reflect the naming within the main GTK+ project, so those familiar with this can skip this section. Most of the examples so far used just gtk, which is clearly the main package to use for building a user interface but, as we saw before, glib may be important too (for things not specifically about widgets).

Let's look at what each namespace covers and see where it might be useful in application development:

gdk	GDK stands for GIMP Drawing Kit; it's a low-level component of GTK+ that handles the details of rendering on each platform that is supported. This provides an abstraction of the operating system details, therefore allowing other areas of GTK+ to be platform agnostic. This package will be useful if your application needs to draw any custom elements.
gdkpixbuf	Pixbuf refers to an in-memory buffer containing pixel data for rendering images. This package provides some convenience functions for managing images that can be loaded into a Go-GTK application. Of note is the `gdkpixbuf.NewPixbufFromData` function, which, combined with the `make_inline_pixbuf` tool, allows the loading of images embedded in the application.
gio	`gio` represents an input/output abstraction for GTK+ applications. It provides access to local and remote files with a consistent API.
glib	`glib` is the supporting library for all GTK+ features and applications. It implements the object-oriented system as well as various data structures and utilities. As the Go language defines many of these natively, the glib package within Go-GTK is responsible for translating from Go to glib (C) structures. This is where thread management and message passing are handled, but most of these features are hidden by the higher-level functions of the library.
gtk	The main namespace for widgets in the GTK+ library. As we've already seen, it presents a cross-platform toolkit for creating graphical applications, which is made possible by the other packages listed here.
pango	**Pango** is a font rendering library, which provides high-quality text glyphs for GTK+ applications. It's unlikely that you would need to call any of these APIs directly; it is mainly used internally for rendering text within GTK+.

Having looked at the main packages within Go-GTK (and seen that an application will probably only need to use `gtk`, `glib`, and `gdk`), we will see how this comes together in a larger application.

Sample application

It's time to dust off the GoMail application design again and adapt it for GTK+ widgets. As the andlabs UI application (when run on Linux) was using GTK+, it would seem logical to start from there. However, this time we are not limited by the *lowest common denominator* design constraint, which the native cross-platform design of andlabs worked around, so let's start from scratch and see what GTK+ can do.

Layout

Basic layout with GTK+-based applications uses a familiar vertical and horizontal box model. Go-GTK (as a straightforward binding to this API) exposes this same functionality. We lay out the GoMail main window using a vertical box to position the menu and toolbar above the main content. Our main content is then a horizontally split pane created with `gtk.NewHPaned()` (where **H** refers to the horizontal layout, not the bar orientation, which is vertical). Before looking at the details, here's the basic layout code for the main window. The toolbar and menu creation code is omitted for brevity but can be found in the example code repository:

```
package main

import "github.com/mattn/go-gtk/gtk"

const padding = 3

func main() {
   gtk.Init(nil)
   window := gtk.NewWindow(gtk.WINDOW_TOPLEVEL)
   window.SetTitle("GoMail")
   window.Connect("destroy", func() {
      gtk.MainQuit()
   })

   list := gtk.NewTreeView()
   list.AppendColumn(gtk.NewTreeViewColumnWithAttributes("Inbox",
gtk.NewCellRendererText(), "text", 0))
   meta := gtk.NewHBox(false, padding)

   labels := gtk.NewVBox(true, padding)
   labels.Add(gtk.NewLabel("To"))
   labels.Add(gtk.NewLabel("From"))
   labels.Add(gtk.NewLabel("Date"))
   values := gtk.NewVBox(true, padding)
   values.Add(gtk.NewLabel("email"))
   values.Add(gtk.NewLabel("email"))
   values.Add(gtk.NewLabel("date"))
   meta.Add(labels)
   meta.Add(values)

   content := gtk.NewTextView()
   content.GetBuffer().SetText("email content")
   content.SetEditable(false)

   detail := gtk.NewVBox(false, padding)
   detail.PackStart(gtk.NewLabel("subject"), false, true, 0)
```

```
        detail.PackStart(meta, false, true, 0)
        detail.Add(content)

        split := gtk.NewHPaned()
        split.Add1(list)
        split.Add2(detail)

        vbox := gtk.NewVBox(false, padding)
        vbox.PackStart(buildMenu(), false, true, 0)
        vbox.PackStart(buildToolbar(), false, true, 0)
        vbox.Add(split)

        window.Add(vbox)
        window.SetBorderWidth(padding)
        window.Resize(600, 400)
        window.ShowAll()
        gtk.Main()
}
```

There are two things of note in this code. First is the `padding` constant defined at the top of the file. The box model doesn't define a standard spacing and so we pass this constant each time the layout requires some visual padding. The second important lesson is the difference between the `Add(IWidget)` and `PackStart(IWidget, bool, bool, uint)` methods on the boxes. The `Add` method simply appends the widget to the container (`gtk.Box` inherits from `gtk.Container`) and it'll cause the child to expand to fill the space available. For a menu bar and toolbar, we don't desire a vertical expansion so we use the `PackStart` method, which allows more control over behavior. The first Boolean parameter controls expansion; by passing `false`, we instruct the container that the widget shouldn't take up any free space.

The second Boolean controls fill and states whether or not the widget should fill any space available after any space calculations have been performed, so passing `true` specifies that our toolbar should be full width. In `gtk.VBox`, the expand parameter refers to vertical stretch and the fill applies to horizontal.

We also need to add some content to the list view, which requires the creation of a model to represent the content we will present. As the content will be a single column with no parent/child relationship, we can use `gtk.ListStore`, rather than the more complex `gtk.TreeStore`. The way that content is set into a model is by using an iterator and applying values to each row of data. For the purpose of this layout, we add `email1` and `email2` to the 0th (first) column of the view:

```
model := gtk.NewListStore(gtk.TYPE_STRING)
list.SetModel(model)

var iter gtk.TreeIter
model.Append(&iter)
model.SetValue(&iter, 0, "email1")
model.Append(&iter)
model.SetValue(&iter, 0, "email2")
```

The toolbar API is simple to use and, by utilizing the stock icons included in GTK+, provides standard icons for many common actions. As some of our buttons are non-standard (`Reply` and `Reply All`), we set the toolbar style to show icons and labels; later, we can add some custom icons. Each item can have its action set using the `OnClicked()` function or by connecting the `clicked` signal:

```
toolbar := gtk.NewToolbar()
toolbar.SetStyle(gtk.TOOLBAR_BOTH)
item := gtk.NewToolButtonFromStock(gtk.STOCK_NEW)
item.OnClicked(showCompose)
toolbar.Add(item)
```

The rest of the icons can be added similarly. The menu code is slightly more complicated; each drop-down menu (whether a sub-menu or a main menu) needs to be created with `gtk.NewMenu()`, and its items added as shown. Each top-level menu then needs to have a new menu item created (for example, `gtk.NewMenuItemWithLabel()`) and the menu connected using `SetSubmenu()`. The constructed menu can then be appended to the menu bar:

```
menubar := gtk.NewMenuBar()
fileMenu := gtk.NewMenuItemWithLabel("File")

menu := gtk.NewMenu()
item := gtk.NewMenuItemWithLabel("New")
item.Connect("activate", showCompose)
menu.Append(item)

fileMenu.SetSubmenu(menu)
menubar.Append(fileMenu)
```

With all of this code in place (and a few more items in the toolbar and menu), we have a basic application layout that should look familiar. As you can see, we are already benefiting from the additional features of a larger widget toolkit with standard icons and more complete styling and layouts:

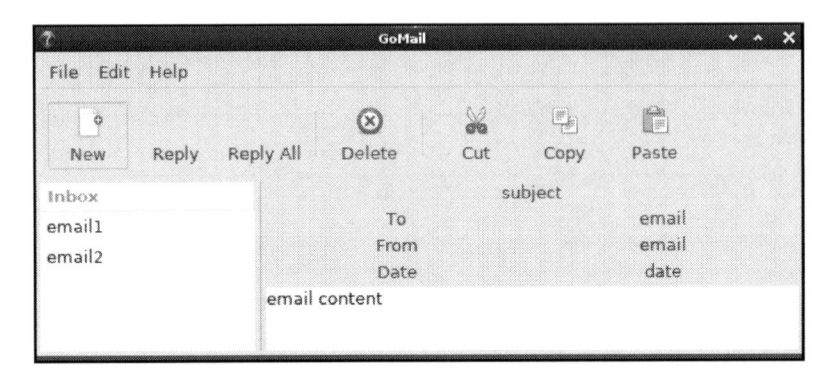

The basic layout of GoMail using Go-GTK before we make any style adjustments

The layout, particularly of the email details panel, can be improved using `label.SetAlignment(0, 0)` to set a left alignment, and the content of a label can be made bold by using the markup capability of the `pango` library; just call `label.SetMarkup(fmt.Sprintf("<b>%s</b>", label.GetText()))`. The preceding code was focused on the basic layout, so these tweaks have been left out. The additional details are included in the example code repository and the completed interface can be seen in the later section about themes.

Compose layout

The code to display the compose dialog should look very familiar by now. The window is created as `gtk.WINDOW_TOPLEVEL` because Go-GTK only allows a choice of top-level or popup (that is, floating content), rather than child windows such as a dialog. We set up a destroy function that will close the window rather than exiting the application.

The rest of the layout code is the usual vertical box for each item with a horizontal box for the `to` label, which is left of the input field:

```
func buildCompose() {
    window := gtk.NewWindow(gtk.WINDOW_TOPLEVEL)
    window.SetTitle("New GoMail")
    window.Connect("destroy", func() {
        window.Destroy()
    })
```

```
    vbox := gtk.NewVBox(false, padding)
    subject := gtk.NewEntry()
    subject.SetText("subject")
    vbox.PackStart(subject, false, true, 0)
    toBox := gtk.NewHBox(false, padding)
    toBox.PackStart(gtk.NewLabel("To"), false, true, 0)
    email := gtk.NewEntry()
    email.SetText("email")
    toBox.Add(email)
    vbox.PackStart(toBox, false, true, 0)

    content := gtk.NewTextView()
    content.GetBuffer().SetText("email content")
    content.SetEditable(true)
    vbox.Add(content)

    buttonBox := gtk.NewHBox(false, padding)
    buttonBox.PackEnd(gtk.NewButtonWithLabel("Cancel"), false, true, 0)
    buttonBox.PackEnd(gtk.NewButtonWithLabel("Send"), false, true, 0)
    vbox.PackEnd(buttonBox, false, true, 0)

    window.Add(vbox)
    window.SetBorderWidth(padding)
    window.Resize(400, 320)
    window.ShowAll()
}
```

As you can see with `buttonBox`, we've made use of the `PackEnd()` function described before to right-align the buttons at the bottom of the compose window. We also make use of the `padding` definition from the main window to provide consistent spacing for our widgets. Running the preceding code should load a window similar to this:

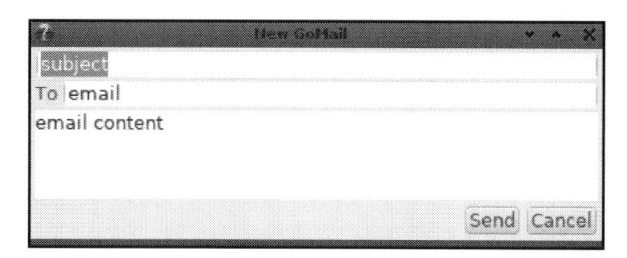

The GoMail compose window with Go-GTK

Now that we have the basic layout and input fields prepared, let's connect to some content using our test email server.

Signaling

In a traditional GTK+ application, it would be possible, even recommended, to make use of the built-in signal handling capabilities. A new signal could be created, which would then be emitted by the application at an appropriate time; components could connect to this signal and respond appropriately. However, the ability to create signals is not exposed through the Go-GTK API and so we will use callbacks like the previous examples.

To load our test server, we first update the `main()` function to set up a server and pass it to the user interface creation code. We then set the content to show the current message from our test server:

```
func main() {
    server := client.NewTestServer()
    main := new(mainUI)
    main.showMain(server)
    main.setEmail(server.CurrentMessage())
    gtk.Main()
}
```

This makes use of a new helper function that will set the content of the email detail panel. We will call this from our list selection code later as well:

```
func (m *mainUI) setEmail(message *client.EmailMessage) {
    m.subject.SetText(message.Subject)
    m.to.SetText(message.ToEmailString())
    m.from.SetText(message.FromEmailString())
    m.date.SetText(message.DateString())

    m.content.GetBuffer().SetText(message.Content)
}
```

To set the content of the email list, we store the iterator and the model in our application struct when created, so they can be referenced later. The following helper function handles the details of prepending an item to the email list. This function is called on each message in `server.ListMessages()` to set up the initial list:

```
func (m *mainUI) prependEmail(message *client.EmailMessage) {
    m.listModel.Prepend(&m.listIter)
    m.listModel.SetValue(&m.listIter, 0, message.Subject)
}
```

The last part of the basic communication with the user interface is to handle the selection of items in the tree view. To handle this, our application must implement `gtk.GtkTreeSelecter`, which has a single `Select()` function. The following implementation will suit our needs. Firstly, note that this can be called for selection and deselection, so we need to check that the item is not currently selected. Then, we use the path specified when the callback is invoked to determine the row that was clicked. This row number is used to get the email from the server list of messages. We can then call our helpful `setEmail()` function:

```
func (m *mainUI) Select(selection *gtk.TreeSelection, model *gtk.TreeModel,
path *gtk.TreePath, selected bool) bool {
   if selected { // already selected, just return
      return true
   }

   row := path.GetIndices()[0]
   email := m.server.ListMessages()[row]

   m.setEmail(email)
   return true
}
```

For the select handler to be called, we must register it on `gtk.ListView` when it is created:

```
var selecter gtk.GtkTreeSelecter
selecter = mainUI
list.GetSelection().SetSelectFunction(&selecter)
```

Now, the user interface should be complete. We need to handle background updates when new emails arrive.

Thread handling

Before we can correctly handle background processing with Go-GTK (or any GTK+ implementations), we must correctly initialize the thread handling portions of the underlying libraries (`glib` and `gdk`). These lines should be entered at the start of an application's `main()` function:

```
glib.ThreadInit(nil)
gdk.ThreadsInit()
gdk.ThreadsEnter()
gtk.Init(nil)
```

Once the thread handling has been set up, we can write background code that will communicate with the user interface. This code must execute on the same thread that the application was created with. To ensure this, we use the helper functions, `gdk.ThreadsEnter()` and `gdk.ThreadsLeave()`, around the code we wish to execute. For our application to add new messages to the end of our email list when they arrive, add the following code immediately before calling `gtk.Main()` to start the application:

```
go func() {
    for email := range server.Incoming() {
        gdk.ThreadsEnter()
        main.prependEmail(email)
        gdk.ThreadsLeave()
    }
}()
```

This completes the implementation of our GoMail application in Go-GTK, but how can we compile the app for different platforms?

Cross compilation

Compiling a Go-GTK based application for additional platforms requires requires additional C compilers to be installed so that CGo can create the necessary binary output. The steps for completing this, if you haven't done so already, are in the `Appendix`, *Cross-Compiler Setup*. You'll also need to have GTK+ installed, which should obviously already be the case. As the *Cross compilation* section of `Chapter 4`, *Walk - Building Graphical Windows Applications*, andlabs UI already stepped through the details, so we won't repeat them here. The process is identical due to andlabs UI's use of the GTK+ library for some target platforms. Be sure to set the appropriate `GOOS`, `GOARCH`, `CGO_ENABLED`, `CC`, and `CXX` environment variables.

Before we wrap up our exploration of the toolkit, we should look at the benefits provided by its theming capabilities.

Theming

One of the large benefits of using a GTK+ (or Qt)-based API is that the widget set can be themed. Users are able to install any number of themes (or write their own) to control how applications look. While this can add a testing overhead, they will behave the same across all platforms so the burden is somewhat reduced.

Let's see a few different themes applied to our GoMail application illustrated here, starting with a great light theme named `Clearlooks`.

- The Clearlooks theme on Linux:

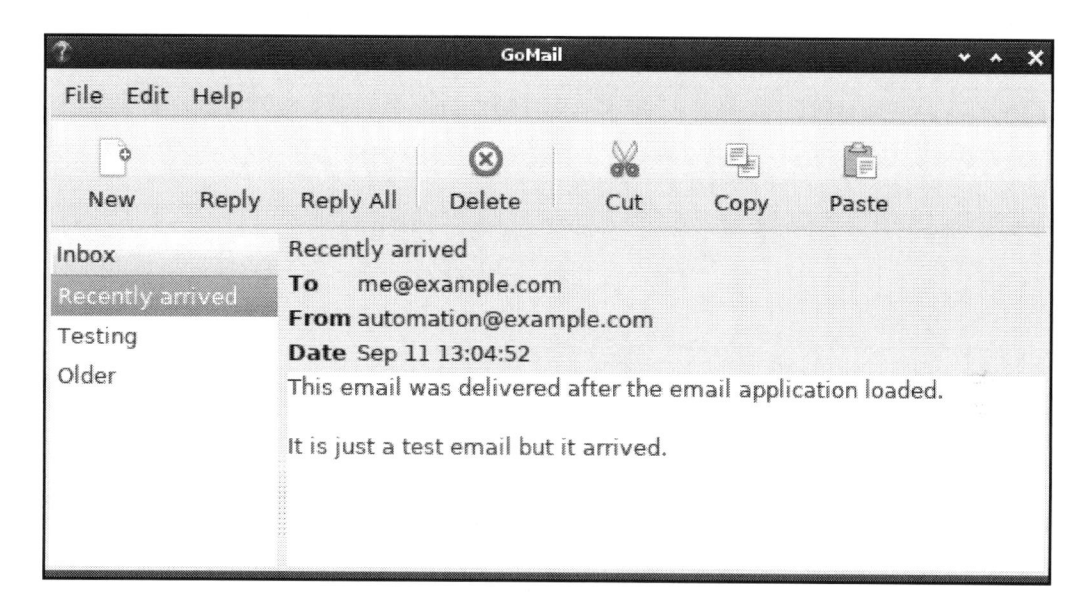

- Compose in Clearlooks:

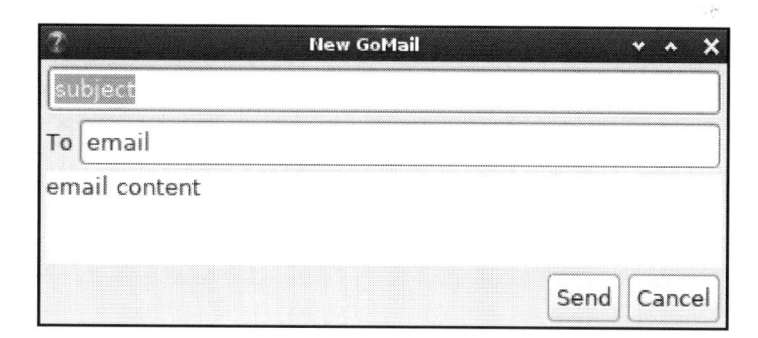

On Windows, the default theme looks more like the standard widgets, though the user can load any other GTK+ theme. Notice that the default icons are also different, more in-keeping with the operating system standards.

- The Windows default theme:

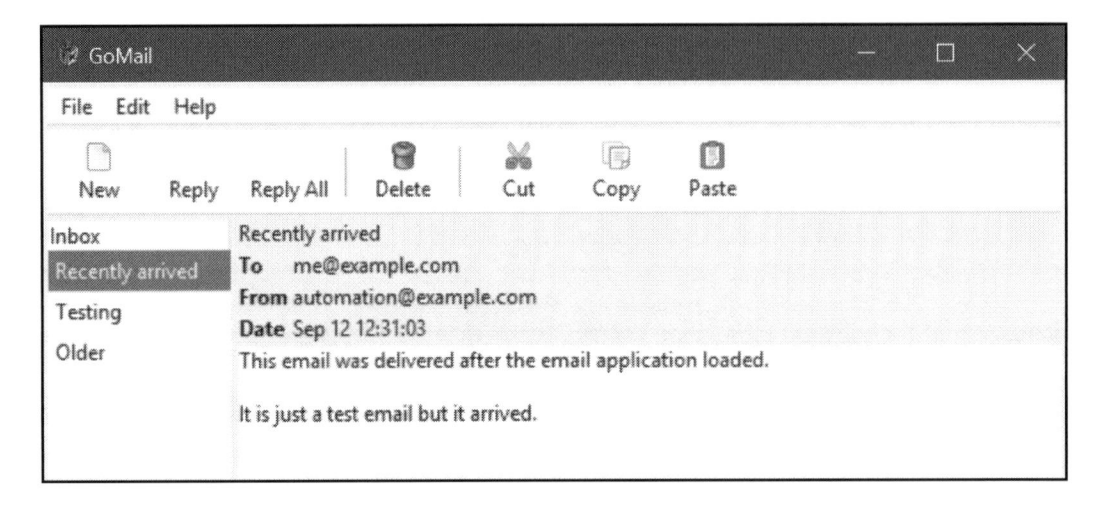

- Compose with Windows:

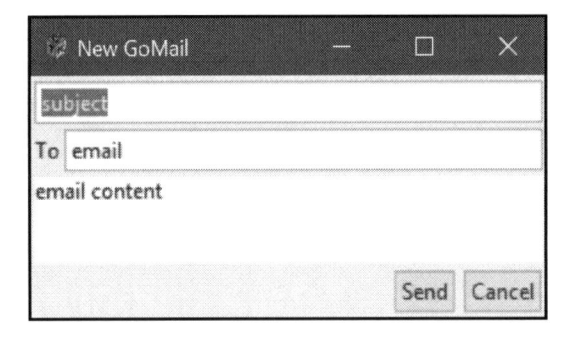

There are also many dark themes; *Arc Dark* is very popular.

- Arc Dark theme running on Linux:

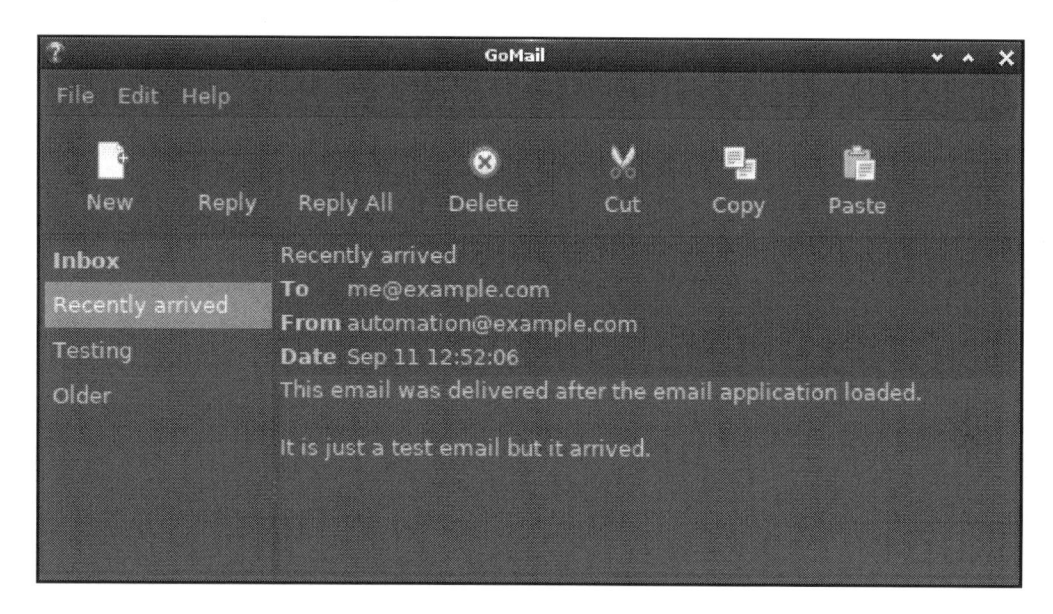

- Ark Dark compose window:

Many themes are designed for nostalgia, including this CDE theme, which is based on a colorful desktop environment from the 1990s.

- Running a CDE theme for the old-school look:

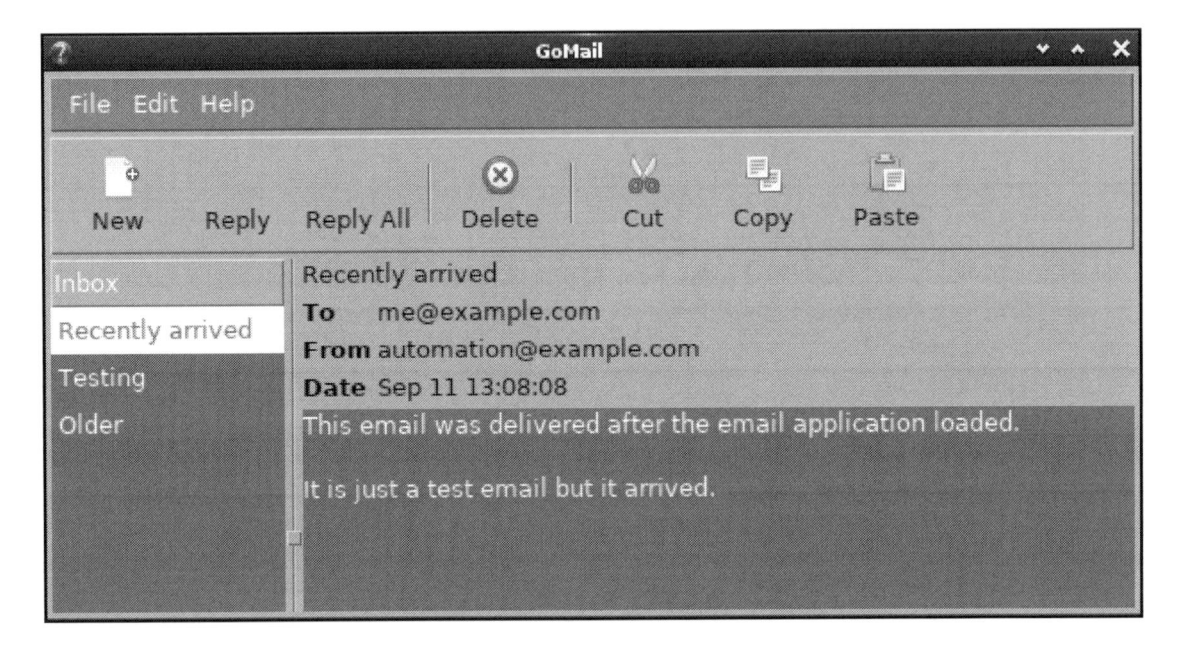

- Composing in a CDE theme:

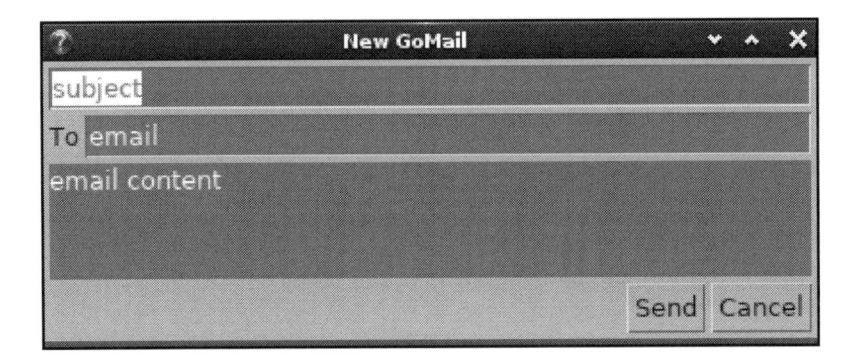

As you can see, the colors of the user interface elements can vary significantly but the layouts are largely consistent. If you look at the buttons (`Send` and `Cancel` on the compose window), there's also a difference between how rounded some edges are. Applications built with Go-GTK should work well with any theme loaded, but it is advisable to check various different configurations as part of your quality assurance process.

Summary

In this chapter, we explored the details of the GTK+ toolkit and how it is made available to Go through go-GTK. We looked at how to get it set up on macOS, Windows, and Linux and how the applications look and behave exactly the same across these platforms. We explored the API design, its various components, and how its event driven model is exposed to developers.

We then returned to the GoMail application from `Chapter 4`, *Walk - Building Graphical Windows Applications*, and `Chapter 5`, *andlabs UI - Cross-Platform Native UIs*, rebuilding it using the Go-GTK library. As the API provides access to most GTK+ features, we found that the application looks more complete than the GTK+ based application created by the Linux driver within andlabs UI used in `Chapter 5`, *andlabs UI - Cross-Platform Native UIs*. We implemented some basic thread and signal handling within the application to handle user input and background events. Lastly, we explored how the powerful GTK+ theme engine could style the created application user interface.

By now, you should be familiar with the Go-GTK library, and how it leverages the underlying GTK+ toolkit and allows the quick development of GUI applications with Go. These applications will differ from the operating system standard look and feel, but are close to standard application design and so should be familiar to most users. If the interface widget design or API wasn't quite what you were looking for, then read the next chapter, where we look at an alternative to GTK, the Qt framework.

Go-Qt - Multiple Platforms with Qt

Similar to the Go-GTK library we explored in the previous chapter, qt by therecipe allows you to write cross-platform graphical applications with a single Go code base. It leverages Qt, a multi-platform application framework that's designed for rapid delivery of applications to desktop and embedded computing environments. Like GTK+, it's designed to draw widgets that are familiar to the end user but aren't reliant upon the operating system's provided toolkit. Additionally, Qt provides a different look for mobile and embedded devices where users expect a different style of presentation. All of this is controlled within the framework so the developer can concentrate on developing a single application.

In this chapter, we'll look at the details of therecipe/qt, the most widely adopted Qt binding for the Go language. We'll cover the following:

- The history and aims of the Qt framework
- How the API is designed and bridged into Go
- Creating an application using therecipe/qt library
- The theming capabilities of Qt applications

By the end of this chapter, you'll be familiar with the capabilities of the Qt framework and its support of many different platforms. Through the exploration of some example applications and our GoMail application, you'll learn how the Go bindings of therecipe provide access to these features for development in Go. You should also have an understanding of whether the Qt framework is a good fit for your next application.

Qt background

The Qt framework was created in 1991 by a company named Trolltech (now called the Qt Company). The KDE Linux desktop is based on Qt and its increase in popularity may be a key reason why Qt development became more widespread. As a platform that's, in part, aimed at embedded devices, the typical developers using Qt are different to those for the GTK+ framework. Additionally, the tooling and support available is better developed due to their commercial backing.

The Qt framework is released in two separate distributions, one commercial and one open source (known as dual licensing). In this manner, they can support open source-compliant applications for free, while providing unrestricted usage for closed source commercial projects. Before the year 2000 (with the release of 2.2), the source code for the free distribution had been under various licenses that some groups considered incompatible with common open source initiatives. For the 2.2 release, it was changed to GPL licensing, which settled any concerns about the group's commitment to true open source freedoms. In 2007, Qt 4.5 was released and they added LGPL as an option for developers who prefer the more permissive license.

In 2011, the Nokia company founded the Qt Project in a move to open up the development and road map of the Qt libraries. Qt's largest market is in embedded devices, such as cars and appliances, the technology being utilized by large companies such as Tesla and Mercedes Benz:

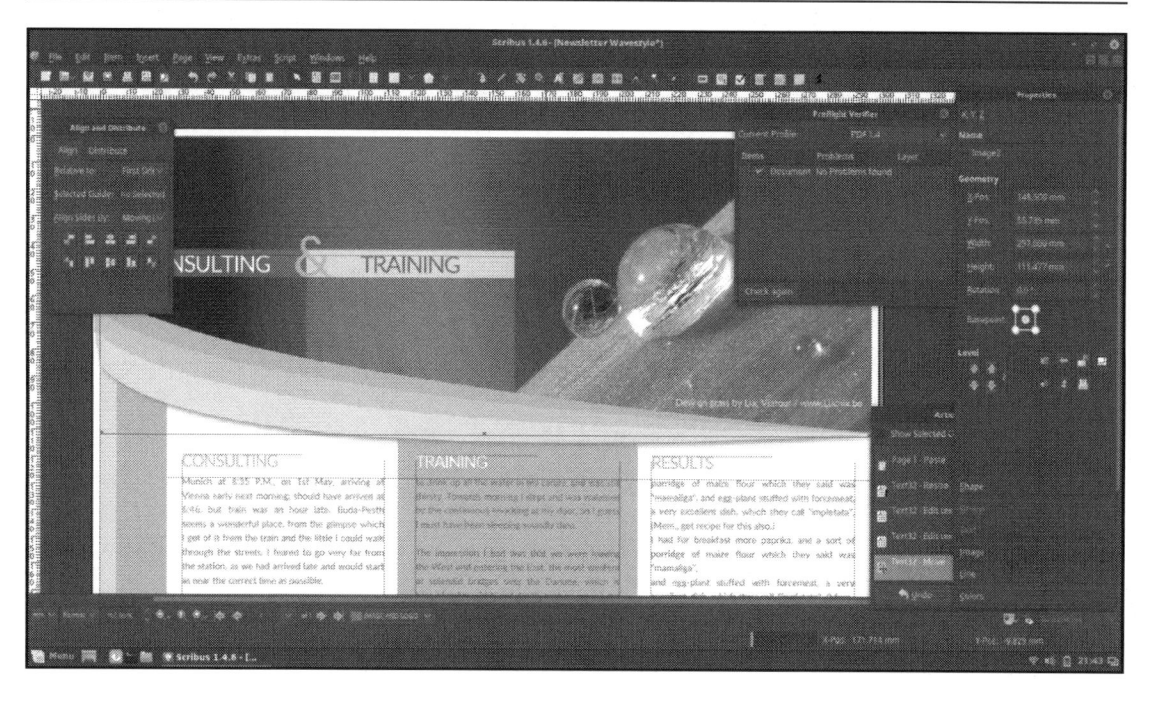

Scribus is a popular desktop publishing application written with Qt (image copyright: Henrik Hüttemann)

The Go bindings by therecipe (whose real name isn't attached to the project), along with many contributors, aims to bring the Qt API along with its substantial list of supported platforms to the Go language. The project supports building applications for Windows, macOS, and Linux desktop computers but also Android, iOS, and many other mobile and embedded devices.

Getting started with therecipe/qt

To begin our exploration of Qt and the binding to Go, we'll build a simple *hello world* application. To be able to do so, we first need to install therecipe/qt, which depends on various prerequisites that we must first set up.

Prerequisites

As with Go-GTK, we'll be relying on a native library that requires that we both set up the CGo functionality and install the Qt library appropriate for the current platform.

Preparing CGo

The Qt Go bindings, like many of the other toolkits featured in this book, require the presence of CGo to utilize native libraries. On a full development system, it's likely that this is already set up. If you're unsure or would like a reminder of how to set up the CGo dependencies, please check the Appendix, *Setting Up CGo*.

Installing Qt

The Qt website (`www.qt.io/download`) offers various methods of installation, including a customized online installer available to anyone with a Qt account (which is free to sign up for). Typically, a Qt installation comes with Qt Creator (the project IDE), the GUI designer, additional tools, and examples. Visiting the preceding site will automatically detect your system and suggest the most appropriate download (this is normally the best option).

> Be aware that the Qt installation can be quite large. If you don't have at least 40 GB of space on your hard drive, you need to make a little space before installing.

Some operating systems offer Qt libraries and tools as part of their package manager, which often provides a more lightweight installation that'll automatically stay up to date. However, this option doesn't deliver the complete feature set of the Qt development tools, and the Qt bindings discussed in this chapter default to using the standard Qt installation provided by the online installer.

macOS

On Apple macOS, the best approach to installation is to use the installer application available at the Qt download site. Visit `www.qt.io/download` and download the macOS installer. Once it has downloaded, open the package and run the program inside; this will install the selected compilers, tools, and supporting applications. If you encounter any errors during installation, the first step would be to check that your Xcode installation is complete and up to date (for more information, see the *Installation Details* appendix).

Windows

Installing on Windows is more straightforward than some of the other toolkits we've looked at, as the Qt installer has a `mingw` package bundled to set up most of the compiling requirements (though it's still recommended to have your own compiler set up for the binding phase next). To install it, go to the download page listed previously and access the Windows installer. Run the downloaded executable and follow the onscreen instructions. It's recommended to install to the default location. Once that's done, you're ready to set up the bindings.

Linux

Using the online installer from `https://www.qt.io` is the easiest approach, though it may be possible to install through your system's package manager (if you want to try the package manager approach, then first read the Qt Linux documentation at `https://github.com/therecipe/qt/wiki/Installation-on-Linux`). On most Linux platforms, the Qt downloads website will correctly detect the platform and offer a simple run installer. After downloading the file, you should make it executable and then run it:

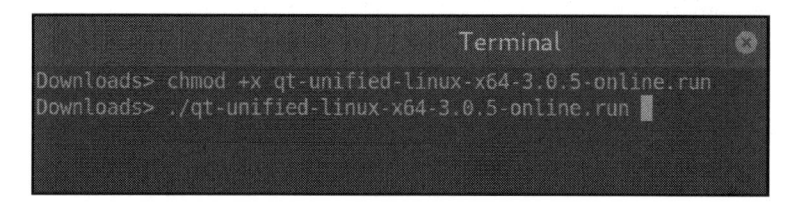

```
Downloads> chmod +x qt-unified-linux-x64-3.0.5-online.run
Downloads> ./qt-unified-linux-x64-3.0.5-online.run
```

On Linux, you need to make the install file executable and run it

This will start the installer just as on macOS; from here, follow the onscreen instructions and complete the installation.

License / Qt account

When it comes to the login screen, then you should enter your Qt account details if you have them. If you qualify for their open source license (GPL or LGPL), you can skip this step—to do so; make sure the email and password fields are empty.

Installing qt (the bindings)

To use qt (the Go Qt bindings), we need to download the project and its dependencies and then run a setup script to configure and compile the library. If using Windows, it's recommended to use the MSYS2 Terminal described in the Appendix.

> If you installed the Qt download to anything other than the default location, then make sure to set up the `QT_DIR` environment variable to the location you chose.

First, the library and its dependencies should be installed using the `go` tools, by running `go get github.com/sirupsen/logrus` and `go get github.com/therecipe/qt`.

Once the download has completed, we need to run the `qtsetup` tool, which is included in the qt project; so, within the `cmd/qtsetup` folder, execute `go run main.go`. Using a Linux Terminal, it should look something like this:

```
chapter7/hello> go get github.com/sirupsen/logrus
chapter7/hello> go get github.com/gopherjs/gopherjs
chapter7/hello> go get golang.org/x/crypto/ssh
chapter7/hello> go get github.com/therecipe/qt
chapter7/hello> cd $GOPATH/src/github.com/therecipe/qt/cmd/qtsetup
chapter7/hello> go run main.go
```

Executing the qtsetup script for therecipe/qt bindings

Once this process completes, the bindings should be ready to use. If you encounter errors, then it's probably because the Qt tools aren't correctly installed or the location was customized and you forgot to set the `QT_DIR` environment variable.

Build

To build our first qt application with Go, let's make another *Hello World* application. As with previous examples, we'll make use of a simple vertical box layout within a single application window. The following code should be sufficient to load your first application:

```go
package main

import (
    "os"

    "github.com/therecipe/qt/widgets"
)

func main() {
    app := widgets.NewQApplication(len(os.Args), os.Args)

    window := widgets.NewQMainWindow(nil, 0)
    window.SetWindowTitle("Hello World")

    widget := widgets.NewQWidget(window, 0)
    widget.SetLayout(widgets.NewQVBoxLayout())
    window.SetCentralWidget(widget)

    label := widgets.NewQLabel2("Hello World!", window, 0)
    widget.Layout().AddWidget(label)

    button := widgets.NewQPushButton2("Quit", window)
    button.ConnectClicked(func(bool) {
        app.QuitDefault()
    })
    widget.Layout().AddWidget(button)

    window.Show()
    widgets.QApplication_Exec()
}
```

Let's note a few details from this code snippet. You'll see that each of the widget constructor functions takes (typically) two parameters, each is the parent widget and a `flags` parameter. Additional types passed in will usually be added before these values with a note in the function name that there are additional parameters. For example, `widgets.NewQLabel2(title, parent, flags)` is equivalent to `widgets.NewQLabel(parent, flags).SetTitle(title)`. Additionally, you'll see that the layout is applied to a new `widgets.QWidget` through `SetLayout(layout)`, and that's set to the window content through `window.SetCentralWidget(widget)`.

Go-Qt - Multiple Platforms with Qt

To load the display and run the application, we call `window.Show()` and then `widgets.QApplication_Exec()`. This file is built in the usual way with `go build hello.go`:

```
[chapter7/hello> ls -lh
total 8
-rw-r--r--  1 andy  staff   674B 16 Sep 17:19 hello.go
[chapter7/hello> go build hello.go
[chapter7/hello> ls -lh
total 193144
-rwxr-xr-x  1 andy  staff    94M 16 Sep 17:29 hello
-rw-r--r--  1 andy  staff   674B 16 Sep 17:19 hello.go
chapter7/hello>
```

Building is simple though the output file is rather large

The file built is quite large due to the size of the Qt framework. This will be reduced significantly when packaging for a specific distribution. This topic will be covered in depth in `Chapter 14`, *Distributing your Application*.

Run

The output of the build phase is a binary that can be executed on the current computer, either on the command line or by double-clicking in a file manager. Additionally, you could execute it directly with `go run hello.go`—either way, you should see a simple window, as shown here:

qt Hello on Linux

Running on macOS

At this stage, the binaries can be executed on a computer with the same architecture that also has Qt installed. We'll look at wider distribution later in this chapter. Before that, let's take a deeper look into the Qt API and how the qt bindings work.

Object model and event handling

The Qt framework is written using the C++ language, and so much of its architecture will be familiar to those who've coded in C++ before. It's important to note that Go isn't a complete object-oriented language and, as such, doesn't match these capabilities directly. In particular, we should look at inheritance as it's important to the Qt object model.

Inheritance

The Qt API is a fully object-oriented model that makes heavy use of the inheritance model. While Go doesn't truly support object-oriented inheritance in the traditional manner, its composition approach is very powerful and works well in its place. The result means that you probably won't notice the difference! This only comes into play if you wish to implement a custom widget, which is out of scope for this chapter.

Memory management

As you'll have noticed in the preceding example, each widget expects the parent to be passed to the constructing function. This enables the Qt framework to handle the tidying up, and freeing of memory when a tree of widgets is removed. `QObject` (which is the base object for all of the Qt API) keeps track of its child objects and so, when being removed, can remove its children too. This makes the creation and deletion of complex widget hierarchies easier to handle correctly. To make use of this feature, you should always remember to pass the parent object to a widget's constructor (the Go functions starting with `New...`), despite the fact that passing `nil` may look like it's working.

Signals and slots

Qt is, like GTK+, an event-driven framework and uses signals extensively to handle event management and data communications. In Qt, this concept is split into signals and slots; a signal is what will be generated when an event occurs and a slot is what can receive a signal. The action of setting a slot to receive a signal is called **connecting** and this causes a slot function to be called when its connected signal is invoked. In Qt, these are typed events meaning that each signal has a list of type parameters associated with it. When the signal is defined, this type is set and any slot wishing to connect to the signal will need to have the same type.

In qt Go code, signals and slots are defined using struct tags such as `_ func(string) `signal:"mySignal"`` and `_ func(string) `slot:"mySlot"``, which provide metadata to the Go type system, much as our JSON example in Chapter 3, *Go to the Rescue!*. Given a struct, `s`, which defines these properties, we could set a function to execute when `mySignal` is fired with the following code:

```
s.ConnectMySignal(
    func(msg string) {
        log.Println("Signalled message", msg)
    }
)
```

Signals and slots are what power user interfaces generated with Qt Designer and are the recommended way of handling multi-threaded applications. A signal may fire from a background thread and the user interface code can connect this signal to its own slot—in essence, listening for the signal. When the signal fires, any associated data (parameters to the signal) will be passed from one thread to another so it can be used safely within the GUI updates. In many ways, this is similar to how Go channels work, which we've discussed extensively in Chapter 3, *Go to the Rescue!*.

As qt is a lightweight binding to the Qt API, the Go-specific documentation is minimal but you can find out a lot more about the Qt design and all of the classes available in the official documentation available at https://doc.qt.io/qt-5/classes.html.

Now that we know how a Qt application and the qt Go implementation are set up, let's explore a more complete application by returning to our GoMail example.

Sample application

To look at a more complete application, we'll dust off the original designs for the GoMail application—after all, they were created with Qt Designer in the first place. We'll recreate the exact layout generated in Chapter 4, *Walk - Building Graphical Windows Applications*, and explain the implementation as we go.

Layout

For the first time in our GoMail examples, we have a toolkit that provides all of the layouts required to match the user interface we designed at the beginning of Section 2, *Toolkits Using Existing Widgets*. That's perhaps no surprise, as it was created using the Qt tools, but it's a chance to explore the more complete set of layouts provided by Qt and made available using the qt bindings. The most useful ones are the following:

Layout	Description
box	The box layout is very familiar by now; it lays out widgets in a horizontal or vertical box. Therefore, it's created with `widgets.NewQVBoxLayout()` or `widgets.NewQVBoxLayout()` accordingly.
form	This is a convenience layout that's basically a two-column grid where all of the widgets in the left column are labels. This is styled accordingly to produce the design we saw in Qt Creator.
grid	This layout represents a flexible grid layout so that cells aren't forced to all be the same size but instead rows and columns flex to accommodate the minimum size of items packed into the grid.
spacer	While not strictly a layout, the spacer item can be used in layouts to create visual space. Constructed using `widgets.NewQSpacerItem(width, height, hPolicy, vPolicy)`, it's possible to add various different types of space using this helpful class.
stacked	A stacked layout sets all child objects to be the full size of the containing widget, but ensures that only one can be visible at a time. The `SetCurrentWidget()` and `SetCurrentIndex()` functions can be used to control which child is visible. This is very useful for implementing tabbed panels or paged controls.

Using this knowledge, we can re-create the GoMail browse interface using pure Qt widgets. A lot of this code will be familiar by now, but there are a number of notable differences. Firstly, you can see that layouts (as listed previously) are typically set on `widgets.QWidget` rather than creating a whole new widget for their own purpose. This approach means that the number of different widgets can be kept lower, but it also causes some functionality to be attached to the layout and not the widget. For example, the `widgets.NewQFormLayout()` we set on the `detail` widget is designed to lay out form components, and as such has helper functions to add rows (`form.AddRow3`, for example). To use these functions, we must keep a reference to the layout (the `form` variable in this code) to operate on. You can also see that `AddWidget()` is called on `widget.Layout()` rather than on `widget` directly.

This snippet contains most of the code to create our basic layout. Some of the toolbar and menu code (which is rather repetitive) has been left out, but it can be found in the code repository that accompanies this book. We start with the imports and a basic skeleton for creating a menu bar:

```
package main

import (
    "github.com/therecipe/qt/core"
    "github.com/therecipe/qt/gui"
    "github.com/therecipe/qt/widgets"
    "os"
)

func buildMenu() *widgets.QMenuBar {
    menu := widgets.NewQMenuBar(nil)

    file := widgets.NewQMenu2("File", menu)
    ...
    menu.AddMenu(file)

    ...

    return menu
}
```

And similarly, we can create a new toolbar using built-in icons:

```
func buildToolbar() *widgets.QToolBar {
    toolbar := widgets.NewQToolBar("tools", nil)
    toolbar.SetToolButtonStyle(core.Qt__ToolButtonTextUnderIcon)
    toolbar.AddAction2(gui.QIcon_FromTheme2("document-new", nil), "New")

    ...
```

```
        return toolbar
}
```

And lastly, we lay out the main content of the window:

```
func main() {
    widgets.NewQApplication(len(os.Args), os.Args)

    window := widgets.NewQMainWindow(nil, 0)
    window.SetWindowTitle("GoMail")

    widget := widgets.NewQWidget(window, 0)
    widget.SetLayout(widgets.NewQVBoxLayout())
    window.SetMinimumSize2(600, 400)
    window.SetCentralWidget(widget)

    window.SetMenuBar(buildMenu())
    widget.Layout().AddWidget(buildToolbar())

    list := widgets.NewQTreeView(window)
    list.SetModel(core.NewQStringListModel2([]string{"email1", "email2"}, widget))

    detail := widgets.NewQWidget(window, 0)
    form := widgets.NewQFormLayout(detail)
    detail.SetLayout(form)
    form.AddRow5(widgets.NewQLabel2("subject", detail, 0))
    form.AddRow3("From", widgets.NewQLabel2("email", detail, 0))
    form.AddRow3("To", widgets.NewQLabel2("email", detail, 0))
    form.AddRow3("Date", widgets.NewQLabel2("date", detail, 0))
    form.AddRow5(widgets.NewQLabel2("content", detail, 0))

    splitter := widgets.NewQSplitter(window)
    splitter.AddWidget(list)
    splitter.AddWidget(detail)
    widget.Layout().AddWidget(splitter)

    window.Show()
    widgets.QApplication_Exec()
}
```

The preceding code is similar in structure to the previous chapter (as GTK+ and Qt APIs have many similarities), though the naming will remind you of Chapter 4, *Walk - Building Graphical Windows Applications*, and the Walk example. Clearly, as Walk is based largely on Qt, the naming is often the same, but the qt APIs being used here don't offer the same declarative syntax and so must be created using the function-based constructors.

Go-Qt - Multiple Platforms with Qt

This example introduces two new qt packages, `core` and `gui`. As you can see from the example, we use the `core` package with data models (which many of the more complex widgets make use of). The `gui` package provides helpful additions to make a user interface more compelling; in this instance, we're looking up standard icons using the `gui.QIcon_FromTheme2` function. In a more complete application, we could provide fallback icons that would complete the **Reply** and **Reply All** toolbar buttons:

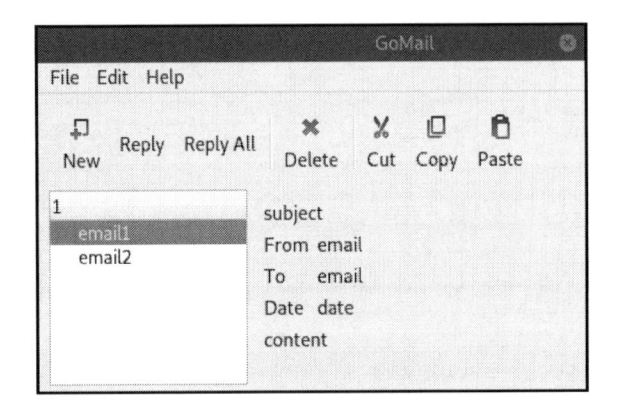

The complete layout of our GoMail application using qt

As you can see from this screenshot, a qt application can look polished with even the most basic of code. You may notice the **1** above our email list instead of **Inbox**; this is due to a limitation in `core.QStringListModel` used for this layout example and should be addressed in our full implementation.

The compose layout

The GoMail compose layout is even simpler: we use `widgets.QFormLayout` again, though the `To` field is the only line with a label included. For this simpler window, we create `widgets.QDialog` and set the layout directly on the dialog widget. To add the buttons at the bottom of the screen, we use a new `widgets.QWidget` with the layout set to `widgets.NewQHBoxLayout()` to lay the buttons out horizontally. To manage the right alignment, we first include `widgets.NewQSpacerItem()` in the button box before the buttons. Note lastly that we call `SetDefault(true)` on the `send` button so it becomes the default action:

```
package main

import "github.com/therecipe/qt/widgets"
```

```
func showCompose() {
    dialog := widgets.NewQDialog(nil, 0)
    dialog.SetModal(false)
    dialog.SetWindowTitle("New GoMail")

    form := widgets.NewQFormLayout(dialog)
    dialog.SetLayout(form)
    dialog.SetMinimumSize2(400, 320)

    form.AddRow5(widgets.NewQLineEdit2("subject", dialog))
    form.AddRow3("To", widgets.NewQLineEdit2("email", dialog))
    form.AddRow5(widgets.NewQTextEdit2("content", dialog))

    buttons := widgets.NewQWidget(dialog, 0)
    buttons.SetLayout(widgets.NewQHBoxLayout())
    buttons.Layout().AddItem(widgets.NewQSpacerItem(0, 0,
widgets.QSizePolicy__Expanding, 0))
    buttons.Layout().AddWidget(widgets.NewQPushButton2("Cancel", buttons))
    send := widgets.NewQPushButton2("Send", buttons)
    send.SetDefault(true)
    buttons.Layout().AddWidget(send)
    form.AddRow5(buttons)

    dialog.Show()
}
```

From the preceding code, we get the following desired outcome—a simple and familiar compose dialog window:

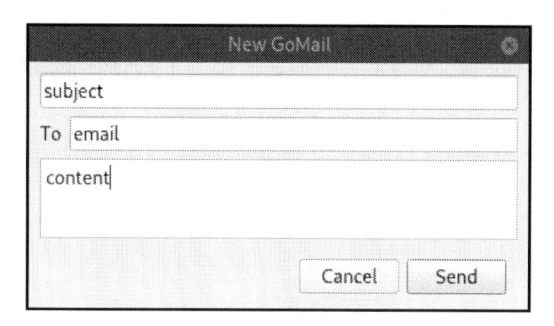

The email compose dialog using qt widgets

Now that the layout is complete, let's connect our test email server to show some email data.

Signalling

To complete the interaction of our GoMail examples, we'll make use of the standard signals and slots within qt. Firstly, we need to set up an instance of our test email server and load the data. We add a `setMessage(*client.EmailMessage)` function to set the content of our labels, which can be called on the loading of our GUI and when the email list is clicked:

```
func (m *mainUI) setMessage(message *client.EmailMessage) {
    m.subject.SetText(message.Subject)
    m.to.SetText(message.ToEmailString())
    m.from.SetText(message.FromEmailString())
    m.date.SetText(message.DateString())

    m.content.SetText(message.Content)
}
```

The code to handle clicking on the email list looks something like the following snippet. We're creating an anonymous function and connecting it to the `selectionChanged` signal. Remember to check whether there are no selected indexes before finding the selected row number:

```
list.ConnectSelectionChanged(func(selected *core.QItemSelection, _
*core.QItemSelection) {
    if len(selected.Indexes()) == 0 {
        return
    }

    row := selected.Indexes()[0].Row()
    m.setMessage(m.server.ListMessages()[row])
})
```

Next, we need to update our toolbar and menu to open the compose dialog when **New** is clicked. The `triggered` signal is the one to connect to; we need to wrap `showCompose()` in an anonymous function as the signal type passes a `bool` flag (for the checked status) that we want to ignore. The code is identical for toolbars and menus:

```
new := file.AddAction("New")
new.ConnectTriggered(func(_ bool){showCompose()})
```

Similar code is used to handle button presses, which send a `clicked` signal; our compose dialog, c, will connect an anonymous function to compose an email, send it, and hide the dialog when **Send** is clicked:

```
send.ConnectClicked(func(_ bool) {
    email := c.createEmail()
    c.server.Send(email)
```

```
    c.dialog.Close()
})
```

Thread handling

As shown in the preceding click handlers, the multi-threaded aspects of a complex application are handled by the signal-slot design in Qt. Code executed in a slot will be running on the correct thread to do graphical updates. Additionally, any data passed as part of the signal definition can be accessed in a thread-safe manner. We'll make use of this property to handle our background email notifications.

To set this up, we create a new custom signal. This is made possible by the `qtmoc` tool, which comes with therecipe/qt bindings. We'll update our `mainUI` struct definition to inherit from `core.QObject` (this is a requirement) and then define an anonymous function with the `signal` tag, which defines the name of the signal:

```
core.QObject
_ func(message *client.EmailMessage) `signal:"newMail"`
```

Once this is set up, you should run the `qtmoc` tool in the current directory; this generates various methods including the `ConnectNewMail()` and `NewMail()` methods (the slots connecting method and signal trigger respectively), as well as a new constructor. Once this is complete, we must update our code to use the newly generated constructor (if your signals don't trigger slots, then this step was probably missed):

```
main := NewMainUI(nil)
```

We then add new code to connect `prependEmail(client.EmailMessage)` to the `newMail` signal. Once that's connected, we listen to the `server.Incoming()` channel and, each time a message arrives, we send the signal using the generated `NewMail(client.EmailMessage)` function:

```
main.ConnectNewMail(main.prependEmail)
go func() {
    for email := range main.server.Incoming() {
        main.NewMail(email)
    }
}()
```

With this code in place, our background code will trigger the appropriate handlers and all updates occur on the correct thread for immediate updates to the screen.

Cross-compilation

Compiling a qt-based application for another desktop platform isn't currently supported in the same way that we've compiled other examples. There's an alternative approach, however, using Docker as a deployment method. Setting up the tools and running a build in this way is out of scope for this chapter, but you can read more about deploying qt apps at `github.com/therecipe/qt/wiki/Deploying-Application`.

Theming

The Qt theme (known as *Style* in Qt terminology) can be adjusted similarly to GTK apps in the previous chapter. Before Qt 5, the current theme could be configured using a standard setup application but in Qt 5, the aim was to fit in with the current desktop—therefore, the application style will adapt to blend in. It's possible to override these settings on a per-application basis. As our application passes the command-line parameters in our `QApplication` constructor (`widgets.NewQApplication(len(os.Args), os.Args)`), we inherit some helpful options, such as `-style=OtherStyle`.

Another default parameter that can be very powerful for applications is `-reverse`. This option will tell all layouts to work in a right-to-left orientation instead of the default left to right:

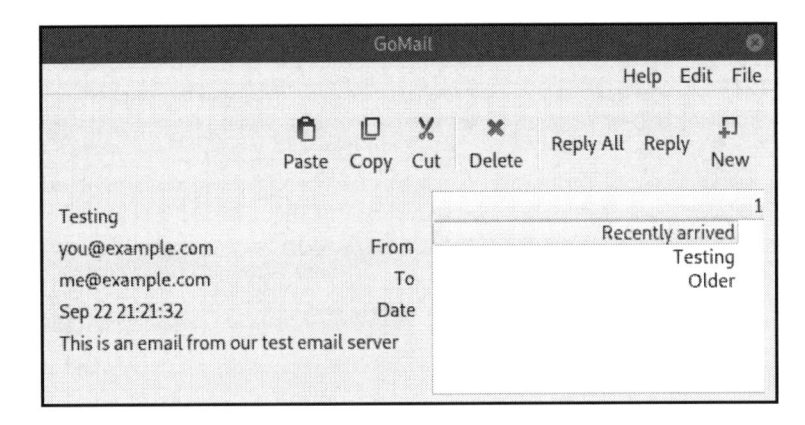

GoMail with reversed layout

Summary

In this chapter, we explored the popular Qt toolkit, its history, and how we can use it to build attractive graphical applications with Go. We saw how easy it is to create a GUI that works identically across many supported platforms.

Through exploring our GoMail application, we found how the powerful layout and built-in standard icons help to quickly build an attractive user interface. The tools provided as part of therecipe's qt bindings allowed us to create custom signals to handle our background processing and avoid multi-threading issues. We'll look further into the distribution of these Go apps for multiple operating systems in Chapter 14, *Distributing Your Application*.

In Section 3, *Modern Graphical Toolkits*, we leave behind the familiar toolkits that make use of standard widget sets. We'll look at various widget toolkits that have either been designed from scratch for cross-platform delivery or to be a great match for the Go programming language.

Section 3: Modern Graphical Toolkits

In the four chapters of `Section 2`, *Toolkits Using Existing Widgets*, we explored various graphical toolkits that provide a Go application different ways to work with existing widget sets. These toolkits provide Go APIs for either native widgets (such as CommonControls in Windows or the Cocoa widgets in macOS) or existing cross-platform toolkits (GTK+ and Qt). These widget sets are tried and tested, often supported by commercial companies, and have established developer tools to support their features (though not all functionality is available to the Go bindings). Applications built using these GUI APIs will vary in look according to the platform they are running on. This may, or may not, be desirable behavior.

In `Section 3`, *Modern Graphical Toolkits*, will look at graphical toolkits designed specifically for the Go language. As part of their design, each of these aim to look and feel identical across all the operating systems they support. Doing so means breaking from traditional widget design and layout to some extent, and most of these APIs have taken the opportunity to bring in inspiration from more modern sources to design their solution.

As libraries that are designed specifically for the Go language, they fit well with the standard libraries, making them easy to learn and integrate with other Go packages. As part of a cross-platform toolkit, they also aim to reduce the complexity of cross-compiling applications for easier distribution. Applications built with these toolkits are typically small, meaning quick download times, and can be expected to run quickly due to less code being loaded than more established cross-platform solutions.

The following chapters will be covered in this section:

- `Chapter 8`, *Shiny – Experimental Go GUI API*
- `Chapter 9`, *nk – Nuklear for Go*
- `Chapter 10`, *Fyne – Material Design-Based GUI*

8
Shiny - Experimental Go GUI API

Shiny is an experimental GUI library designed from scratch and written purely in Go. It was created to explore what's possible when building a cross-platform GUI for the Go language. It is not an official GUI toolkit for Go (though it was created by developers at Google) but provides a solid basis for graphical applications on most supported Go platforms.

This chapter explores how to use the Shiny project to build cross-platform graphical applications without the need for C libraries or pre-installed dependencies. The following topics will be covered in this chapter:

- The design principles of the Shiny project and its widgets
- How the toolkit is built to support multiple platforms without external drivers or native libraries
- Building a basic graphical application that can easily cross-compile to different systems
- Creating a a complete application using Shiny

At the end of this chapter, you should be well-versed in this experimental new API.

Background and the vision for Shiny

The Shiny project was created in an effort to understand how a graphical application toolkit could be created to be in keeping with the Go idiom. Therefore, it is important that its API and methodologies should match the Go language semantics and standard library, its dependencies should be only pure Go libraries or existing system routines, and it should provide a modern approach to developing an application GUI. Much of this is only possible if you start from scratch, as you can tell from the toolkit bindings we saw in Section 2, *Toolkits Using Existing Widgets* of this book. It lives in the `golang.org/x/exp/shiny` repository—an experimental extension to the Go libraries.

The project was started as an investigation by Nigel Tao, a Go developer who had been working on `golang.org/x/mobile` (on which Shiny depends), as he wanted to see desktop applications supported by a new API. After substantial development, it was proposed that this be added as an experimental project within the `golang.org` repositories, which was accepted in 2015. It is expected that, at some future point, the commonality between `golang.org/x/mobile` and `golang.org/x/exp/shiny` will be captured in a separate project, leaving the mobile and desktop specific portions in their respective projects.

The project's development has slowed in recent years but it remains a strong foundation for graphical applications to be built upon. Whether the project will see a resurgence or instead become the base upon which another is built is unclear at this time. Either way, it is an excellent low-level graphical API for Go and so we will look into the details of it and start to build a sample application.

Design and supported platforms

The Shiny project has been designed to ensure good separation between the widget code and the lower-level rendering code that widgets utilize. It is also built with the understanding that graphical drivers may be useful on more than a single platform and could potentially be changed or added to over time.

Architecture

The Shiny API is split into two layers, a lower layer that handles graphical buffers and rendering, and a higher layer where the widget and layout code is located. Each layer has clear responsibilities and their separation helps to maintain a clean API.

Lower layer

The lower layer of the Shiny API is responsible for creating a render context for each platform supported. It is also responsible for handling input from keyboard and other peripheral devices. The main concepts of the graphical presentation are **Buffer**s, **Texture**s, and **Window**s:

- **Buffer:** A buffer refers to an array of pixel data in memory. This could be a loaded image, a canvas for drawing, or any other graphical data that needs to be presented within an application.
- **Texture:** A texture is a handle to a snapshot of graphical state that's ready to be rendered. It will not be accessible to the application. A texture may be rendered immediately (such as the current widget state) or stored and rendered many times in the future (such as an image).
- **Window:** A window is the location of an application's graphical output. Textures are rendered to the window after certain transformations (determined by the driver) have been applied.

In normal application flow, the code of a graphical user interface will update a widget or layout state—resulting in a buffer's contents being updated. This buffer will then be uploaded to a texture in preparation for being drawn by the driver. The texture will then be rendered to the application window, potentially through transformations within the driver or the underlying platform's graphical implementation. If you are familiar with how OpenGL works, then the processes will seem quite familiar—this is no coincidence, as the approach is well-proven and one of the Shiny drivers uses the OpenGL APIs. For most application developers, the existence of textures will not be visible or important, but it can help to consider the process when optimizing your code.

The driver also handles user interactions, encapsulating them as `mouse.Event` and `key.Event` structures (defined in `x/mobile/event`). A `widget.Widget` can register to receive these events, using a filter that will determine which are relevant to that object, and mark them as handled. Alternatively, an application could access the event queue directly from `screen.Window`, where calling `NextEvent()` would wait until another event occurs. An application that takes this approach should be aware of the vast number of events that can be generated by Shiny (see *Example* in the *Getting started* section later in this chapter). When working with events, the Shiny project includes a powerful gesture package, that enables you to filter on `gesture.Event`, which describes more intent-based information than lower-level data. Helpful event types include `gesture.TypeDrag`, `gesture.TypeIsLongPress`, and `gesture.TypeIsDoublePress` (the event type is accessible through `Event.Type` on gesture events).

Higher layer

Higher-layer APIs are focused on widgets and the overall layout and behavior of a graphical user interface. Working at this level, a developer wouldn't expect to be dealing with buffers and events but with high-level concepts such as buttons, text areas, and layouts. The types and functions defined at this layer (within the `widget` package) are designed to be easy to understand from a high level and includes graphical user interface concepts that will be familiar to most developers.

The Shiny widgets (detailed further in the *Widgets and material design* section later in this chapter) are all written in pure Go and encapsulate any widget logic (such as input handling), as well as rendering (by implementing the `node.PaintBase()` or `node.Paint()` functions). This allows the user interface code to remain completely detached from the drivers for better testing and to promote consistency across all supported operating systems.

Supported platforms

The Shiny project currently supports Windows, macOS, Linux, DragonFly BSD, and OpenBSD. Other BSD distributions or Unix systems that use X11 (see the following discussion of drivers) may work but are not officially supported at this time.

The code required to support an operating system is relatively lightweight if one of the existing drivers is able to run. For example, if OpenGL is installed on a not-yet-supported platform, then you may be able to add the operating system-specific code to wire it in. In this situation, a platform-specific Go file would need to open a window and handle any platform-specific input or device setup for the OpenGL window.

On a platform where an existing driver does not currently work, it would be a tremendous amount of work to add support. As well as the window- and user-interaction code, it would be necessary to write the graphical renderer and presentation layer from scratch or provide an API bridge to an existing one. Such an implementation would have to handle the complete set of draw primitives and transformations utilized by the main Shiny code (such a list is outside the scope of this book).

Drivers currently included

Shiny has three complete drivers at the time of writing (**win**, **gl**, and **x11**) and each of these drivers must implement all of the input and output capabilities of the Shiny toolkit. The output portion of a driver is required to define a suitable `screen.Texture` provider so that buffers can be uploaded ready for rendering and to handle the rendering process. On the input side, a driver must handle mouse and keyboard events and translate them into `golang.org/x/mobile` types that can then be filtered by the Shiny event-handling code. The details of each driver are as follows:

- **gl:** The most commonly used driver, built on top of the cross-platform OpenGL, it makes use of this standard API for graphical display. Many operating systems provide this functionality, though it should be noted that this may not be supported on all devices.
- **win:** The win driver is built specifically for the Microsoft Windows operating system to work without the OpenGL APIs. Rendering is provided by the **Graphics Device Interface** (**GDI**).
- **x11:** The X11 driver provides support for the standard graphical desktop platform on Linux and Unix. It communicates directly with the *XServer* and uses the **SHared Memory** (**SHM**) extension for communicating image data efficiently.

Between these drivers, there is at least one render definition for all of the operating systems supported by the toolkits described earlier in this book, and potentially more. These details shouldn't be a concern day to day when programming with Shiny but it helps to understand possible extensions in the future.

Getting started with Shiny

In keeping with the design of Shiny to not depend on any native libraries or system dependencies, there are no prerequisites to using it. So, we can jump straight into getting the library installed and see it in action.

Setup

Installing the Shiny library is as simple as installing the Go files from `golang.org/x/exp/shiny` and its `x/mobile` and `x/image` dependencies. As these are top-level projects, you may see a warning about no Go files—you can ignore this, as the APIs will be installed:

```
chapter8/hello> go get -u golang.org/x/exp/shiny
package golang.org/x/exp/shiny: no Go files in /home/andy/Code/Go/src/golang.org/x/exp/shiny
chapter8/hello> go get -u golang.org/x/mobile
package golang.org/x/mobile: no Go files in /home/andy/Code/Go/src/golang.org/x/mobile
chapter8/hello> go get -u golang.org/x/image
package golang.org/x/image: no Go files in /home/andy/Code/Go/src/golang.org/x/image
chapter8/hello> ls -la $GOPATH/src/golang.org/x/exp/shiny/
total 52
drwxr-xr-x 13 andy users 4096 Oct 26 15:56 .
drwxr-xr-x 17 andy users 4096 Oct 26 15:56 ..
drwxr-xr-x  6 andy users 4096 Oct 26 15:56 driver
drwxr-xr-x 12 andy users 4096 Oct 26 15:56 example
drwxr-xr-x  2 andy users 4096 Oct 26 15:56 gesture
drwxr-xr-x  4 andy users 4096 Oct 26 15:56 iconvg
drwxr-xr-x  2 andy users 4096 Oct 26 15:56 imageutil
drwxr-xr-x  4 andy users 4096 Oct 26 15:56 materialdesign
drwxr-xr-x  2 andy users 4096 Oct 26 15:56 screen
drwxr-xr-x  2 andy users 4096 Oct 26 15:56 text
drwxr-xr-x  2 andy users 4096 Oct 26 15:56 unit
drwxr-xr-x  3 andy users 4096 Oct 26 15:56 vendor
drwxr-xr-x  6 andy users 4096 Oct 26 15:56 widget
chapter8/hello>
```

Getting x/exp/shiny will download the package contents

No extra libraries or system configuration are required.

Example

Before we start building an application, let's load an example project to check that Shiny is installed and working correctly. The project provides various example projects—we will check the one called *basic*. Simply change to the `examples/basic` directory and run `main.go`:

```
> cd $GOPATH/src/golang.org/x/exp/shiny/example/basic/
> go run main.go
got lifecycle.Event{From:StageDead, To:StageAlive, DrawContext:<nil>}
got lifecycle.Event{From:StageAlive, To:StageVisible, DrawContext:<nil>}
got size.Event{WidthPx:1024, HeightPx:768, WidthPt:1024, HeightPt:768, PixelsPerPt:1.3333334, Orientation:0}
got paint.Event{External:false}
got lifecycle.Event{From:StageVisible, To:StageFocused, DrawContext:<nil>}
got lifecycle.Event{From:StageFocused, To:StageVisible, DrawContext:<nil>}
```

Launching the basic Shiny example

After launching, you should see the following window and (as illustrated in the preceding) the output of all of the events triggered by the application. The size of the window may vary depending on the operating system you are running, due to driver default values:

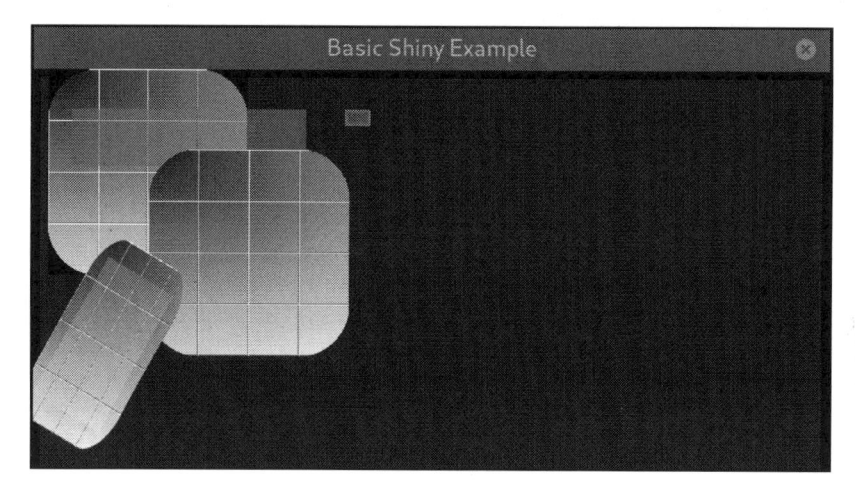

A rather unconventional example application

As you can see, this example application is unlike the other toolkits we've explored. This represents the main focus of the Shiny project as primarily a technology demo.

Cross-compiling

As a project that aims to be written purely in Go, one of its goals is to be just as easy to cross-compile for different platforms as it is to build for the current operating system. In cases where the Shiny driver for the operating system is pure Go (as is currently the case for **windows** and **x11**, used by Linux and BSD), compiling for a specific operating system is as simple as using the `GOOS` parameter, as described in Chapter 3, *Go to the Rescue!*:

Compiling Linux and Windows binaries from a Linux Command Prompt

The **gl** driver that provides hardware-accelerated rendering (used by macOS and Linux) depends on a system API that is not currently available without CGO and so is more challenging to cross-compile. Through the toolkit design, it's possible to use the **x11** driver for a Unix target platform if CGO is not available—so Linux or BSD can still be cross compiled.

> Note that cross-compiling a Shiny application for Linux will result in an application that does not have graphical acceleration enabled. This can be overcome by using `CGO_ENABLED=1` and installing various libraries but it is easily forgotten, so it's advisable to set up a dedicated Linux build environment.

This means that, from macOS, we can cross-compile both Linux and Windows executables by simply setting the appropriate `GOOS` variable as would be expected:

```
[chapter8/hello> go build hello.go
[chapter8/hello> file hello
hello: Mach-O 64-bit executable x86_64
[chapter8/hello> GOOS=linux go build hello.go
[chapter8/hello> file hello
hello: ELF 64-bit LSB executable, x86-64, version 1 (SYSV), statically linked, w
ith debug_info, not stripped
[chapter8/hello> GOOS=windows go build hello.go
[chapter8/hello> file hello.exe
hello.exe: PE32+ executable (console) x86-64 (stripped to external PDB), for MS
Windows
chapter8/hello>
```

Cross-compiling for macOS

With Windows and Linux (and some BSD flavours), all cross-compiling completes without CGO, therefore, we only need to look at macOS as a special case. To cross-compile successfully for macOS, we must add `CGO_ENABLED=1` to our build, which will then look for the required system libraries. Clearly, these are not normally available and so we must set up our development environment to provide the required APIs.

The procedure for setting up the clang binary and required API bundles for macOS cross-compiling is a complicated process, but if you worked through `Chapter 5`, *andlabs UI - Cross-platform Native UIs*, this will already be set up. If you've jumped straight to this chapter, then you may need to follow the steps in the `Appendix`, *Cross-Compiler Setup*, under *Cross-compiling for macOS with cgo*. Once that's complete, you should have a new compiler available named `o32-clang`, which is able to link to macOS Foundation APIs.

To build the application, we now set up the `GOOS` and `CGO_ENABLED` flags as before, but also specify the compiler to use through an extra `CC` environment variable, setting it to `o32-clang`. With that configuration complete, we can build a macOS Shiny application from our Linux Terminal:

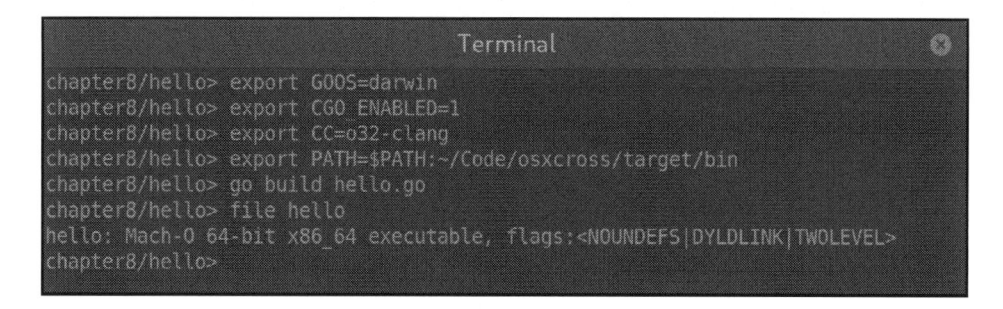

```
chapter8/hello> export GOOS=darwin
chapter8/hello> export CGO_ENABLED=1
chapter8/hello> export CC=o32-clang
chapter8/hello> export PATH=$PATH:~/Code/osxcross/target/bin
chapter8/hello> go build hello.go
chapter8/hello> file hello
hello: Mach-O 64-bit x86_64 executable, flags:<NOUNDEFS|DYLDLINK|TWOLEVEL>
chapter8/hello>
```

Building a macOS application from a Linux terminal

Applications built in this manner will have full OpenGL acceleration as though they were built directly on a macOS computer.

Now that we've seen all of the details for building with Shiny, let's explore how these applications are designed.

Widgets and material design

Before we can start a simple application, we need to understand more about Shiny widgets and how their visual design impacts development. The other toolkits that we've looked at didn't need this understanding to start using the API, but the experimental status of the higher-level APIs in Shiny means that even a *hello world* application requires some understanding of how the toolkit functions.

Before we get into the details of the widgets that Shiny provides and how to work with them, let's take a look at the design and iconography of the Shiny project. This design takes a different approach to the toolkits we've previously looked at in this book, but it should be familiar to any Android app developers or users of the Google product suite.

Design

Material design, if you are not already familiar with the concept, can be defined as follows:

> ... an adaptable system of guidelines, components, and tools that support the best practices of user interface design"

```
-material.io
```

The design principles will be familiar to anyone with an Android smartphone or tablet and are somewhat similar to the user interface design adopted by Microsoft for recent releases of the Windows operating system, which support tablets and touch screen user input. The approach aims to help developers quickly create beautiful applications and to ease communication between developers and designers. The *design language* also helps to promote a consistent user experience in a world where applications are trying to stand out with their own brand design.

An application that utilizes the material design principles will not look identical to all of the others, but will have sufficient similarities that a user should have no trouble understanding how it works. Colors, layouts, and navigation can be different from one interface to another, as long as they follow the guidelines set out. Material design includes some standard color palettes and advice for creating custom ones for your needs. Layouts and navigation widgets similarly have standard implementations, but these can be extended and used to suit the context. These standard widgets are called *material components* and have been created for Android, iOS, Flutter, and the web—Shiny is one potential approach to bringing them to desktop:

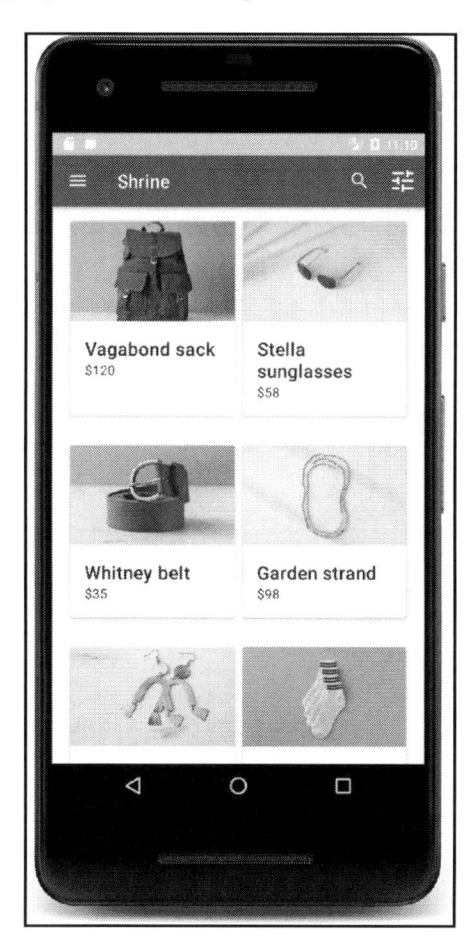

An Android app demonstrating material design. Image copyright: Google.

Shiny - Experimental Go GUI API

There are many tools online to help you learn about and adopt material design principles. They can be found on the material design website at `material.io`. Let's explore a few of the details that are at the core of the Shiny API.

Icons

The material design project has created a standard set of icons that are freely available to use in any application. Integrating these clear, concise icons into your user interface adds simple-to-understand hints that are consistent with other applications and can alleviate the need for too much text in the resulting user interface. Shiny bundles the most commonly used icons in the `materialdesign/icons` package and they can be referenced by name through the API. To see the list of names and the icons, you can run the Shiny *IconGallery* example (pictured in the following screenshot):

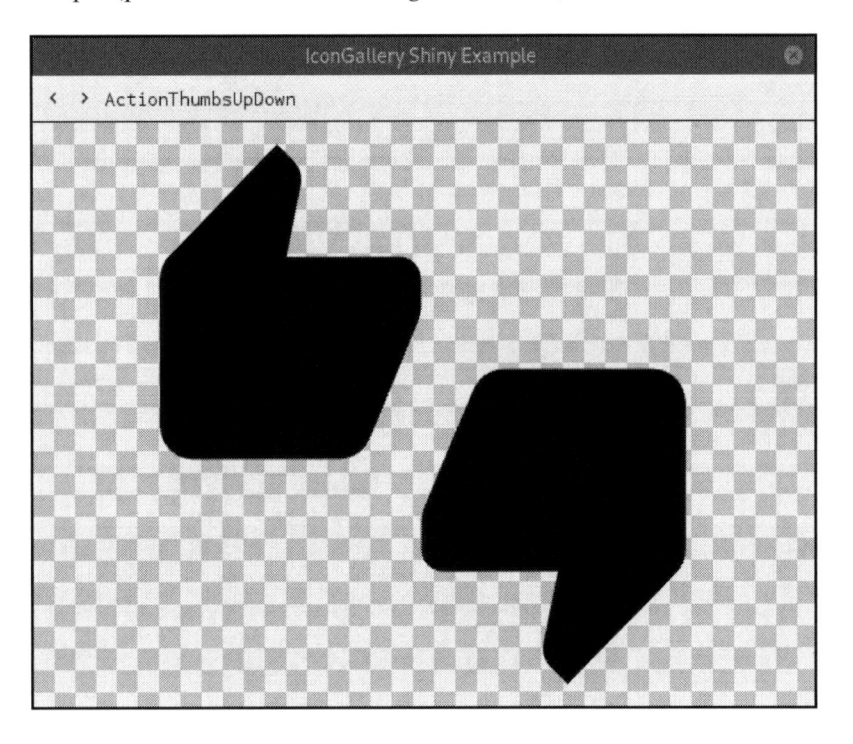

Shiny includes the material icon set as vector graphics

The icons can be painted within a `node.PaintBase()` method by creating an `iconvg.Rasterizer` instance for `node.PaintBaseContext` and calling `iconvg.Decode()` for the icon reference (these icons are stored in the compact IconVG format). Examples of this code in action can be found later in the chapter (or in the Shiny example code).

Themes

One of the central concepts in material design is the color palette—while it does not mandate the colors that an application can use, it has very clear rules about color choice and combinations that work. Designers are encouraged to pick a primary color from the standard palettes (used in most user interface elements) and a secondary color (for highlights and accents) that complement each other. For each color, there are standard light and dark variants, which can add depth to an application interface. You can explore these through the online color tool at `material.io/tools/color`.

The palette that Shiny uses follows this approach; the available colors are:

- `theme.Foreground`: The standard foreground color for the theme—used for text and icons
- `theme.Background`: The standard background color for containers
- `theme.Neutral`: A background color for smaller areas that should be distinct from the background
- `theme.Light`: A lighter version of the neutral color
- `theme.Dark`: A darker version of the neutral color
- `theme.Accent`: The main color from the secondary palette, used for highlighting key elements

Colors in the Shiny API are passed using the `theme.Color` type instead of the golang `color.Color` type. This ensures that the colors used are from the theme palette. From a theme color type, you can call the `Color()` function to get a standard color type or the `Uniform()` function to get `image.Uniform` which is used to draw filled rectangles in a `Paint()` function.

Applications can choose to use the built-in theme (`theme.Default`) or to provide their own. Any type that implements `theme.Theme` can be used in the rendering of a Shiny GUI.

Widgets

As a project that has focused more on the capabilities of cross-platform graphical rendering on the lower layer, Shiny toolkit does not come with many standard widgets. A lot of work has gone in to setting up the building blocks so that applications can provide their own widgets, but if you are looking to use built-in types, the list provided by the `widget` package is as follows:

- **Flow:** This is a container that lays out its children along a horizontal or vertical axis (set in `Flow.Axis` or `NewFlow()`).
- **Flex:** Actually, in a `flex` sub-package, this is a container that lays out its children according to the CSS flexbox algorithm. As with `widget.Flow`, the parameters for the layout are set on the `flex.Flex` container.
- **Image:** This widget renders a golang `image.Image` onscreen. Its dimensions are specified separately to the image.
- **Label:** This is a simple widget for displaying a line of text with a theme color (for example, `theme.Foreground`).
- **Padder:** An invisible widget that contains a child widget and displays it with a specified amount of space around the horizontal or vertical dimensions (or both).
- **Sheet:** A sheet provides the buffer on which all other widgets will draw. Any widgets that are not children of a Sheet may not be rendered. Multiple sheets are required if content should move independently, such as a scroll view.
- **Sizer:** A sizer is an invisible widget that contains a child widget but overrides its size. This can be used to specify a different natural size than the default for an existing widget.
- **Space:** An invisible widget that takes up available space. Placed between two widgets, they will become left- and right- aligned, or by placing `widget.Space` either side of a widget, it will become centered.
- **Text:** A multi-line text widget for displaying more complicated text than `widget.Label`.
- **Uniform:** This is a simple widget that draws a rectangle of a solid color from the theme palette (for example, `theme.Background`).

There is also an advanced widget named `glwidget.GL`, which renders a **OpenGL for embedded systems (GLES)** `framebuffer` into a Shiny application. This is not commonly required for traditional applications but it's a great additional feature to support.

Despite the length of the preceding list, you'll probably notice that it does not provide all the widgets we have used in other chapters. For this reason, we will build a different sample application. This time, one that's a better fit for the toolkit's capabilities. Before that, however, let's return to *getting started* and creating a hello world application.

Getting started continued

Now that we have explored a little of how Shiny is designed and its current constraints, we can implement our first graphical application and see it run.

Code

Let's get started with writing a simple *hello world* window, as in the previous chapters. This code is a little more complicated than in previous examples due to the low-level nature of the toolkit at this time. As well as defining the window, label, and button, we will need to set up a background layer and measure the minimum size for the containing window:

```
package main

import (
    "golang.org/x/exp/shiny/driver"
    "golang.org/x/exp/shiny/screen"
    "golang.org/x/exp/shiny/widget"
    "golang.org/x/exp/shiny/widget/theme"

    "log"
)

func main() {
    driver.Main(func(s screen.Screen) {
        label := widget.NewLabel("Hello World!")
        button := newButton("Quit",
            func() {
                log.Println("To quit close this window")
            })

        w := widget.NewFlow(widget.AxisVertical, label, button)
        sheet := widget.NewSheet(widget.NewUniform(theme.Neutral, w))

        w.Measure(theme.Default, 0, 0)
        if err := widget.RunWindow(s, sheet, &widget.RunWindowOptions{
            NewWindowOptions: screen.NewWindowOptions{
                Title: "Hello",
```

Shiny - Experimental Go GUI API

```
            Width: w.MeasuredSize.X,
            Height: w.MeasuredSize.Y,
         },
      }); err != nil {
         log.Fatal(err)
      }
   })
}
```

In the preceding code, you can see the flow layout (`widget.NewFlow()`), a background layer (`widget.NewSheet()`), and the measurement initialization (`w.Measure()`). With Shiny, `widget.Sheet` is required underneath any widgets so they can paint correctly. On a simple application, a single sheet should be sufficient, but on a more complex user interface where items move independently (that is, scrolling), additional sheets will probably be required.

Supporting code

As you may have noticed, the preceding code has two issues, both relating to the `Quit` button. Firstly, the `func()` that's called does not actually exit the application. This is a current limitation of the Shiny lifecycle code. It can be worked around with a custom lifecycle, but this is not recommended due to the large amount of code that would be required. Secondly, you may notice that `newButton()` is a local function and not part of the `widget` package. One of the widgets currently missing from the toolkit list is a standard button, therefore, we must define one ourselves. This can be done by adding the code described as follows:

First, we define the custom node; it must begin by inheriting from `node.LeafEmbed`. We add fields for the text label it'll contain and the `onClick` function that should be called when it is tapped. We should also add a convenience method to construct the button. This needs to set the `node.Embed.Wrapper` field, as that should never be `nil`:

```
type button struct {
   node.LeafEmbed

   label    string
   onClick  func()
}

func NewButton(label string, onClick func()) *button {
   b := &button{label: label, onClick: onClick}
   b.Wrapper = b
```

```
        return b
}
```

To define a suitable area for the button to take up, we need to implement the `Measure()` function. This will update a cached size (`node.Embed.MeasuredSize`) that's used for the interface layout:

```
const buttonPad = 4

func (b *button) Measure(t *theme.Theme, widthHint, heightHint int) {
    face := t.AcquireFontFace(theme.FontFaceOptions{})
    defer t.ReleaseFontFace(theme.FontFaceOptions{}, face)

    b.MeasuredSize.X = font.MeasureString(face, b.label).Ceil() + 2*buttonPad
    b.MeasuredSize.Y = face.Metrics().Ascent.Ceil() + face.Metrics().Descent.Ceil() + 2*buttonPad
}
```

To display content onscreen (this actually paints to an underlying `widget.Sheet` described earlier), we add a `PaintBase()` function. For our button, we will paint a `theme.Foreground` colored rectangle as a base and use the `theme.Background` color for the text (so our button stands out from other text). Note that, before actually painting, we remove the `node.MarkNeedsPaintBase` mark from the object so that it will not be redrawn on the next interface redraw:

```
func (b *button) PaintBase(ctx *node.PaintBaseContext, origin image.Point) error {
    b.Marks.UnmarkNeedsPaintBase()
    face := ctx.Theme.AcquireFontFace(theme.FontFaceOptions{})
    defer ctx.Theme.ReleaseFontFace(theme.FontFaceOptions{}, face)

    draw.Draw(ctx.Dst, b.Rect.Add(origin).Inset(buttonPad), theme.Foreground.Uniform(ctx.Theme), image.Point{}, draw.Src)
    d := font.Drawer{
        Dst:  ctx.Dst,
        Src:  theme.Background.Uniform(ctx.Theme),
        Face: face,
        Dot:  fixed.Point26_6{X: fixed.I(b.Rect.Min.X + buttonPad), Y: fixed.I(b.Rect.Min.Y + face.Metrics().Ascent.Ceil() + buttonPad)},
    }
    d.DrawString(b.label)

    return nil
}
```

Shiny - Experimental Go GUI API

Lastly, a button needs a click handler. We can implement the `OnInputEvent()` function so that Shiny can send events to the button. Here, we check to see whether the event's a `gesture.Event`, and if so, see that its type is `gesture.TypeTap`. If these conditions are met, and we have an `onClick` handler registered, then call `b.onClick()`:

```
func (b *button) OnInputEvent(e interface{}, origin image.Point) node.EventHandled {
    if ev, ok := e.(gesture.Event); ok {
        if ev.Type == gesture.TypeTap && b.onClick != nil {
            b.onClick()
        }

        return node.Handled
    }

    return node.NotHandled
}
```

That concludes the code required to fulfill a hello world GUI app with Shiny (the complete code is in this book's code repository). Let's now build and run the application.

Build and Run

Building our Shiny hello world app is simple as Shiny has no native dependencies—we can simply build or run the `hello.go` file directly. Additionally, as many platform drivers are written without CGo, we can easily cross-compile for those operating systems. The following screenshot illustrates building for Linux and then Windows with no additional setup:

Building our hello app and running it with no CGo is easy

Note that building for macOS would require some additional setup, as its driver uses CGo (as described in the preceding *Cross-compiling* section of *Getting started*).

However you build or run the application, you should see a little window, something like the following:

Hello world with Shiny

We could refine the visuals of our app, but instead, we will move on to a larger application to demonstrate the capabilities of Shiny.

Building a user interface

To explore the capabilities of the Shiny toolkit, we will build another complete graphical application. As the development of Shiny has been focused on the lower layer of graphical APIs, an application such as GoMail would involve the creation of many custom widgets. Instead, we will look at a more graphically-oriented application—an image viewer.

Design

To get an idea of how the image viewer should look, we will make a rough design that we can follow. The online tool Balsamiq (`balsamiq.com`) is a good way to rapidly create wireframes that will suit this purpose. Take a look at the following export. It includes a navigation bar along the top, a directory listing on the left, and a full-size image view on the right:

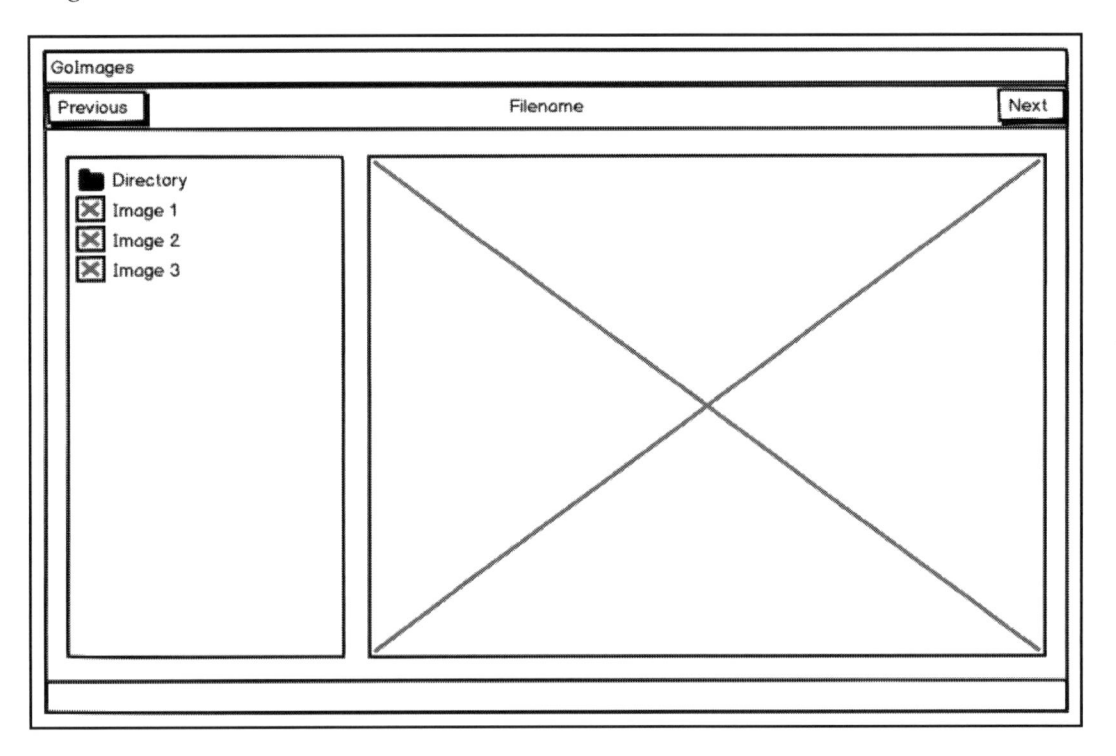

A mockup of the GoImages application using the Balsamiq tool

Clearly, this image has a far lower level of detail than the design tool we used in `Chapter 4`, *Walk – Building Graphical Windows Applications* (back at the beginning of `Section 2`, *Toolkits Using Existing Widgets*) for our GoMail design, but this is intentional. Each toolkit in `Section 3`, *Modern Graphical Toolkits* of this book has a very different look, set by its theme definition and by using a rough design we can build an implementation using the best practice for each of them.

Layout

To get started, we will implement the layout. The easiest way to set this up for the application we designed is to use horizontal and vertical flow layouts. Before creating the layout, we should define those widgets that will be included. For now these are represented by the placeholders created in `makeBar()` and `makeList()`—each of which simply creates a label to show the purpose. We also want to ensure that the items are padded according to our design. To do this with Shiny, we use `widget.NewPadder()` and a defined unit, `padSize`. We also define a `spaceSize` used later for the central padding:

```
package main

import (
    "golang.org/x/exp/shiny/driver"
    "golang.org/x/exp/shiny/screen"
    "golang.org/x/exp/shiny/unit"
    "golang.org/x/exp/shiny/widget"
    "golang.org/x/exp/shiny/widget/node"
    "golang.org/x/exp/shiny/widget/theme"

    "image"
    "log"
    "os"

    _ "image/jpeg"
)

var padSize = unit.DIPs(20)
var spaceSize = unit.DIPs(10)

func makeBar() node.Node {
    bar := widget.NewUniform(theme.Neutral,
        widget.NewPadder(widget.AxisBoth, padSize,
            widget.NewLabel("Navigation")))

    return widget.WithLayoutData(bar,
        widget.FlowLayoutData{ExpandAlong: true, ExpandAcross: true})
}

func makeList() node.Node {
    return widget.NewUniform(theme.Background, widget.NewLabel("File list"))
}
```

[205]

Shiny - Experimental Go GUI API

To show the image in our layout, we can use `widget.Image`, but first we need to load an image from the filesystem—a helper function, `loadImage()`, is defined to handle this for the application. When loading an image, don't forget to import the appropriate decoder (in this case, `image/jpeg`):

```go
func loadImage(name string) image.Image {
    reader, err := os.Open(name)
    if err != nil {
        log.Fatal(err)
    }
    defer reader.Close()

    image, _, err := image.Decode(reader)
    if err != nil {
        log.Fatal(err)
    }

    return image
}
```

With that in place, we're ready to implement the layout. The main method constructs the widget tree and creates `widget.Sheet` to manage their rendering. This is passed to `widget.RunWindow()` to show the contents and run the application. The main layout elements are `body` (a horizontal flow) and `container` (the vertical flow, containing the navigation and the body). Note how a `nil` child is passed to `widget.NewPadder()` between the file list and the image viewer to approximate widget spacing. You can also see that the child widget of `sheet` is actually a `theme.Background` colored rectangle created using `widget.NewUniform()` – this helps to ensure that we have a consistent background color if any widgets leave part of their area unpainted. The container then fills the space by being the uniform's child widget:

```go
func main() {
    driver.Main(func(s screen.Screen) {
        image := loadImage("shiny-hall.jpg")

        body := widget.NewFlow(widget.AxisHorizontal, makeList(),
            widget.NewPadder(widget.AxisHorizontal, spaceSize, nil),
            widget.NewImage(image, image.Bounds()))
        container := widget.NewFlow(widget.AxisVertical, makeBar(),
                    widget.NewPadder(widget.AxisBoth, padSize, body))
        sheet := widget.NewSheet(widget.NewUniform(theme.Background,
    container))

        container.Measure(theme.Default, 0, 0)
        if err := widget.RunWindow(s, sheet, &widget.RunWindowOptions{
            NewWindowOptions: screen.NewWindowOptions{
```

```
                Title:  "GoImages",
                Width:  container.MeasuredSize.X,
                Height: container.MeasuredSize.Y,
            },
        }); err != nil {
            log.Fatal(err)
        }
    })
}
```

Running the preceding code should result in a window showing the following contents, which broadly matches the layout we designed before. As we progress through this chapter, we will add the content to each area and polish each part of the interface:

The GoImages layout with the navigation bar and file list placeholders

[207]

Navigation

To create the navigation bar in our design, a horizontal flow layout is the right tool for the job. We can use `widget.Spacer` to create the gaps between the buttons and the label and to ensure the filename is centered within the space available. A helper method, `expandSpace()`, is added to create a new spacer that will expand along the flow layout axis. We also define the `previousImage()` and `nextImage()` functions, which will execute when the buttons are pressed:

```
func previousImage() {}

func nextImage() {}

func expandSpace() node.Node {
   return widget.WithLayoutData(widget.NewSpace(),
      widget.FlowLayoutData{ExpandAlong: true, ExpandAcross: true,
AlongWeight:1})
}
```

With those functions defined, we can lay out the navigation bar. We define the `prev`, `next`, and `name` items and add them to a `widget.AxisHoriontal` flow container that includes `expandSpace()` elements to space the items. To create buttons, we are using the same `newButton()` function as earlier in this chapter (due to the Shiny widget API not having a standard button defined). We use `theme.Neutral` for the background container for this section and we set the whole bar to expand along the horizontal axis:

```
func makeBar() node.Node {
   prev := newButton("Previous", previousImage)
   next := newButton("Next", nextImage)
   name := widget.NewLabel("Filename")

   flow := widget.NewFlow(widget.AxisHorizontal, prev, expandSpace(),
      widget.NewPadder(widget.AxisBoth, padSize, name), expandSpace(),
next)

   bar := widget.NewUniform(theme.Neutral, flow)

   return widget.WithLayoutData(bar,
      widget.FlowLayoutData{ExpandAlong: true, ExpandAcross: true})
}
```

Chapter 8

The preceding code should update the navigation bar, as follows. As we've defined the buttons ourselves, they can be customized to use the border style if preferred (the full code listing is available in this book's code repository):

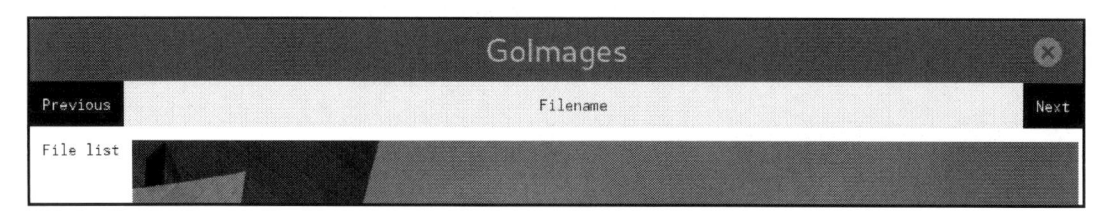

The updated navigation bar with left- and right- aligned buttons

File list

As Shiny does not define a list widget, we will construct one using another vertical flow container. Each item within this list will be a custom cell widget that displays an icon on the left with the filename text left-aligned in the remaining space. First, we will update our `makeList()` function to add some dummy data. Each item is a new cell, created using `makeCell()` (which is defined later). The items are laid out as a list using `widget.NewFlow()` on the vertical axis:

```
func makeList(dir string) node.Node {
    parent := makeCell(dir, nil)
    cell1 := makeCell("Filename 1", loadImage("shiny-hall.jpg"))
    cell2 := makeCell("Filename 2", loadImage("shiny-hall.jpg"))
    cell3 := makeCell("Filename 3", loadImage("shiny-hall.jpg"))
    return widget.NewFlow(widget.AxisVertical, parent, cell1, cell2, cell3)
}
```

As you can see, the first item in the list is the name of our directory, which needs a different icon. We can load a standard icon from the Shiny icon collection using the `iconvg` package, specifically, `iconvg.Rasterizer` and `iconvg.Decode()`. Using the following helper function, we can load the `icons.FileFolder` icon into an image so it can be drawn using the same functions as images we load from the filesystem:

```
func loadDirIcon() image.Image {
    var raster iconvg.Rasterizer
    bounds := image.Rect(0, 0, iconSize, iconSize)
    icon := image.NewRGBA(bounds)
    raster.SetDstImage(icon, bounds, draw.Over)

    iconvg.Decode(&raster, icons.FileFolder, nil)
```

[209]

Shiny - Experimental Go GUI API

```
        return icon
}
```

The last part of our layout code is the `makeCell()` function. In this case, it's a simple wrapper around the creation of a `cell` widget. When this function is passed a `nil` icon, it will set up the directory icon using the helper above. When an icon is passed, then it creates an `onClick` function that will load the image in the main view:

```
func makeCell(name string, icon image.Image) node.Node {
    var onClick func()
    if icon == nil {
        icon = loadDirIcon()
    } else {
        onClick = func() {chooseImage(icon)}
    }

    return newCell(icon, name, onClick)
}
```

The details of our cell widget are very similar to the button we created earlier and so most of the code is omitted. The next excerpt shows its `PaintBase()` function, which draws the icon and text to screen. It calculates the ratio of an image so that it can be correctly painted within the cell. The text is then drawn like the button code, but with a space between it and the image we painted.

To make this work, a simple `scaleImage()` function is also needed, which uses `draw.ApproxBiLinear` to resize the graphic to fit with reasonable performance:

```
func (c *cell) PaintBase(ctx *node.PaintBaseContext, origin image.Point) error {
    c.Marks.UnmarkNeedsPaintBase()
    face := ctx.Theme.AcquireFontFace(theme.FontFaceOptions{})
    defer ctx.Theme.ReleaseFontFace(theme.FontFaceOptions{}, face)

    ratio := float32(c.icon.Bounds().Max.Y)/float32(c.icon.Bounds().Max.X)
    if c.icon.Bounds().Max.Y > c.icon.Bounds().Max.X {
        ratio = float32(c.icon.Bounds().Max.X)/float32(c.icon.Bounds().Max.Y)
    }
    scaled := scaleImage(c.icon, iconSize, int(float32(iconSize)*ratio))

    draw.Draw(ctx.Dst, c.Rect.Add(origin), scaled, image.Point{}, draw.Over)
    d := font.Drawer{
        Dst:  ctx.Dst,
        Src:  theme.Foreground.Uniform(ctx.Theme),
        Face: face,
        Dot:  fixed.Point26_6{X: fixed.I(c.Rect.Min.X + origin.X + iconSize + space),
```

```
            Y: fixed.I(c.Rect.Min.Y + origin.Y +
face.Metrics().Ascent.Ceil())},
    }
    d.DrawString(c.label)

    return nil
}

func scaleImage(src image.Image, width, height int) image.Image {
    ret := image.NewRGBA(image.Rect(0, 0, width, height))

    draw.ApproxBiLinear.Scale(ret, ret.Bounds(), src, src.Bounds(),
draw.Src, nil)

    return ret
}
```

All this code comes together to create a file listing with an image preview, as shown in the following screenshot:

The completed file list on the left with placeholder content

Image view

The `widget.Image` type draws an image to the buffer at the same resolution as it was loaded (a pixel in the source image matches a pixel on screen). What we need to do for the image viewer is scale it to fit the available space. To do this, we create a new custom widget named `scaledImage`. The code is very similar to the Shiny image widget but with a more complicated `PaintBase()` function.

This function calculates `imgWidth` and `imgHeight` to fit within the current bounds of the widget and maintain the aspect ratio of the source image. It then scales the image using the `scaleImage()` helper function defined earlier, ready to paint at the correct resolution. Lastly, `offset` is calculated so that the image is centered within the available space:

```
func (w *scaledImage) PaintBase(ctx *node.PaintBaseContext, origin image.Point) error {
    w.Marks.UnmarkNeedsPaintBase()
    if w.Src == nil {
        return nil
    }

    wRect := w.Rect.Add(origin)
    ratio := float32(w.Src.Bounds().Max.X)/float32(w.Src.Bounds().Max.Y)
    width := wRect.Max.X - wRect.Min.X
    height := wRect.Max.Y - wRect.Min.Y

    imgWidth := int(math.Min(float64(width), float64(w.Src.Bounds().Max.X)))
    imgHeight := int(float32(imgWidth)/ratio)

    if imgHeight > height {
        imgHeight = int(math.Min(float64(height), float64(w.Src.Bounds().Max.Y)))
        imgWidth = int(float32(imgHeight)*ratio)
    }

    scaled := scaleImage(w.Src, imgWidth, imgHeight)
    offset := image.Point{(imgWidth-width)/2, (imgHeight-height)/2}

    draw.Draw(ctx.Dst, wRect, scaled, offset, draw.Over)
    return nil
}
```

Chapter 8

To avoid a blank space being left by the preceding calculations, let's add a checkered pattern typical in many other image applications. To make this possible, we create a custom image type named `checkerImage` that simply returns pixels from the `At()` function based on a regular checker pattern. As images are bounded, we need to add a `resize()` function so the image can expand to fill the space:

```
var checkers = &checkerImage{}

type checkerImage struct {
    bounds image.Rectangle
}

func (c *checkerImage) resize(width, height int) {
    c.bounds = image.Rectangle{image.Pt(0, 0), image.Pt(width, height)}
}

func (c *checkerImage) ColorModel() color.Model {
    return color.RGBAModel
}

func (c *checkerImage) Bounds() image.Rectangle {
    return c.bounds
}

func (c *checkerImage) At(x, y int) color.Color {
    xr := x/10
    yr := y/10

    if xr%2 == yr%2 {
        return color.RGBA{0xc0, 0xc0, 0xc0, 0xff}
    } else {
        return color.RGBA{0x99, 0x99, 0x99, 0xff}
    }
}
```

To include the checker pattern, we simply need to update the end of the `PaintBase()` function of `scaledImage`. Before the image itself is drawn, we set the checker pattern to expand to the correct size and paint it onto the background. The checkers are drawn with the `draw.Src` mode and the image is then drawn over the top using the `draw.Over` mode:

```
func (w *scaledImage) PaintBase(ctx *node.PaintBaseContext, origin image.Point) error {

    ...

    checkers.resize(width, height)
    draw.Draw(ctx.Dst, wRect, checkers, checkers.Bounds().Min, draw.Src)
```

```
        draw.Draw(ctx.Dst, wRect, scaled, offset, draw.Over)
        return nil
}
```

With all of this code in place, we have an updated application that correctly fills the layout we designed and scales and positions the placeholder image we have to fit within the available space:

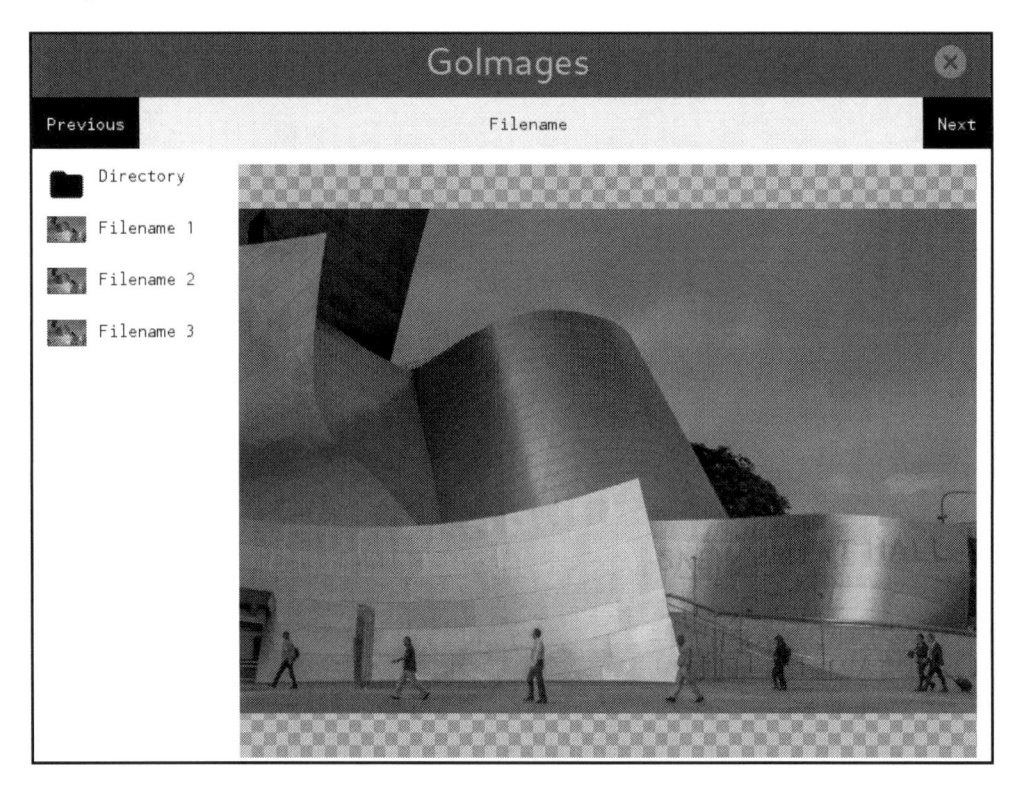

The interface updated to show images centered at the correct aspect ratio

That's the majority of our graphical code complete. Next, we will make the necessary additions to load real content from the local filesystem.

Communicating with the GUI

Now that we have a user interface up and running, we need to load some real data and display it. We start this task by obtaining a list of image files for the requested directory and updating the user interface to list those instead of the placeholder information. Remember, at this stage, to add the extra image imports so we can decode all of the images that we will then filter for in a new getImageList() function:

```go
import (
    _ "image/jpeg"
    _ "image/png"
    _ "image/gif"
)

var names []string

func getImageList(dir string) []string {
    files, _ := ioutil.ReadDir(dir)

    for _, file := range files {
        if file.IsDir() {
            continue
        }

        ext := strings.ToLower(filepath.Ext(file.Name()))
        if ext == ".jpg" || ext == ".jpeg" || ext == ".png" || ext == ".gif" {
            names = append(names, file.Name())
        }
    }

    return names
}
```

The listing shows a fairly simple algorithm for checking each item in a directory and adding it to a names list if the filename looks like a image file that we support. Simple filename extension checking should be sufficient for our purposes here. We add these filenames to a global list for later use in the user interface.

Once we have a list of supported files, we can update the existing `makeList()` function. The new version iterates over the `files` list and adds a new cell for each item. The `makeCell()` function does not need any additional work to use this new content, but we do pass the array index for use later in the button handlers. We also save the `images` loaded in memory for display when selected:

```
var images []image.Image

func makeList(dir string, files []string) node.Node {
    parent := makeCell(-1, filepath.Base(dir), nil)
    children := []node.Node{parent}

    for idx, name := range files {
        img := loadImage(path.Join(dir, name))
        cell := makeCell(idx, name, img)
        children = append(children, cell)
        images = append(images, img)
    }

    return widget.NewFlow(widget.AxisVertical, children...)
}
```

To update the main image displayed, we need to add a new function to our `scaledImage` widget. This new `SetImage()` function sets the image reference to be displayed and marks the widget for painting. Updating the `node.MarkNeedsPaintBase` mark means that the widget will be repainted next time there is a graphical paint event (we will discuss paint events in more detail shortly):

```
func (w *scaledImage) SetImage(img image.Image) {
    w.Src = img
    w.Mark(node.MarkNeedsPaintBase)
}
```

To make use of this new function, we update our `chooseImage()` code to set the image selected. We also need to store a reference to the `scaledImage` widget created to call the function on:

```
var view *scaledImage

func chooseImage(idx int) {
    view.SetImage(images[idx])
}
```

Chapter 8

When the image is changed, we also need to set the correct filename to the label above the image. To do so, we will add a reference to the `widget.Label` object and set its `Text` field. After updating this property, we also need to set the `node.MarkNeedsMeasureLayout` flag, as the text may have a different size to the previous content. We use the `names` array and the index variable passed into `chooseImage()` to look up the content. This could also be accomplished by creating a list of items using a new object type that stores the image, name, and metadata in a single list, but the approach of multiple indexed lists is easier to explain in smaller code samples:

```
var name *widget.Label
var index = 0

func chooseImage(idx int) {
    index = idx
    view.SetImage(images[idx])

    name.Text = names[idx]
    name.Mark(node.MarkNeedsMeasureLayout)
    name.Mark(node.MarkNeedsPaintBase)
}
```

We also need to fill in the empty `previousImage()` and `nextImage()` functions that the header buttons call. A simple helper function called `changeImage()` is added to handle image switching based on an offset from the current image (either 1 or –1). Each button callback calls this with the appropriate offset:

```
func changeImage(offset int) {
    newidx := index + offset
    if newidx < 0 || newidx >= len(images) {
        return
    }

    chooseImage(newidx)
}

func previousImage() {
    changeImage(-1)
}

func nextImage() {
    changeImage(1)
}
```

Shiny - Experimental Go GUI API

With this in place, the `main()` function can include a call to `chooseImage(0)` to load the first image found in the directory. Of course, you should check that there is at least one image before you do this.

The last change is to determine which directory to show images for when the application loads. The previous `main()` function is renamed `loadUI()` (which takes a directory parameter to pass into `getImageList()` and `makeList()`). A new main function is created that parses command-line arguments to allow the user to specify a directory. The following code will print out a helpful usage hint if some unexpected parameters are passed (or if `--help` is specified) and if no parameters are found, it will show the current working directory (using `os.Getwd()`):

```
func main() {
    dir, _ := os.Getwd()

    flag.Usage = func() {
        fmt.Println("goimages takes a single, optional, directory parameter")
    }
    flag.Parse()

    if len(flag.Args()) > 1 {
        flag.Usage()
        os.Exit(2)
    } else if len(flag.Args()) == 1 {
        dir = flag.Args()[0]

        if _, err := ioutil.ReadDir(dir); os.IsNotExist(err) {
            fmt.Println("Directory", dir, "does not exist or could not be read")
            os.Exit(1)
        }
    }
    loadUI(dir)
}
```

With these modifications, we've created a complete image viewer application that displays thumbnails for a whole directory of images and one large image view. By tapping on items in the list, or using the **Next** and **Previous** buttons, you can switch between the images available. While this works, it can be quite slow to load in a large directory. Next, we'll explore how this can be improved:

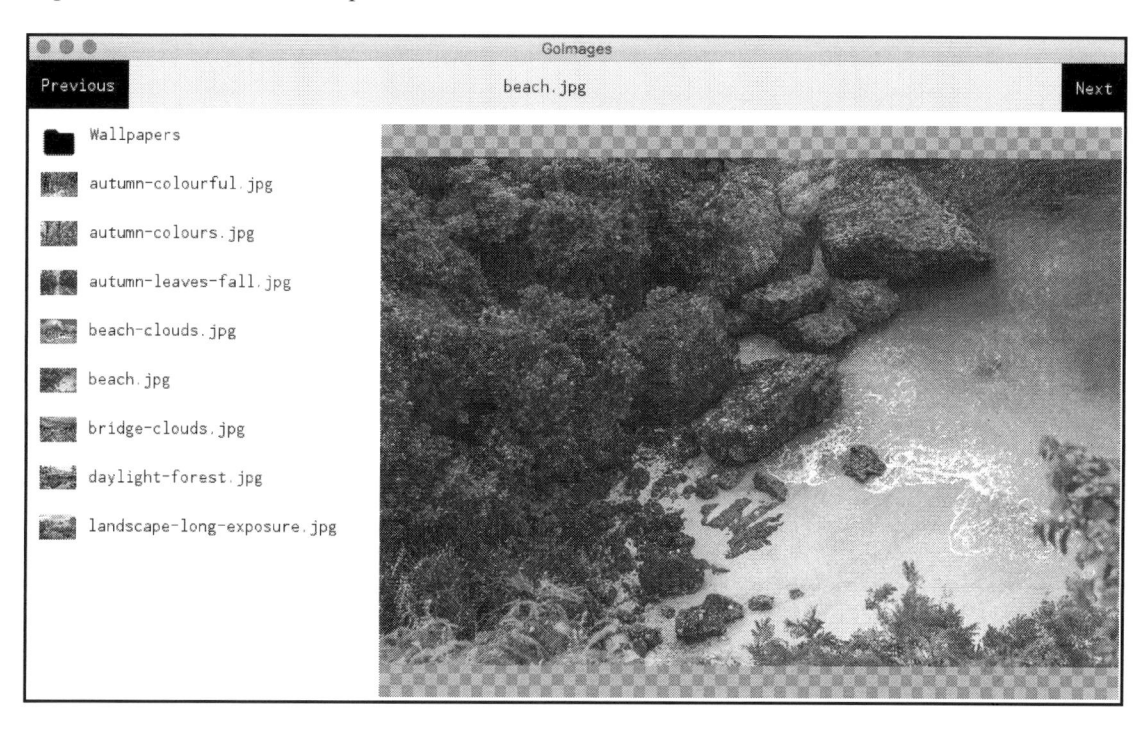

The completed GoImages application running on macOS

Background processing

Image processing, even just loading the images to be viewed, is a CPU-intensive task, so if we open a directory with a lot of pictures, the application will be very slow to load. We can fix this delay by moving our image loading to work in the background while we load the user interface. Thankfully, creating new threads for asynchronous processing is very simple with Go (as we explored in Chapter 3, *Go to the Rescue!*), but we also need to ensure that the user interface is updated accordingly.

Shiny - Experimental Go GUI API

To delay the loading of images until there is processing power available, we can replace uses of `loadImage()` with a replacement `asyncImage` type that will handle the heavy lifting. The main image loading code will be moved into a private `load()` function that's called from `newAsyncImage()` using `go img.load()`, therefore starting it in the background:

```
type asyncImage struct {
    path     string
    img      image.Image
    callback func(image.Image)
}

func (a *asyncImage) load() {
    reader, err := os.Open(a.path)
    if err != nil {
        log.Fatal(err)
    }
    defer reader.Close()

    a.img, _, err = image.Decode(reader)
    if err != nil {
        log.Fatal(err)
    }

    a.callback(a.img)
}

func newAsyncImage(path string, loaded func(image.Image)) *asyncImage {
    img := &asyncImage{path: path, callback:loaded}
    go img.load()

    return img
}
```

With the definition of an asynchronous image loader, we can replace the use of `image.Image` with `asyncImage`. The important thing to remember is that the image in the `img` field will be `nil` until the `load()` function has completed. Be sure that any code using images checks for `nil` data before processing. The first function we update is `makeCell()` so that it no longer accepts an image parameter. Instead, we pass a `loaded` callback function to set the image once it is loaded. We update `makeList()` to replace the cell creation code with the following:

```
cell := makeCell(idx, name)
i := idx
img := newAsyncImage(path.Join(dir, name), func(img image.Image) {
    cell.icon.SetImage(img)
```

```
        if i == index {
            view.SetImage(img)
        }
    })
```

This code will ensure that thumbnails are shown once the image has loaded but also that, if the image is the current selection, it updates the main image `view` as well.

If you run the application at this point, you will notice that some images are loaded while others may not be. This is due to us not having signaled to Shiny that a re-paint is necessary. The marks that were applied to the widgets to force them to be repainted do not actually trigger the painting of the interface; it simply marks them as needing to be painted the next time a re-paint is triggered:

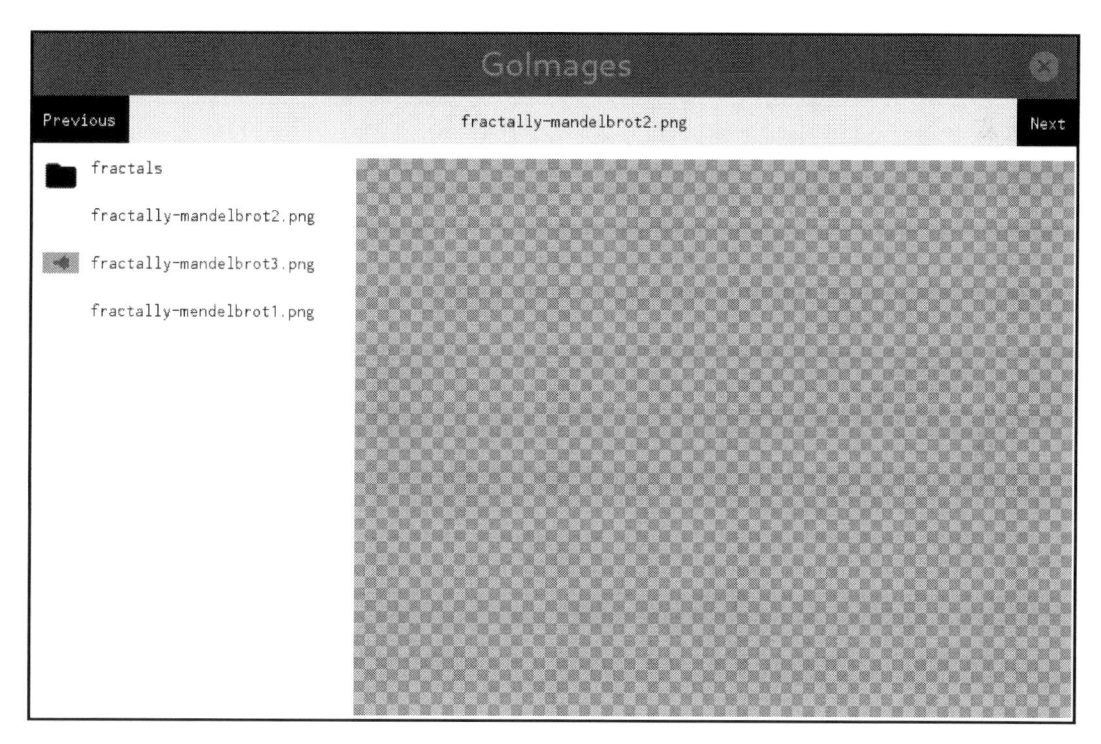

A partial rendering when loading images in the background

Shiny - Experimental Go GUI API

There is no easy way to signal Shiny to refresh the user interface, so we will make a `refresh()` function for convenience. This should be called when the text for a filename is updated and when a different (or lazy-loaded) image is set on the `scaledImage` widget:

```
func chooseImage(idx int, img image.Image) {
    ...

    name.Mark(node.MarkNeedsPaintBase)
    refresh(name)
}

func (w *scaledImage) SetImage(img image.Image) {
    w.Src = img
    w.Mark(node.MarkNeedsPaintBase)

    refresh(w)
}

func refresh(_ node.Node) {
    // Ideally we should refresh but this requires a reference to the window
    // win.Send(paint.Event{})
}
```

Unfortunately, at this point, we can't proceed further without a significant amount of extra code. This is a limitation of the recommended `widget.RunWindow()` function that we used to load our interface. The window reference that we would need to send the paint event to is not available outside the Shiny package. To resolve this issue, it would be necessary to use the `NewWindow()` function on the `screen.Screen` instance, passed into the `driver.Main()` function—but to do so would mean completely re-implementing the event loop as well, which is a lot of work.

The reason we didn't notice the issue when setting the main image earlier is because, when the application is receiving user events (mouse moves and so on), its event loop runs. Each time an iteration of the loop completes, the user interface is repainted. Sending the `paint.Event` previously illustrated would also cause this to happen. Therefore, it follows that the interface will update after background image loading if the user is currently interacting with the GUI (even just moving the mouse over it). It's left as an exercise for the reader to implement the replacement lifecycle to resolve this issue, if desired.

Summary

In this chapter, we looked at our first modern widget toolkit, Shiny, which has been designed specifically for the Go language. We explored its design principles and how it manages to support cross-platform graphical application development without the need for external dependencies. We also saw that its design makes use of powerful features of the Go language, such as concurrency and the standard library.

The graphical design principles behind Shiny provide a new interpretation of the desktop application GUI, which will be familiar to users of the Android mobile operating system (due to them using the same material design approach). While exploring its graphical capabilities, we saw that the widget set is currently in its early stages and so isn't yet ready to support the GoMail application we've been creating in previous chapters. To explore the capabilities of the Shiny toolkit, we instead developed an image viewer application, which is better suited to the current feature set. We saw how powerful the rendering capabilities of Shiny are, but also that there are a few challenges around creating a rich application user interface.

In the next chapter, we will look at another toolkit that takes a modern approach to the widget toolkit. Nuklear also helps developers to create cross-platform graphical user interfaces but does so from an embedded user interface approach. We'll explore the Go bindings for this library, named `nk`.

9
nk - Nuklear for Go

Nuklear is a lightweight widget library that focuses purely on the graphical interface. It provides a rich widget toolkit that renders identically across all supported platforms. Originally designed for embedded systems, it avoids the complications of application life cycles and windows and managing user interaction to keep its API focused and completely platform-independent. Its implementation has no dependencies and achieves this by avoiding a platform-specific render library or operating system drivers.

This chapter will cover the following topics:

- The design and purpose of the Nuklear project
- Getting set up with Nuklear and the Go bindings, nk
- How to create a render context and use the toolkit widgets
- Building a complete application using nk

By the end of this chapter, you'll have created an nk-based application using an OpenGL backend that will work across all mainstream desktop operating systems.

Background and design of Nuklear

Nuklear was designed to build graphical user interfaces for embedded applications and games. It aims to be lightweight and completely platform agnostic. It manages this by leaving the window management, operating system-specific methods, and even the render driver to separate modules or the applications that use the library. Many of these features are provided by add-on modules; due to Nuklear's popularity, there are many render drivers to choose from (some are operating system-specific and others work across multiple platforms). Nuklear has been made available within the public domain, which also makes it an attractive option for embedding within commercial software.

nk - Nuklear for Go

Nuklear provides many widgets, layouts, and features for creating rich application GUIs that can also be skinned to suit the application design. The following screenshot is an example of the standard interface design: more can be found in the gallery section of the project website at `https://github.com/vurtun/nuklear#gallery`:

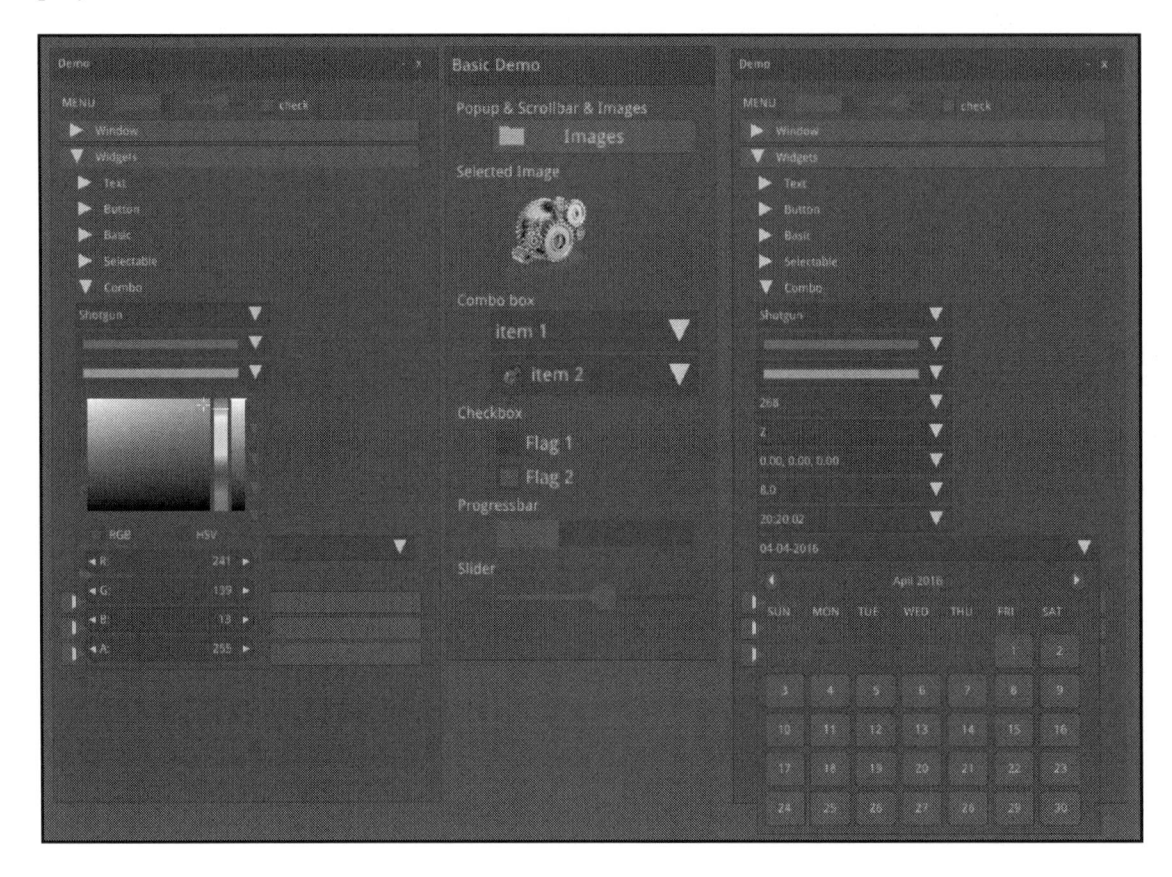

A screenshot of Nuklear widgets from the project website (Copyright: Micha Mettke)

Alongside the differences that the Nuklear design has to other toolkits we've explored, there's a larger distinction—Nuklear is an *immediate mode* GUI toolkit. In comparison, the other toolkits we've worked with in this book have all been *retained mode* user interfaces. With a retained mode API, the developer describes the application GUI by creating objects such as buttons and input boxes, arranging them in layouts, and then the toolkit will draw these features to screen. When an event occurs, the toolkit will change the state of an item and the resulting graphical changes will be reflected onscreen, optionally sending the changes to the application code.

When using an immediate mode library, there's no state retained. The application developer doesn't create buttons and widgets for later use; instead, these widgets are defined during the render process purely for the next graphical update. At a glance, this may seem inefficient but it's actually a very good match for how graphical render pipelines function and so can be far more efficient. It's also a less memory-intensive process as there's no additional structure in memory representing the whole application GUI. The main impact of this decision, as we'll see later, is how the code that creates a GUI is laid out and how events are handled. Rather than try and describe this further, you can see it in action later in this chapter (in the *Code* section of *Getting started with nk*).

Rendering and platform support

The core of the Nuklear library's flexibility is its modular design. The library doesn't render to screen nor does it manage user input; such functionality is provided by modules that accompany the library. An application will typically utilize the core Nuklear library for widgets and layout as well as one of its render modules to control the opening of windows, rendering, and handling user input.

Rendering modules

The Nuklear project includes many rendering modules that provide support for various different environments or operating systems. At the time of writing, you can choose from the following backends:

- Windows:
    - **Graphics Device Interface (GDI)**
    - GDI+
    - **Direct3D (D3D)**
- Linux or Unix:
    - X11
    - X11 OpenGL
- Games development:
    - Allegro
- Cross-platform development:
    - **Simple DirectMedia Layer (SDL)**
    - **Simple and Fast Multimedia Library (SFML)**
    - **Graphics Library Framework (GLFW)**

Some of the renderers are 3D accelerated and others aren't, some focus on embedded and low power devices, others for desktop or smart phone type devices. As the GLFW module supports most desktop operating systems (and some smart phones), we'll use this module for the following chapter. If you choose to use a different module, then the application life cycle code should be adapted, but the nk code we'll explore remains the same.

Supported platforms

With such a wide range of renderers available for the toolkit, Nuklear offers exceptional coverage for various different operating systems. With support available for Windows, Linux, macOS, BSD, iPhone, and Android, it offers better support for multiple platforms than other libraries we've explored. By selecting the cross-platform GLFW Nuklear module, we've reduced the possible number of platforms slightly but it'll still support Windows, macOS, and Linux desktop applications as well as Android for mobile applications.

The GLFW library has Go bindings that work alongside the OpenGL Go bindings (both are by the same authors). For most platforms, they don't rely on any external packages or libraries being installed. This is a huge benefit to getting up and running fast with nk, as we don't need to install additional packages or configure our development environment. So, let's get started.

Getting started with nk

To use GLFW and Go-GL, we'll need to link to some C APIs; however, these aren't (on most systems) external libraries. The fact that the only native dependency is the OpenGL native library (which is typically part of the operating system), and any intermediate libraries are embedded within the Go projects, means that all we need to prepare is CGo.

Prerequisites

As the renderer we'll use for nk requires access to native C APIs, we'll need CGo to be correctly functioning for our applications to build. On most platforms, this simply means installing a compatible C compiler. This is only a development dependency and there's no installation required for the users of applications that we build with nk (other than an OpenGL compatible system). If you've worked through previous chapters of this book, then you probably have this set up already. If not, or you're unsure, then follow the steps in the `Appendix`, *Installation Details*, in the *Setting up CGo* section.

Some platforms will require additional development files to be installed for the operating system-specific portions of the code to compile correctly. macOS and Windows developers can skip this section as the development environment for CGo provides all that's required. Linux or Android developers may require additional steps, as follows.

Linux

To use nk on Linux, we need to ensure some additional development headers are installed. Due to the GLFW dependency on Xorg for window management and input handling, we'll need to be able to compile against its libraries. If your distribution packages development headers separately to the library, you'll need to ensure that they're installed for compilation to succeed. The required package is called `xorg-dev` on Debian or Ubuntu, `xorg-server-devel` for Arch Linux, and `xorg-x11-server-devel` on Fedora or CentOS.

Therefore, one of the following should correctly install the development dependencies:

- For Debian or Ubuntu, use this:
  `sudo apt-get install xorg-dev`
- For Arch Linux (this will probably already be installed), use the following:
  `sudo pacman -S xorg-server-devel`
- For Fedora or CentOS, use this:
  `sudo yum install xorg-x11-server-devel`

If the `sudo` command can't be found, then try `su -c` instead. Once this library is installed, you should be able to follow the setup steps in the next section and run an nk example application.

macOS and Windows

Once you have Go and CGo set up on your computer, there are no additional prerequisites so you can jump to the following *Setup* section.

Android

To build an Android app using nk, there are some additional steps required. Development of mobile apps is out of scope for this book but, for the curious, these steps are included to get you started. First, you must have the Android **Software Development Kit** (**SDK**) and **Native Development Kit** (**NDK**) installed. The easiest way may be to install Android Studio (available from https://developer.android.com/studio/) and use the built-in SDK Manager (under **SDK Tools**) to install the NDK packages as well:

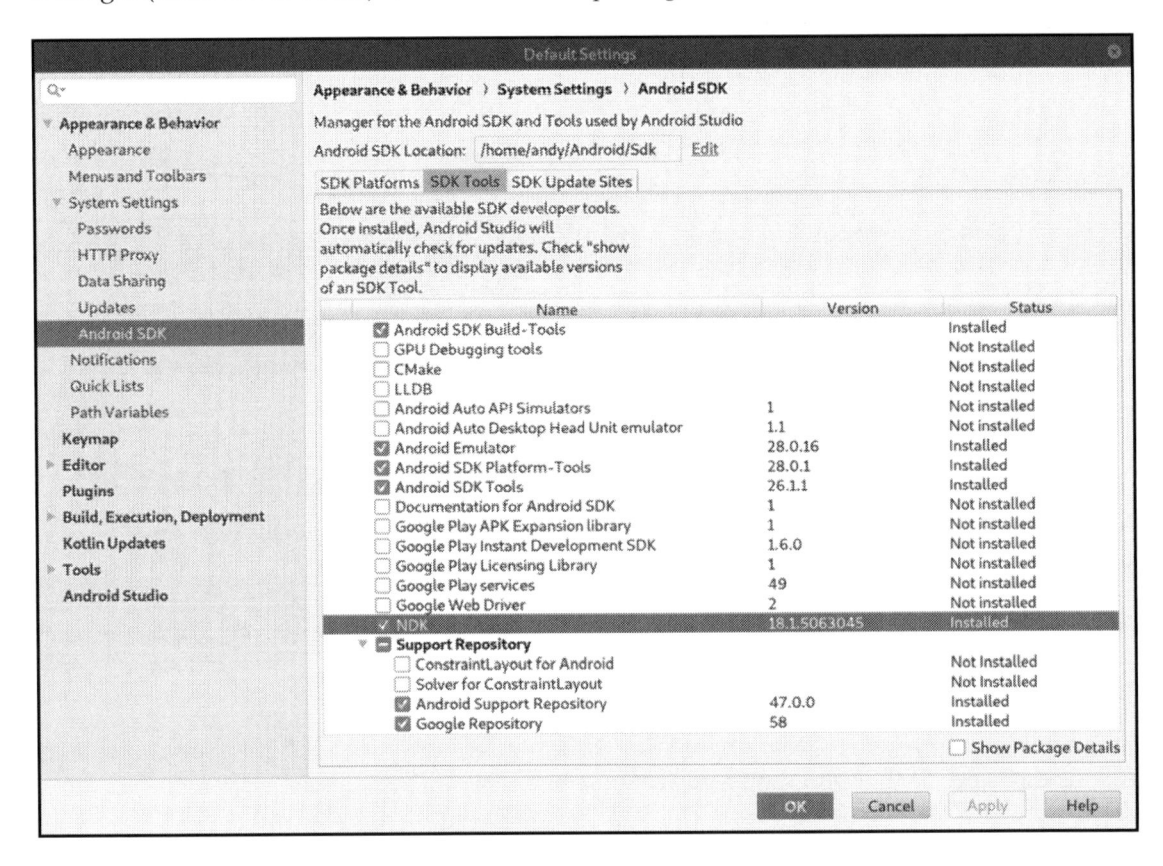

Ensure that the NDK package is installed and up to date for Android nk development

The following steps will be needed to complete the `nk-android` build, which should result in a complete development environment. Building the toolchain requires `ANDROID_HOME` and `NDK` environment variables to be set and your `PATH` to be updated correctly. You may not need to set up all of these environment variables as they may already be configured if you've completed previous Android projects. Further documentation is available at https://github.com/golang-ui/nuklear#android-demo:

```
chapter9/android> cd $GOPATH/src/github.com/golang-ui/nuklear/cmd/nk-android
chapter9/android> export ANDROID_HOME=/home/andy/Android/Sdk
chapter9/android> export NDK=$ANDROID_HOME/ndk-bundle
chapter9/android> export PATH=$PATH:$NDK/build/
chapter9/android> make toolchain
/home/andy/Android/Sdk/ndk-bundle/build/tools/make_standalone_toolchain.py \
    --api=21 --install-dir=/home/andy/Code/Go/src/github.com/golang-ui/nuklear/cmd/nk-android/toolchain \
    --arch=arm --stl libc++
chapter9/android>
```

Setting up an Android environment and building the nk-android toolchain

This should prepare your desktop for Android development using nk and Go. The rest of this chapter focuses on desktop development, but if the tools are working correctly, you should be able to adapt the instructions to Android NDK-based deployment.

Now that the prerequisites for your platform are complete, let's set up nk and run our first example application.

Setup

Setting up the `nk` package to use Nuklear from Go is as simple as installing the `github.com/golang-ui/nuklear/nk` package with the standard `go` tools:

```
chapter9/hello> go get -u github.com/golang-ui/nuklear/nk
chapter9/hello>
```

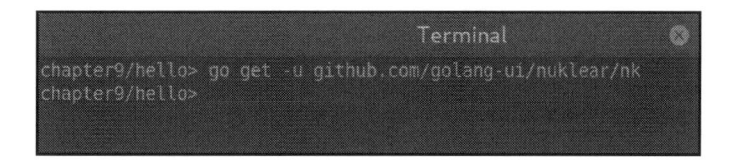

Installing nk is straightforward if you already have CGo up and running

Now that you have the library installed, let's run an example to see nk in action.

nk - Nuklear for Go

Example

The Go Nuklear bindings project provides an example application to demonstrate some widgets; we can use this to quickly check that things are working. With the previous setup steps complete, running the demo is as simple as installing the Go project and running it. The code is located in the `cmd/nk-example` sub-project of `github.com/golang-ui/nuklear`; we can use `go install` to download and install the example and run it using `nk-example`:

```
chapter9/hello> go install github.com/golang-ui/nuklear/nk
chapter9/hello> go install github.com/golang-ui/nuklear/cmd/nk-example
chapter9/hello> nk-example
2018/11/12 11:38:38 glfw: created window 400x500
2018/11/12 11:38:47 [INFO] button pressed!
```

Installing and running a nuklear example is trivial once CGo is set up

Running the preceding commands should result in the following example window appearing on your screen. This example shows some of the widgets provided by the Nuklear toolkit, including embedded windows:

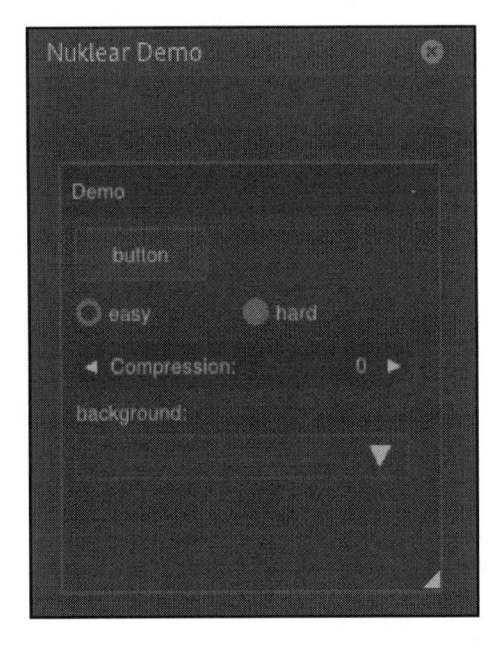

The nk-example application running on Linux

[232]

Code

To get started with our first nk application, there's a certain amount of setup code we need to write. Nuklear is focused on delivering a graphical toolkit API and not the operating system-specific code such as managing windows and user input. To avoid having to write all of that code ourselves, we'll use the `glfw` Go bindings to create and show a window for our application. The following code will set up an application window and show it (without any content). We also need to call `runtime.LockOSThread()` as this setup code must all execute on the main thread:

```
package main

import "runtime"
import "github.com/go-gl/glfw/v3.2/glfw"
import "github.com/go-gl/gl/v3.2-core/gl"

func init() {
    runtime.LockOSThread()
}

func main() {
    glfw.Init()
    win, _ := glfw.CreateWindow(120, 80, "Hello World", nil, nil)
    win.MakeContextCurrent()
    gl.Init()

    ...
}
```

After initializing `glfw`, we need to create a window, which `glfw.CreateWindow()` handles for us. We specify the window size and title in the first three parameters. The fourth parameter is used for fullscreen windows; by passing a `*glfw.Monitor` reference, we request a window that fills the specified monitor in its default video mode. The final parameter is related to *context sharing*, passing an existing `*glfw.Window` reference requests that this new window shares the same graphical context to reuse textures and other resources. We then make the new window current so that its context is used in the following code. Note that the window may not exactly match the requested parameters (exact window size or monitor modes may not be supported), so it's important to check these values after creation rather than assume the result.

The other setup we must do is to create an OpenGL context that the Nuklear code can utilize. For this task, we'll import the `go-gl` library (by the same authors as the `glfw` Go bindings). We initialize the OpenGL library ready to use the context from the window that was created by `glfw`.

nk - Nuklear for Go

Additionally, the nk package needs to be initialized and we need to set up a default font. Thankfully, Nuklear has a standard font packaged but we need to run some code to set it as the default (or load a custom one for our application):

```go
import "github.com/golang-ui/nuklear/nk"

func main() {
    ...

    ctx := nk.NkPlatformInit(win, nk.PlatformInstallCallbacks)
    atlas := nk.NewFontAtlas()
    nk.NkFontStashBegin(&atlas)
    font := nk.NkFontAtlasAddDefault(atlas, 14, nil)
    nk.NkFontStashEnd()
    nk.NkStyleSetFont(ctx, font.Handle())

    ...
}
```

With all of the setup done, the window still looks the same as we haven't yet rendered any content. To actually run a Nuklear application, we need to add a run-loop that handles event management and GUI refreshing. The following code isn't the simplest possible event loop (it would be possible to use `for !win.ShouldClose() { ... }`, but that would consume a whole CPU!), but it's reasonably efficient for the brevity. It sets up a loop that will check for any events and then refresh the user interface 30 times a second. The following code block completes our basic nk `main()` function:

```go
import "time"

func main() {
    ...

    quit := make(chan struct{}, 1)
    ticker := time.NewTicker(time.Second / 30)
    for {
        select {
        case <-quit:
            nk.NkPlatformShutdown()
            glfw.Terminate()
            ticker.Stop()
            return
        case <-ticker.C:
            if win.ShouldClose() {
                close(quit)
                continue
            }
            glfw.PollEvents()
```

```
            draw(win, ctx)
        }
    }
}
```

The preceding code will run our application, but we haven't defined the user interface. The call to a `draw()` function in the preceding code is the secret, so we should implement that now. Let's look at the method in two parts: first, the GUI layout and second, the actual rendering. To set up our interface, we create a new *frame* (imagine a single snapshot of a video) that will be drawn on the next refresh of the user interface. After calling `nk.NkPlatformNewFrame()`, we can set up our interface; any code between `nk.NkBegin()` and `nk.NkEnd()` will be part of our UI update for the frame we just started. We can find out whether re-drawing is needed by checking the returned `update` variable; if it's 0, then no changes have occurred and we can skip the UI code.

Inside the `if update > 0 { ... }` block, we lay out the application interface, two rows each containing a single cell. In the first row (created with `nk.NkLayoutRowStatic()`), we add an `nk.NkLabel` containing the text *Hello World!*. In the second, we create a **Quit** button using `nk.NkButtonLabel()`. As this is an immediate mode user interface, we don't retain a reference to the button to check its state, nor do we pass an on-click handler; we simply check the return value from the widget draw function. The value that's returned will be greater than 0 if the button has been clicked; and so we can place code inline that will tell the window to close and thereby close the application:

```
const pad = 8

func draw(win *glfw.Window, ctx *nk.Context) {
    // Define GUI
    nk.NkPlatformNewFrame()
    width, height := win.GetSize()
    bounds := nk.NkRect(0, 0, float32(width), float32(height))
    update := nk.NkBegin(ctx, "", bounds, nk.WindowNoScrollbar)

    if update > 0 {
        cellWidth := int32(width-pad*2)
        cellHeight := float32(height-pad*2) / 2.0
        nk.NkLayoutRowStatic(ctx, cellHeight, cellWidth, 1)
        {
            nk.NkLabel(ctx, "Hello World!", nk.TextCentered)
        }
        nk.NkLayoutRowStatic(ctx, cellHeight, cellWidth, 1)
        {
            if nk.NkButtonLabel(ctx, "Quit") > 0 {
                win.SetShouldClose(true)
            }
        }
```

```
        }
    }
    nk.NkEnd(ctx)

    ...
}
```

Lastly, at the end of the `draw()` function, we need to ask our OpenGL viewport to render the created user interface. To do this, we set up the OpenGL viewport using `gl.Viewport()`—as you can see, we use the width and height parameters from the actual window size rather than assuming the size we requested at the beginning of this code is correct. Once the viewport is set up, we clear it and set a background color (using `gl.ClearColor()`). The main render work is handled by `nk.NkPlatformRender()`, which takes the frame that we defined previously and draws it into the current graphical context. This function requires that we specify buffer sizes for the vertex and element buffers. We pass numbers that will be large enough for our demonstration purposes.

Finally, we cause the content to be shown by calling `win.SwapBuffers()`. As `glfw.Window` is *double buffered*, we've been drawing to a back buffer that's currently off-screen. By calling swap, we're moving the back buffer to the screen and setting the previously shown front buffer to be hidden, ready for the next frame to be drawn:

```
func draw(win *glfw.Window, ctx *nk.Context) {
    ...

    // Draw to viewport
    gl.Viewport(0, 0, int32(width), int32(height))
    gl.Clear(gl.COLOR_BUFFER_BIT)
    gl.ClearColor(0x10, 0x10, 0x10, 0xff)
    nk.NkPlatformRender(nk.AntiAliasingOn, 4096, 1024)
    win.SwapBuffers()
}
```

That should complete the code for our *hello world* application. There was a lot of setup but the UI definition code was relatively succinct, so building more complex interfaces won't be much more work.

Build and run

Simply build or run `hello.go` and you'll see the expected **Hello World** window. Clicking the **Quit** button will tell the window to close which in turn will exit the application:

Hello world with nk

Cross-compiling

Compiling an nk-based application for a different operating system can be a complicated process due to its requirement to use CGo to communicate with native OpenGL libraries. However, if you've worked through Chapter 5, *andlabs UI - Cross-platform Native UIs*, or Chapter 8, *Shiny - Experimental Go GUI API*, this should already be set up. If you've jumped straight to this chapter, then you may need to follow the steps in the Appendix, in the *Cross-Compiler Setup*. Once that's complete, you should have new compilers available (named o32-clang for macOS or x86_64-w64-mingw32-gcc for Windows) that are able to link to macOS Foundation APIs and Windows system calls respectively.

To build the application, we now set up the GOOS and CGO_ENABLED flags as before, but also specify the compiler to use through an extra CC environment variable, setting it to o32-clang for the Darwin OS or x86_64-w64-mingw32-gcc for Windows. With that configuration complete, we can build our nk application for macOS and Windows from our Linux Terminal:

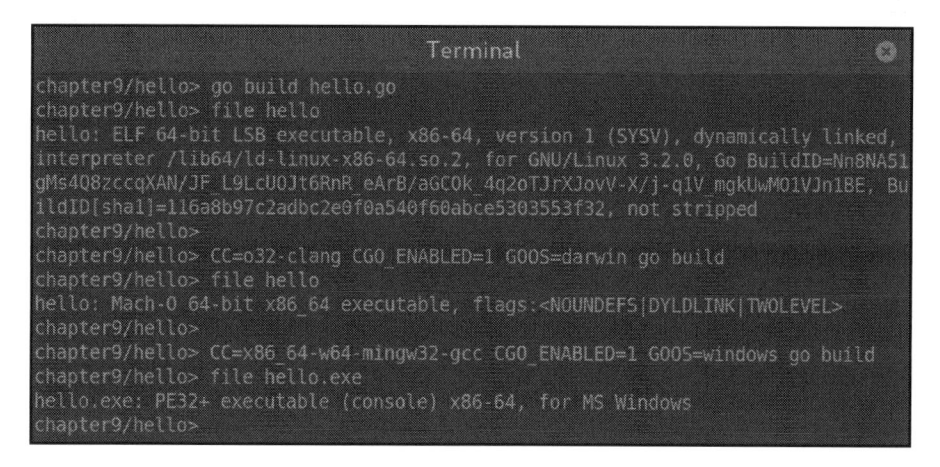

Compiling for Linux, macOS, and Windows from a Linux Terminal

Now that we've built our first nk application, let's look further into what the underlying Nuklear library supports for building application GUIs.

Widgets, layout, and skinning

As the Nuklear library focuses purely on the widget aspects of an application toolkit, its capability in this area is comparable to that of more established application libraries. As you'll see in the following, there's a long list of widgets that can be included in any Nuklear application. As the nk bindings expose all of the library functionality, these features are all available to an nk application as well.

The GUI functionality is split into three broad areas: **widgets** (the main user interface elements), **drawing** (for drawing directly to the canvas), and **layout** (for arranging elements on screen). In this section, we'll look at each area in turn, starting with the main widgets.

Widgets

The Nuklear widgets (and the nk API presenting them) should in many ways be familiar. Sensible naming allows for many of these features to be discovered while programming in your favorite IDE, but let's explore the main widgets and how they function:

Widget name	Description
NkButtonLabel	A standard push button widget, the API reports when it has been clicked. See NkButtonImage also (to use an image instead of a text label) and NkButtonImageLabel to include both.
NkCheckboxLabel	A checkbox displays a familiar box next to the label that's either checked or not. The API reports when its value has changed.
NkColorPicker	This is a special button that opens a color picker. This form returns the currently selected color, or you can use NkColorPick, which reports when the value changes.
NkComboBox	This is a combobox container for dropping down a selection. Each item within it can contain text, an image, or both (see the APIs beginning with NkComboItem).

Chapter 9

NkGroup(Begin/End)	This adds a grouping for widgets in an interface. A group has a title and a scrollbar, if required. To manually control the scroll behavior, you can instead use `NkGroupScrolledBegin`. The widgets declared between begin and end will be included. The begin function returns > 0 if the contents should be drawn.
NkImage	This displays a simple image in the interface.
NkMenubar(Begin/End)	For add a menu bar to the user interface, this requires the use of the various APIs beginning with `NkMenu` and `NkMenuItem` as well. The begin function returns > 0 if the contents should be drawn.
NkPopup(Begin/End)	This displays a popup over the current content; the widgets declared between begin and end will be included. The begin function returns > 0 if the contents should be drawn.
NkRadioLabel	A radio selection is like a combobox but offers multiple possible values, each added using this function. The return value indicates whether the specified item has been selected.
NkSlider(Int/Float)	The `NkSlider` functions add a slide bar with specified minimum, maximum, and current values. The API reports when the value has changed. An alternative format, `NkSlide(Int/Float)`, returns the current value.
NkTexteditString	This is a text entry widget. This function requires a buffer to edit; this can more easily be set through `NkEditStringZeroTerminated()`. There are also many helpful APIs starting with `NkTextedit` that can be used to manage the text content.
NkTree(Push/Pop)	Tree widgets can be used to allow sections of the user interface to be expanded and collapsed or to present tree-based data on the screen. Functions beginning with `NkTreePush` mark the start of a new tree section and `NkTreePop` ends that section (or the root of the tree). The `TreeType` named `TreeNode` marks a user interface style tree and `TreeTab` is for data style tree.
Window (NkBegin, NkEnd)	A window is required to contain all widgets within Nuklear (anything declared outside this scope will be ignored or cause an error). A window is declared with `NkBegin` or `NkBeginTitled` and marked as complete with `NkEnd`. Various window management functions are available and they start with `NkWindow`.

As you can see, many of these widgets are straightforward. The more complex ones have semantics for opening and closing their definition that become familiar over time. This is due to the immediate mode nature of the API and its design to not retain any state. Common semantics are for containers to return a value greater than 0 when they need to be drawn. Similarly, items that respond to user events will return a non-zero value when they have been activated or changed.

[239]

Now that we've explored the widgets available, let's look at how we can arrange elements in our GUI.

Layout

The layout system for Nuklear follows a simple rows and columns approach. To lay out widgets, each item should be within a row; columns are implicitly created when widgets are added according to the parameters set in the row configuration. When widgets are added to a row that's full, a new one will be automatically created with the same parameters as the previous. A new row may be started to change the parameters or to finish a previous row without filling the remaining columns. The basic layout is controlled by the NkLayoutRow API as described here; there's also a helpful template-based layout in `NkLayoutRowTemplate`, which we'll explore after that. Lastly, `NkLayoutSpace` allows directly setting widget locations and sizes—we'll explore that last.

NkLayoutRow

The easiest approach to layout is to start a new row using `NkLayoutRowDynamic()` or `NkLayoutRowStatic()`. Both functions specify the number of cells in the row. The difference between the two is that the dynamic row allocation will split all of the space between the cells and resize them all as the window or container changes size. With a static arrangement, the sizes of all cells will remain the same irrespective of the container size. Widgets added after a row is started will append to the row, until it's full; if further widgets are appended, then a new row will be created for the new widgets. This continues until `NkLayoutRowEnd()` is called, or a different row configuration is started using one of these alternative functions.

Some added control is made possible by using the `NkLayoutRowBegin()` function to start a row; this specifies the row height and number of columns, but not how the columns will be sized. Cells are added to the row before widgets are appended by calling `NkLayoutRowPush()`; this sets a size or ratio for the next cell and should be followed by the declaration of a widget to fill the cell. This type of row should also conclude by calling `NkLayoutRowEnd()`.

Lastly, it's possible to call `NkLayoutRow` directly to set up the parameters for the following rows, static or dynamic sizing, and specified height or ratio with a specified number of columns.

NkLayoutRowTemplate

A more powerful way to lay out rows is to use the template mechanism available. By calling `NkLayoutRowTemplateBegin()`, it's possible to set the template for all rows that follow. Column sizing is defined using one of three template functions.
Firstly, `NkLayoutRowTemplatePushStatic()` specifies that widgets in this column should be of a fixed width. `NkLayoutRowTemplatePushDynamic()`, like the definition of dynamic allocation without templates, will split the row width among dynamic columns (this could be as little as 0 if no space is available). Finally, there's an additional call to the `NkLayoutRowTemplatePushVariable()` function; this will ensure that widgets get their minimum required space and will take up any extra space available (or split evenly across other variable width columns).

At the end of the template specification, you must call `NkLayoutRowTemplateEnd()`; this will indicate that any widgets added will start the creation of layout rows that follow the declared template. As before, if there are more widgets that fit in a row, then a new row will automatically be created and widgets will start to be added on this new row. Unlike the regular row layout functions before that specified the number of columns in a row, using this method will add as many widgets to a row as items exist in the template definition.

NkLayoutSpace

Lastly, the space layout offers full control over the positioning and size of the items in your Nuklear application. The layout is started and ended like the previous row-based layout; use `NkLayoutSpaceBegin()` to start a space-based layout and `NkLayoutSpaceEnd()` to finish the layout. Before each widget you wish to add to your interface, call the `NkLayoutSpacePush()` function, passing `NkRect`, which specifies the size and position for the next widget to be added.

As well as the layout control functions, there are a number of helper functions that use the `NkLayoutSpace` API prefix. The most useful is `NkLayoutSpaceBounds()`—if called within a space layout, it'll return the total space that's available to work within. This is important if you wish to right- or bottom-align or position your widgets centrally within available space.

Those are all of the layout options that the nk API provides; let's look now at the drawing capabilities of the library.

Drawing

The drawing API presents a fairly standard **two-dimensional** (2D) vector graphics library that's mostly used by the higher level widgets. As it's part of the public API, it's also possible to use them in your application.

Command queue

To draw custom areas of an application, our application will be interacting directly with the Nuklear draw command queue (the list of items to draw for rendering a frame of the user interface) so care is recommended. You can get access to `nk.CommandBuffer`, which is needed for each draw command by using the `NkWindowGetCanvas()` function. It's important that this is only called when a window is active (after `NkBegin` and before `NkEnd`). The positional values will need to be aware of other widgets and layouts loaded, which can get complicated very fast—it's easiest to draw using these commands only in an otherwise empty window so that you avoid drawing over other widgets.

Draw functions

If you want to go ahead and make use of these draw commands directly, you can use the following:

Stroke function	Fill function	Notes
NkStrokeLine()		Draw a single line segment in the specified color.
NkStrokeCurve()		Draw a single curve segment in the specified color.
NkStrokeRect()	NkFillRect(), NkFillRectMultiColor()	Draw a rectangle (or square) outline, or solid rectangle in the specified color(s). To draw an outlined, filled rectangle, call `NkFillRect()` and then `NkStrokeRect()` using the same coordinates. `NkFillRectMultiColor()` is a quick way to draw gradients in a rectangle.
NkStrokeCircle()	NkFillCircle()	Draw a circle (or ellipse) outline or fill in the specified color.
NkStrokeArc()	NkFillArc()	Outline, or fill, an arc around a central point in the specified color.
NkStrokeTriangle()	NkFillTriangle()	Draw a triangle outline or a solid triangle in the specified color.
NkStrokePolyline()		Draw a series of line segments in the specified color.
NkStrokePolygon()	NkFillPolygon()	Outline or fill a shape with a list of points defining its boundary.
NkDrawImage()		Draw an image into a specified rectangle and background color.
NkDrawText()		Draw a text string with the specified background and foreground colors.

Now that we've explored all of the widgets and drawing capabilities, we could jump right in to building a full application. However, Nuklear has one other cool feature that we should look at: the ability to change the interface design using skinning.

Skinning

As well as defining its own style for the widgets included, Nuklear supports **skinning**—loading a theme to change how applications look. This is a powerful feature—very similar to the themes that we saw with GTK+ and Qt, but selected by the application instead of the end user. Any nk application developer looking to set up skinning for their application may find that it isn't easy to do—this is due to the way that most configuration is expose through C structures from the underlying Nuklear API. While these elements are mostly available through the Go API binding, it requires a lot of pointer conversion and unsafe assignments that could affect the stability of your application. It would be possible, however, to write some C code and include it in your application using CGo.

The following C code is extracted from a Nuklear skinning example in case a developer wishes to include a custom skin in their application and is willing to embed C in their Go code. The example uses a single texture image that defines all of the different images that together define the theme. Firstly, the texture must be loaded into the current OpenGL context and then the individual areas identified within the loaded texture, as follows:

```
glEnable(GL_TEXTURE_2D);
media.skin = image_load("../skins/gwen.png");
media.check = nk_subimage_id(media.skin, 512,512,
nk_rect(464,32,15,15));
media.check_cursor = nk_subimage_id(media.skin, 512,512,
nk_rect(450,34,11,11));

...
```

The preceding code excerpt specifies only two sub-textures where, in real-life usage, there would be many more. After the textures are loaded, we define a style struct pointer that matches the widget to theme (here, we're skinning the checkbox). The value of this pointer is then set to the location of the loaded style configuration (this is where it becomes very difficult to re-create in pure Go code). For each field in the struct, an appropriate image or color should be set:

```
{struct nk_style_toggle *toggle;
toggle = &ctx.style.checkbox;
toggle->normal = nk_style_item_image(media.check);
toggle->hover = nk_style_item_image(media.check);
toggle->active = nk_style_item_image(media.check);
toggle->cursor_normal = nk_style_item_image(media.check_cursor);
toggle->cursor_hover = nk_style_item_image(media.check_cursor);
toggle->text_normal = nk_rgb(95,95,95);
toggle->text_hover = nk_rgb(95,95,95);
toggle->text_active = nk_rgb(95,95,95);}
```

nk - Nuklear for Go

The same technique should be applied for all widgets that will be used in the application to be skinned. This is a lot of work and even the toolkit author warns against it at this time due to its time-consuming nature! Following is the style texture for the *Gwen* skin and a screenshot of an application with this theme loaded:

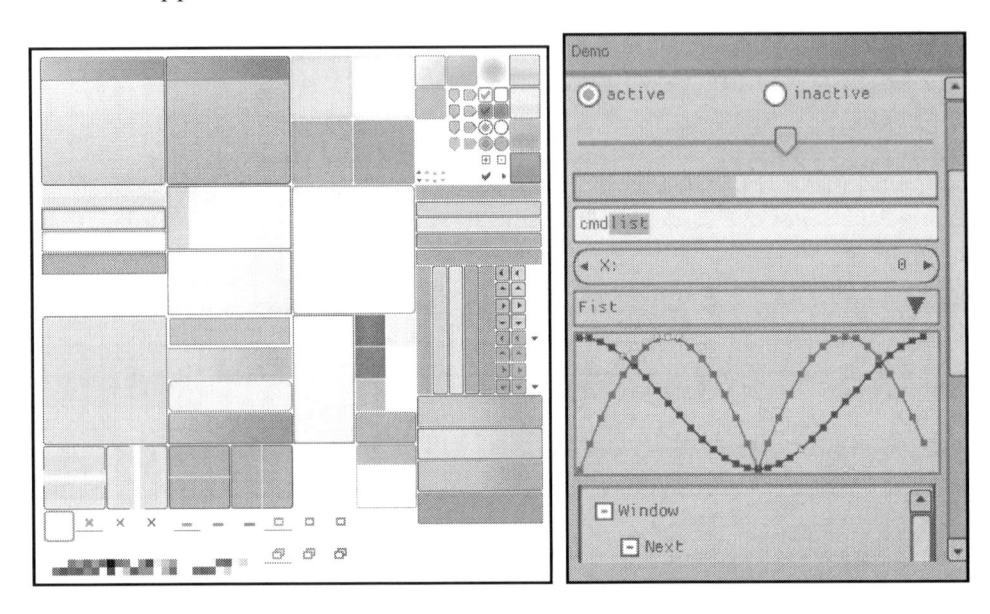

The Gwen skin is used to demonstrate Nuklear skin capabilities (left); The Gwen skin in action (right)

A complete implementation can be found in the examples repository at https://github.com/vurtun/nuklear/blob/master/example/skinning.c.

Building a user interface

Let's return to our GoMail application again to try out the nk API. Nuklear is an established toolkit with a lot of functionality so it should be able to build the user interface just as well as previous examples. What we'll see as we build out this user interface is how different an immediate mode toolkit is, in how the code is arranged and how event handling is managed.

We can start by copying the hello world application so we don't have to re-work all of the setup code and life cycle management. As this application is going to contain many more graphical elements, we need to increase the buffer sizes that set using `NkPlatformRender()`. Replace the original line with the following for this example. In your own applications, this may need to be higher still—if the number is too low, you may notice graphical elements not showing or disappearing when popups and menu items appear:

```
nk.NkPlatformRender(nk.AntiAliasingOn, 512 * 1024, 128 * 1024)
```

Layout

We'll begin with the basic application layout; to start with, we update our `draw()` function to call a separate `drawLayout()` function where we'll add our new code. This new function will need to be passed the height of the window to correctly fill the vertical space, as you'll see later:

```
func draw(win *glfw.Window, ctx *nk.Context) {
    nk.NkPlatformNewFrame()
    width, height := win.GetSize()
    bounds := nk.NkRect(0, 0, float32(width), float32(height))
    update := nk.NkBegin(ctx, "", bounds, nk.WindowNoScrollbar)

    if update > 0 {
        drawLayout(win, ctx, height)
    }
    nk.NkEnd(ctx)

    gl.Viewport(0, 0, int32(width), int32(height))
    gl.Clear(gl.COLOR_BUFFER_BIT)
    gl.ClearColor(0x10, 0x10, 0x10, 0xff)
    nk.NkPlatformRender(nk.AntiAliasingOn, 512 * 1024, 128 * 1024)
}
```

The preceding code is fairly standard for painting a window with nk. Let's jump straight into our new layout code.

Main email window

We start with a simple layout function called `drawLayout()`. This will set up the basic application layout similar to the GoMail design we created in Chapter 4, *Walk - Building Graphical Windows Applications*. The beginning of the code sets out space for the menu and toolbar that will expand to stretch the width of our window. We then start a template layout using `NkLayoutRowTemplateBegin()` to have a fixed size column on the left for our email list and a wider, variable width column on the right that will expand as our window resizes:

```
func drawLayout(win *glfw.Window, ctx *nk.Context, height int) {
    toolbarHeight := float32(36)
    nk.NkLayoutRowDynamic(ctx, toolbarHeight, 1)
    nk.NkLabel(ctx, "Toolbar", nk.TextAlignLeft)

    nk.NkLayoutRowTemplateBegin(ctx, float32(height)-toolbarHeight)
    nk.NkLayoutRowTemplatePushStatic(ctx, 80)
    nk.NkLayoutRowTemplatePushVariable(ctx, 320)
    nk.NkLayoutRowTemplateEnd(ctx)

    nk.NkGroupBegin(ctx, "Inbox", 1)
    nk.NkLayoutRowDynamic(ctx, 0, 1)
    nk.NkLabel(ctx, "Item1", nk.TextAlignLeft)
    nk.NkLabel(ctx, "Item2", nk.TextAlignLeft)
    nk.NkLabel(ctx, "Item3", nk.TextAlignLeft)
    nk.NkGroupEnd(ctx)

    ...
```

> Notice that, while the width of our layout can adjust automatically, the height isn't quite as flexible. For this example, we pass in the height of the window and deduct from that the height we're allocating for the toolbar. This total is passed to our template layout so it'll expand to the remaining window height.

In the first column of the main layout, we add a new group named "Inbox" for our email list and add three simple label items that represent the loaded list. Next, we add another group that will occupy the second space in the template layout. This code sets up a mix of one and two column rows that will display email content.

We open the group and set up a simple dynamic row with a single column using `NkLayoutRowDynamic()`, inserting the `NkLabel` subject in that cell. Next, we add another template layout so we can have a narrow, fixed width column for our labels and a variable width column for the values. After that, `NkLabel` for the label and value can be inserted to form a grid. Lastly, we start another single column dynamic row for the main email content:

```
    ...
    nk.NkGroupBegin(ctx, "Content", 1)
    nk.NkLayoutRowDynamic(ctx,0, 1)
    nk.NkLabel(ctx, "Subject", nk.TextAlignLeft)
    nk.NkLayoutRowTemplateBegin(ctx, 0)
    nk.NkLayoutRowTemplatePushStatic(ctx, 50)
    nk.NkLayoutRowTemplatePushVariable(ctx, 320)
    nk.NkLayoutRowTemplateEnd(ctx)
    nk.NkLabel(ctx, "From", nk.TextAlignRight)
    nk.NkLabel(ctx, "email", nk.TextAlignLeft)
    nk.NkLabel(ctx, "To", nk.TextAlignRight)
    nk.NkLabel(ctx, "email", nk.TextAlignLeft)
    nk.NkLabel(ctx, "Date", nk.TextAlignRight)
    nk.NkLabel(ctx, "date", nk.TextAlignLeft)
    nk.NkLayoutRowDynamic(ctx,0, 1)
    nk.NkLabel(ctx, "Content", nk.TextAlignLeft)
    nk.NkGroupEnd(ctx)
}
```

Running the preceding code, along with the necessary boilerplate code from our *Hello world* example, should show a single window, looking a lot like the following:

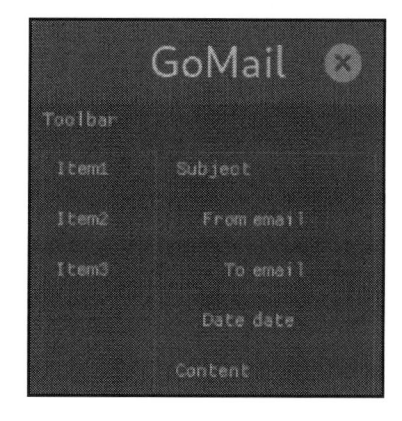

The basic GoMail layout created with the nk API

[247]

Email compose dialog

To start our compose window layout, we create a new `drawComposeLayout()` function that (for testing) we can call instead of `drawLayout()` from the `draw()` function. Before we can add the text edit widgets that the email compose UI will use, we need to create buffers to manage the content they'll edit. Remember that this is an immediate mode toolkit so, to remember any state, we must provide the data storage. This is where the compose window will store the subject, email address, and content for a new email message:

```
var composeSubject = make([]byte, 512, 512)
var composeEmail   = make([]byte, 512, 512)
var composeContent = make([]byte, 4096, 4096)
```

It's also helpful to our user to provide a hint (often called a placeholder) for the user—to do this, we need to copy some data into the buffers before the draw loop begins:

```
copy(composeSubject[:], "subject")
copy(composeEmail[:], "email")
copy(composeContent[:], "content")
```

Now let's look at the layout for the email compose window. The layout is similar to the content of our email display group in the previous layout code, setting up a dynamic row for the subject widget followed by a row template for the *To* label and email address entry. Instead of `NkLabel()`, this time we're creating a text entry widget using `NkEditStringZeroTerminated()` with a number of parameters. The `nk.EditBox|nk.EditSelectable|nk.EditClipboard` flags tell Nuklear that we're setting up an edit box where the text can be selected and interact with the system clipboard. We also need to tell the widget which buffer it should edit (in this case `composeSubject`) and what the maximum number of characters should be (which we set to the length of the buffer `int32(len(composeSubject))`). This is then repeated for the email and content input widgets:

```
func drawComposeLayout(ctx *nk.Context, height int) {
    nk.NkLayoutRowDynamic(ctx, 0, 1)
    nk.NkEditStringZeroTerminated(ctx,
        nk.EditBox|nk.EditSelectable|nk.EditClipboard,
            composeSubject, int32(len(composeSubject)), nil)
    nk.NkLayoutRowTemplateBegin(ctx, 0)
    nk.NkLayoutRowTemplatePushStatic(ctx, 25)
    nk.NkLayoutRowTemplatePushVariable(ctx, 320)
    nk.NkLayoutRowTemplateEnd(ctx)
    nk.NkLabel(ctx, "To", nk.TextAlignRight)
    nk.NkEditStringZeroTerminated(ctx,
        nk.EditBox|nk.EditSelectable|nk.EditClipboard,
```

```
        composeEmail, int32(len(composeEmail)), nil)
    nk.NkLayoutRowDynamic(ctx, float32(height-114), 1)
    nk.NkEditStringZeroTerminated(ctx,
 nk.EditBox|nk.EditSelectable|nk.EditClipboard,
        composeContent, int32(len(composeContent)), nil)
```

...

Lastly, we need to add the buttons to the bottom of the screen—we use another row template for this. The variable space in this layout is set to be the size of the row, minus the size of our buttons, so that the buttons will align to the right. We insert an empty `NkLabel` in the first cell to work as a spacer. The two `NkButtonLabel()` function calls set up the buttons at the bottom-right of the layout:

...

```
    nk.NkLayoutRowTemplateBegin(ctx, 0)
    nk.NkLayoutRowTemplatePushVariable(ctx, 234)
    nk.NkLayoutRowTemplatePushStatic(ctx, 64)
    nk.NkLayoutRowTemplatePushStatic(ctx, 64)
    nk.NkLayoutRowTemplateEnd(ctx)
    nk.NkLabel(ctx, "", nk.TextAlignLeft)
    nk.NkButtonLabel(ctx, "Cancel")
    nk.NkButtonLabel(ctx, "Send")
}
```

With that layout code created, we can show the window and see an email **Compose** window like the following screenshot:

The basic Compose layout with the nk toolkit

Toolbar and menu

Adding a menu to an nk window is accomplished using `NkMenubarBegin()`, `NkMenuBeginLabel()`, and `NkMenuItemLabel()`, among others. The only difficult step in setting up a menu is that we also need to add an appropriate layout for the bar and its items. It's important (in fact, mandatory) that the bar is in a layout where y=0, so we immediately add a new row layout using dynamic sizing with `NkLayoutRowBegin()`. Then, we push the cell size for this layout using `NLayoutRowPush()`.

A menu item is opened using `NkMenuBeginLabel()` and we must check the return value for this function—0 means that the menu is hidden. If it returns a non-zero value then we should lay out the menu below the bar. We start a new dynamic row layout with a single column using `NkLayoutRowDynamic()` to contain each menu item. Each menu item is then added using `NkMenuItemLabel()` with the appropriate label string. The return value for this function indicates whether the item has been clicked. If we get a non-zero value, then we should action the item—as shown by the
Quit item. Lastly, if the menu is open, we must close it again with `NkMenuEnd()`:

```
nk.NkMenubarBegin(ctx)
nk.NkLayoutRowBegin(ctx, nk.LayoutStaticRow, 25, 3)
nk.NkLayoutRowPush(ctx, 45)
    if nk.NkMenuBeginLabel(ctx, "File", nk.TextAlignLeft, nk.NkVec2(120, 200)) > 0 {
        nk.NkLayoutRowDynamic(ctx, 25, 1)
        nk.NkMenuItemLabel(ctx, "New", nk.TextAlignLeft)
        if nk.NkMenuItemLabel(ctx, "Quit", nk.TextAlignLeft) > 0 {
            win.SetShouldClose(true)
        }

        nk.NkMenuEnd(ctx)
    }

    ...
```

Further menus (Edit and Help, for example) can simply be added by starting another block with `NkMenuBeginLabel()`. For the complete listing, you can see the code repository for this book: chapter9/gomail.

Adding a toolbar is less straightforward as the Nuklear toolkit has no direct toolbar support. We'll simulate this by adding a row of buttons that are of fixed size and left-aligned in the bar. To do this, we open a new static row layout, specifying the desired size of the buttons as the cell width (and the correct number of columns). We then add each button with `NkButtonLabel()` passing a button label. Ideally, we would use `NkButtonImage()`, but there are no standard toolbar icons available. We could package the required icons ourselves and load the images, but there's currently little support for loading an image from Go code; a proposal exists to add `NkImageFromRgba()`, but at the time of writing, this doesn't exist. Implementing that image loading is out of scope for this chapter:

```
...

toolbarHeight := float32(24)
nk.NkLayoutRowStatic(ctx, toolbarHeight, 78, 7)
nk.NkButtonLabel(ctx, "New")
nk.NkButtonLabel(ctx, "Reply")
nk.NkButtonLabel(ctx, "Reply All")

nk.NkButtonLabel(ctx, "Delete")

nk.NkButtonLabel(ctx, "Cut")
nk.NkButtonLabel(ctx, "Copy")
nk.NkButtonLabel(ctx, "Paste")

...
```

Each of these buttons returns, an `int` value, like the preceding menu items, that indicate whether it was clicked. We'll add the button handling in the next section, *Communicating with the GUI*. With this code in place, we see a complete user interface for our email browse window:

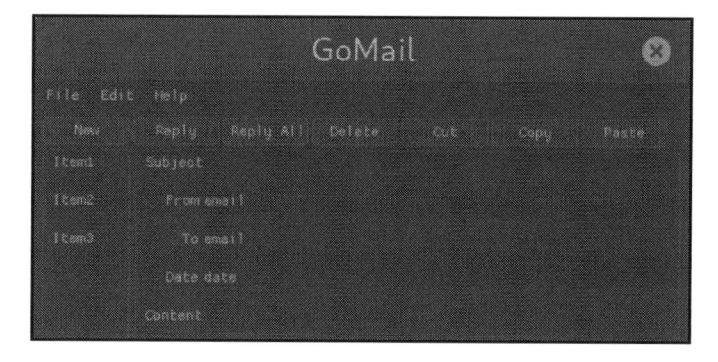

The completed layout of our compose window

Communicating with the GUI

Now that we have all of the layout completed, we need to connect up a data source and handle the appropriate interaction events. We start by importing the `client` email package used in the previous examples. Once imported, we set up a new test server and cache the current message (this will be changed later by clicking an item). As outlined before, we must save all state within the application code, not the user interface:

```
import "github.com/PacktPublishing/Hands-On-GUI-Application-Development-in-Go/client"

var server = client.NewTestServer()
var current = server.CurrentMessage()
```

Updating the email list group is as simple as wrapping the label creation in a `for` loop that iterates the range of `server.ListMessages()`:

```
nk.NkGroupBegin(ctx, "Inbox", 1)
nk.NkLayoutRowDynamic(ctx,0, 1)
for _, email := range server.ListMessages() {
   nk.NkLabel(ctx, email.Subject, nk.TextAlignLeft)
}
nk.NkGroupEnd(ctx)
```

The content is loaded from the `client.EmailMessage` that we saved as `current`, as follows:

```
nk.NkLabel(ctx, ui.current.Subject, nk.TextAlignLeft)
...
nk.NkLabel(ctx, "From", nk.TextAlignRight)
nk.NkLabel(ctx, string(ui.current.From), nk.TextAlignLeft)
nk.NkLabel(ctx, "To", nk.TextAlignRight)
nk.NkLabel(ctx, string(ui.current.To), nk.TextAlignLeft)
nk.NkLabel(ctx, "Date", nk.TextAlignRight)
nk.NkLabel(ctx, ui.current.DateString(), nk.TextAlignLeft)
...
nk.NkLabel(ctx, ui.current.Content, nk.TextAlignLeft)
```

For the main interface, the last interaction is the menu and toolbar buttons; each of the relevant functions returns > 0 when the item has been activated. We can add a click handler to the menu items as we did with the **Quit** item earlier:

```
if nk.NkMenuItemLabel(ctx, "Quit", nk.TextAlignLeft) > 0 {
   win.SetShouldClose(true)
}
```

The same pattern can be used for toolbar buttons. For the **New** button, we set a compose window to appear when it's tapped. As we need to maintain all state locally, you'll see that the button tap here is setting a `composeUI` instance (a custom type for the compose state); this will be used in the following to decide whether we should open a compose window:

```
if nk.NkButtonLabel(ctx, "New") > 0 {
    compose = newComposeUI(this)
}
```

As the Nuklear backends typically don't support multiple native operating system windows, we need to load our compose window within the main GoMail user interface. After the main interface layout code has run, we can insert a new check for the `compose` value that we set before. When this value is `nil`, we have no compose window to show, but when it has been set, we'll create a second window within the first:

```
...
nk.NkEnd(ctx)

if compose != nil {
    drawCompose(ctx)
}

...
```

The preceding code executes after the main window (marked by `NkEnd()`). If a compose state is set, we'll need to call the new `drawCompose()` function:

```
func (ui *mainUI) drawCompose(ctx *nk.Context) {
    bounds := nk.NkRect(20, 20, 400, 320)
    update := nk.NkBegin(ctx, "Compose", bounds, nk.WindowNoScrollbar |
 nk.WindowBorder | nk.WindowTitle | nk.WindowMovable | nk.WindowMinimizable)

    if update > 0 {
        compose.drawLayout(ctx, 296)
    }

    nk.NkEnd(ctx)
}
```

This new function sets up a sub-window and then calls the `drawComposeLayout()` that we defined earlier—now renamed `drawLayout()` within a new `composeUI` type. We need to encapsulate the compose state (the data buffers we declared earlier) in a separate type; this allows us to track changes made in multiple compose windows (as the compose window has no state).

To change email based on the selected item in the list, we can change `NkLabel` to `NkSelectableLabel`. This widget takes an additional parameter for whether or not it's selected and will return a non-zero value if the selection is changed to the specified item. The update list code should look like this (a little extra code is required to convert from `bool` into `int32`):

```
for _, email := range ui.server.ListMessages() {
    var selected int32
    if email == ui.current {
        selected = 1
    }
    if nk.NkSelectableLabel(ctx, email.Subject, nk.TextAlignLeft,
&selected) > 0 {
        ui.current = email
    }
}
```

With all of our data loaded and the compose window opened from the **New** toolbar or menu item, we see something like the following:

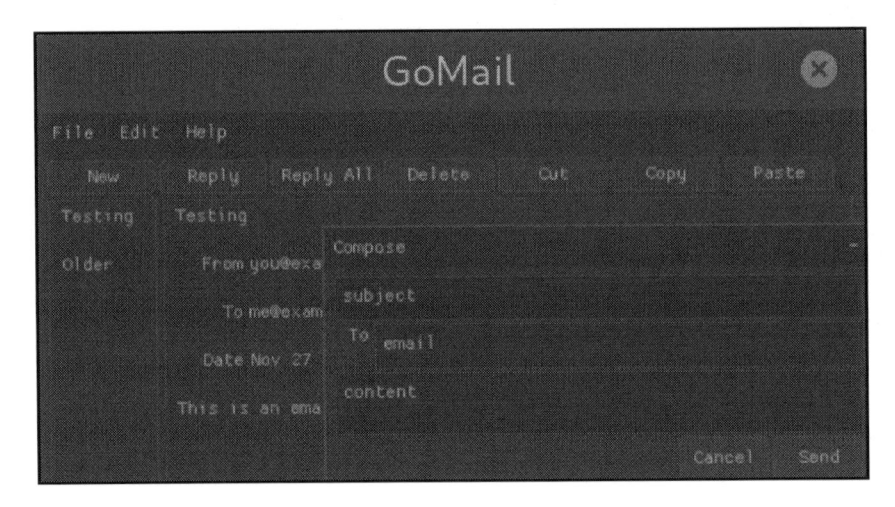

Our completed GoMail app with nk showing a compose window

Background processing

One of the benefits of an immediate mode user interface toolkit is that there's no hidden state. When we see a new email arrive, we don't have to communicate the change to a list widget (or equivalent) to instruct it to add a new row. As long as the model data updates when an event occurs, there's no additional work to do. Our nk code will automatically add the new data on the next frame and so the user interface will refresh accordingly.

This also means that we don't have to handle multiple thread complications in our user interface code. If you ensure that any model data is thread-safe (using standard Go tools) then the user interface will continue to render from the main thread on each refresh. It's a requirement that all render code runs on the same thread, but that's unlikely to be a problem due to the way the toolkit is designed.

Summary

In this chapter, we looked at the second toolkit of three that were designed to break away from the traditional toolkits that we looked at in Section 2, *Toolkits Using Existing Widgets*. The Nuklear project primarily targets embedded applications but we saw that, in many ways, it's a possible fit for desktop applications. Its bespoke widget design means that applications will look identical across all supported operating systems, which is a longer list than Shiny—including Android for mobile development.

We explored how the Nuklear framework is designed and how it interacts with various backends that provide the actual drawing and user input implementation. We examined the main API features, including its drawing capabilities, the widgets it includes, and the layout algorithms that it provides for constructing user interfaces. We then implemented the same GoMail project that was created in Chapter 4, *Walk - Building Graphical Windows Applications*, through to Chapter 7, *Go-Qt - Multiple Platforms with Qt*, working through the nk APIs and features to create a complete application. There were many differences when working with an immediate mode GUI framework but, in many ways, it was easier to implement our basic application.

In the next chapter, we'll look at **Fyne**, the last toolkit that we'll explore in detail. As with Shiny, it's a material design inspired widget library but, similar to Nuklear, its focus is on providing a complete widget toolkit.

10
Fyne - Material Design-Based GUI

Fyne is a UI toolkit and application API designed to be easy to use. Its interface design follows the material design principles, providing cross-platform graphics that appear identical on all supported platforms. This chapter explores how to write graphical applications for multiple platforms with Fyne.

We'll cover the following topics:

- The vision and design of the Fyne project
- Building a simple Fyne-based application for multiple platforms
- API design and the widgets provided by Fyne
- How to create a complete application using Fyne

By the end of this chapter, you should have an understanding of Fyne project's ambitions and will have built multiple cross-platform graphical applications using the toolkit.

Background and vision for Fyne

The Fyne project was created by Andrew Williams (the author of this book) in response to growing criticism of the complexity in existing graphical toolkits and application APIs. It was designed with the aim of being easy to use, and the Go language was chosen for its powerful simplicity. Like the Shiny project we explored in `Chapter 8`, *Shiny – Experimental Go GUI API*, its APIs benefit from being created specifically for the Go language.

Fyne - Material Design-Based GUI

As with the other widget toolkits in `Section 3`, *Modern Graphical Toolkits*, it facilitates the building of graphical applications that look identical across all platforms, rather than adopting the look and feel of the operating system.

> *"Fyne's APIs aim to be the best for developing beautiful, usable, and lightweight applications for desktop and beyond."*
>
> `github.com/fyne-io/fyne/wiki/Vision`

The toolkit was initially built using the Enlightenment Foundation Libraries (EFL: `enlightenment.org/about-efl`) to facilitate cross-platform rendering. Since then, Fyne has moved to an OpenGL-based driver, much like the nk package from the previous chapter. This makes for a much simpler setup and means that there are no runtime dependencies for apps created with Fyne. Before we examine the toolkit in detail, let's see how to set up a simple Fyne application.

Getting started with Fyne

Before we start building a Fyne application, we will step through the installation and run an example application. For most systems, the setup is as simple as installing the `fyne.io/fyne` package using standard Go tools. For some systems, however, there are development prerequisites to check, so let's start there.

Prerequisites

For the majority of platforms, there are no installation requirements to begin using Fyne. On macOS and Windows, the toolkit uses built-in OpenGL capabilities, so you can skip straight to the following *Setup* section (however, if you are developing for the first time on macOS, examine the following notes). If you are working with Linux (or another Unix system), then it may be necessary to install a number of system header files.

Linux

To compile on Linux, you will need to have the Xorg and GL (*mesa* or similar) headers installed (this is not required for running the applications). The specifics will vary from system to system, but the most common requirements are as follows:

- Debian / Ubuntu:
  `libgl1-mesa-dev` **and** `xorg-dev`

- Fedora / CentOS:
  `libX11-devel`, `libXcursor-devel`, `libXrandr-devel`, `libXinerama-devel`, `mesa-libGL-devel`, and `libXi-devel`
- Arch Linux:
  `mesa`

On a development computer these packages may well already be installed, but if you have compile errors later in this chapter, the first thing to check would be that these packages, or their equivalent for your system, are installed correctly.

macOS

For developing on macOS, you must have the Xcode command-line tools installed. If you've been working with C or CGo previously, then this is probably already set up; if not, then you may need to execute the `xcode-select --install` command:

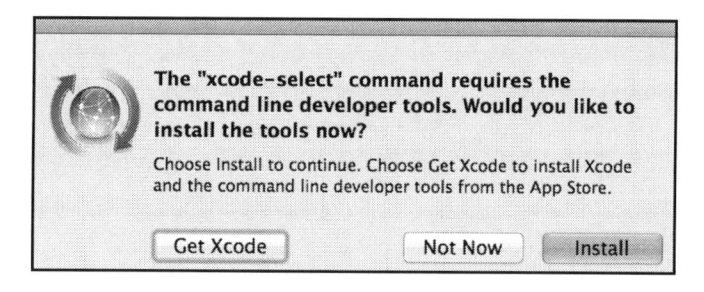

If you don't already have the command-line tools installed, then xcode-select will display this prompt

Setup

Setting up the Fyne API for use is as simple as downloading it using the `go get` command. The project is accessed from its base import name, `fyne.io/fyne`:

Installing Fyne is easy once CGo is set up

Example

The Fyne toolkit comes with an example application built in that can be used to explore its features and assets. We can use this to verify that the setup is working. Simply use the Go tools to install the application and then run it using the `fyne_demo` command:

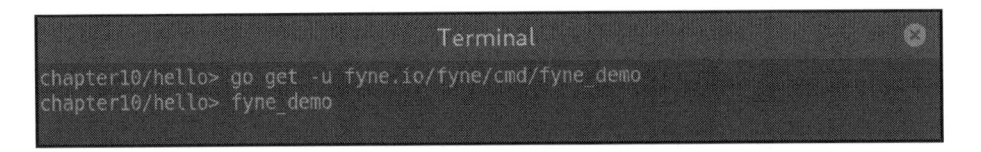

```
chapter10/hello> go get -u fyne.io/fyne/cmd/fyne_demo
chapter10/hello> fyne_demo
```

Install and run the fyne_demo command from the project repository

Running the demo application opens a single window that offers various options to explore. If we tap on a few items, additional windows will open and you should see something like this:

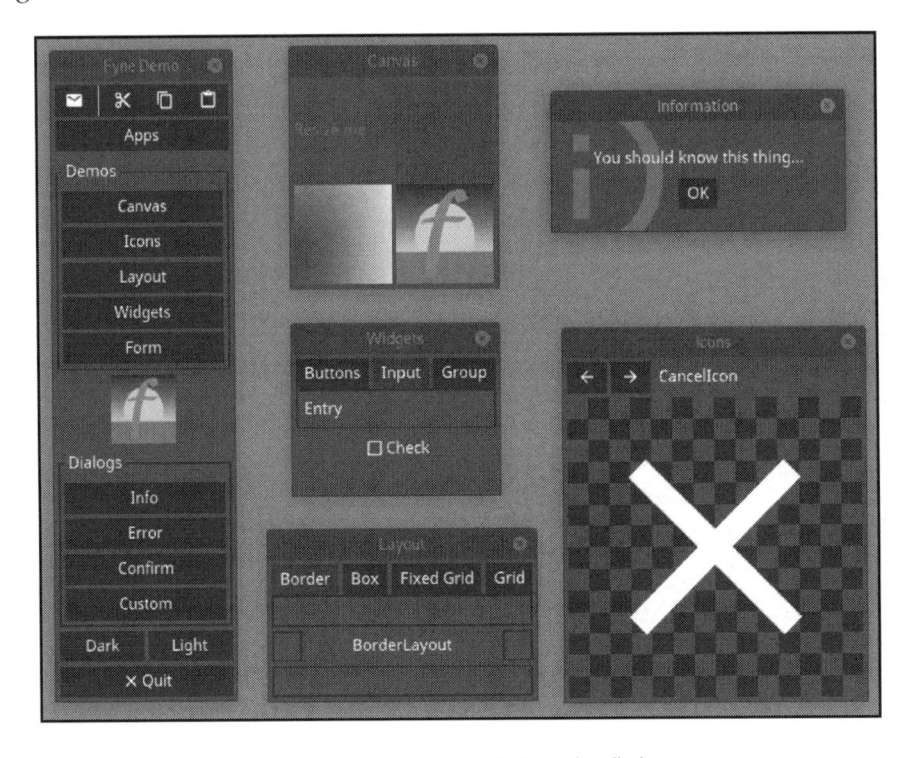

Some of the features demonstrated in Fyne's example application

Code

The basic *Hello World* application with Fyne is quite succinct, as the application setup is encapsulated in a single call. The entry point, `app.New()`, provided by the `app` sub-package, sets up a new application that we use to open a new window. The `widget` sub-package defines the various widgets available that we can add to our new window:

```
package main

import "fyne.io/fyne/app"
import "fyne.io/fyne/widget"

func main() {
    app := app.New()

    win := app.NewWindow("Hello World")
    win.SetContent(widget.NewVBox(
        widget.NewLabel("Hello World!"),
        widget.NewButton("Quit", func() {
            app.Quit()
        }),
    ))

    win.ShowAndRun()
}
```

As you can see in the preceding code block, the newly created `fyne.Window` has its content set to a new `widget.VBox` that provides the basic layout. Into this, we add a *Hello World!* label using `widget.NewLabel()` and a **Quit** button using `widget.NewButton()`. The second parameter to the button is `func()`, which will be called when the button is tapped.

Lastly, we call `ShowAndRun()` on the window we created. This function will show the window and start the application `event` loop. It is shorthand for `win.Show()`; `app.Run()`.

Fyne - Material Design-Based GUI

Build and run

This simple application can be run directly with `go run hello.go`, or built using `go build hello.go` and then run using the compiled binary:

Compiling or running directly works the same on any supported system

Running the code should produce a simple app that looks like the following. Clicking the **Quit** button or closing the window will exit the application:

Running Hello World on macOS

Cross compiling

Due to the dependency on CGo, compiling for a platform other than the one you are developing in is, unfortunately, not as simple as setting the `GOOS` environment variable. Building for a different platform requires an installation of the C compiler for the target operating system. If you've been working through the previous chapters, then this may already be set up, but if not, then the process is documented in `Appendix 2`, *Cross-Compiler Setup*.

Once you have the appropriate compiler installed, then the build process is configured by setting the `GOOS`, `CGO_ENABLED`, and `CC` environment variables. You may also need to update your path—it's advisable to put this in your Terminal or shell configuration:

Building from Linux for macOS and Windows is a case of using the correct compiler

Now that we've explored the details of getting up and running and compiling for multiple platforms, let's look more at how Fyne is designed and organized.

Rendering and vector graphics

The Fyne widgets (much like those in the Nuklear library in Chapter 9, *nk – Nuklear for Go*) are made up of simple graphical objects that the render drivers are responsible for drawing. The driver is included as part of the package, and so no additional setup is required to start an application. Similar to the Shiny toolkit (that we explored in Chapter 8, *Shiny – Experimental Go GUI API*), the iconography is all vector-based, which Fyne uses to create scalable user interfaces that adapt to the device screen density.

Vector graphics

Vector graphics refers to images that are made up of lines and shapes rather than a collection of pixels (referred to as raster graphics). Whilst these images can be slower to load, they're excellent for drawing perfect images at any scale. As computer screens and smart phones have continued to increase their pixel density, measured in **Dots Per Inch** (**DPI**), it has become more difficult to produce raster graphics that look good on all devices. Platforms such as iOS have historically approached this by requiring multiple files of the same content at different resolutions—such as Icon.png, Icon@2x.png, and Icon@3x.png (which could be, for example, 60 x 60, 120 x 120, or 180 x 180 pixels, respectively)—so that the closest match image for the screen can be used. With a vector icon, you would provide a single image, Icon.svg (**Scalable Vector Graphics**), that can be drawn at exactly the resolution required for a sharp image.

Fyne - Material Design-Based GUI

The Fyne toolkit uses vector graphics throughout so that applications built using it can scale appropriately for any computer screen. When an application starts, it calculates the pixel density (DPI) of the current screen and sets an appropriate scale for the application. Additionally, when a Fyne window is moved to a screen with a different resolution, the content (and window containing it) will re-size accordingly. This means that when an application running on a laptop (typically, a high-resolution screen) moves to an external monitor (usually a lower resolution), the window will be resized to a smaller number of pixels to try and maintain a consistent size for the user. If you wish to override the scale that's auto detected, then it is possible to set a `FYNE_SCALE` environment variable before launching the application.

An example of setting scale values—notice the crisp text and icons:

FYNE_SCALE=0.5

FYNE_SCALE=2.5

In some situations, it may be appropriate to use a raster image instead of a vector. This is usually helpful if you want to draw exactly as many pixels as are visible in the space available. An example of this may be found in image manipulation programs or when drawing the result of a complex calculation. For these situations, there is a type of image within the Fyne API (created with `canvas.NewRaster()`) that provides this functionality. One of the examples provided by Fyne is a fractal viewer, where each pixel is calculated and drawn using the raster image feature:

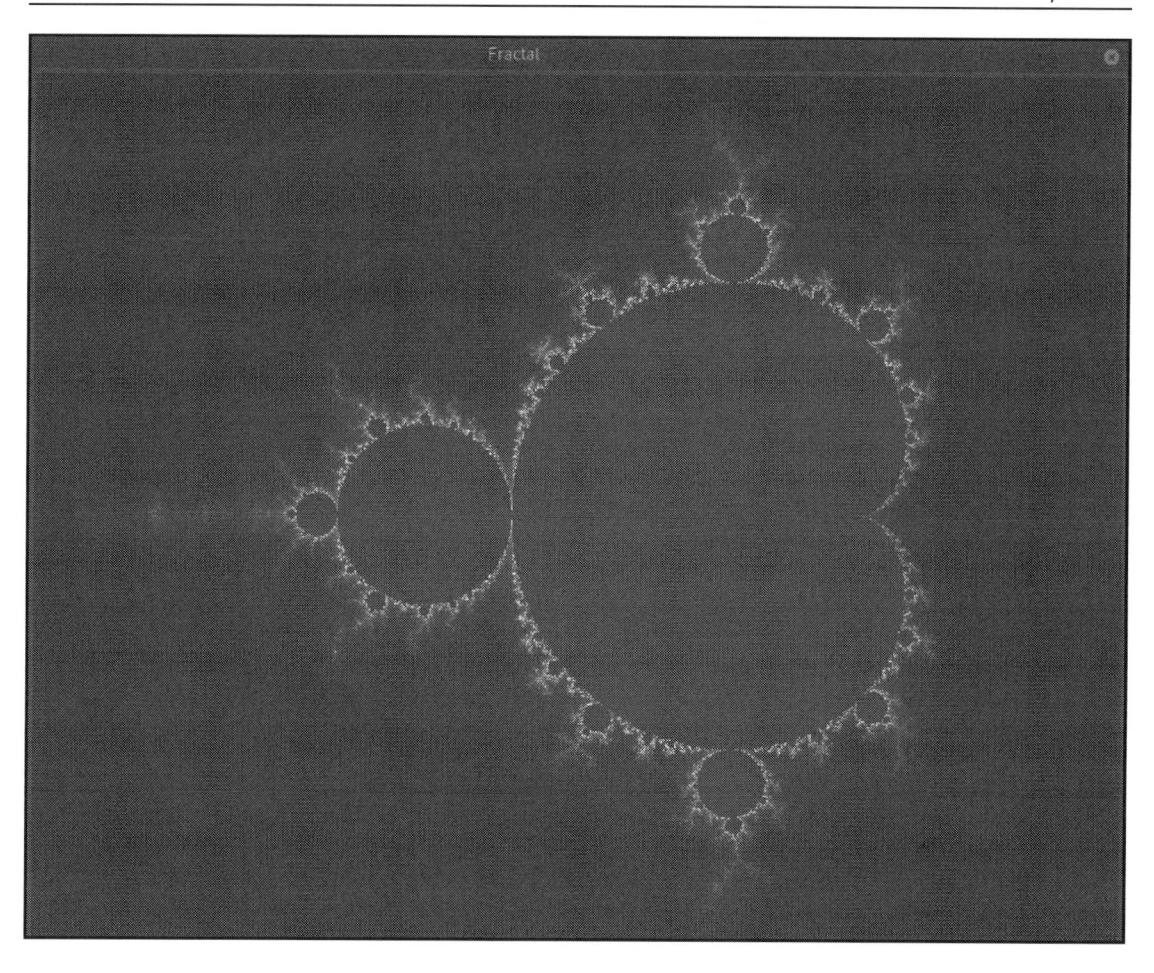

A mandelbrot fractal calculated per-pixel for the output device. Observe the level of detail

Drivers

A driver in Fyne is responsible for rendering the text, canvas objects, and images, as well as handling window management and user input. The drivers are also required to handle any thread management behind the scenes. By adopting this design, it is possible for background processes or asynchronous events to update the user interface without any of the thread management code that is common in many graphical toolkits.

The default driver for Fyne uses Go-GL and the Go GLFW bindings, which means it has the same dependencies as the examples we worked through in the previous chapter, *nk – Nuklear for Go*. If your computer, and that of your target customers, supports OpenGL (which includes all recent desktop computers, most laptops, smart phones, and tablets, and beyond), then you don't need any additional libraries or support packages. Having the appropriate Go developer tools installed (see *Prerequisites* within the *Getting started with Fyne*, discussed earlier) is all you need, and there are no runtime requirements for users of your apps.

If you wish to build for an older computer, or one that does not have support for OpenGL, it is possible to use the alternative `efl` driver. This driver uses the Enlightenment Foundation Libraries to handle rendering, window management, and user input in a cross platform manner. Their years of development for a wide range of platforms (alongside desktop platforms, they support Playstation, Tizen, Samsung Gear watch, and various set-top boxes) means that applications could potentially run on a wider range of devices. To run using this driver, just add `-tags efl` to any go build or run command, such as `go run -tags efl hello.go`. While this driver does offer better multi-platform support, it also requires that the EFL libraries are installed both on the developer's computer and the target device. For this reason, it is often not the preferred approach when working with Fyne.

Supported platforms

Although the different Fyne drivers have potentially different supported platforms, the core toolkit just supports a standard set of operating systems. At the time of writing, this covered macOS, Windows, Linux, and BSD variants. Any operating system-specific code understands how applications should function on each of these target. Unlike the other toolkits in `Section 3`, *Modern Graphical Toolkits*, Fyne is designed to provide APIs for managing applications as well as their graphical interfaces. For example, `app.OpenURL()` allows an application to launch an external document in the default browser for each supported system.

Now that we've explored the Fyne project background, as well as its design and operating system support, let's explore the APIs it provides to application developers.

Canvas, widgets, and layouts

The Fyne API is divided into various sub-packages for basic drawing definition, container layout, high-level widgets, and theme description. In this section, we will look at each in turn. These packages provide the implementation details that are useful from an application developer point of view, and they typically implement generic interfaces. These interface definitions are at the top level of the hierarchy and include things such as `fyne.CanvasObject` (which is implemented by any object that can be added to a canvas), `fyne.Container` (that describes how multiple objects can be grouped and laid out), and `fyne.Resource` (representing an embedded application resource, such as an icon or font). Additionally, there are some math and geometry utilities as well as definitions for event and text handling.

There are additional packages that we will not cover, including `dialog` (helpful classes for common dialog windows), `driver` (which is where drivers are loaded from), and `test` (which provides helpful test facilities). Let's explore the other, more commonly used, packages.

Canvas (drawing)

The `canvas` package includes definitions of all of the basic drawing objects that Fyne understands. Each of these types defines a number of fields that represent the configuration, such as color, size, and visibility. These are the objects that a Fyne driver will iterate over, drawing each to create the rendered user interface:

Circle	This is a circle, or ellipse, defined by the bounding top-left to bottom-right rectangle. It could be created with `NewCircle()` or `&Circle{}`. It isn't commonly used in most applications.
Image	An image may be a vector or bitmap-based image loaded from a file (with `NewImageFromFile()`) or embedded resource, or it may be an image generated dynamically to fill available space (using `NewRaster()` and a `func(w, h int) *image.Image` callback).
Line	This is a simple line that draws from one position to another. It isn't commonly used unless drawing diagrams.
Rectangle	The basic building block for widgets, a rectangle draws an area with a specified color. Create with `NewRectangle()` or `&Rectangle{}`.
Text	The text canvas primitive draws a single string to screen in a specified color and alignment. It does not handle any special characters or formatting. It can be created directly using `&Text{}` or with the helper `NewText()` function.

The preceding list makes up the primitive drawing elements of the Fyne canvas. Next, we look at how layouts can be used to position them within a container.

Layout

Multiple objects in Fyne are grouped in a `fyne.Container` type and its child objects are laid out by `fyne.Layout`. Various standard layouts are provided, as detailed in the following table. A layout provides two functions: first, it manages the size and position for a list of `fyne.CanvasObject` objects; and second, it must define the minimum size required to fit all of the objects it arranges:

`BorderLayout`	The border layout places a specific canvas object at each of the top, bottom, left, and right edges of a container. Any other objects in the container will fill the central space.
`BoxLayout`	The box layout is either vertical or horizontal (created with `NewVBoxLayout()` or `NewHBoxLayout()` functions). It will arrange items in a list, each at their minimum height (vertical) or width (horizontal), and the other dimension will expand to the container edge. A box layout may also contain a spacer that will expand to fill available space (normally created with `NewSpacer()`).
`FixedGridLayout`	The fixed grid layout specifies the size of every cell and then arranges them in rows within the available space. A new row is created when the next widget would have extended beyond the container width.
`GridLayout`	The grid layout has a specified number of columns and each child object will be the appropriate fraction of the container width. The height is defined similarly, depending on the number of child canvas objects. For example, with five objects in two columns, there will be three equal height rows.
`MaxLayout`	This is the simplest layout. Every item is set to the same size to fill the available space. Be careful to specify container objects in the correct order (the first will be drawn under any subsequent items). For example, a button may simply be a rectangle with text positioned above where both should expand equally.

It is also possible to write a custom layout by implementing the `fyne.Layout` interface. The `MinSize()` function should determine the size required (probably respecting the `MinSize()` function of the child objects) and the `Layout()` function calls `Move()` and `Resize()` on child objects to configure the display for rendering.

Whilst containers and layouts are useful, most of our time will be spent with higher-level widget definitions, so let's see what is available.

Widgets

Fyne widgets are divided into two parts: the behavior, which is what the main API exposes, and the renderer, which controls how a widget will look. Unless you are building a custom widget, it is not recommended to access the render functionality (hidden behind the `widget.Renderer()` utility function). Customization of the user interface, if required, should be managed using the `theme` package (refer to the next section).

All widgets can be created using their constructing function (such as `NewButton("text", callback)`) or using the initializer syntax, such as `&Button{Text: "text", OnTapped: callback}`. If the latter is used, then fields can also be set immediately after the widget is initiated until it is first rendered. After a widget is shown, setter functions, such as `SetText()`, should be used to ensure that the GUI is updated to reflect the changes. Widget fields can still be useful—if you want to update multiple properties at once, you can set the appropriate fields to be applied in a single refresh. Just be sure to call `widget.Refresh(myObject)` once you've applied the changes.

The full list of widgets at the time of writing is as follows:

Box	This is a simple widget that uses a `layout.BoxLayout` to arrange the child objects in horizontal or vertical lists.
Button	The basic button contains text and/or an icon and will call a passed `func()` when it is tapped.
Check	A check widget displays a label next to a check box and triggers a `func(bool)` callback if it is toggled.
Entry	A text entry widget for single- or multiple-line input.
Form	The form widget lays out a simple data form, with labels in one column and input widgets on the other. Setting `OnSubmit` or `OnCancel` fields for callbacks will include the appropriate buttons on an additional row.
Group	A visual grouping of child objects. A line is drawn around the items and a title label is drawn above them.
Icon	A simple widget for drawing a themed icon. Create it with an icon resource (refer to *Themes* in the following section), and it will adapt to the current theme configuration.
Label	This is a simple text widget that draws using the current theme text color and updates if that changes.
PasswordEntry	The same as for the preceding `Entry` widget, but the text is hidden as * characters.
TabContainer	Similar to a standard container, except that it can display different contents. Each child container is associated with a tab button that, when pressed, will show the appropriate content.
Toolbar	A toolbar widget shows a row of icon buttons, optionally separated with `NewToolbarSpacer()` (an invisible space) or `NewToolbarSeparator()` (a thin line to show the grouping).

It is possible to implement your own widgets—all they need to do is implement the `fyne.Widget` interface. As well as the basic `fyne.CanvasObject` functions, a widget must also define a `CreateRenderer()` function returning a `fyne.WidgetRenderer` instance. A widget renderer is similar to a container object, but it also has a background color and should reflect the current theme (the required `ApplyTheme()` function will be called on all widgets if the theme is changed). As we've mentioned it many times, let's now explore more of what a Fyne theme provides.

Themes

The `theme` package is an implementation of a material design inspired user interface. It provides the color palette, icons, font, and spacing information required to display the Fyne user interface:

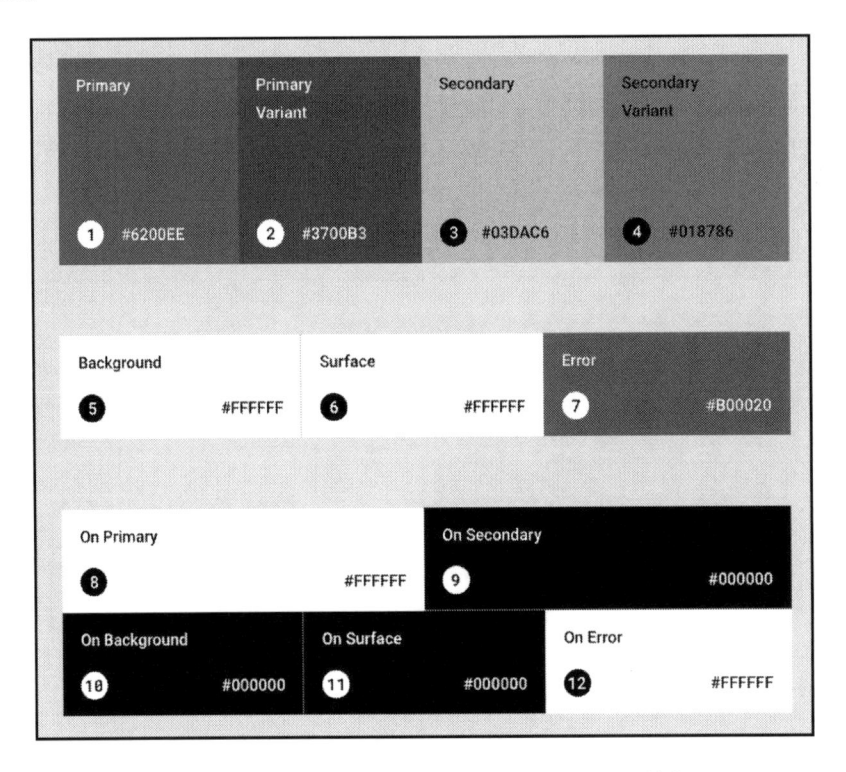

The "baseline" material design color palette. Fyne uses a blue/gray variant by default

Widgets utilize the theme package extensively to match the current settings. For example, a button will be colored `theme.ButtonColor()` (unless it is a primary button, in which case it's `theme.PrimaryColor()`) and a label text is `theme.TextColor()`. Fyne also packages a standard font that can be accessed using `theme.TextFont()` (and variations), but these are not often needed. Instead, use `fyne.TextStyle` properties on a text object or label. However, `theme.TextSize()` and `theme.Padding()` are useful ways to match the user interface style in a custom widget.

Fyne themes also provide a collection of material design icons that can be used in any application, for example, `theme.ContentPasteIcon()`. Icons loaded from a theme will adapt to a new theme loading when used with any standard widgets. These icons are bundled with the toolkit and do not require any installation or additional items to be shipped with an application.

Any time you use a theme method, it's important to realize that the result may change over time—a new theme could be loaded or the user may change the configuration. To handle this correctly, you should implement `fyne.ThemedObject`, which requires a single function, `ApplyTheme()`. Inside this function, you should re-apply any theme-based values that were accessed. This functionality is handled automatically by widgets, so it is not commonly required that an application handles theme changes.

Packaged themes

The Fyne toolkit provides two themes to match a user's preference—a light theme and a dark theme. To change the theme for an application, the environment variable, `FYNE_THEME`, can be set to *light* or *dark*. If you are implementing a custom widget, it's advisable to test it with at least these two themes:

The default dark theme

The alternative light theme

At the time of writing, Fyne does not provide the ability to download user-created custom themes, but this may change in the future. It is, however, possible for an application to be displayed using its own theme. After implementing the `fyne.Theme` interface, you should pass an instance of the type to your application configuration using `app.Settings().SetTheme()`.

Building a user interface

To explore the Fyne toolkit further, let's build our latest version of the GoMail application designed in `Chapter 4`, *Walk – Building Graphical Windows Applications*. We will start by setting out the basic application layout.

Layout

Creating a complex layout with Fyne is a case of combining multiple containers, each of which are using one of the layouts provided. It would be possible to write our own layout to set up the interface with a single container, but for this exploration, we will use only the built-in components. Let's start by creating the main application window.

Main email window

To load the first window of a Fyne application, we must create a new application instance using `app.New()`. After that, we can call the `NewWindow()` function on this application object. The returned `fyne.Window` object allows us to control the window on screen and to set its content:

```
import "fyne.io/fyne/app"

func main() {
   mailApp := app.New()
   browse := mailApp.NewWindow("GoMail")

   ...
}
```

Next, we will create the required widgets for our GUI. This starts by adding the widget import line, and then we add the declarations to the `main()` function created previously. A toolbar is added using `widget.NewToolbar()` (we will add items to it later). For the email list on the left, we create a new titled group using `widget.NewGroup()` with the title `Inbox`. Into this group we add placeholder labels using `widget.NewLabel()`.

Chapter 10

Then, we create new labels for the content and subject of the email to display. We set the text of the subject label using a `fyne.TextStyle` declaration. Lastly, we set up the grid layout for our email metadata using `widget.NewForm()`. A form widget matches our design of where we list rows with a bold text label next to the widget it describes. To the form, we append the **To**, **From**, and **Date** items, shown as follows:

```
import "fyne.io/fyne/widget"

func main() {
    ...

    toolbar := widget.NewToolbar()
    list := widget.NewGroup("Inbox",
        widget.NewLabel("Item1"),
        widget.NewLabel("Item2"),
        widget.NewLabel("Item3"),
    )
    content := widget.NewLabel("Content")
    subject := widget.NewLabel("subject")
    subject.TextStyle = fyne.TextStyle{Bold:true}

    meta := widget.NewForm()
    meta.Append("To", widget.NewLabel("email"))
    meta.Append("From", widget.NewLabel("email"))
    meta.Append("Date", widget.NewLabel("date"))

    ...
}
```

Now that we have defined all of the widgets, we need to lay them out appropriately. In Fyne, we typically use a `fyne.Container` object and optionally pass a layout to control how it is set up. There are also some helper widgets that provide easier-to-use APIs, such as `widget.NewVBox()` used in the following section (that sets up a container where items are arranged in a vertical list).

In both containers in this code snippet, we are using `BorderLayout`. When calling `layout.NewBorderLayout()`, we pass the objects that should be positioned in the top, bottom, left, and right positions of the layout (or `nil` if they are to be left empty). Any items that are included in the container not listed in a particular position will be arranged to fill the center of the layout, taking up all remaining space. Remember that items to be placed in one of the border sections should also be passed into the `fyne.NewContainerWithLayout()` function as subsequent parameters, as this controls which objects will be drawn within the container. Refer to the following section to see how `subject` and `box` are passed to the layout as well as the container, as we wish them to be positioned by the layout and drawn by the container.

[273]

In the first container (`detail`), we've set the `subject` label to stretch along the top and the `box` containing our metadata and content to be left-aligned within the container. The following container (`container`) is our overall application layout and it positions the `toolbar` at the top, the email `list` on the left, and the `detail` container fills the remaining space for the layout (since it is not specified as a border parameter):

```
import "fyne.io/fyne"
import "fyne.io/fyne/layout"

func main() {
    ...

    box := widget.NewVBox(meta, content)
    detail := fyne.NewContainerWithLayout(
        layout.NewBorderLayout(subject, nil, box, nil),
        subject, box)
    container := fyne.NewContainerWithLayout(
        layout.NewBorderLayout(toolbar, nil, list, nil),
        toolbar, list, detail)

    ...
}
```

With all of the containers and layouts defined, we need to complete the window by setting its content and optionally specifying a size. You may not have to call the `Resize()` function on a window—its default size will be the appropriate size to fit all of the widgets and containers at their minimum size.

Finally, we call `ShowAndRun()` on the window, which will cause the window to appear and the application's main loop to start. Any subsequent windows can simply call `Show()` (since an application should only start once):

```
    ...

    browse.SetContent(container)
    browse.Resize(fyne.NewSize(600, 400))
    browse.ShowAndRun()
}
```

Running the preceding code (which can be found in the source code repository for this book) should result in a window much like the following:

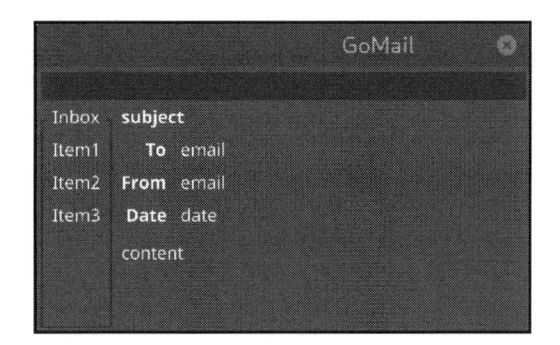

The basic application layout with Fyne. The bar at the top is an empty toolbar

Compose dialog

To start our secondary window, the compose dialog, we could use the custom dialog feature in Fyne (created with `dialog.ShowCustom()`). However, all dialog windows in Fyne are of a fixed size, and we would like the compose window to be flexible. Instead, we will create a new window, as in our `main()` function, using `app.NewWindow()`. To do this, we will need to pass the app instance into a new `ShowCompose()` function (as windows are created from the app object):

```
func ShowCompose(app fyne.App) {
    compose := app.NewWindow("GoMail Compose")
    
    ...
}
```

Next, we create the widgets for the compose window. We will use `widget.NewEntry()` for each of the text entry components. For the multiple-line message widget, we could set `Entry.MultiLine` to `true`, but instead, we use the `widget.NewMultiLineEntry()` helper function. In each instance, we use `Entry.SetPlaceHolder()` to set a placeholder value (that will display as a hint, until the user enters their own text).

[275]

Two new buttons are created using `widget.NewButton()`, one with a "`Send`" label, and the other with "`Cancel`". We keep a reference to the `send` button so that we can set `Button.Style` to `widget.PrimaryButton`. This highlights the button as the window default action. Lastly, we create a new horizontal box for the button bar using `widget.NewHBox()`. Into that, we first add a spacer to right-align the buttons (using `layout.NewSpacer()`), and then we include the **Cancel** and **Send** buttons:

```
func ShowCompose(app fyne.App) {
    ...

    subject := widget.NewEntry()
    subject.SetPlaceHolder("subject")
    toLabel := widget.NewLabel("To")
    to := widget.NewEntry()
    to.SetPlaceHolder("email")

    message := widget.NewMultiLineEntry()
    message.SetPlaceHolder("content")

    send := widget.NewButton("Send", func() {})
    send.Style = widget.PrimaryButton
    buttons := widget.NewHBox(
        layout.NewSpacer(),
        widget.NewButton("Cancel", func() {
            compose.Close()
        }),
        send)

    ...
}
```

Finally, we set up the layout of the window. Once again, this is a non-trivial layout due to Fyne's simple layout options. We use `layout.NewBorderLayout()` to specify which components should stretch and which should be placed around them. The `top` layout places the subject along its top edge and aligns the `to` field left of the expanding `toLabel`. The second layout, `content`, positions the `message` editor in the center, with the `top` layout above and the `buttons` bar below.

[276]

We then set the content of the new `compose` window, set it to a default size (larger than the `minSize()` calculated by the layouts), and call `Show()`. Remember that, this time, we do not use `ShowAndRun()`, since the application is already running:

```
func ShowCompose(app fyne.App) {
    ...

    top := fyne.NewContainerWithLayout(
       layout.NewBorderLayout(subject, nil, toLabel, nil),
       subject, toLabel, to)

    content := fyne.NewContainerWithLayout(
       layout.NewBorderLayout(top, buttons, nil, nil),
       top, message, buttons)

    compose.SetContent(content)
    compose.Resize(fyne.NewSize(400, 320))
    compose.Show()
}
```

Although we don't have a `compose` button yet, this code can be invoked from the `main()` function immediately before the `browse.ShowAndRun()` just for test purposes (remember to remove this line afterward). The result should be something like the following:

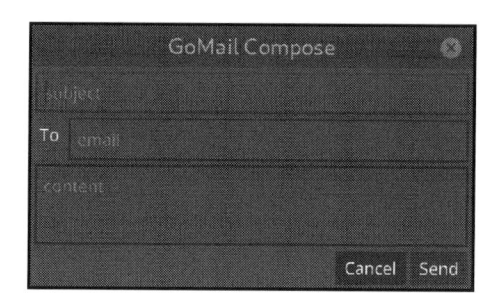

Our compose dialog box using basic Fyne components

Toolbar and menu

Unfortunately, Fyne has no menu bar support (although it is proposed in the following project issue: https://github.com/fyne-io/fyne/issues/41). We also cannot easily create one from simpler components, as there is currently no support for pop-over widgets. Therefore, we will just add a toolbar (as in some previous examples).

Fyne - Material Design-Based GUI

Using Fyne's built-in iconography (from the material design project), we can quickly create an attractive toolbar. To set up the toolbar, we will create a new function, `buildToolbar()`, that will create the toolbar and add the items to it. We pass in the application instance so that the **Compose** item can pass it into the `ShowCompose()` function we created earlier.

The toolbar constructing function takes a list of `ToolbarItem` objects (any widget or type that implements `widget.ToolbarItem`). It is also possible to call `Append()` or `Prepend()` after the toolbar is created. For each item that should appear in the toolbar, we pass an action item using `widget.NewToolbarAction()`. A toolbar action takes a `fyne.Resource` parameter (the icon) and a `func()` that's called when the item is tapped. For resources, we use the theme API to access standard icons that are packaged in the framework. Additionally, we add a separator to group actions using `widget.NewToolbarSeparator()`:

```
func buildToolbar(app fyne.App) *widget.Toolbar {
    return widget.NewToolbar(
        widget.NewToolbarAction(theme.MailComposeIcon(), func() {
            ShowCompose(app)
        }),
        widget.NewToolbarAction(theme.MailReplyIcon(), func() {
        }),
        widget.NewToolbarAction(theme.MailReplyAllIcon(), func() {
        }),
        widget.NewToolbarSeparator(),
        widget.NewToolbarAction(theme.DeleteIcon(), func() {
        }),
        widget.NewToolbarAction(theme.CutIcon(), func() {
        }),
        widget.NewToolbarAction(theme.CopyIcon(), func() {
        }),
        widget.NewToolbarAction(theme.PasteIcon(), func() {
        }),
    )
}
```

To use this new method, we update the toolbar creation code in the `main()` method to read simply `toolbar := buildToolbar(mailApp)`. With these changes in place, we see a full toolbar using the material design icons at the top of the main window, shown as follows:

The built-in Fyne toolbar provides default icons for many actions

Communicating with the GUI

Setting up the user interface to show real data and perform the appropriate interactions is as simple as setting text values and filling in click handlers. To begin with, we will add two helper methods.

Loading emails

The first new function, `setMessage()`, will simply call `SetText()` on each of our `widget.Label` elements. This requires saving a reference to the `to`, `from`, `date`, `subject`, and `content` label widgets that were created earlier in this section. Their content can be updated using the `SetText()` function as follows:

```
func setMessage(email *client.EmailMessage) {
    subject.SetText(email.Subject)

    to.SetText(email.ToEmailString())
    from.SetText(email.FromEmailString())
    date.SetText(email.DateString())

    content.SetText(email.Content)
}
```

We will also create another helper function, `addEmail()`, to add a new email to the list. This is a change from the initial list of `widget.Label`s that we added to `widget.Group`—we are using buttons to utilize their built-in click handling. The button created in this function sets the label to be the email subject, as before, and calls the new `setMessage()` function if it is tapped:

```
func addEmail(email *client.EmailMessage) fyne.CanvasObject {
    return widget.NewButton(email.Subject, func() {
        setMessage(email)
    })
}
```

Then, the list code is updated to call the new `addEmail()` function when we load the user interface:

```
list := widget.NewGroup("Inbox")
for _, email := range server.ListMessages() {
    list.Append(addEmail(email))
}
```

Those are the only changes that we need to implement in order to make the browser interface functional. Now, let's add the appropriate handling code to the compose window.

Sending email

To complete the work on the compose view, we need to update the buttons callback. For the cancel button, all that's necessary is to call `Close()` on the window object. In the click handler for the send button, we will construct a new email and send it using the server object's `Send()` function. The `client.NewMessage()` function handles creation of the email object. All we need to do is use the `Entry.Text` field for each input in order to access the current state:

```
send := widget.NewButton("Send", func() {
   email := client.NewMessage(subject.Text, content.Text,
      client.Email(to.Text), "", time.Now())
   server.Send(email)
   compose.Close()
})
send.Style = widget.PrimaryButton
buttons := widget.NewHBox(
   layout.NewSpacer(),
   widget.NewButton("Cancel", func() {
      compose.Close()
   }),
   send)
```

With this code in place, the application should function in exactly the same way as the previous examples we've built. Although the compose window does not look any different, our email browser window now has some real data in that should look like this:

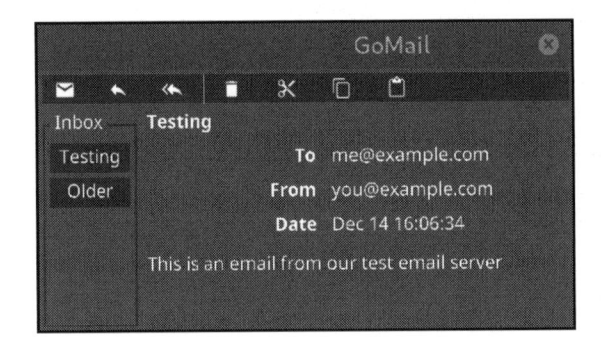

The completed GoMail interface in Fyne's default dark theme

[280]

As Fyne provides two built-in themes, we can also see how the application looks if users prefer a light colored theme. By setting the `FYNE_THEME` environment variable to "light", we can load the alternative theme, demonstrated as follows:

You can either set FYNE_THEME in the environment or pass it to the run command

Setting the correct theme value will result in a light version of the application loading instead:

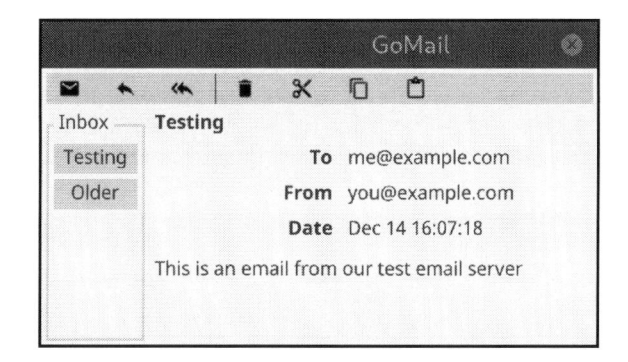

Our GoMail interface with the light Fyne theme

Before we complete this application, we should also cover the background processing portion—to handle when a new email arrives.

Background processing

Background processing that updates the user interface does not require any special thread handling code with Fyne. You can execute the full set of graphical and widget commands in any goroutine—the toolkit will take care of any system thread management.

Fyne - Material Design-Based GUI

To add incoming emails to the list in our application, all we need to do is call `addEmail()` for the new `client.EmailMessage` and pass that to the `list.Prepend()` function. The code is as straightforward as the following:

```
go func() {
   for email := range server.Incoming() {
      list.Prepend(addEmail(email))
   }
}()
```

That completes our basic GoMail application. Given the Fyne project's similarities to the Shiny toolkit that we explored in `Chapter 8`, *Shiny – Experimental Go GUI API*, let's also see how we could rebuild the image viewer application.

Building an image viewer

Since the Fyne toolkit includes a canvas API and image handling similar to the Shiny project, it makes sense to also compare with the image viewer application that we created in `Chapter 8`, *Shiny – Experimental Go GUI API*. Let's start, as usual, with the basic application layout.

Layout

As we will be working with canvas APIs, as well as widgets and layouts, we will need to start by importing most of the Fyne sub-packages. In addition to *canvas*, where we get the basic image APIs, we will also use the `theme` package for accessing icons and the `app` package to launch our application. We don't need to import the image libraries, such as `image/jpeg`, because Fyne image widgets import them for us:

```
import (
   "fyne.io/fyne"
   "fyne.io/fyne/app"
   "fyne.io/fyne/canvas"
   "fyne.io/fyne/layout"
   "fyne.io/fyne/theme"
   "fyne.io/fyne/widget"
)
```

As with any Fyne application, we start by creating an application using `app.New()` and then create a window for the application by calling `NewWindow()` with an appropriate title:

```
func main() {
    imageApp := app.New()
    win := imageApp.NewWindow("GoImages")

    ...
}
```

Next, we will create the widgets for the main layout. To achieve a visually distinct navigation bar, let's use a toolbar as in the GoMail application. In addition to standard icon buttons, we also add a spacer (with `widget.NewToolbarSpacer()`) so that the second button is right aligned in the bar. We will come back to the navigation later to add the filename display and functionality.

Next, we use the `widget.Group` widget to visually group the file listing (we could use the `widget.Box` widget if the border-less look is preferred). Into the group, we append various labels that will serve as file placeholders. Lastly, we load the image view to show the placeholder file. The `canvas.NewImageFromFile()` function handles all of the image loading for us, as can be seen in the following code block:

```
func main() {
    ...

    navBar := widget.NewToolbar(
        widget.NewToolbarAction(theme.NavigateBackIcon(), func() {}),
        widget.NewToolbarSpacer(),
        widget.NewToolbarAction(theme.NavigateNextIcon(), func() {}))
    fileList := widget.NewGroup("directory",
        widget.NewLabel("Image 1"),
        widget.NewLabel("Image 2"),
        widget.NewLabel("Image 3"))
    image := canvas.NewImageFromFile("shiny-hall.jpg")

    ...
}
```

For this application, a simple `layout.BorderLayout` will provide exactly the layout we are looking for. We create a new layout with `navBar` at the top and `fileList` on the left. The container also includes `image`, which will be stretched to fill the remaining space:

```
func main() {
    ...

    container := fyne.NewContainerWithLayout(
```

```
            layout.NewBorderLayout(navBar, nil, fileList, nil),
            navBar, fileList, image,
    )
    ...
}
```

Lastly, we set this container to be the content of our window, resize the whole window to be larger than the calculated minimum size, and show it. As before, we use `ShowAndRun()` as a shortcut to running the application with this first window:

```
func main() {
    ...
    win.SetContent(container)
    win.Resize(fyne.NewSize(640, 480))

    win.ShowAndRun()
}
```

With all of this code in place, the example can be run. You should see a window very much like the following (assuming you are using the default dark theme):

A basic image viewer layout using default Fyne widgets

Navigation

To complete the navigation bar, we need to also display the filename in the middle of the bar. As you may have noticed, there is no toolbar widget that allows the showing of text, but we can create our own. Every item in a toolbar implements the `widget.ToolbarItem` interface, so we can create a new type that follows this pattern. By implementing `ToolbarObject()` (the only function this interface requires), we can return the appropriate label to display:

```
type toolbarLabel struct {
}

func (t *toolbarLabel) ToolbarObject() fyne.CanvasObject {
    return widget.NewLabel("filename")
}
```

While we are updating the navigation bar, we should create placeholder functions that will handle the button presses for "previous" (left arrow) and "next" (right arrow). An empty parameter list matches the function type for a `widget.Button` callback, so these are simply as follows:

```
func previousImage() {}

func nextImage() {}
```

Lastly, we update the navigation bar creation to use the new `toolbarLabel` type that we created. By adding a second spacer widget, we are asking the layout to center the label as well as retain the right alignment of the **next** button:

```
navBar := widget.NewToolbar(
    widget.NewToolbarAction(theme.NavigateBackIcon(), previousImage),
    widget.NewToolbarSpacer(),
    &toolbarLabel{},
    widget.NewToolbarSpacer(),
    widget.NewToolbarAction(theme.NavigateNextIcon(), nextImage))
```

With these changes in place, running the code should result in the following updated navigation bar. We will return to this later to set the correct filename, but for now, we shall move on to the file listing on the left of the interface:

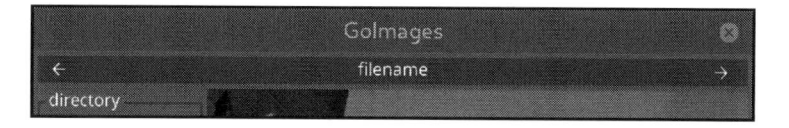

The navigation bar created using customized toolbar components

File listing

As the Fyne list widgets do not support icon and text combinations, we will need to construct one from basic components. Within the file group, we update each item to call a new function, `makeRow()`, that will be defined later on. We pass the filename to this function so that it can load the image and display a suitable caption:

```
fileList := widget.NewGroup("directory",
    makeRow("shiny-hall.jpg"),
    makeRow("shiny-hall.jpg"),
    makeRow("shiny-hall.jpg"))
```

The new `makeRow()` function will return a horizontal box widget containing the image preview and caption text. The preview image is loaded using `canvas.NewImageFromFile()` and a suitable size is set using `SetMinSize()`. To be consistent in terms of sizing, `theme.IconInlineSize()` is used for height and a 50% larger width—assuming most pictures are landscape. Finally, this is returned in a horizontal box, along with a new label widget, using `widget.NewHBox()`:

```
func makeRow(text string, file string) fyne.CanvasObject {
    preview := canvas.NewImageFromFile(file)
    iconHeight := theme.IconInlineSize()
    preview.SetMinSize(fyne.NewSize(int(float32(iconHeight)*1.5), iconHeight))

    return widget.NewHBox(preview, widget.NewLabel(text))
}
```

With these changes in place, you should see the same interface with icon previews before each filename. Before we are done with the layout, let's polish the image view and see how we can maintain the image aspect ratio:

Placeholder files and image thumbnails added to the interface

Image view

To complete the image viewer layout, we need to look at the main image view. The default behavior for images in Fyne is that they'll expand to fill the available space (this is the `canvas.ImageFillStretch` mode). However, we want the image to maintain its aspect ratio, as well as remain within the bounds of the viewing area. We will also add a background pattern as we did in the Shiny example in Chapter 8, *Shiny – Experimental Go GUI API*.

Firstly, we create a new image for the background pattern. Fyne provides a helper method to create an image that's drawn dynamically called `canvas.NewRasterWithPixels()`. It takes a single parameter, which is the pixel calculation function that returns `color.Color` for the pixel requested. Its parameters are `x, y, width, height` (all `int` variables). This means that we can use just the `x` and `y` coordinates, or we can perform calculations based on the width and height values (that specify the number of pixels on each axis).

In our checker pattern implementation, we simply return a light or dark gray color to make a pattern of squares. The blocks are 10 x 10 pixels in size and we calculate which square a pixel coordinate is within, as follows:

```
func checkerColor(x, y, _, _ int) color.Color {
    xr := x/10
    yr := y/10

    if xr%2 == yr%2 {
        return color.RGBA{0xc0, 0xc0, 0xc0, 0xff}
    } else {
        return color.RGBA{0x99, 0x99, 0x99, 0xff}
    }
}
```

The checker pattern image is created by passing our `checkerColor` function to the `canvas.NewRasterWithPixels()` function. This variable can now be used like any other `canvas.Image` type:

```
checkers := canvas.NewRasterWithPixels(checkerColor)
```

Additionally, the main image view should be set to maintain its aspect ratio within the available space. To do so, we set the `FillMode` field of the `image` variable to `canvas.ImageFillContain`. Like the CSS3 definition, this will center the image at the largest scaled size that fits within the space:

```
image := canvas.NewImageFromFile("shiny-hall.jpg")
image.FillMode = canvas.ImageFillContain
```

Lastly, the checker pattern image is added to our layout. By passing it before the main image object, we specify that it is layered lower in the draw order, and therefore set as a background. Notice that any item not listed as specifically positioned in a border position is sized to fill the remaining space. In this way, our image view is drawn above the background and both are set to fill the space inside our border widgets:

```
container := fyne.NewContainerWithLayout(
    layout.NewBorderLayout(navBar, nil, fileList, nil),
    navBar, fileList, checkers, image,
)
```

Updating the code with these changes results in the completed image viewer layout, which should look like the following:

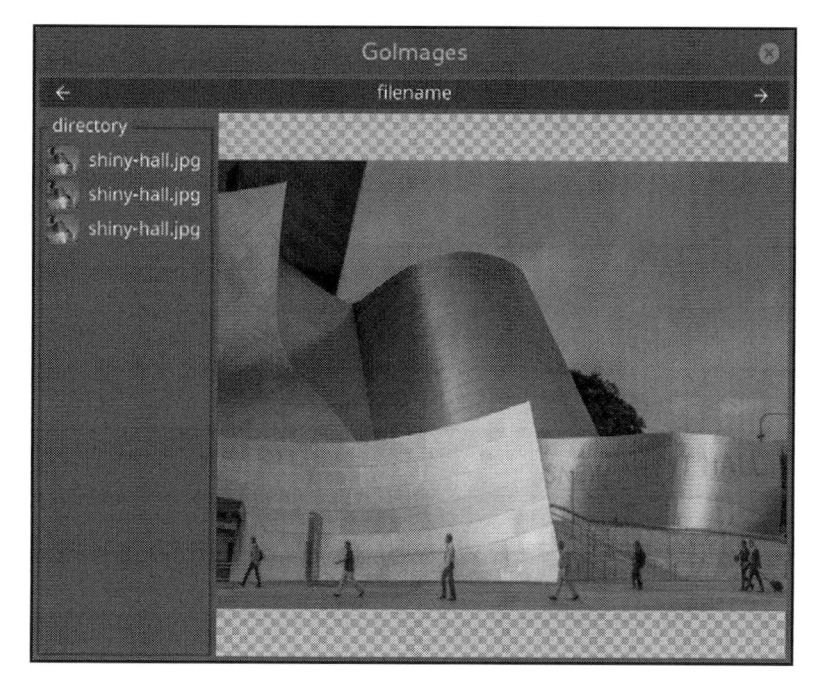

Centering the image over a checkerboard pattern

Communicating with the GUI

To add the code that handles updating the GUI and responding to user events, we will need to save references to some widgets that have been created; mainly the `widget.Label` toolbar and the main view, `canvas.Image`. By storing these references, we can update their content later.

Additionally, we will add a `[]string` to list `images` for the directory we are accessing and save `int index` of the current image so that we can calculate the previous and the next. Once those are created, we can fill in the content of our `previousImage()` and `nextImage()` functions to call a new `chooseImage()` function that will update the display:

```
var images []string
var index int
```

Fyne - Material Design-Based GUI

```
var image *canvas.Image
var label *widget.Label

func previousImage() {
   if index == 0 {
      return
   }

   chooseImage(index-1)
}

func nextImage() {
   if index == len(images)-1 {
      return
   }

   chooseImage(index+1)
}
```

The `chooseImage()` function accesses the file path from the image list that will be loaded later and uses this information to update our user interface. From `path`, we call `label.SetText()` to show the filename and then set `image.File` to update the path for the main image display:

```
func chooseImage(id int) {
   path := images[id]
   label.SetText(filepath.Base(path))
   image.File = path
   canvas.Refresh(image)
   index = id
}
```

To most easily implement the click handling behavior in order to choose an image from the list, we will change from `widget.Label` to `widget.Button` items. As the buttons have a different color background, we should tidy up the display by
using `layout.BorderLayout` so that the buttons fill the available space. Finally, because buttons are taller than labels, we update the `minSize()` preview code to be relative to the button's minimum height rather than the previous inline icon size defined by the theme:

```
func makeRow(id int, path string) fyne.CanvasObject {
   filename := filepath.Base(path)
   button := widget.NewButton(filename, func() {
      chooseImage(id)
   })

   preview := canvas.NewImageFromFile(path)
   iconHeight := button.MinSize().Height
```

[290]

```
        preview.SetMinSize(fyne.NewSize(int(float32(iconHeight)*1.5),
           iconHeight))

        return fyne.NewContainerWithLayout(
           layout.NewBorderLayout(nil, nil, preview, nil),
           preview, button)
    }
```

Next, we need to add a `getImageList()` function that will access the list of images in a directory. The contents of this function are identical to the same function in Chapter 8, *Shiny – Experimental Go GUI API*, so it is omitted here for brevity. With that in place, we can update our `makeList()` function, which now takes a `dir` parameter, to load the image file list and create the new rows using `makeRow()`, as well as populating our stored `images` list:

```
    func makeList(dir string) *widget.Group {
        files := getImageList(dir)
        group := widget.NewGroup(filepath.Base(dir))

        for idx, name := range files {
           path := filepath.Join(dir, name)
           images = append(images, path)

           group.Append(makeRow(idx, path))
        }

        return group
    }
```

We then update the creation of the `fileList` in `main()` function to pass a directory path to load:

```
    fileList := makeList(dirpath)
```

As with the previous GoImages code, we can use the built-in `flag` handling to allow users to specify the directory to display. The code is listed here and we can invoke it simply by setting the preceding `dirpath` variable to the result of `parseArgs()` (if you add this code, remember to import the `flag`, `fmt`, and `os` packages):

```
    func parseArgs() string {
        dir, _ := os.Getwd()

        flag.Usage = func() {
           fmt.Println("goimages takes a single, optional, directory parameter")
        }
        flag.Parse()
```

Fyne - Material Design-Based GUI

```
    if len(flag.Args()) > 1 {
        flag.Usage()
        os.Exit(2)
    } else if len(flag.Args()) == 1 {
        dir = flag.Args()[0]

        if _, err := ioutil.ReadDir(dir); os.IsNotExist(err) {
            fmt.Println("Directory", dir, "does not exist or could not be read")
            os.Exit(1)
        }
    }

    return dir
}
```

Updating all of the preceding code should result in our complete image viewer application. If you'd prefer to access the complete code, this can be downloaded from this book's source code repository on GitHub:

Our completed image viewer showing a wallpaper directory

As with the previous GoMail example, we can load this interface using the light theme by specifying `FYNE_THEME=light` in the command-line environment:

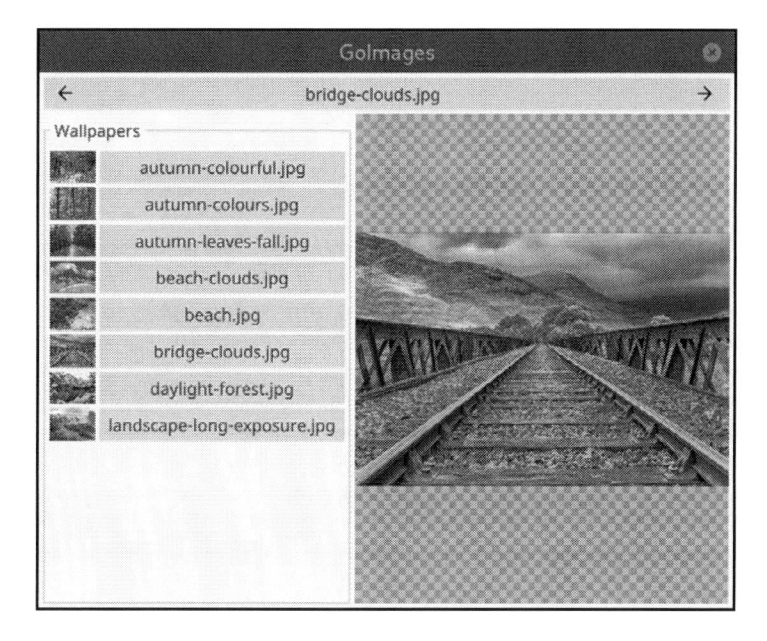

The same app and directory with the Fyne light theme

Background processing

With Fyne a lot of image handling is already processing on multiple threads, but that may not be enough for image-intensive applications. In this GoImages app, there are many images being loaded before the user interface is displayed. We can update the image handling to allow the GUI to display faster. To do so, we once again create a new `asyncImage` type, that loads the image on a background thread before displaying it. Whereas Shiny was passing the images directly to the rendering, here, we are providing them to a `canvas.Image` object, so the code is slightly different.

Fyne - Material Design-Based GUI

We start by creating the basic `asyncImage` type—its main work is in the `load()` function, which will run on a background thread. The `loadPath()` function sets up the path to the file to be loaded and starts the background processing. Notice that once we've changed the image data, we need to call `canvas.Refresh()` to ensure the interface updates—there is no need for any thread-handling code, since Fyne will deal with that for us:

```go
type asyncImage struct {
    path   string
    image  *canvas.Image
    pixels image.Image
}

func (a *asyncImage) load() {
    if a.path == "" {
        return
    }
    reader, err := os.Open(a.path)
    if err != nil {
        log.Fatal(err)
    }
    defer reader.Close()

    a.pixels, _, err = image.Decode(reader)
    if err != nil {
        log.Fatal(err)
    }

    canvas.Refresh(a.image)
}

func (a *asyncImage) loadPath(path string) {
    a.path = path
    go a.load()
}
```

As this async image loader will be providing raw image data to the image widget, we also need to implement the `image.Image` API. In each of the methods, we check to see whether the `pixels` variable has been set (it will be `nil` until the image is loaded), returning the appropriate value or a sensible fallback:

```go
func (a *asyncImage) ColorModel() color.Model {
    if a.pixels == nil {
        return color.RGBAModel
    }

    return a.pixels.ColorModel()
}
```

```
func (a *asyncImage) Bounds() image.Rectangle {
    if a.pixels == nil {
        return image.ZR
    }

    return a.pixels.Bounds()
}

func (a *asyncImage) At(x, y int) color.Color {
    if a.pixels == nil {
        return color.Transparent
    }

    return a.pixels.At(x, y)
}
```

Lastly, our `asyncImage` type would benefit from a convenience constructor to set up the `image` widget that will render. We also begin the loading of the first image file, `path`, on a background thread:

```
func newAsyncImage(path string) *asyncImage {
    async := &asyncImage{}
    async.image = canvas.NewImageFromImage(async)
    async.loadPath(path)

    return async
}
```

To complete the use of our asynchronous image loader, we update the `chooseImage()` function to set the new path. With this change, the application will be loading all images on a background thread instead of on the main loop. Go will distribute this across our processors appropriately to make use of the available CPU:

```
func chooseImage(id int) {
    path := images[id]
    label.SetText(filepath.Base(path))
    async.loadPath(path)
    index = id
}
```

Running this new version of the application will load noticeably faster. You'll also see the images appear as the loading of each file is completed. By using the simple `canvas.Refresh()` call after we load each image, we ensure that the user interface updates appropriately.

Summary

In this chapter, we looked at the last of the toolkits to be explored in this book, Fyne. We learned how it was created specifically for Go so as to make it simple to build graphical applications. We quickly got set up with the toolkit and explored how to build applications that will run identically on macOS, Windows, and Linux.

We looked at the architecture of the Fyne toolkit and its use of vector graphics to provide scalable graphical interfaces. By learning the features of the `layout`, `canvas`, and `widget` packages, we saw how to quickly build basic user interfaces. We also saw how Fyne provides two different themes, *light* and *dark*, which will be used based on user settings or environment variables.

Applying this knowledge, we built the sixth version of our GoMail application, which included built-in material design icons and avoided any thread-handling complexities. We also explored the image APIs and background processing capabilities by re-building the GoImages application designed in `Chapter 8`, *Shiny – Experimental Go GUI API*.

Now that we've explored the main toolkits available, we will move to `Section 4`, *Growing and Distributing Your Application*. In the final part of this book, we change focus to topics that apply to all graphical applications, regardless of the toolkit used. We will explore topics that help polish and distribute complete graphical user interfaces, starting with `Chapter 11`, *Navigation and Multiple Windows*.

Section 4: Growing and Distributing Your Application

Throughout `Section 2`, *Toolkits Using Existing Widgets*, and `Section 3`, *Modern Graphical Toolkits*, we have looked in detail at the most popular toolkits available for building graphical applications with the Go language. Each framework has a different background and vision and many vary in the platforms they support. You may already have a strong idea about which is the best API for your next application, but irrespective of the technology you plan to use, there are many other things to consider in building and managing a growing or complex graphical application.

In this section, we will look at various topics related to more substantial GUIs than those that we explored in the earlier chapters. We will cover what you will need to consider when designing more complicated graphical interfaces, and how to manage them on different platforms. Concurrency and network programming are often a challenge when applications connect to modern cloud and distributed services, so we will look at how these can be integrated into applications using the Go language and standard libraries.

At the end of this section, we will turn to managing your code and applications as they grow. We will cover best practices for developing graphical applications and how they apply to the Go language. Lastly, we will prepare our applications for distribution, looking at how the benefit of cross-platform development can lead to complications when we want to deploy our software.

The chapters in this section are as follows:

- `Chapter 11`, *Navigation and Multiple Windows*
- `Chapter 12`, *Concurrency, Networking, and Cloud Services*
- `Chapter 13`, *Best Practices in Go GUI Development*
- `Chapter 14`, *Distributing Your Application*

11
Navigation and Multiple Windows

Through the last seven chapters, we've explored how to build a fairly simple graphical user interface using different toolkits and technologies. In each example, we saw benefits to the widget and API design but also challenges that are often faced when picking a toolkit. In this chapter, we're shifting focus to the planning and implementation of a more complex GUI—the sorts of challenges that will be encountered irrespective of the toolkit and technology selected.

In this chapter, we'll cover the following topics:

- Planning the workflow of a more complex GUI
- Window management and notifications for a clean user experience
- Operating system-specific details and how to adapt a cross-platform application

At the end of this chapter, you'll have examined the bigger picture questions of application flow and navigation in a more complex graphical application. You'll have thought about how your GUI will fit within the current platform's flow and how to notify or engage the user as appropriate. So, let's get started by looking at the navigation of a complex application.

Planning application layout

Planning a large graphical application can seem like a daunting task, if you're thinking about all of the different users of your software and the varied devices it'll be used on. Or, it may seem quite straightforward if your ambitions can be realized by using standard design applications (such as Qt Creator or Glade for GTK+) that can generate code from a drag-and-drop interface. Unsurprisingly, creating a great user experience for your application interface will probably take a while to explore, plan, and design for the best result. The largest complexity is likely the navigation or overall layout of the application—we'll look first at layout techniques across multiple platforms.

Standard layouts

Each of the toolkits we've explored provide standard layout components that help to organize widgets and interface elements in neat, standardized arrangements. When you think about the naming of these layouts, however (for example, VBox, Border, and Frame), they typically describe fine-grained control rather than higher-level design concepts. For this section, we need to step back a little and think about the overall flow of an application, what will be the most used parts of the application, and what should the user see when they first load the user interface.

As discussed in `Chapter 2`, *Graphical User Interface Challenges*, desktop applications have been standardized around a fairly common layout: menu, toolbar, palettes, and content. As applications have grown more complicated, there have been attempts to fit more functions and features into this space to allow users to gain access to the full feature set of these increasingly powerful applications. Since the rise in popularity of smart phones and mobile applications, there has been a lot of discussion about better use of screen real estate and how to make a great user experience with limited resources.

Research into the use of screens, readability of content, and related topics is now commonplace in relation to web design as well. Topics such as *How eye scanning impacts visual hierarchy in UX design* are often seen on recommended reading lists for those looking to improve their site's usability or user retention. With this in mind, we, as desktop or cross-platform application creators, should probably be thinking much more carefully about how our software is presented and whether the traditional methods fit with our specific use cases.

Some GUI toolkits are beginning to provide higher-level layouts that reflect intention rather than a static visual layout. For example, `UISplitViewController` in Apple's iOS presents a list view and detail view side by side when space is available or one view at a time (the detail view slides on when the list is tapped) when screens are smaller:

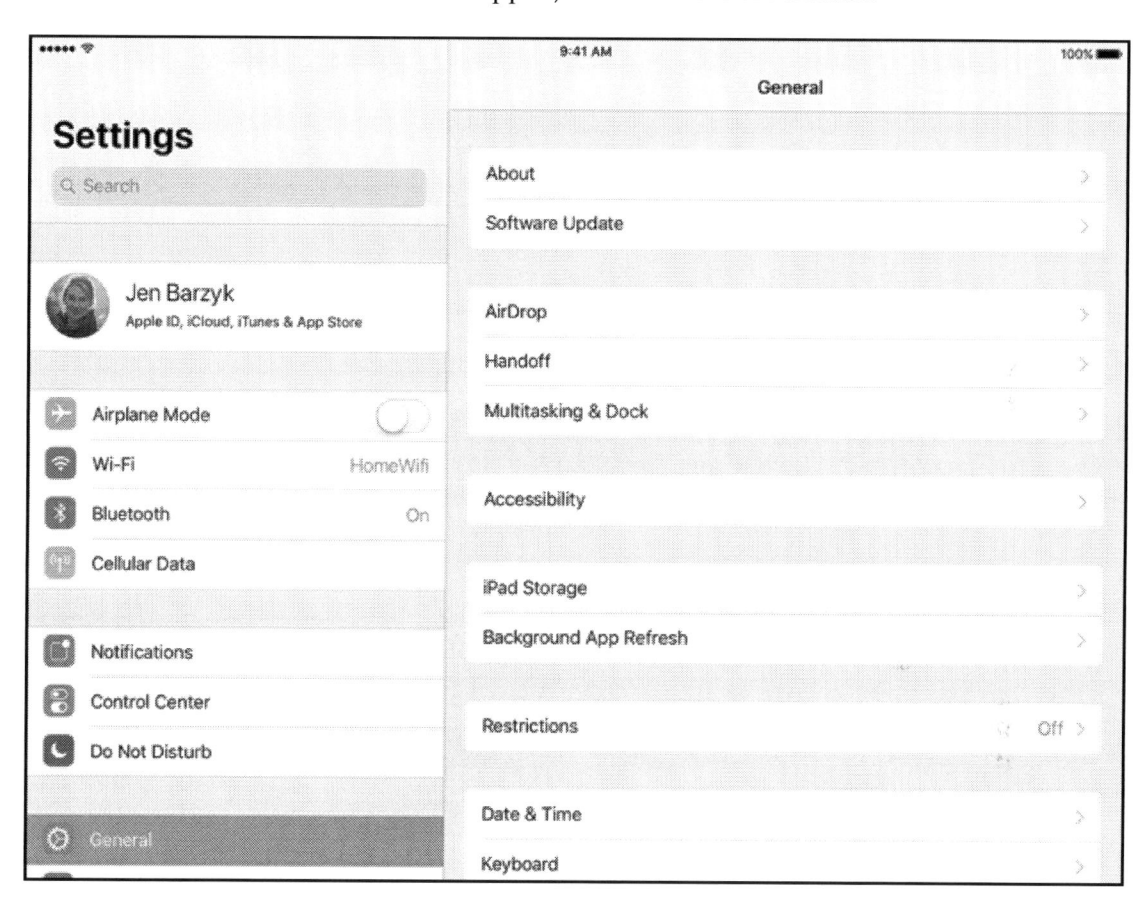

An iOS split pane used for iPad settings app
(Image copyright: Apple)

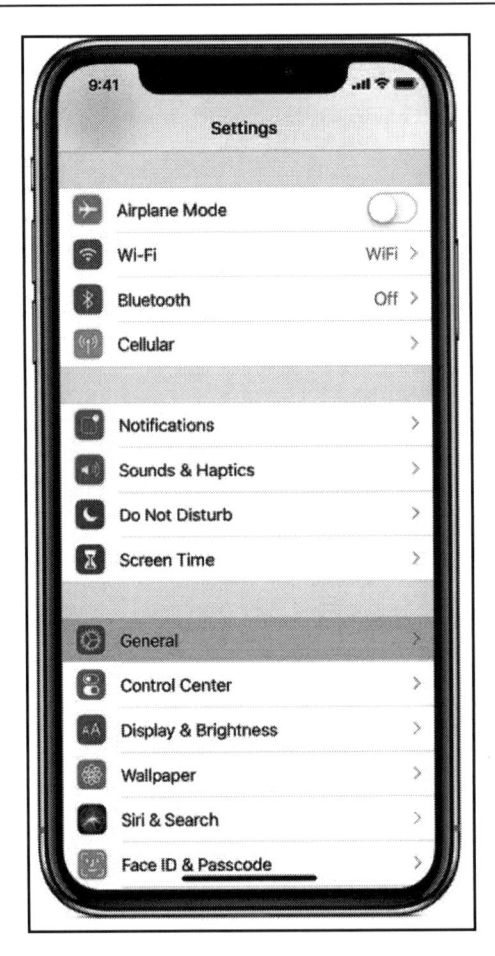

Navigation and Multiple Windows

The same split pane on an iPhone
(Image copyright: Apple)

Where possible, these should be used in your application so your interface is configured appropriately for the current device, but there may be further customization needed. Let's look at some of the factors that impact more complex layout design.

Device form factors

While primarily a consideration for mobile and modern portable devices, an application layout should be designed with the physical design of the device in mind. Visual and interaction technologies on the desktop have remained largely consistent for 25 years, leading to standardized interface designs—but this too is changing. Computers are now more commonly shipping with ultra high definition screens, many of which are also touch surfaces. If your approach to cross-platform application development is to also include mobile devices, you will need to consider the small screen sizes as well as orientation of the device.

Of course, the screen isn't the only factor to consider; it's now also common for input devices to vary. A mouse and keyboard is probably the main configuration for user input but many portable computers now have a *tablet mode* where touch input is a replacement for the mouse and a virtual keyboard can appear for text input. If this is a configuration you want to support, then your layout will need to work when parts of the screen (probably the bottom edge) is covered with the virtual keyboard. More importantly, finger-based input (most commonly called *multi-touch*) is far richer than a point and click approach; will your application aim to support *pinch to zoom* or *touch rotation*? If you intend to support these sorts of features, then make sure your chosen framework supports *input gestures*. Each toolkit is evolving rapidly and so the details have been omitted from this book as it would be out of date by publication.

In addition to the full device capabilities, a traditional desktop application can be moved around and made different sizes or orientations by many user actions—should your design aim to accommodate these changes in configuration? When displaying applications side by side on a tablet device, you'll see how powerful the different layouts can be when implemented correctly.

Responsive or adaptive design

To be able to suit a wide variety of devices, it normally won't be possible to use a single user interface design. Therefore, some form of adaptation to the current environment will probably be necessary. There are two main schools of thought with regard to adapting to variations in screen and device capability: responsive and adaptive designs. Both aim to provide an appropriate user experience with an interface that feels native to the current device. While these principles currently refer mostly to web application design, they can also be applied to native applications, especially if designing for multiple platforms.

Navigation and Multiple Windows

When following adaptive principles, application designers will choose a limited set of device configurations to design for, typically a mobile device (possibly in multiple orientations), a tablet device, and a regular desktop. By designing for these categories, the amount of time spent designing for specific devices is reduced, focusing only on these defined configurations. When focusing on a small number of variations, the design can be perfected for these different use cases, creating a very smooth experience. When implemented this way, an application will detect which category of device it's running on and load the appropriate layout (sometimes this is handled automatically by the framework). This approach has been exemplified by Apple's iOS SDK (user interfaces are defined for iPhone, iPhone Plus, and iPad), the correct user interface will be loaded and a single application can execute with any configuration. The limitation of the adaptive approach is that *intermediate* devices, ones that are smaller or larger than expected (or with unusual configurations), will probably not look or function as the user may expect.

Responsive design, on the other hand, aims to define a single user interface that responds to the current device configuration. Layouts created in this manner will typically have certain trigger values or inflection points that determine the visibility of elements or the positioning and sizing of items that should always be shown (in CSS, this is usually done with *media queries*). The responsive technique is becoming more popular in designing websites that wish to provide a good experience on a huge range of different devices; it probably won't provide the perfect user interface that adaptive design aims for, but it does cater for every device from the smallest, least capable to the full desktop experience. This approach maps well to the cross-platform approach that's likely part of the intention of a team developing application GUIs with Go because we don't usually know the devices that our software will be run on ahead of time.

The toolkits explored in this book offer some amount of support for responsive layouts. Grids that lay out the content according to the space available and the screen layout are a good place to start. Some are pushing further into this space by providing semantic layouts that'll adapt correctly to the current device:

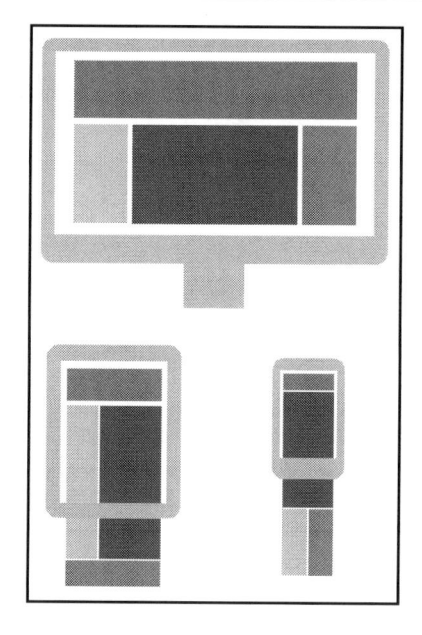

An example of a possible responsive layout at three different sizes

Custom layouts

It's likely that your application has requirements that are different to standard layouts or more complicated than the toolkit's API supports. Using standard layouts where possible is recommended but that doesn't have to mean giving up on your ideal application design. Every toolkit supports custom layouts in some manner that you can make use of to fill the gaps in the available standard layouts. When implementing a custom layout in this manner, the basic approach is to set a fixed position for each component within the parent container. To better adapt to the available screen space, remember to factor in the current width and height of the interface; it's often easier to implement using ratios or percentages rather than absolute values (for example, a list component is 25% of the screen width or content columns are 1/3 of the available space).

In more advanced toolkits, there's also a *constraints-based* layout available, one that lays out components based on configured equations instead of hardcode values. The standard algorithm for constraints layouts is named Cassowary and is fully documented at `http://overconstrained.io/`. The basic principle is that each layout value can be defined as the result of an equation in the form `item1.attr1 = item2.attr2 × multiplier + constant` (such as `button.top = content.bottom × 1.0 + 25`). Constraints-based layouts (also known as **auto layouts**) are standard in iOS and Android but not so common in desktop toolkits. Modern GUIs often include this functionality as standard but using this functionality in others such as Qt and GTK will require the integration of third-party projects (as these aren't currently available through Go bindings, the integration is out of scope for this chapter):

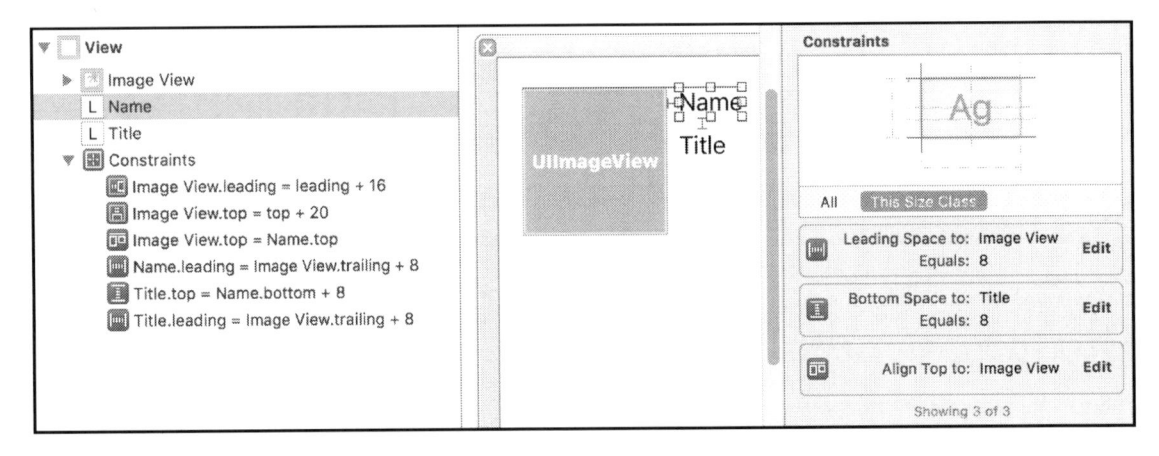

Adding constraints to a label with Xcode (image copyright: Big Nerd Ranch, LLC)

Navigating your application

Consistent and easy-to-follow navigation through a complex application is hard to attain but doing it well can lead to dramatically improved user experience. A typical application has a core set of functionality—which should always be easy to access—and a larger set of additional tools and helpful features that are used less frequently. Keeping the balance between core features and additional functionality is something that many applications haven't yet solved. Overcrowded toolbars and very long menus are problems we encounter on a regular basis:

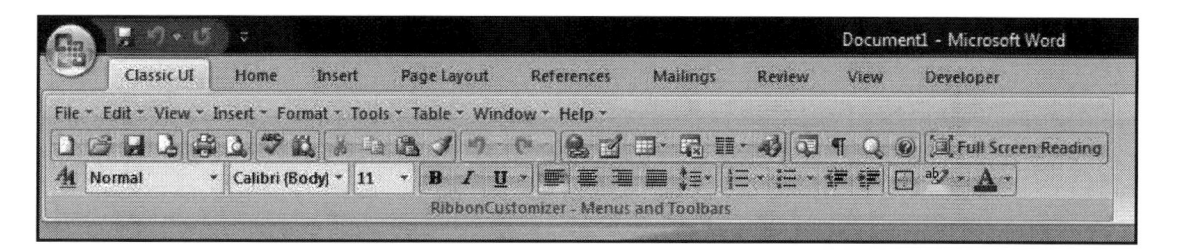

Menus, toolbars, shortcuts, and drop-down lists all above a document in Microsoft Office 2007

Finding ways to limit the various options onscreen should lead to less user confusion. It's the responsibility of an application designer to make a clear and easy-to-use interface, not to present all of the options and expect users to learn how to navigate. There are various methods for adjusting a user interface to focus on the essential or most useful features; we'll explore them in the following sections.

Progressive disclosure

In larger applications (as previously illustrated), it's likely that the number of features available can't easily be presented in a minimal user interface. When that's the case, application designers will have a new challenge in creating a smooth learning curve for new users. How can an application's user interface be designed both for a complex feature set and to be easy to learn by people who are new to the product?

Progressive disclosure is a technique for helping to focus a user's attention and facilitate learning a complex system. This is achieved by hiding functionality or data that isn't necessary to support the task at hand. Commonly, this is implemented by starting with a basic set of functionality visible and expanding as the user explores areas beyond the basics. Triggers to expand the functionality available may be accessing a new menu item, an **Advanced** button, or simply using the application for a certain time or adding sufficient data.

Example 1 – Microsoft Edge

A standard feature of popular web browsers is the developer tools that they include—but this isn't core functionality. When building their new web browser, Edge, Microsoft decided to focus on the core features, hiding more advanced functionality, such as developer tools, from the average user.

Navigation and Multiple Windows

If enabled through a single menu item (the **...** menu, then **F12 Developer Tools**) or the *F12* keyboard shortcut, the developer features are switched on. From then on, the browser will present developer features in all of the expected places, creating a much richer application feature set:

The default Edge context menu

F12 or Developer Tools menu item:

After developer tools are enabled

Example 2 – Skyscanner flight search

The main functionality of the Skyscanner service (https://www.skyscanner.net/) is to search through the many flights available, matching a certain criteria based on price, time, location, and so forth. After finding a suitable journey in the (initially minimal looking) mobile app, a user would normally go through a booking process to purchase their flights.

If they aren't ready to make the purchase, a user of the application can *favorite* a flight combination for later. Upon doing this, a menu will appear in the application from which favorite searches can be returned to. If these searches are visited many times, then another new feature called *watched flights* appears, which allows more advanced holiday planners to monitor the varying prices of their searches.

Menus and toolbars

When there are many items that you wish to provide to users of your application, a menu or toolbar are convenient options, but should be used carefully and sparingly. Too many options added to a toolbar can add to the cluttered *ribbon* user interface from Microsoft Office, as previously displayed. Likewise, adding a menu item for every feature will probably lead to cognitive overload as users spend too much time trying to find an item or remember where it's located.

Toolbar

A toolbar is ideally suited for actions that'll be used on a regular basis. For example, in our email application **Reply** will be a popular action, as will **New** and **Delete**. Grouping toolbar items together by similarity (for example, **Reply** and **Reply All** or **Cut**, **Copy**, and **Paste**) will help users to find your shortcuts quickly. Ordering these groups by likelihood of use will mean that, if the user interface is smaller than expected, then the most useful features will still be visible. To provide access to tools that don't fit onto the screen, you can use an overflow item (where it pops out a list of not-visible items), make the tool bar scrollable, or provide access in a different place, such as a menu or second row.

Toolbars are popular in most form factors of devices, from small phones up to large desktop applications. The main difference is clearly the number of items that can be included. If you're including toolbars in a responsive or adaptive layout, you may consider a more complex strategy than leftmost-visible. For example, in an email application, if only five items can be displayed, then removing **Reply All** so **Delete** can be seen might be a good approach; the user could always choose to reply to all in the compose window after pressing **Reply**.

Navigation and Multiple Windows

Many applications choose to allow items in the toolbar to be rearranged, a feature that's provided by some graphical toolkits (for example, UIKit for Apple's iOS devices and AppKit for their desktop applications):

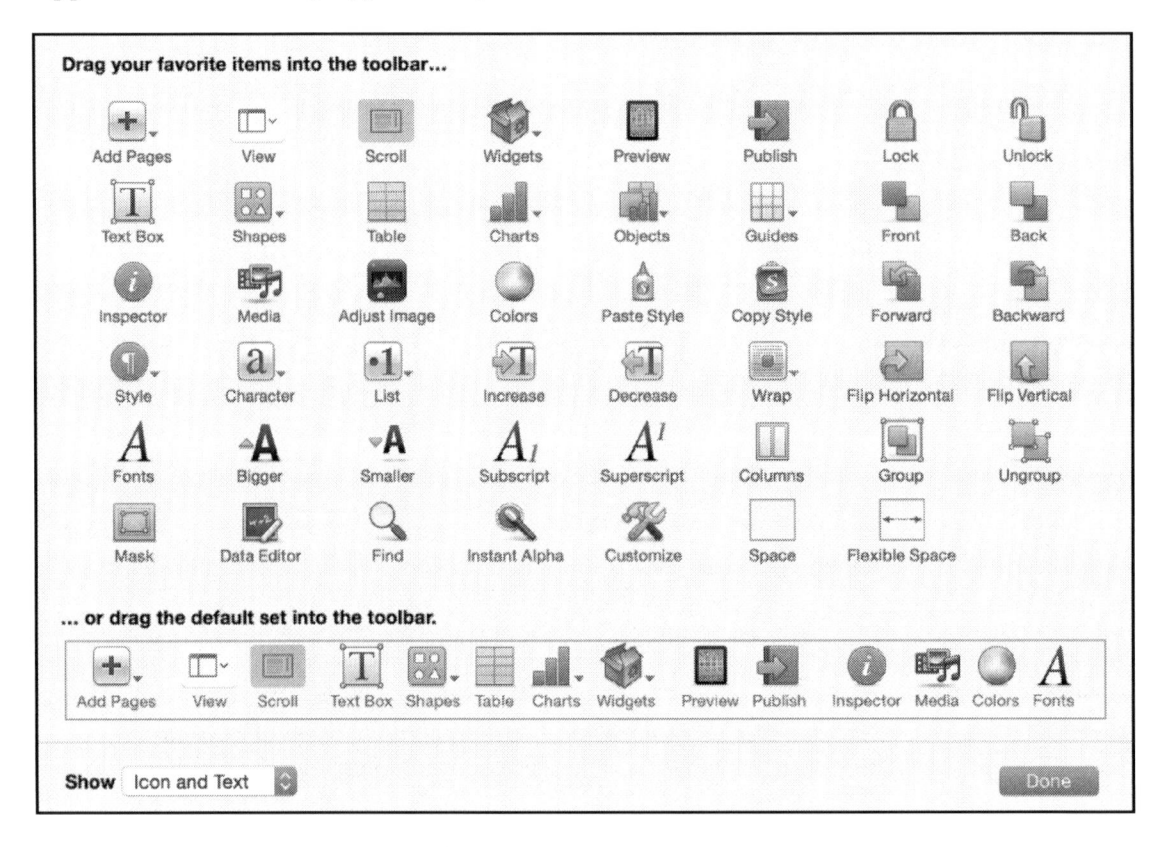

A sample user interface for customizing toolbars in macOS (image copyright: Apple)

Menu

Menu bars have traditionally been thought of as the right location to place all otherwise absent feature access in an application. With a long list of items in a growing number of menu headings, an application menu can quickly become hard to navigate. This is generally considered to be due to the number of items that an average human can hold in their short-term memory. Experiments by George Miller in 1956 suggested that the number of objects that can typically be held in working memory is between five and nine (seven plus or minus two—Miller's "Magical Number"). More recent estimates have shown that this number is typically lower, closer to just four or five items.

Chapter 11

Taking this into consideration, we can understand why it's important to keep menus fewer and shorter—at every step of navigating, there should be no more than nine options available—and far less, if possible.

The presentation of a menu varies from one platform to another with the standard top of the window or top of the screen being most common on the desktop, and an icon at the top-left of the screen (known as the hamburger) most prevalent on mobile layouts. What you'll notice, regardless of the layout, is that the top-level list will be around five items and, if further options are required, the menus that cascade down won't be much longer than that. If you find your menus becoming overwhelmingly long, perhaps consider task-specific toolbars or other grouping of context-relevant shortcuts, possibly opened from a single menu item.

Whatever design you choose for making features available, please remember the user's main focus or the current context.

You don't want to end up overwhelming them to the point that there's significant thinking required at every step of the way:

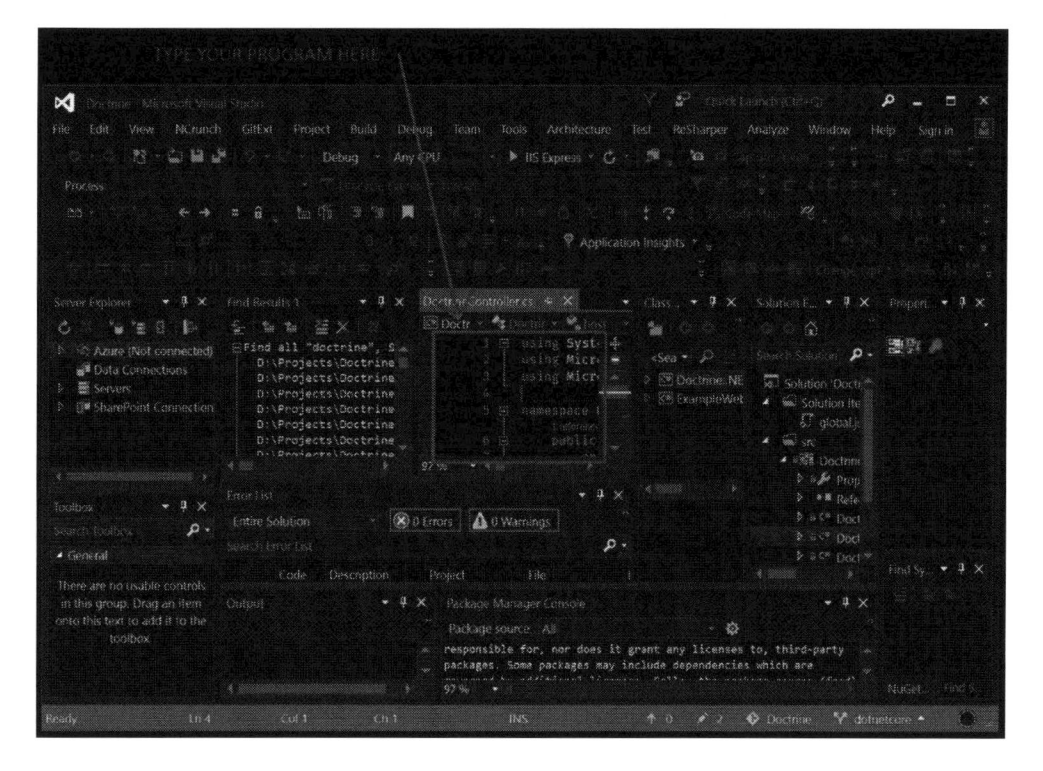

Visual Studio with all of its viewers and toolbars switched on (copyright Dylan Beattie)

Multiple windows

One more approach that can help your application to be easier to navigate is to split the content into multiple windows. Each will be a different view of your application, within which the appropriate toolbars or menus can be presented for the current context. As shown in our GoMail examples, we compose new messages in a separate window; this allows us to group editing-related items close to the input fields and allows us to simultaneously be drafting multiple messages without cluttering our email browse window.

Of course, multiple windows won't necessarily have the same semantics on different platforms. If we were to take the same approach on a smart phone device, it would be common for the compose window to be presented as an overlay to the existing application. Whether the user can switch between that mode and the browse window may be down to the operating system's design or we may decide that, when running on a smaller device, the compose window should be a *modal* window (that is, it blocks access to the parent window. This is discussed further later).

Yet another approach that we saw in `Chapter 2`, *Graphical User Interface Challenges*, was to have multiple windows for the main focus of the applications. These peripheral windows are typically for toolbars or detailed information/control of the content in the main window and can be particularly helpful in content creation-based applications. With the content expanding to fill the whole of the main window, the toolbars and context actions have been placed in separate windows to keep the user focused. This type of layout and navigation is usually adopted in *pro* applications where the user knows the domain well. The added complexity of this approach can lead to confusion for early users of a product and so we, as application designers and developers, should be mindful of the number of windows or different layouts and contexts we present in our user interface.

Window types and keeping things clean

Managing multiple windows will become essential for any application, either through part of a layout design like the preceding, or for presenting important information to the user to gain their attention or receive their input. For each window that's displayed in your application, it's important to know whether its appearance should attract their immediate attention, support what's already onscreen, or simply be something that can be attended to later. Knowing the intention of each window shown will help to support, rather than impede, the user workflow and keep your application's user experience clean.

Standard dialogs

The most common reason to show an additional window during application flow is to ask the user for additional input or confirmation, or to alert them of (typically unexpected) events. These are standard interactions and so it's usually most effective to use, where possible, the provided dialog windows defined by the toolkit being used. Using the provided APIs will generally provide the most consistent user experience and will almost certainly lead to less code in your application as well.

The types of standard dialogs provided by a toolkit will normally include file handling (open and save), progress (when the user must wait), message (to show warnings or errors), and a confirmation dialog (to ask an immediate question). On more advanced toolkits, you can also expect to find dialog APIs to help with color selection, font selection, document printing, and even a standardized **About** window. The following APIs are great places to get started with some of the toolkits we covered earlier in this book (with namespace included if it's not the default):

	walk	andlabs UI	GoGTK	qt	Fyne
open	ShowOpen	OpenFile	NewFileChooserDialog	widgets.NewQFileDialog	
save	ShowSave	SaveFile	NewFileChooserDialog	widgets.NewQFileDialog	
progress				widgets.NewQProgressDialog	dialog.NewProgress
message		MsgBox MsgBoxError	NewMessageDialog	widgets.NewQMessageBox widgets.NewErrorMessage	dialog.ShowInformation dialog.ShowError
confirm				widgets.NewQMessageBox	dialog.ShowConfirmation
input				widgets.NewQInputDialog	
color				widgets.NewQColorDialog	
font			FontSelection	widgets.NewQFontDialog	
print				printsupport.NewQPrintDialog	
about			NewAboutDialog		
custom	NewDialog		NewDialog	widgets.NewQDialog	dialog.ShowCustom

It's often useful to show a small selection or confirmation window that isn't in the preceding list (either because your requirements are different or the toolkit hasn't implemented that feature). This can be achieved by creating a new window, packing the content, and showing it, but the recommended method is to use the custom dialog API instead. Showing a dialog instead of a standard window allows the toolkit to configure the window to best effect. This typically involves setting it to be a non-resizable, topmost window that's *modal* (meaning the user can't interact with the window underneath until the dialog is dismissed).

Modal windows

As suggested previously, a modal window is one that blocks user input to the window that it's above. This typically means it's placed in the center of a parent window and the window below will be disabled or grayed out, focusing the user interaction on the new dialog window. This is typical of dialog windows as they're designed to appear only when the user can't continue with the current task until the information, confirmation, or progress is completed (at which point the dialog disappears and control returns).

To function in this way, a modal window is usually passed the parent window that it should occlude. The input will be forced to the new modal window (depending on the desktop environment and configuration, this may not be the case if the parent window isn't currently the topmost application) to interact with the new interface. Different platforms can present modal windows using various styles; some will look like a regular window (often with maximize and minimize buttons disabled), others will present the content embedded within the current window, and others (such as macOS) can present them appearing from the title bar of the parent window. Using the built-in API for custom dialogs will mean that these visual styles are consistent within your application.

There may be a reason, however, that your application requires a new window to take focus in a different type of workflow. For these cases, a toolkit often allows the *modality* of a window to be set directly. This can be a powerful feature but be sure to consider whether there isn't a better API to manage this flow, or whether a custom dialog window may be a better fit.

Window hints

The properties of a window (referred to as *hints* on many systems) allow an application to indicate certain desired attributes to the operating system that'll control how a window is presented. For various reasons (including user experience and even security), an application can't mandate how and when a window will be presented in most situations; therefore, it's important to remember that these hints may not be enforced.

Sizes

The most common hints set are related to size—the minimum and possibly maximum size that your user interface should occupy. Minimum size is almost universally supported; every graphical system will try to allow an application to use as much space as it claims to need. Be sure to have sensible sizes though as, especially when targeting multiple different platform types, the minimum size shouldn't be bigger than the screen available! To avoid this situation, the operating system will probably show your application windows smaller than requested so that the user doesn't have the problem of accessing portions of the user interface that are off-screen. For this reason alone, it's recommended that the minimum size set is truly the smallest size that your GUI will operate correctly.

So that an application is proportioned correctly when first loaded, it's common to set a default or preferred size (typically through `SetDefaultSize()`, `SetSize()`, or `Resize()`). This means that, as much as possible, your application will load at a sensible size, but smaller if the screen isn't large enough. In the example of our *New GoMail* email compose window, we can set a good default for typing a large email while having a sensible minimum size (probably calculated by the toolkit) that allows access to all of the input fields.

Additionally, it may be helpful to set a maximum size for your window; while not used as often as minimum or default sized, this can be helpful. Most commonly, this is helpful if you want your window to remain small (such as a toolbox or information window) or expand only in one direction (to allow only height adjustments, or set the minimum and maximum width to the same value). It's also helpful in presenting custom dialog boxes to set the minimum and maximum size to the same value, hence requesting that the window be a fixed size. Some toolkits make this easier by providing a `SetFixedSize()` function.

Other hints

There are many other types of properties or hints that can be set on windows to help guide users through an application. Depending on the toolkit, it may be possible to set the window type. This is usually handled automatically when displaying a dialog window (as they can have special properties) but may not be handled for other types of window creation. Check out the window API in your chosen toolkit to see whether you can set the type of window when doing things such as creating a toolbox window or information panel that should belong to a parent window somehow.

The most instructive window hint is the icon that's displayed in places such as the task bar, application switcher, and possibly the window border. On some systems, the default icon is that of the application, and in others it's a window specific image. Generally, it's a good idea to set the same icon on your application windows and application icon, which may be handled by the toolkit you're using. Setting a different icon for a window should be reserved for times when the window serves a different purpose to the main window. To avoid user confusion, window icons that differ from the main one should indicate through style or content which main icon they relate to. Setting a window icon is usually achieved by calling `window.SetIcon()` or `widget.SetWindowIcon()` (for top-level widgets). In some cases, `application.SetDefaultIcon()` may allow you to set the icon for all windows with a single call.

Setting the application icon is platform-specific and is explored further in `Chapter 14`, *Distributing Your Application*. It's important to be aware that some systems allow custom icon themes to be loaded. In this case, a custom application or window icon may be less familiar to the user, so you may consider including some branding within the application itself.

Notifications and task status

As we saw earlier, it's part of most toolkit APIs to provide easy ways to open dialog windows for displaying information, progress reports, and errors to gain a user's attention. However, with great power comes great responsibility; it's important to not interrupt the workflow unless it's really necessary. Think of the many **File download complete!** or **Please wait for update to download...** dialog windows you've had to wait for or dismiss and you'll be thinking in the right direction.

So what's the solution? Let's look at how to present non-critical alerts or background progress to the user in a less obstructive manner.

Minor alerts

Many messages that should be presented to the user probably aren't crucial and so should probably not interrupt their flow. The information may not be important enough to warrant displaying another window or it may be time-based, and so if the app isn't active, it may no longer be relevant when they come back. A better approach to this sort of information is present in most operating systems: a notification area.

Initially presented as part of a system tray, notifications are displayed as a bubble or call-out area that can catch a user's attention if they're ready to be distracted or could be ignored otherwise. The more modern way for this to be presented is a notification area (which may not always be visible) in which all application notifications are placed. This provides a way to group all messages for later processing at a more convenient time. A preview is normally shown so it's a good idea to keep the message short.

Notifications can be created using built-in APIs for many of the frameworks we've discussed, such as `NewQSystemTrayIcon().ShowMessage()` in Qt or `NewNotifyIcon().ShowMessage()` in Walk. Using these functions will typically display the notification in the current platform's default notification area, leading to a consistent user experience. This, however, means that even on GUI toolkits that aim to be completely consistent across multiple platforms, this code will behave differently, so be sure to test all supported platforms and bear the differences in mind when writing documentation:

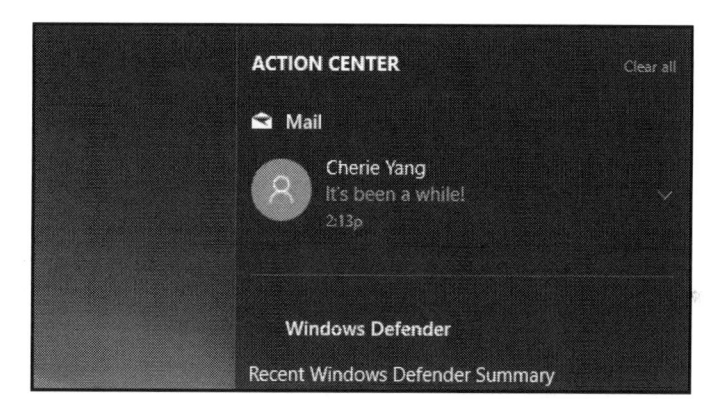

Notifications appear in the Action Center on Windows 10 (Image copyright: Microsoft)

Background progress

The progress dialog windows provided by Qt, Fyne, and others are ideal for showing the user how much longer they need to wait for a critical process to complete (such as opening a large file, buffering a movie, or loading the required data from a website). What they aren't suitable for is reporting the progress of a task that can run while the user continues their task in the application. For that purpose, we should consider displaying the information elsewhere on the application or screen.

Many systems are starting to add support for reporting task progress in a standard area, such as the notification space described earlier. Unfortunately, this isn't yet commonplace across enough operating systems for toolkits such as those we've explored to provide support; therefore, we must use another approach. There are two common strategies to communicating task progress for such background processes, and it probably depends on whether you expect multiple tasks to be running concurrently or not.

For applications where a single background task may run (such as an IDE running a build, or a to-do list synchronizing with its server), the traditional approach is to embed a progress bar in the application somewhere. This would be shown when the background task starts and then disappear once it's completed. Such visual queues are usually in a status bar or other information area where the user's eye typically travels when looking for ancillary information.

If your application is regularly going to have multiple background events running, such as file downloads or image conversions, it's usual to see a new window or tool panel appear when tasks are running. This user interface addition would normally list all of the active tasks with their progress and hide them once complete. As these are non-critical to the current workflow, it's important not to show the elements over the current work—indeed, some applications (such as Apple's Safari web browser) don't even show this window unless the user requests detailed information on the download progress:

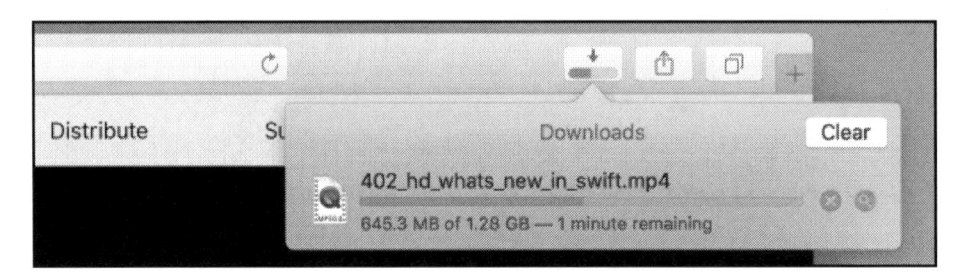

The download list in Safari isn't visible by default but will provide details if requested (image copyright: Apple)

Platform-specific considerations

Despite the broad similarities in how most widget toolkits work across the platforms they support, there are some differences in operating system behavior. Whether due to a desire to stand out against the competition or through a belief that their approach is a better user experience, these distinctions should be taken into consideration. In this section, we'll explore some significant differences in platform approaches.

Window grouping

In the taskbar of Windows 10 and most versions of macOS, all of an application's windows are grouped under a single icon. This makes the user interface less cluttered, but it does mean that an application that opens many windows may be a little harder to navigate as there isn't a simple icon click to show a specific window. Add to this the behavior of macOS and Ubuntu Linux (or other distributions using the Gnome desktop) to group windows under a single icon in the task switcher (keyboard *Alt + Tab*) as well. With Gnome, you can explore the windows under an icon by pressing the down arrow key or using the mouse, but on macOS, you need to use an alternative keyboard combination (*Alt +~*) to cycle the windows of an application.

This trend to group windows may impact the design of applications that present multiple windows; if every time you launch the application, it opens three windows, then; after opening three documents, you could have nine windows open. The most common approach in this situation is to have supporting windows open just once, making their tools or information assume the context of the current document (probably the topmost window). However, this may add complexity to your application as it would need to communicate with other instances of the software that are already open.

Application instances

Although somewhat hidden in a modern task switcher, it can be noticed that some operating systems prefer to have just one instance of an application open rather than launching many (for example, one per document). When developing applications for macOS, it's encouraged to only have one copy running at any time-attempting to run a second instance of the same application will normally result in the original window being brought to the front. If your application is aiming to support platforms where the *concurrent instances* semantics are different, time should be spent deciding how your application should behave. Will your design work the same way on all platforms or adapt to the current environment?

To change behavior according to platform, it's possible to detect the operating system at runtime, but normally the operating system is the defining factor, and so you can make use of Go's built in build tags discussed in `Chapter 3`, *Go to the Rescue!*. For example, we could have two different files that control how an application is opened: `launch_darwin.go` will be used when compiling for macOS and `launch_other.go` will run on other platforms. An example of setting this up may go as follows.

Navigation and Multiple Windows

Firstly, we create a file that handles the standard mechanism (called `launch_other.go`); opening a file or a new document will create a window with an appropriate document and show it:

```
// +build !darwin
package main

type app struct {
}

func (a *app) openFile(file string) {
   newWindow(openDocument(file)).Show()
}

func (a *app) openBlank() {
   newWindow(newDocument()).Show()
}
```

Then, we make a version for macOS (named `launch_darwin.go`), which first checks for a running instance. If one is found, we call some **RPC (remote proceedure call)** functions to open files in the running application, otherwise we load the window as before:

```
package main

import (
   "log"
   "os"
)

type app struct {
}

func (a *app) openFile(file string) {
   running := getFirstInstance(a)
   if running != nil {
      log.Println("Found running app, opening document", file)
      running.openFile(file)
      os.Exit(0)
   } else {
      newWindow(openDocument(file)).Show()
   }
}

func (a *app) openBlank() {
   running := getFirstInstance(a)
   if running != nil {
      log.Println("Found running app, opening blank document")
```

```
        running.openBlank()
        os.Exit(0)
    } else {
        newWindow(newDocument()).Show()
    }
}
```

The main function of the app that launches this will probably be to parse the command-line parameters to determine whether a filename has been passed, such as the following:

```
func main() {
    app := &app{}

    if len(os.Args) <= 1 {
        app.openBlank()
    } else {
        app.openFile(os.Args[1])
    }
}
```

The details of `getFirstInstance()` and the RPC code are out of scope for this chapter but can be found in the `chapter11/singleapp` folder in this book's code repository. This model may be supported by some toolkits, but there are also projects that aim to make this easier, such as https://github.com/marcsauter/single.

Extra features

In some cases, it isn't possible to find equivalent behavior or user interface elements on every platform your application or toolkit supports. In these cases, you may find the toolkit providing operating system-specific extensions that can be used in your application code. If you make use of these platform-specific items, you'll need to ensure that your code still functions correctly on other target systems. This would normally be handled by the build constraints such as the preceding, where some implementations may have no or reduced functionality to match the lowest common denominator.

Such a platform extension is Qt Windows Extras, which provides the taskbar icon progress API and a method for providing a *jump list* (a set of shortcuts from the application icon). This project can be found at http://doc.qt.io/qt-5/qtwinextras-index.html.

Summary

In this chapter, we explored techniques for designing and programming more complex graphical applications. While looking at principles for complex layouts and deep navigation structures, we compared how common applications deal with these challenges and noted the types of complex user interfaces to avoid. To provide a richer, consistent user experience in these applications, we investigated the APIs that provide standard dialog windows and allow developers to configure application windows to be consistent with the application workflow.

Background task progress and system notifications should be visible but not interrupt the user's workflow. We explored how to use toolkit widgets and common techniques to provide this balanced communication. To further integrate with the current operating system, we explored the differences between, and additional features provided by, desktop platforms so that applications can match system semantics while maintaining a single code base for cross-platform development.

In the next chapter, we'll turn our attention to the background operations and networking features provided by Go and how to use them effectively in graphical application. We'll return to our GoMail examples and extend them using cloud services for a richer user experience.

12
Concurrency, Networking, and Cloud Services

So far, we've been focusing on designing and building the graphical elements of applications. Most modern software isn't complete without a solid connection to internet services and networking features. Adding dependencies to remote services could affect the stability of an application if it isn't correctly managed. Concurrency is also a key part of managing an interaction with remote services; we'll need to add more advanced task handling to manage these various communication channels.

In this chapter, we'll explore the following topics:

- Thread handling and managing the user interface
- Including remote resources in your application
- Connecting to cloud services and handling error cases
- Maintaining user experience when the network disconnects

By the end of this chapter, you should be able to integrate remote resources and cloud services into your application. You'll also see how to maintain a responsive user interface despite this new functionality relying on network connections that may be unreliable or unavailable. The addition of long-running background processes and the communication challenges they can cause will be completely solved as your application is updated to manage data from a multitude of sources.

Concurrency, threads, and GUI updates

Goroutines are a very powerful tool for running concurrent operations and background tasks, especially if they're short-running. As we move more application logic and data handling to background processes, we need to add appropriate safeguards to ensure that errors are handled and that the user interface is kept up to date.

Managing long-running processes

A goroutine is typically created so that code flow continues while another task completes in the background. If these tasks start to be used for application-critical tasks or to handle important data, especially if these tasks could take a long time, we need to manage them more carefully. The main consideration is how to shut down background tasks gracefully if the application exits. This may not seem essential, and for some tasks it may not be, but if the process is involved in data integrity, we want to be certain that early termination doesn't cause problems.

Signaling shutdown

To demonstrate the problem, let's start with a simple goroutine demo; we'll launch three threads that print progress. For each thread, we'll print Started followed by . until the thread stops, at which point Ended will be printed:

```
package main

import (
    "fmt"
    "time"
)

func tick() {
    fmt.Println("Started")

    for _ = range time.NewTicker(time.Second).C {
        fmt.Print(".")
    }

    fmt.Println("Ended")
}

func main() {
    go tick()
    go tick()
    go tick()

    time.Sleep(5 * time.Second)
}
```

If you run this code, you'll see the following output. The threads start and tick as expected and, after a 5 second timeout, the program exits. No Ended messages are seen:

```
chapter12/goroutines> go run unterminated.go
Started
Started
Started
.............chapter12/goroutines>
```

The output of unterminated goroutines

As you can see from this simple demo, the goroutines aren't gracefully terminated; they simply stop running. If we're writing complex data, sending a message to a remote server, or waiting for an important response, this would probably result in data corruption or other unexpected results. Let's look at how to signal goroutines to stop when our application terminates.

We start by creating a simple channel called stop that's passed into each goroutine. When the application is ready to exit, we'll signal each thread so it can finish its work by closing this channel. We update the tick function to check whether this new channel is closed and if so, it'll exit. To allow the code to complete before the application exits, we must add a new pause at the end of main() for the cleanup. The updated code looks like this:

```
package main

import (
    "fmt"
    "time"
)

func tickUntil(stop chan(struct{})) {
    fmt.Println("Started")

    ticker := time.NewTicker(time.Second).C
    for {
        select {
        case <-ticker:
            fmt.Print(".")
        case <-stop:
            fmt.Println("Ended")
            return
        }
    }
}
```

Concurrency, Networking, and Cloud Services

```
func main() {
    stop := make(chan(struct{}))

    go tickUntil(stop)
    go tickUntil(stop)
    go tickUntil(stop)

    time.Sleep(5 * time.Second)
    close(stop)

    time.Sleep(10 * time.Millisecond)
}
```

Running this should display the following output, which is what we were looking for in the first place:

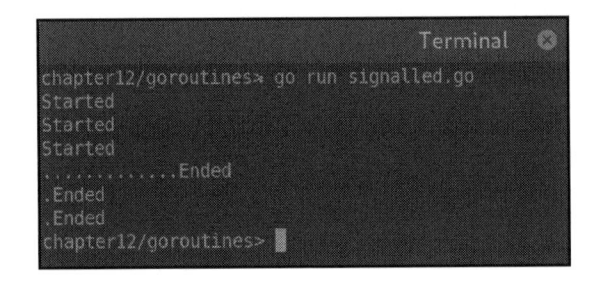

With a signal channel, our threads can end just before the program exits

Checking completion

The preceding example technically works, but depending on a timer to wait for threads to complete isn't reliable. If the threads need to wait for a response or are part way through a long calculation, we'll still have potential corruption if the timer elapses. The solution is to have the goroutine signal once the cleanup is complete. This can be done with sync.WaitGroup or by using another channel.

For our completed thread example, we create sync.WaitGroup, which is passed to each of the tick threads. Before we start the goroutine, we increment the number of threads to wait on using wg.Add(1). Once each thread is complete, they mark that using wg.Done(). Our application is then free to call wg.Wait() immediately before exiting, safe in the knowledge that it won't prematurely terminate any of the grouped background processes.

The following code demonstrates signaling and waiting for multiple goroutines:

```go
package main

import (
    "fmt"
    "sync"
    "time"
)

func tickAndEnd(stop chan (struct{}), wg *sync.WaitGroup) {
    wg.Add(1)
    go func() {
        fmt.Println("Started")

        ticker := time.NewTicker(time.Second).C
        for {
            select {
            case <-ticker:
                fmt.Print(".")
            case <-stop:
                fmt.Println("Ended")
                wg.Done()
                return
            }
        }
    }()
}

func main() {
    stop := make(chan (struct{}))
    wg := &sync.WaitGroup{}

    tickAndEnd(stop, wg)
    tickAndEnd(stop, wg)
    tickAndEnd(stop, wg)

    time.Sleep(5 * time.Second)
    close(stop)

    wg.Wait()
}
```

The output of this is almost exactly the same as the previous version, but the specific timing of the threads ending is slightly different:

Waiting for our goroutines to complete instead of waiting a set time

Communicating through channels

As we've seen in earlier chapters, goroutines offer powerful but simple concurrent operation. Most of these examples have been generating output or responding to user requests, but long running processes are often generating data that needs to be utilized by the application. In this example, we see how a channel can be used to effectively gather data from multiple threads to aggregate and report.

Our example is a simple tool that'll get the disk usage of a directory. For each element within this directory, we'll start a goroutine (`dirSize()`) that'll calculate the space used by the directory and the files it contains. This function returns the result through a channel so the application can use the information once it's available:

```
package main

import (
    "fmt"
    "os"
    "path/filepath"
)

type sizeInfo struct {
    name string
    size int64
}

func dirSize(path string, result chan sizeInfo) {
    var size int64
```

```
    filepath.Walk(path, func(_ string, file os.FileInfo, err error) error {
        if err == nil {
            size += file.Size()
        }

        return nil
    })

    result <- sizeInfo{filepath.Base(path), size}
}
```

Within the `reportUsage()` function, we start as many goroutines as there are files reported in the specified directory. The code then prints the usage result from each goroutine when it completes using `for info := range result`, and then terminates when every result is returned (`if results == len(files) {break}`), adding a simple total before we exit:

```
func reportUsage(path string) {
    f, _ := os.Open(path)
    files, _ := f.Readdir(-1)
    f.Close()

    result := make(chan sizeInfo)
    for _, file := range files {
        go dirSize(filepath.Join(path, file.Name()), result)
    }

    var total int64
    results := 0
    for info := range result {
        total += info.size
        fmt.Printf("%s:\t%d\n", info.name, info.size)

        results++
        if results == len(files) {
            break
        }
    }
    fmt.Printf("\nTotal:\t\t%d\n", total)
}
```

[329]

Lastly, we add a `main()` function that simply parses arguments to initialize the `reportUsage()` function. If no argument is specified, we'll report for the current directory reported by `os.Getwd()`:

```
func main() {
    path, _ := os.Getwd()

    if len(os.Args) == 2 {
        path = os.Args[1]
    }

    fmt.Println("Scanning", path)
    reportUsage(path)
}
```

Running this example may return immediately, but if you invoke it on a large directory, it may take some time to complete. By doing this, you can see that each printed appears as soon as the related goroutine completes, and the total is always last to appear. The preceding listing doesn't include some boilerplate number formatting seen in the resulting screenshot (that can be found in this book's code repository):

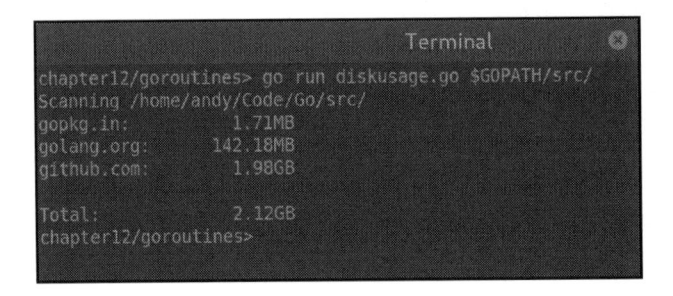

```
chapter12/goroutines> go run diskusage.go $GOPATH/src/
Scanning /home/andy/Code/Go/src/
gopkg.in:        1.71MB
golang.org:    142.18MB
github.com:      1.98GB

Total:           2.12GB
chapter12/goroutines>
```

Reporting the usage of a directory: typically smaller items appear first as they're faster to calculate

Graphical updates from goroutines

Communicating with the graphical interface (in most frameworks) means managing threads correctly. In the preceding example, we could have updated a GUI within the `dirSize()` method, adding a row to a table, for instance. In theory, that would have avoided the need for a channel and the struct that we passed back to the `reportUsage()` function. However, changing threads is a (relatively) slow process depending on other application activities, and moreover we should try to separate our logic and processing from the user interface code. Doing so will make it easier to reuse code later and possibly to change toolkit if our requirements change.

Our design to handle most of the user interaction in a single function means that our actual directory usage code is completely separate from our user interface. Let's update the preceding example to generate a graphical output instead. We'll use Go-GTK this time, as its thread handling is quite explicit:

```
func gtkReportUsage(path string, list *gtk.ListStore, totalLabel
*gtk.Label) {
    f, _ := os.Open(path)
    files, _ := f.Readdir(-1)
    f.Close()

    result := make(chan sizeInfo)
    for _, file := range files {
        go dirSize(filepath.Join(path, file.Name()), result)
    }

    var total int64
    results := 0
    for info := range result {
        var listIter gtk.TreeIter
        total += info.size

        gdk.ThreadsEnter()
        list.Append(&listIter)
        list.SetValue(&listIter, 0, info.name)
        list.SetValue(&listIter, 1, formatSize(info.size))
        gdk.ThreadsLeave()

        results++
        if results == len(files) {
            break
        }
    }

    gdk.ThreadsEnter()
    totalLabel.SetText(fmt.Sprintf("Total: %s", formatSize(total)))
    gdk.ThreadsLeave()
}
```

Notice that our replacement usage reporting method has two instances of `gdk.ThreadsEnter()` and `gdk.ThreadsLeave()`; each time we update the user interface, we must switch to the `gdk` main thread. As in previous Go-GTK examples, we need to also update the main method to correctly initialize thread handling:

```
func main() {
    glib.ThreadInit(nil)
    gdk.ThreadsInit()
```

Concurrency, Networking, and Cloud Services

```
    gdk.ThreadsEnter()
    gtk.Init(nil)

    window := gtk.NewWindow(gtk.WINDOW_TOPLEVEL)

...

    gtk.Main()
}
```

The full user interface creation is omitted from this chapter for brevity, but can be found in this book's source code (in `chapter12/goroutines/gtkdiskusage.go`). It's a requirement of most graphical toolkits that background processes switch to the main or graphics thread when updating the user interface. Some, such as Fyne, don't have this requirement, which you can see in an alternative version of the example (also available in this book's code repository at `chapter12/goroutines/fynediskusage.go`). Instead of wrapping GUI calls in thread handling code, we simply call `list.Append()` or `label.SetText()` from the background code and the interface will update accordingly:

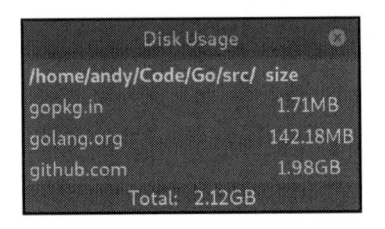

A GTK interface for the disk usage example

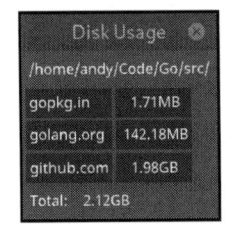

The same disk usage example using Fyne

[332]

Network resources and caching

Accessing remote resources, on a local network or from a server across the internet, is likely to play a part in most applications. Unfortunately, it's also the source of a significant number of potential issues: slow responses, unexpected data, or no data at all. Let's look at some ways we can work to create a robust application even when we need to use the network and integrate cloud services.

Loading remote resources

Accessing resources in Go is normally through a byte stream, either locally (for embedded resources or file system access) or remotely (for HTTP requests and data from a remote server). As the method for reading local and remote data is similar, we can load remote resources in most of the places where local or embedded assets have been used.

Images

Following the stream-based design, the Go `image` package decodes images from a stream. By connecting to a remote stream and reading the bytes from the request, we can easily render an image from a web server. The following code uses the Fyne `canvas.NewImageFromImage()` function to render a Go decoded image, which we've loaded from the https://golang.org/doc/gopher/frontpage.png URL using `image.Decode()`:

```
package main

import (
    "image"
    _ "image/png"
    "io"
    "log"
    "net/http"

    "fyne.io/fyne"
    "fyne.io/fyne/app"
    "fyne.io/fyne/canvas"
)

func readStream(url string) io.ReadCloser {
    res, err := http.Get(url)
    if err != nil || res.StatusCode != 200 {
        log.Fatal("Error reading URL", err)
```

```
    }

    return res.Body
}

func remoteImage(url string) image.Image {
    stream := readStream(url)
    defer stream.Close()

    m, _, err := image.Decode(stream)
    if err != nil {
        log.Fatal("Error reading image", err)
    }

    return m
}

func main() {
    app := app.New()
    w := app.NewWindow("Remote Image")

    img :=
canvas.NewImageFromImage(remoteImage("https://golang.org/doc/gopher/frontpage.png"))
    img.SetMinSize(fyne.Size{180, 250})
    w.SetContent(img)
    w.ShowAndRun()
}
```

As you would expect, this application opens a single window with the image loaded as its content:

Loading a file from the internet

But this only works appropriately when the internet connection is behaving correctly and, even then, may take longer than the user expects to load. Before we look at strategies to improve this, let's see how to do the same for data downloaded from a web service.

JSON

To explore how to work with remote data from a web service, we shall start by adapting our web service example from Chapter 3, *Go to the Rescue!*. The code is slimmed down and updated to use the same `readStream()` function as created for the preceding image example. The resulting code is very basic but demonstrates how easily we can decode JSON data into a struct using built-in Go features:

```
type Person struct {
    Title      string `json:"title,omitempty"`
    Firstname  string `json:"firstname"`
    Surname    string `json:"surname"`

    Username   string `json:"username"`
    Password   string `json:"-"`
}

func main() {
    fmt.Println("Downloading...")
    stream := remote.ReadStream("http://echo.jsontest.com/title/Sir/" +
        "firstname/Tom/surname/Jones/username/singer1/")
    defer stream.Close()

    person := &Person{}
    json.NewDecoder(stream).Decode(person)
    fmt.Println("Decoded:", person)
}
```

Using a single method for our resource loading enables us to put more robust error handling in a central place. Until we've made those improvements, our application will crash if the request fails (no internet or server error, for example):

Image failure when there's no network connection

JSON can't be accessed when offline either

While these errors could be handled better, we would still have downloaded no content. An image not loading may not matter, situations when the connection but missing JSON data would probably reduce the functionality of our application. What we should aim for is to better handle situations where the connection isn't present or isn't responding correctly.

Caching resource data

Our first approach to providing a better experience when an internet connection is slow or unreliable is to implement a caching mechanism for our remote resources. With this in place, a single online run of the application would be sufficient to defend against connectivity problems as it'll populate the cache data. The bonus is that, on repeated runs of the application, it'll be much faster to load these resources.

Building on the previous image example, we implement a new function, cacheStream(), which we'll call instead of readStream(). A helper function called cacheFileName() establishes a file location to use for the cache based on a url parameter. Every time we request a URL using this function, it'll attempt to load a cached copy from that location; if it's present, then io.ReadCloser to this location will be returned directly. If the cache file isn't present, then we use the original readStream() function to download the content into the cache file and then return a stream to the cache file as before:

```
func cacheFileName(u string) string {
    id, _ := url.Parse(u)
    file := filepath.Base(id.Path)
    return path.Join("/tmp/", fmt.Sprintf("%s:%s", id.Hostname(), file))
}

func cacheStream(url string) io.ReadCloser {
    cacheFile := cacheFileName(url)
    if _, err := os.Stat(cacheFile); !os.IsNotExist(err) {
        fmt.Println("Found cached file at", cacheFile)
        file, _ := os.Open(cacheFile)
```

```
        return file
    }

    fmt.Println("No cache found, downloading")
    stream := readStream(url)
    writer, _ := os.Create(cacheFile)
    io.Copy(writer, stream)
    stream.Close()
    writer.Close()

    fmt.Println("Saved to", cacheFile)
    stream, _ = os.Open(cacheFile)
    return stream
}
```

This implementation is just an illustration of how this can be done; if it were to be used in a production application, you would need to use a better cache location and handle potential thread issues.

> In the 1.11 release of Go, there's a new os.UserCacheDir() function. However, it's often wise to wait for a while before relying on new functionality as not everyone will have upgraded yet.

The benefit of the stream-based approach is that we can use it for assets other than images. Just like the image example, we can update our JSON code to use cacheStream() instead of readStream(), and our data will be downloaded once and then read from the local file by the cache code:

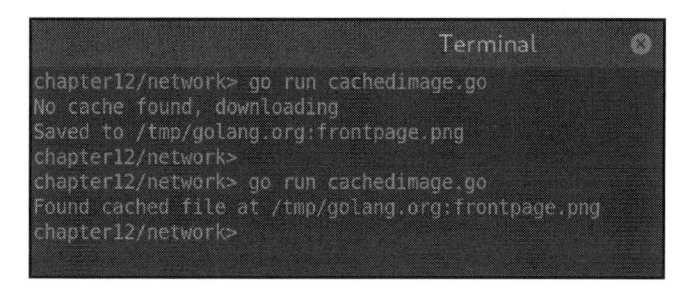

```
chapter12/network> go run cachedimage.go
No cache found, downloading
Saved to /tmp/golang.org:frontpage.png
chapter12/network>
chapter12/network> go run cachedimage.go
Found cached file at /tmp/golang.org:frontpage.png
chapter12/network>
```

Caching our remote image means better resilience of the application

Concurrency, Networking, and Cloud Services

By caching the JSON, our application can function if the network fails

These examples should help to work with remote resources in your application, but are relatively simple examples. How do we work with more complicated cloud services?

Connecting to cloud services

There are many frameworks and libraries available that aim to help you to work with cloud services in Go. However, if you ask the Go community which is best, they'll probably suggest that you stick with the built-in packages. Doing so may seem strange for anyone coming from C or Java (or many other languages created before internet connected applications became commonplace), but the standard library for Go is very capable. We'll explore here how to work with the provided tools and add cloud service-based functionality to our code without additional dependencies.

Encoding

To start looking at this, we'll return to the `EmailMessage` model defined in the `client` package at https://github.com/PacktPublishing/Hands-On-GUI-Application-Development-in-Go/tree/master/client, which was imported in previous chapters. By adding simple hints to this object, we can correctly serialize and deserialize in both JSON and XML formats with ease.

JSON

As the convention in JSON is for map keys to be in lowercase, we add hints to our struct of the `json:"subject"` form that tell the json package how to handle the field names within the struct. The updated definition should look like the following code:

```
type EmailMessage struct {
    Subject string      `json:"subject"`
    Content string      `json:"content"`
    To      Email       `json:"to"`
    From    Email       `json:"from"`
    Date    time.Time   `json:"sent"`
}
```

To aid in testing, let's also add a String() function to the definition for easier debugging later:

```
func (e *EmailMessage) String() string {
    format := "EmailMessage{\n  To:%s\n  From:%s\n  Subject:%s\n  Date:%s\n}"
    return fmt.Sprintf(format, e.To, e.From, e.Subject, e.Date.String())
}
```

Once this is in place, we can add some code that demonstrates the usage. Firstly, let's construct a new EmailMessage object and encode it to JSON. The encoding is very simple, and is illustrated as follows. We just create a new json.Encoder instance (that will output to the standard output), set the indent values (for improved readability), and ask it to encode our struct:

```
fmt.Println("To JSON:")
encoder := json.NewEncoder(os.Stdout)
encoder.SetIndent("", "  ")
encoder.Encode(email)
```

Decoding a struct from JSON is also simple. We connect to a URL, open a stream using code from earlier in this chapter (the URL is omitted here for brevity), and defer the closing of the stream. Then, a new json.Decoder instance is created from this stream and we ask it to decode into the email struct. We'll then output the data (using the preceding helpful String() function) to see the result:

```
stream := readStream(urlOmitted)
defer stream.Close()

email := &EmailMessage{}
json.NewDecoder(stream).Decode(email)
fmt.Println("Downloaded:", email)
```

Running all of that'll result in some pretty easy-to-read output that shows we've successfully created, encoded, and then decoded JSON data for our struct:

```
chapter12/cloud> go run json.go
Constructed: EmailMessage{
  To:hi@example.com
  From:me@example.com
  Subject:Welcome to this message
  Date:2018-10-09 10:38:53.522448065 +0100 BST m=+0.001121525
}
To JSON:
{
  "subject": "Welcome to this message",
  "content": "This email is written directly in the Go file.",
  "to": "hi@example.com",
  "from": "me@example.com",
  "sent": "2018-10-09T10:38:53.522448065+01:00"
}
Downloaded: EmailMessage{
  To:you@example.com
  From:me@example.com
  Subject:Testing
  Date:0001-01-01 00:00:00 +0000 UTC
}
chapter12/cloud>
```

JSON data from a struct and from a WebService

XML

Working with XML is very similar to JSON. In fact, as XML and Go share the semantics of capitalizing their public variable names, there's less mapping annotation required, so the struct only requires a single mapping tag:

```
type EmailMessage struct {
    Subject string
    Content string
    To      Email
    From    Email
    Date    time.Time `xml:"Sent"`
}
```

Encoding and decoding are almost identical; obviously, we need to create `xml.Encoder` and `xml.Decoder` rather than the JSON counterparts. The only other difference is the method call to set the indenting (only required for pretty printing):

```
fmt.Println("To XML:")
encoder := xml.NewEncoder(os.Stdout)
encoder.Indent("", "   ")
encoder.Encode(email)
```

And, we can use a web service to provide us with XML to decode (the URL is omitted here for brevity but can be found in this book's source code repository):

```
stream := readStream(urlOmitted)
defer stream.Close()

email := &EmailMessage{}
xml.NewDecoder(stream).Decode(email)
fmt.Println("Downloaded:", email)
```

Executing all of the preceding code will give a similar output to the JSON example but with a different format when encoded. Note also that the variable names start with uppercase letters, which is common in XML:

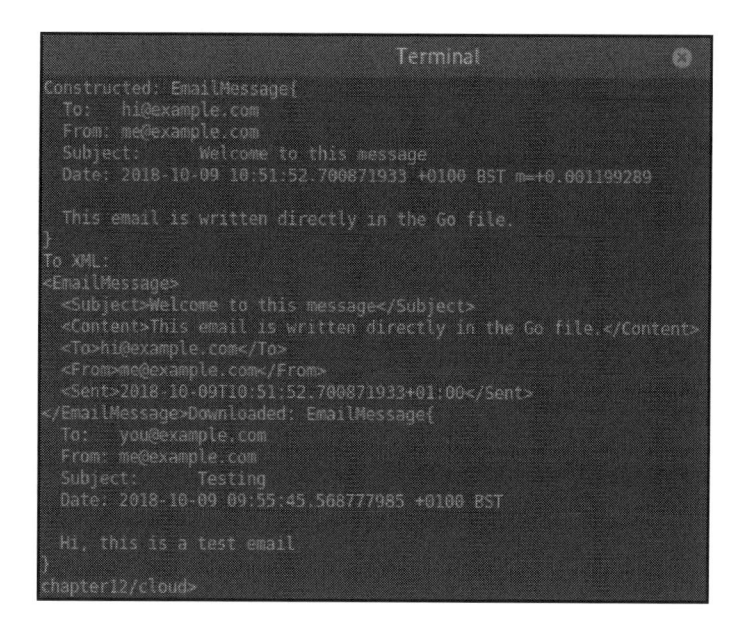

XML data can just as easily be used when communicating with WebServices

Authentication – OAuth 2.0

Authentication is often a requirement for accessing a service over the web—not always for the entire API, but certainly to access privileged user data. Most web-based authentication currently utilizes OAuth 2.0, a framework that allows applications to gain partial access to user data after permission is granted by the user. The authentication will need to show a web page the first time a resource is accessed to explain the request. As a GUI-based application, this workflow is often presented using an embedded browser window to hide the complexity of going to a web page for the permission request. Unfortunately, such functionality isn't built into many of the toolkits we've covered and so we'll instead simply open an external web browser for illustrating the workflow. This should only be required for first usage and, after that, the access granted should be remembered across application runs.

To demonstrate authentication, we'll further progress the client code used in each GoMail example. We'll extend it to read from the Gmail APIs to download messages. For this, you'll need to have a Gmail account and to have created a project in the Google Developer Console and enabled API access, which will generate `CLIENT_ID` and `CLIENT_SECRET`. First of all, we'll create a new function called `authStream()` that'll take a URL `string` parameter and return an `io.ReadCloser` stream like the previous `readStream()` and `cacheStream()` functions.

First request

To return an authenticated stream, we need to check whether authentication is required (a status code of 401 on an HTTP request means just that). If we've already authenticated, then the request will complete as normal and we can just return the request body. If authentication is required, then we must initiate the process by loading a web browser at the correct URL to ask the user for permission; this is completed by a helper function, `openBrowser()`, which can be found in this book's source code repository.

When the browser window opens, the user will be told about the permission being requested and, assuming they accept, the page will redirect to a callback URL. We need to set up a simple web server locally to handle this redirect. To do so, we register a handler at the `/oauth/callback` path and wait for a connection on port 19999.

The server is started, which will cause the function to block until we shut it down later:

```
func authStream(url string) io.ReadCloser {
    ret, err := client.Get(url)

    if err == nil && ret.StatusCode != 401 {
        return ret.Body
    }

    fmt.Println("Requesting authorization")
    openbrowser(conf.AuthCodeURL("state", oauth2.AccessTypeOffline))

    http.HandleFunc("/oauth/callback", callbackHandler)
    server = &http.Server{Addr: ":19999", Handler: nil}
    server.ListenAndServe()

    return retReader
}
```

The callback handler is relatively simple. It's responsible for extracting the authorization code from the redirection and, using this code, requesting a reusable token from the server that sent the single-use code (this is handled by `conf.Exchange()`). Upon the exchange completing, we try once again to connect to the URL originally specified; if we, succeed, then the return stream is set and if not, we fail with the appropriate error. Whatever the outcome, we prompt the user to close the browser window (as web page security dictates this can't be done automatically). After we've returned this content to the user, we'll shut down the server. This returns control to the original `authStream()` function, which will return the newly authenticated request stream:

```
func callbackHandler(w http.ResponseWriter, r *http.Request) {
    queryParts, _ := url.ParseQuery(r.URL.RawQuery)

    authCode := queryParts["code"][0]
    tok, err := conf.Exchange(ctx, authCode)
    if err != nil {
        log.Fatal(err)
    }
    client = conf.Client(ctx, tok)

    ret, err :=
  client.Get("https://www.googleapis.com/gmail/v1/users/me/messages")
    if err != nil {
        fmt.Fprint(w, "<p><strong>Authentication Failed</strong></p>")
        fmt.Fprintf(w, "<p style=\"color: red\">%s</p>", err.Error())
        fmt.Fprint(w, "<p>Please close this window and try again.</p>")
        log.Fatal(err)
    } else {
```

[343]

```
            fmt.Fprint(w, "<p><strong>Authentication Completed</strong></p>")
            fmt.Fprint(w, "<p>Please close this window.</p>")

            retReader = ret.Body
        }

        server.Shutdown(context.Background())
    }
```

The last piece of this puzzle is to set up the OAuth2 configuration and context. We'll be requesting `read-only` authentication scope from the Gmail API and specifying our local server for the callback URL. You'll need to provide values for `CLIENT_ID` and `CLIENT_SECRET` for this to operate correctly. Much of the configuration is helpfully provided by the `google.Endpoint` definition from the `golang.org/x/oauth2/google` package:

```
func setupOAuth() {
    // Your credentials should be obtained from the Google Developer Console
    // (https://console.developers.google.com).
    conf = &oauth2.Config{
        ClientID:     "CLIENT_ID",
        ClientSecret: "CLIENT_SECRET",
        Scopes:
[]string{"https://www.googleapis.com/auth/gmail.readonly"},
        Endpoint:     google.Endpoint,
        RedirectURL:  "http://127.0.0.1:19999/oauth/callback",
    }
    ctx = context.WithValue(context.Background(), oauth2.HTTPClient, client)
}
```

Storing tokens

For a repeat request, we can avoid having the user go through a permission workflow again by reusing the token we've been issued. The token that's returned by `conf.Exchange()` can be persisted and used in subsequent requests. This token contains a reference to refresh the token, which means that, even if the token has expired, the application can probably request a new token automatically.

To store and retrieve the token, we shall use a JSON serialization that's already set up on the `oauth2.Token` type. When the token is originally issued, we'll save it to a file (this could be a database or any other persistence your application has access to). As the `client` object we're using to issue `Get()` requests is shared; we don't need to reload the token for each request. Instead, we can simply load it the next time the application starts. This should mean that, upon a second launch of an example, you'll immediately see the results rather than having to go through the permission request a second time.

And so we update the `callbackHandler()` function to store the token, if it was successfully returned:

```
if err != nil {
    log.Fatal(err)
}
saveToken(tok)
client = conf.Client(ctx, tok)
```

And in our application's `main()` function, we add the token load line immediately after setting up the OAuth configuration:

```
func main() {
    setupOAuth()
    token = loadToken()

    ...
}
```

This loads the stored token (if one exists) into a global variable to be accessed later by the `authStream()` function, which should be updated to check for the token to see whether it has been loaded:

```
func authStream(url string) io.ReadCloser {
    if token != nil {
        fmt.Println("Reusing stored token")
        client = conf.Client(ctx, token)
    }
    ret, err := client.Get(url)

    ...
}
```

Simple implementations of `saveToken()` and `loadToken()` are available in the source code repository. For testing purposes, it's sufficient to print the content to the system output and then copy and paste it into the `loadToken()` function before the next run. With all of this together, we can implement a simple request that'll count the messages in a user's inbox. This function requests a Gmail API that requires authentication and counts the number of items in the resulting JSON message list:

```
func countMessages() {
    in :=
authStream("https://www.googleapis.com/gmail/v1/users/me/messages")
    defer in.Close()

    var content interface{}
    decoder := json.NewDecoder(in)
    decoder.Decode(&content)

    if body, ok := content.(map[string]interface{}); ok {
        list := body["messages"].([]interface{})
        fmt.Println(len(list), "messages found")
    }
}
```

When we run this twice, we see that the first request required the browser to open and confirm the authorization. On the second run, that token is reused and the same content is returned without interrupting the user:

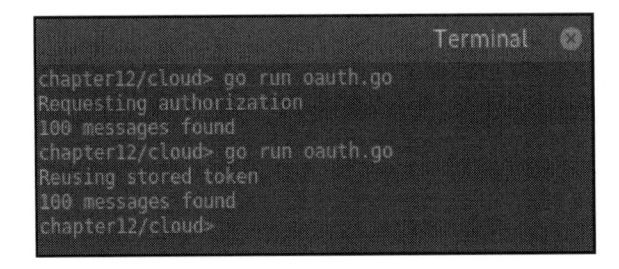

```
chapter12/cloud> go run oauth.go
Requesting authorization
100 messages found
chapter12/cloud> go run oauth.go
Reusing stored token
100 messages found
chapter12/cloud>
```

Requesting OAuth2 authorization the first time opens a browser window: repeat calls use the token we saved

Posting data

Posting data to a web service should be just as easy as changing a `Get()` function call to a `Post()` but there are often complications. Consider our email example and the task of connecting to Gmail. The API is straightforward and we can easily make the request, but the data must be appropriately formatted. Emails have complex encodings when sent to mail servers and we need to implement that to work with the API. The Gmail service requires an RFC 2822 encoded email (which the Go standard library doesn't provide), which is then base64url encoded (the standard library can handle this). Before we can post any email messages, we need to add an encoder to our `EmailMessage` type, as follows:

```
func (e *EmailMessage) ToGMailEncoding() string {
    m := mime.NewMultipartMessage("alternative", "")
    m.SetHeader("Subject", mime.EncodeWord(e.Subject))
    m.SetHeader("From", mime.EncodeWord("Demo") + " <" + string(e.From) + ">")
    m.SetHeader("To", mime.EncodeWord("Demo") + " <" + string(e.To) + ">")
    plain := mime.NewTextMessage(qprintable.UnixTextEncoding,
bytes.NewBufferString(e.Content))
    plain.SetHeader("Content-Type", "text/plain")
    m.AddPart(plain)

    var buf bytes.Buffer
    io.Copy(&buf, m)
    return base64.URLEncoding.EncodeToString(buf.Bytes())
}
```

This code makes use of an external library, `github.com/sloonz/go-mime-message`, and it has been imported as `mime` for convenience. We're using the name `Demo` as we haven't recorded people's names in these examples; you could omit that part if you prefer. To implement the sending of emails, we can check the Google documentation at `https://developers.google.com/gmail/api/v1/reference/users/messages/send` to find out that we need to pass a JSON payload with the encoded data as a value associated with the `raw` key. A simple method should be able to package that and send it to the API:

```
func postMessage(msg *EmailMessage) {
    raw := msg.ToGMailEncoding()
    body := fmt.Sprintf("{\"raw\": \"%s\"}", raw)

    ret :=
authPost("https://www.googleapis.com/gmail/v1/users/me/messages/send",
        "application/json", strings.NewReader(body))
    io.Copy(os.Stdout, ret)
    ret.Close()
}
```

Concurrency, Networking, and Cloud Services

For this code, we need just one more function, `authPost()`. This function will make an authenticated post to our URL passing the content type and request body as the second and third parameters. This method could save the URL, content type, and payload to re-submit if the authorization workflow is required, but often this is unwise or impossible for an HTTP post request and so we simply re-use the token that was generated in the previous `authStream()` function. If you do reuse this token, then you'll need to remember to update the code to request additional permissions; the updated scope should be as follows:

```
Scopes: []string{"https://www.googleapis.com/auth/gmail.readonly",
    "https://www.googleapis.com/auth/gmail.compose"},
```

With this changed, a new token is issued and, with the preceding code in place, we can execute a simple method to send an email using the `postMessage()` function listed previously:

```
func main() {
    setupOAuth()
    token = loadToken()

    msg := &EmailMessage{
        "GoMail Test Email",
        "This is a test email sent from a Go example",
        "test@example.com",
        "me@example.com",
        time.Now() }
    postMessage(msg)
}
```

The preceding `postMessage()` function outputs useful debug information, but that can clearly be switched off and the email can send handle failures in a more appropriate manner:

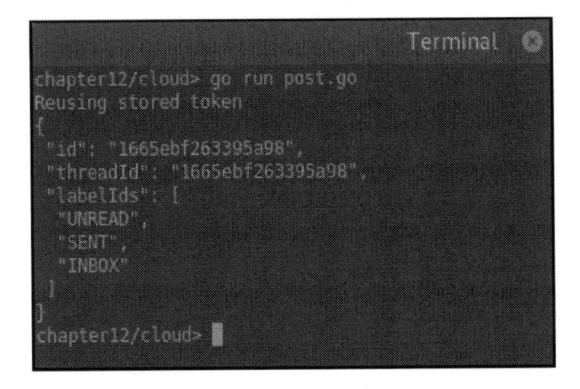

The debug from our email post example: Gmail returns the message and thread ID along with label information

GUI integration

In the previous *Concurrency, threads, and GUI updates* section, we looked at thread management and how to update the user interface from background tasks. Now that we're working with real cloud services, let's look at additional complications that we may need to deal with.

Incoming messages

The client API that has been used to simulate a connection to an email server included the `Incoming()` function, which returned a channel of `EmailMessage` objects. A new message would be sent to this channel each time a new email arrived, and we can use this same model for a real email server connection as well. The email message abstraction works to communicate a standard structure and so all a new email connection (such as the preceding Gmail examples) needs to do is package the incoming data into an `EmailMessage` struct and add it to the channel.

This means the only additional work that we need to do is update the code in the server connection package to monitor for new messages and add some JSON decoding when a new message is detected. All of this can be done without changing a single line of our GoMail example application GUIs. In fact, to activate a real Gmail account instead of our test server "we need to change the `client.NewTestServer()` function call to `client.NewGmailServer()` (a full description of this Gmail provider is available in the final `Appendix`, *Connecting GoMail to a Real Email Server*).

Activity notifications

It can be helpful for users to know when an application is executing code in the background. If, for example, you wanted to include a **Check Email** button in your application, then it may be helpful to indicate when email is being checked so the user knows that pressing the button won't do anything. As a developer, this is most commonly seen in an IDE status bar, indicating that a build is in progress or a packaging task is running. If working on a laptop and fans start to spin, it's useful to know what's executing in the background so that any potential concerns can be put to one side for a while.

To support this type of interface update, we need to track when tasks start and stop. Depending on the type of visual design, there are two strategies we could use: a simple counter of background tasks or a list of running tasks. The former is far easier to implement but the latter is able to report more information to the application user. If you'll just use a spinner or an infinite progress bar, then the first strategy will work well. If, however, you want to add a status bar that shows the current running task, you'll need to go with the second.

Spinner

A spinner (or other simple activity indicator) can be a helpful visualization of whether or not there's background activity. It'll be visible if the number of background tasks is non-zero. To track this, we can implement a simple counter in the application and update it using the `StartTask()` and `StopTask()` functions. A listener or channel would then tell the user interface element that the number of running tasks had changed so it can update the GUI by showing or hiding the visual element.

In a cloud-based application where a background task is using network connections, there's an added benefit: we can insert these task tracking function calls into the network request code. For example, we could update `readStream()` to call `StartTask()` and all of the background tasks will increment the counter. To signal that the task had ended, we would return a wrapper to the stream so that, when `Close()` is called, it can correctly call `StopTask()`.

Status panel

A status panel, which displays the current (or most recent) task, will need us to track the name of a task when it starts. To accurately display which task is still running, we'll also need to track which task ends (otherwise a quick task that starts after a long running one and then stops won't correctly update the status display).

An example implementation would be for the appropriate start function to return a task reference, which is then stopped directly, for example, `task := StartTask("My task name")`, which is then stopped later using `task.Stop()`. A similar listener or channel would be needed, but this time the data would be a task reference instead of the count of background tasks.

Consistent user experience when offline

In modern graphical applications, a good user experience is clearly dependent upon great design and a high level of quality, but it's also important to handle network and service failures. In the *Network resources and caching* section of this chapter, we covered, caching of server responses to be more fault tolerant and to speed up application loading, but that's a small portion of a larger strategy for great offline support.

Caching responses

The response caching code introduced earlier in this chapter can be applied to almost all HTTP requests, but we only used it for HTTP GET. Of the many different types of HTTP requests, only three are deemed to be cacheable (GET, HEAD, and POST), and the HEAD request doesn't return a body and so isn't useful in our application. The POST method is indicative of an action being performed, so in our context (and most others), it's more important to know that it completed, rather than to save the response it caused (see the *Queuing actions* section next). To learn more about the types of HTTP requests, see `https://en.wikipedia.org/wiki/Hypertext_Transfer_Protocol`.

In addition to this, it may not be suitable to cache the response to every GET request. While HTTP is a stateless protocol, the server that you're communicating with may be tracking state that could affect the response to your request. If your application knows that the response to a request will be time sensitive, you could make sure that it skips the cache or set a timeout on that cache entry. Unfortunately, it may not always be possible to know this in advance; this is where HTTP headers (and the HEAD method) can be helpful. By examining the headers of a response, you may see **Last-Modified** or **ETag** metadata (by issuing a HEAD request, you can access this information without the full response data being sent). If the **Last-Modified** header contains a time that's earlier than the creation of your cache entry, then your cache can still be used, otherwise you should remove the cached item and replace it with a fresh request. Using **ETag** is usually more efficient as it doesn't require any date parsing, but you'll need to store the appropriate tag for each cached response. This metadata is used as a unique identity for the response content and, if the data were to be changed in any way, the **ETag** would change as well (at which point you would reset the cache, as mentioned earlier).

If implementing a complete HTTP cache, there are other headers to be aware of as well, most notably `Cache-Control`. If this value is set to `no-cache` or `no-store` (or a combination including those values), the server is indicating that the response must never be cached. This is probably an indication that the content is specific to that request and the time of request, or that there's another reason that issuing the same request again would return a different response body.

With all of these considerations properly addressed, the code to manage a response cache is a lot more complicated than illustrated earlier in this chapter, which is why various Go packages exist to manage the details. Searching in your favorite search engine for *golang http cache* will probably return the most popular results.

Queuing actions

Other HTTP methods, such as POST, PUT, or DELETE, are typically indicative of a user action whereby confirmation that it has been communicated is the main requirement. In these situations, a cache isn't helpful; if requested a second time, the cache could stop our action from reaching the server at all. For this reason, it's uncommon to cache these requests. Moreover, if we're to build a resilient application, we need to plan for unsuccessful requests. In these situations, the server may or may not have received our request and the action may or may not have been processed.

The usual approach to this challenge is to build a queue of outgoing responses. Adding a request to such a queue could be done using *fire and forget*, whereby the user doesn't care when the request is completed, or to add a callback so that appropriate notifications (such as *Email sent*) can be communicated upon completion. Building queues like this with Go is well documented; support for multi-threading, channels, and wait groups makes it a relatively simple task so we'll not go into the details of how this could be executed. What's important, however, is determining whether a request succeeded or failed.

If an HTTP POST (for example) times out or returns with an error of 500 (or above), we must assume it failed. Re-issuing the same request is safe as re-issuing an identical POST shouldn't cause any additional state change if it was successfully completed the first time. A response code from 400 to 499 means that there was a fault with the request and re-trying won't fix the issue. In these cases, it's likely that the user needs to be informed of the failure (and the code should probably log the error to your team somehow).

Be careful not to blindly accept a status code of 200 (OK) as success; many protocols communicate certain failure conditions within the body of a successful HTTP response. Be sure to read the documentation for the API you're using to see how to check for additional errors. For example, a typical `graphql` response may return an HTTP status code 200 but have failed internally; knowing whether to retry in the background or to communicate the error to the application user will be specific to the service and the error encountered. In the following example, the server response helpfully indicated that a retry may help to resolve the issue:

```
{
  "errors" => [
    {
```

```
        "message" => "Temporary storage failure",
        "retry" => true,
        "path" => ["user", "add"],
      }
   ]
}
```

Starting offline

The preceding strategies help to deal with intermittent internet connections, or continuing to work with an application in offline mode after some time online. But what if your application is designed to work offline right from the first usage? If a login isn't required immediately, then you may be able to support an initial offline state; probably not ideal for an email client but it may be expected for a collaborative documentation platform or entertainment system. How can we make use of the techniques we've explored already to provide a great first-use experience if there's no network available?

The simplest approach to this problem is probably to package data with the application so that it can be used as a cache if no recently cached data is available. In this manner, the application could attempt to use a local cache if one exists, then fall back to the application data otherwise, and if neither is available, then attempt to make the remote connection, like the following prototypical function:

```
func cacheFallbackStream(url string) io.ReadCloser {
   stream := cacheStream(url)
   if stream != nil {
      return stream
   }
   stream = resourceStream(url)
   if stream != nil {
      return stream
   }
   return readStream(url)
}
```

In this example, we re-use the `cacheStream()` and `readStream()` functions before and use a new (hypothetical) function named `resourceStream()`, which would encode the URL, look up some bundled resources in the application, and return a stream to one if it's found. An alternative approach is for the first run of an application to extract all of the cached resources it has packaged and set up a local cache, then later code could simply use `cacheStream()` as before. For more information about bundling resources for distribution, see `Chapter 14`, *Distributing your Application*.

Of course, whichever strategy you use, be sure to consider how important it is for the data to be up to date; is falling back to an old cache that's bundled in the application a good strategy for your data? Do you want to update the local copy of this information on a regular basis? If it's important that the data be as fresh as possible, then the preceding function should probably be changed so that `readStream()` is attempted before `resourceStream()` or even `cacheStream()` and a *live* request is attempted if possible. If you take this approach, be sure to consider timeouts and other failure conditions, and handle user expectations appropriately.

Summary

In this chapter, we explored some of the more complex aspects of developing a rich application with long-running background threads and a reliance on remote resources or web services. We first looked at multi-threading and the management of long-running processes, building on the basics of goroutines and thread handling from earlier chapters. We looked at how background processes can be designed to minimize the impact of the code overhead required by some graphical toolkits.

Most of the complexity discussed in this chapter covered working with remote resources and web services. We saw how to implement caching strategies and how they can work to create a more resilient application when network conditions aren't optimal. We also explored authentication of requests (using the common OAuth2 workflow) and connected the GoMail examples to a live Gmail account to read and send emails.

All of these topics help to build robustness into an application and maintain a high quality user experience even when required resources aren't available. In the next chapter, *Chapter 13, Best Practices in Go GUI Development*, we'll move our focus from user experience to great source code and look into best practices for GUI development with Go. We'll also cover how to set up your code for ease of development and collaboration, as well as the tools and processes that'll help along the way.

13
Best Practices in Go GUI Development

The Go language has well-defined practices for formatting, documentation, and code structure. You can find these referenced in many places, for example, `https://golang.org/doc/effective_go.html#formatting` and `https://github.com/golang/go/wiki/CodeReviewComments`. Additionally, there is a strong community drive to encourage writing idiomatic Go, such as `https://dmitri.shuralyov.com/idiomatic-go`. Many of these design decisions are encoded in tools such as `gofmt` and `golint`, which makes it easy for people to learn and maintain standardized code.

In this chapter, we will look beyond these code standards and common conventions to focus on the aspects of best practice that make it easier to maintain and grow GUI-based applications. We will cover the following topics:

- Separation of concerns
- Test-driving UI development
- Continuous integration for GUIs
- Managing platform specifics

The addition of graphical elements to an application often makes it harder to test. In this chapter, we will see that with the correct preparation and structure, we can overcome these challenges and make our code robust and easy to change. Let's start by looking at how to structure a GUI-based application for maintainability.

Separation of concerns

The concept is closely related to the *Single Responsibility Principle* introduced by Robert C. Martin in his principles of Object Oriented Design (`butunclebob.com/ArticleS.UncleBob.PrinciplesOfOod`), which state that:

> "A class should have one, and only one, reason to change."
>
> –Robert C. Martin

In this respect, *concerns* have a wider scope than *responsibilities*, typically influencing your application's design and architecture rather than individual classes or interfaces. Separation of concerns is essential in a graphical application to correctly detach your easily-tested logic from the presentation code, which manages user interaction.

By separating the concerns of an application, it is easier to test subcomponents and check the validity of our software without even needing to run the application. In doing so, we create more robust applications that can adapt to changes in requirements or technology over time. For example, the graphical toolkit that you choose for your application should not be incorporated into, or impact the design of, your business logic. Consider the GoMail examples that we built in previous chapters; we were able to use different toolkits to display our emails, but the code to manage accessing them was never changed. In this way, we kept the software open to change without a huge impact on unrelated areas.

Suggested application structure

As you plan the development of your application, consider how the core concerns could be separated to maintain flexibility. The following suggested structure should provide some inspiration:

`project/`	The root of the project structure. This package should define the interfaces and utility functions used by the rest of the project. These files should not depend on any sub-packages.
`project/logic/`	This package will contain most of your application logic. Careful consideration should be given to which functions and types are exposed, as they will form the API that the rest of your application will depend upon. There may be multiple packages that contain application logic as you separate the application's concerns. An alternative, domain-specific term may be preferred to `logic`.

project/storage/	Most applications will rely upon a data source of some kind. This package will define one or many possible data sources. They will conform to an interface in the top-level project so that data access can be passed between packages of the project.
project/gui/	This package is the only place where your graphical toolkit should be imported. It is responsible for loading your application GUI and responding to user events. It will probably access data provided by a storage package set from the application runner.
project/cmd/appname/	The Go convention for application binaries is that they reside within a cmd/appname sub-package. The actual package for this directory will be main, and it will contain, minimal code that is required to load and run the main application defined within the other packages. It will probably initialize a storage system, load the application logic, and instruct the graphical interface to load.

When writing tests in each of these packages, they will focus on the functionality of the current package. The logic package should have very high unit-test coverage, whereas the storage package may rely more on integration testing (for a refresher on the different types of testing see www.atlassian.com/continuous-delivery/software-testing/types-of-software-testing). The gui package, which is often considered the hardest to test, could directly import the logic package in its tests, but should probably not include the main storage package to validate its functionality. You can read more about the recommended package structure at medium.com/@benbjohnson/standard-package-layout-7cdbc8391fc1.

Following a sensible structure will aid significantly in making your application testable, as many developers are probably already aware. It is often much harder, however, to test the graphical portions of an application. Designing your application to be unit-testable from the beginning will often result in a code base that is better organized and will naturally lead to code that is easier to understand and change. Let's take a look at what **Test-driven Development** (TDD) can teach us about building graphical interfaces.

Test-driving UI development

The effort required to automatically test user interfaces or frontend software is often debated as being far too expensive for the value it returns in avoiding future bugs. However, this is largely rooted in the toolkits being utilized or even the presentation technologies chosen. Without full support for testing in the development tools or graphical APIs, it can indeed be difficult to create simple unit tests without a huge effort. As seen frequently in web-based environments (and some native test frameworks), the only remaining possibility is to run the application and execute test scripts that will perform the validation. They will typically control the user input, simulating mouse actions and keyboard taps, and monitor the resulting behavior of the application under test. If, however, your application and GUI toolkit are architected with testing in mind (for example, using separation of concerns), automated tests should be possible with far less overhead.

Designed to be testable

When setting out the components within a project's UI code (as illustrated in the `gui` sub-package), care should be taken to define types and classes that have a single responsibility and a clear API. Doing so will make it easier to load and test individual components with the standard Go testing tools. If smaller components can be tested, we we can avoid launching the whole application and the required test runners, therefore making the testing process much faster. When a test suite runs quickly, it can be run more frequently and extended more easily, leading to higher test coverage and greater confidence in the software quality.

For a practical example, let's look at the GoMail compose dialog and its **Send** button. Clearly, the dialog box should perform all sorts of validation before sending, and if they pass then send the email. Validation can easily be tested with normal unit tests, but verifying that the send button correctly sends a new email will require the user interface to be tested. In the following example, we will load the compose window, enter some data, and simulate the **Send** button being pressed. By using a test email server, as used through each of the GoMail examples, we can check that the email has been sent by the user interface without needing to communicate with a real email server.

Example application test

We return to the GoMail code of `Chapter 10`, *Fyne – Material-design-based GUI* and create a new file, `compose_test.go`. As the tests are in the same package, we can test internal function definitions rather than relying on exported APIs—this is common with UI code as long as the application is not large enough to warrant separate packages or libraries. We start by adding the test imports; `testing` is required for go test code and `github.com/stretchr/testify/assert` provides helpful assertion functionality. We also import the client email library created for our GoMail examples and finally the Fyne test package, `fyne.io/fyne/test`:

```
package main

import (
    "testing"

    "fyne.io/fyne/test"

    "github.com/PacktPublishing/Hands-On-GUI-Application-Development-in-Go/client"
    "github.com/stretchr/testify/assert"
)
```

Now we can add a test method using the recommended naming pattern of `Test<type>_<function>()`; normally, the function would be a function name, but here we refer to the button title or its action. In the first part of the function, we set up the compose window for testing by calling `newCompose()` and passing it a test application (returned from `test.NewApp()`). We then prepare the state for our test—we record the size of the server outbox and set up an `OnClosed` handler that will report when the window is closed. Finally, we simulate typing an email address into the `compose.to` field using `test.Type()`:

```
func TestCompose_Send(t *testing.T) {
    server := client.NewTestServer()
    compose := newCompose(test.NewApp(), server)
    ui := compose.loadUI()

    pending := len(server.Outbox)
    closed := false
    ui.SetOnClosed(func() {
        closed = true
    })
    address := "test@example.com"
    test.Type(compose.to, address)
```

Best Practices in Go GUI Development

```
    ...
}
```

Once the setup code is complete, we can implement the main test. This starts by using `test.Tap()` to tap the `compose.send` button, which should cause an email to be sent. We first verify that the window was `closed` after the email send completes (the `OnClosed` handler we added records this). Then we check that there is one more email in the `server.Outbox` than before.

If these tests pass, we will move to the final check. The email that was sent is extracted from the outbox so we can examine its content. With one final assertion, we verify that the email address matched what we typed into the *To* input box:

```
func TestCompose_Send(t *testing.T) {
    ...

    test.Tap(compose.send)
    assert.True(t, closed)
    assert.Equal(t, pending + 1, len(server.Outbox))

    email := server.Outbox[len(server.Outbox)-1]
    assert.Equal(t, address, email.ToEmailString())
}
```

Running the preceding test will load the user interface in memory, execute the setup code, and run the tests, and then exit with the results. We run the following test with -v to see each test that is run rather than just a summary. You will notice that testing in this way takes very little time (`go test` reports 0.00 seconds for the test and 0.004 seconds in total); therefore, many more tests could be run on a regular basis to verify the application's behavior:

```
chapter10/gomail> go test -v .
=== RUN   TestCompose_Send
2018/12/30 14:08:59 Send Email to:test@example.com subject:""
--- PASS: TestCompose_Send (0.00s)
PASS
ok      github.com/PacktPublishing/Hands-On-GUI-Application-Development-in-Go/chapter10/gomail 0.004s
chapter10/gomail>
```

Running the user interface test took very little time

[360]

When running the tests, you may notice that this test does not cause any window to be displayed on your computer screen. This is a design feature of many test frameworks for GUI toolkits – it is much faster to run the application without displaying it for test purposes. This is often called **headless** mode and is very useful when running automated tests as part of a **continuous integration** process.

Continuous integration for GUIs

Continuous integration (the regular merging of a team's work-in-progress code to be automatically tested) has become commonplace in software-development teams. Adding this process to your team workflow is shown to highlight issues earlier in the development process, which leads to fixing issues faster and, ultimately, better-quality software. A critical part of this is the automation of tests that exercise the whole of the source code, which includes the graphical user interface.

Approaches to GUI test automation

It is important to organize your code into logical components for development and testing. Using the framework test features (or external support libraries) smaller components can more easily be verified through simple tests. The Go language's built-in support for testing has meant that test coverage is improving; in fact, the popular Go library list, `awesome-go.com`, asks that libraries have a test coverage of at least 80%! GUI toolkits, especially those newer ones discussed in Section 3, *Modern Graphical Toolkits*, need to meet these expectations and allow developers using them to do so as well.

If your chosen framework does not provide the necessary support, it is still possible to automate functional testing. The technique involves running the application from a test script that then performs simulated user actions on the host computer. This is not ideal as it requires the application to be visible on the screen and for the test script to take control of the keyboard and mouse – but it is better than having no GUI testing in place. To work around this inconvenience, it is possible to load a virtual frame buffer (an off-screen display area) in which to run the application. This technique basically creates an invisible *screen* to which the application can draw. Such approaches are typically supported by commercial continuous-integration servers, but setting them up is outside the scope of this book.

Avoiding external dependencies

One thing to be aware of when testing an application, or portions of it, is that there may be external systems involved. A file browser may rely on network connections for some of its work, or an instant messenger app is going to need a server to handle sending and receiving messages. If your code has been organized carefully to separate its concerns, you will already have used interfaces to define the interactions between different components. If this approach is taken, we can use *dependency injection* to provide alternative implementations for areas of an application that should not be included in automated testing.

> *"One of the main goals of decomposing complex problems into smaller modules and implementing these modules are dependencies. A module that relies heavily on a underlying technology or platform is less reusable and makes changes to software complex and expensive."*
> –http://best-practice-software-engineering.ifs.tuwien.ac.at/patterns/dependency_injection.html

When code is properly decoupled from the components that it relies on, it's possible to load different versions of an application for testing. In this manner, we can avoid relying on any external systems or causing permanent changes to a data store. Let's look at a trivial example, a `Storage interface` is defined that will be used to read and write files from a disk:

```
type Storage interface {
    Read(name string) string
    Write(name, content string)
}
```

There is an application runner that invokes a permanent storage and uses it to write and then read a file:

```
func runApp(storage Storage) {
    log.Println("Writing README.txt")
    storage.Write("README.txt", "overwrite")

    log.Println("Reading README.txt")
    log.Println(storage.Read("README.txt"))
}

func main() {
    runApp(NewPermanentStorage())
}
```

Clearly, this application will cause whatever was in an existing README.txt file to be overwritten with the contents of overwrite. If we assume, for example, that this is the desired behavior, we probably don't want this external system (the disk) to be affected by our tests. Because we have designed the storage to conform to an interface, our test code can include a different storage system that we can use in tests, as follows:

```go
type testStorage struct {
    items map[string]string
}

func (t *testStorage) Read(name string) string {
    return t.items[name]
}

func (t *testStorage) Write(name, content string) {
    t.items[name] = content
}

func newTestStorage() Storage {
    store := &testStorage{}
    store.items = make(map[string]string)
    return store
}
```

Following this addition, we can test our application's runApp function without the risk of overwriting real files:

```go
import (
    "testing"

    "github.com/stretchr/testify/assert"
)

func TestMain_RunApp(t *testing.T) {
    testStore := newTestStorage()
    runApp(testStore)

    newFile := testStore.Read("README.txt")
    assert.Equal(t, "overwrite", newFile)
}
```

When running this test, you will see that we get the expected result, and should also notice that no real files have changed. The code from this sample is also available in the book's source code repository in the `chapter13/ci` folder:

See that our TestMain_RunApp completed successfully without writing to our disk

Managing platform specifics

Back in `Chapter 3`, *Go to the Rescue!*, we saw that the Go compiler has built-in support for the conditional inclusion of source files based on a system of environment variables and build tags. As an application adds more functionality, especially from a platform-integration perspective, it is possible that the toolkit you have chosen will not provide all of the functionality you are looking for. When this happens, the code will need to be updated to handle platform-specific functionality. To do so, we will use a variation of the conditional build – using well-named files instead of build tags (as used in `Chapter 11`, *Navigation and Multiple Windows*). This is easier to read at the project level and should indicate clearly which files will be compiled for which platform.

Let's create a simple example: we want to show a notification, but our code only has the ability to do so on macOS (darwin). We will set up a simple `notify()` function that does what we want in the `notification_darwin.go` file:

```
package main

import (
    "log"
    "os/exec"
)
```

```go
func notify(title, content string) {
    cmd := exec.Command("osascript", "-e", "display notification
\""+content+
        "\" with title \""+title+"\"")
    err := cmd.Run()

    if err != nil {
        log.Printf("Error showing notification: %v", err)
    }
}
```

This simple function calls out to the `osascript` tool, a command-line application bundled with macOS that allows the execution of system scripts. As this file ends with the name `_darwin.go`, it will only be compiled when we are building for macOS. To compile correctly when building on other platforms, we need to create another file that will be loaded instead, we will call it `notification_other.go`:

```go
// +build !darwin

package main

import "log"

func notify(title, content string) {
    log.Println("Notifications not supported")
}
```

In this file, we must specify the build condition, as there is no special filename format for *all other platforms*; here, `// +build !darwin` means that the file will be included on any platform other than macOS. The method we provide in this file simply logs that the feature is not supported. Finally, we create a simple application launcher named `main.go` that will call the `notify()` function:

```go
package main

func main() {
    notify("Email", "A new email arrived")
}
```

Running this code on macOS will result in the expected notification appearing:

Our simple notification appearing on macOS

On any other operating system, it will log the fallback error message:

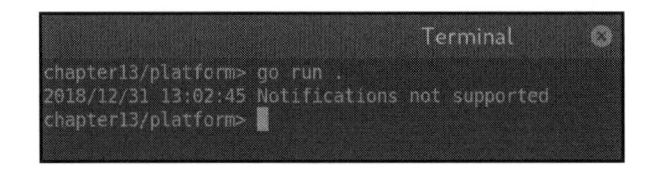

When run on Linux (or Windows or others) we just see the log message

We can handle platform-specific code in a way that should be clear to anyone learning the source code. Another developer could decide to add a `notification_windows.go` file to add support for notifications on Windows. As long as they also update the build rules in `notification_other.go`, the application will continue to work as expected but with the addition of Windows-based notifications. The benefit of this approach is that it did not require any modifications of existing code to add this new functionality.

Summary

In this chapter, we explored some of the tips and techniques for managing a GUI-based application written with Go. By carefully planning the modules of an application and how they interact, we saw that we can make it easier to test and maintain. As higher test coverage is a factor in increasing the quality of software applications, we looked at how we can use these techniques to test our graphical code, which is a notoriously difficult topic. We stepped through an example of writing test code for a simple GUI application that could be run automatically.

From these basic concepts, we looked at how to prepare an application for regular automated testing to constantly check the code for errors (a technique called **Continuous Integration**). By leveraging a well-modularized code base, we can avoid relying on external services or creating accidental side effects when testing our software. We saw how **Dependency Injection** can improve our test reliability and speed up the process for more immediate feedback. Finally, we saw how to apply our knowledge to handling operating-system-specific functionality within our graphical apps.

In the next, and final, chapter, we will look into the last step of the development process: packaging and sharing the compiled application. We will explore the various options available for each platform and how these channels can benefit, or complicate, our cross-platform strategy.

14
Distributing Your Application

By now, you should be familiar with how to build graphical user interfaces for applications using the Go language. The last step of any journey in building a graphical application is distribution. The process of packaging and releasing your completed product can be challenging, especially if you are publishing to multiple platforms, and we will explore these details in this chapter.

While the Go language and the libraries that we've utilized so far in this book make it easy to write software for multiple platforms, there is no escaping the fact that different operating systems require native graphical applications to be in different formats. For developers, it is often easy to forget this, as Go tools build from the source code in a way that's consistent across different systems. To prepare an application for release, we will look at the following topics:

- Preparing metadata and icons for our application
- Bundling assets to fit with Go's *single binary* distribution
- Packaging a completed application for different operating systems
- Uploading to platform marketplaces and app stores

By the end of this chapter, you should be able to package and distribute graphical applications ready to share with your target audience. You'll have worked through the steps to create application packages that can be downloaded or installed exactly as users on each of your distribution platforms expect. We start by gathering all of the information that you will need to complete a distribution for any system marketplace.

Metadata and icons

Before we start on the technical aspects of creating an application release, there are a few prerequisites to consider. The application name is probably set by now, but do you have a great description for it? Do you know how to articulate the key features of your software in a way that will grab the attention of potential users? Have you (or your design team) created a great app icon that will be memorable and somehow indicative of its functionality?

If you will not be distributing through a managed channel such as an app store, you should consider how the application will be discovered by your target audience. There's a lot of discussion and information online about **Search Engine Optimization** (**SEO**) and a growing amount about **App Store Optimization** (**ASO**), so we will not go into detail here. What's clear in the current software climate is that ease of discovery and memorability are now more important than ever before.

Application icon

Picking your icon is probably the single most important part of preparing an application for release. It needs to be memorable and evoke some idea of what the software is for. A great icon should look good when displayed either large or small, and in general, tiny details should be avoided or only used for unimportant aspects of the design. Make sure that your icon is created at a high resolution; 1024 x 1024 pixels is the minimum requirement for an icon to look great on the widest variety of devices. It's also important to consider the use of transparency—depending on the platforms you wish to distribute to, this may or may not be recommended. Most desktop systems allow the use of shaped icons, but not all will allow *semi-transparent* areas.

Take some time to look at popular or commonplace icons on each of the operating systems or desktop environments where you expect your application to be used. Can you match your icon style to each of them successfully? Does it seem like a particular shape or style will be expected by users of these systems? It may be best, or necessary, to create different versions of the graphic for different platforms. Doing so is not a problem, and can be accommodated by passing different icons to the build tools we work with later.

Describing your app

At this stage of development, it's not uncommon to have a little marketing material ready for the software you have created. This is the time to think about how your description could best attract new users. Whether it's through a web search engine or an application marketplace, the text you use is critical for convincing anyone to install your application. As well as the name of the application and its main functionality, make sure you consider how it could benefit your users. What tasks do you expect they'll be trying to complete when searching for the solution you have built? Don't worry about making this text long, but do try to include these important points.

Whether you intend to ship your application via an online store or a simple website, it's advisable to make sure you've completed the metadata before you continue to the release process.

Bundling assets

Go applications are designed to run from a single binary file. This means they can be easily distributed and do not rely on installation scripts. Unfortunately, this benefit results in a cost for developers—we cannot rely on resources being found next to our applications in the way that web or mobile app developers can (as we have been doing during development). To ensure that our applications conform to this design, we must embed any required assets into the application binary. This includes fonts, images, and any other static content that's needed for the application to operate correctly.

go-bindata

GUI-based applications are not alone in needing to solve this challenge so there are many solutions already available. The most commonly utilized tool is called `go-bindata` and is available from `github.com/jteeuwen/go-bindata`. It is a simple utility that converts static files in to Go source code so they can be compiled into an application. This approach is the easiest to work with as the embedded assets become part of the source code and would therefore be checked out and built with the rest of the project. Unfortunately, that package is no longer maintained, even though it is still heavily used in the community. New, actively-maintained versions do exist, but are less popular at this time.

Distributing Your Application

To use this asset packager, we install it from GitHub with `go get -u github.com/jteeuwen/go-bindata/...` and then run the `go-bindata` command passing in the name of the `asset` directory:

```
chapter14/bundle> ls
data
chapter14/bundle> go get -u github.com/jteeuwen/go-bindata/...
chapter14/bundle> go-bindata data/
chapter14/bundle> ls
bindata.go  data
chapter14/bundle>
```

Running go-bindata creates a new file named bindata.go

By including the generated Go file, we have access to a number of newly exported methods. The most important of these are `Asset()` and `MustAsset()`, which each take the name of an `asset` file from the directory that was bundled. The first method looks up the asset and returns the data if it is found or otherwise an error. The latter returns the data but will panic if the named resource cannot be found. With this new functionality, we can load the desired resource from the code, as follows:

`data, err := Asset("shiny-hall.jpg")`

You can also get the list of assets available using the `AssetNames()` command, or load more information about an asset using the `AssetInfo()` command.

packr

An alternative approach is provided by the packr project, hosted at `github.com/gobuffalo/packr`. This utility provides additional functionality over `go-bindata` and other similar tools— the ability to load assets directly from the filesystem while in development. This flexibility can speed up working with many assets, as you no longer have to re-generate the packaged source code after every change. This flexibility, however, requires a slight change in workflow, and it is necessary to use the `packr` command in place of `go` when building the application for installation or release.

To use this bundle technique, we need to install the `packr` tool (using `go get -u github.com/gobuffalo/packr/packr`), which will also ensure the library is installed. Before we can run the build, we need to write the code that looks up our resources, as follows:

```
package main

import "log"
import "github.com/gobuffalo/packr"

func main() {
    box := packr.NewBox("./data")
    data, err := box.Find("shiny-hall.jpg")

    log.Println("datLen", len(data), "err", err)
}
```

After saving this code, we can run as normal, for example, `go run main.go`, and it will load the resources from the filesystem. When we want to install the app or build for release, we have to use the `packr` command instead, such as `packr install`. This command will find all of the resource directories we reference, bundle them into Go code, and then build the application including the additional code:

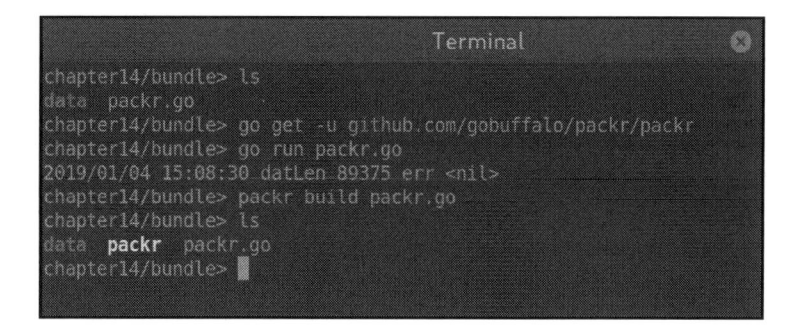

We can run code as normal but must use packr at build time.

As you can see in the preceding screenshot, there was no extra step when developing and it works just like any other Go code. When building the application for release, we use the `packr` command to bundle the `assets` into the executable during the build process.

Distributing Your Application

rsrc

If your application is built using Walk or another Windows-specific toolkit, you may consider the `rsrc` tool. `rsrc` is used to bundle manifest files and icon files within an executable file. The process involves running the tool to generate a `.syso` file, which is then compiled into the final binary output when running `go build`. This is the same process described in Chapter 4, *Walk – Building Graphical Windows Applications*, for embedding the applications manifest file. We also use the tool later in this chapter to embed an application icon for distributing to Windows.

To package icons into the application, you can run `rsrc -ico myicon.ico, anothericon.ico`, and then re-build your app. Resources embedded in this way can be accessed using `walk.NewIconFromResource("myicon.ico")`. This is a helpful method of embedding icon resources if you are writing applications specifically for Windows. If you intend to work with multiple target platforms, it is less likely to be useful as your macOS or Linux executable will not be able to access these icons.

fyne bundle

The previous tools will work with any of the Go GUI frameworks, but if you are using the Fyne toolkit, you can make use of its own bundling utility (within the `fyne` command that is part of the Fyne project). The benefit of using this specific tool when working with a Fyne-based application is that it generates `fyne.Resource` definitions for each of the embedded resources. This makes it easier to pass an asset into various Fyne APIs. The process for `fyne bundle` is similar to `go-bindata`—running the utility converts assets from the filesystem into the Go source code, which can then be compiled into applications. The biggest difference is how we then reference the assets, that is, through declared variables instead of a lookup system.

The `bundle` command is part of the `fyne` executable and takes the file to embed as its main parameter. It prints the result to the system output so we use console redirection (>) to send the generated Go source code to a suitable file:

The Fyne bundle command outputs to stdout so we redirect output to a Go file

Once the file is generated (or appended to an existing file), we can reference it using the created symbol (of the `*fyne.StaticResource` type, which implements `fyne.Resource`). This can be used like any other resource, so we can load it as an image in the following way:

```
image := canvas.NewImageFromResource(resourceShinyHallJpg)
```

The generated variable name may not be ideal for your usage, but it can be changed using an additional command parameter. For example, if you wanted to export this new symbol, you could uppercase the name using `-name ShinyHall`. To bundle a directory, you can either pass the directory name instead of a filename or run the command repeatedly for individual files with an additional `-append` parameter.

Building a release

Now that your code is complete, you have all of the metadata prepared, and you've embedded the asset files, it's time to actually build the release. We will look at this process in three stages, as follows:

1. Deciding which platforms to release for and setting up the tools
2. Building the binary files for release
3. Preparing the actual packages that you will distribute

Assuming that you will be distributing to multiple operating systems, there may be some preparatory stages to go through before you can build all of the release binaries.

Distributing Your Application

Preparing

If you've got to this chapter with the intention of using the Walk framework and therefore distribute only to the Windows operating system, you can skip this preparation step as you don't need any additional compilation tools. All of the other toolkits that we have explored in this book require CGo for some functionality. The C compiler to enable CGo should already be set up for the platform you are developing on, but there is additional work needed to enable cross-compilation to other platforms. If you have a separate operating system installation for the development of each of your target platforms, then you can skip this step.

For this section, we assume development on a preferred operating system, and therefore the need to cross-compile for additional target platforms. Doing this will require installing a GCC compatible compiler for each target platform (for example, a Linux-based developer may need to install compilers for Windows and macOS).

Compiler installation

Each additional platform (with a different operating system to the current one) will require a C compiler to be installed. The ones recommended throughout this book are as follows (along with the CC environment variable to use them with CGo):

Target Platform	CC=	Download	Notes
macOS (darwin)	o32-clang	github.com/tpoechtrager/osxcross/	You will also need the macOS SDK (see osxcross documentation)
Windows	x86_64-w64-mingw32-gcc	On macOS: brew.sh/ On Linux: use your package manager	macOS: install mingw-w64 package Linux: package names vary
Linux/BSD	gcc-linux	On macOS: brew.sh/ On Windows: cygwin.com/install.html	macOS: Install FiloSottile/musl-cross/musl-cross Windows: Install gcc-linux package

> Installing cross-compilation tools can be complicated—be sure to read the documentation on each download page and check your environment configuration after installing.
> Full details of how to install and set up each of these compilers can be found in Appendix 2, *Cross-Compiler Setup*.

Building

With all of the appropriate compilers and libraries installed, we can continue to the build phase. For each of the target operating systems, you will need to run through these steps with the correct environment variables set. It is recommended to build for one platform and then complete the packaging step listed in the following table before changing to the next configuration. This is because the release binary for one platform may overwrite another (for example, macOS and Linux binaries have the same name when compiled). Note that when building a release for the current platform, you can omit the CGO_ENABLED and CC environment variables:

Target Platform	GOOS=	CGO_ENABLED=	CC=	Notes
macOS	darwin	1	o32-clang	Make sure you've prepared the SDK and copied it to the osxcross tarballs/ directory.
Windows	windows	1	x86_64-w64-mingw32-gcc	A different CC or compiler may be required if you change GOARCH.
Linux	linux	1	gcc-linux	On macOS you may need to use x86_64-linux-musl-gcc for CC.

With these environment variables set appropriately, we can execute the build command. You may also want to set GOARCH to specify a different CPU architecture, but doing so is beyond the scope of this chapter. If you are using the Packr asset bundler, then you will need to use the packr build command, otherwise the go build command can be executed. This will typically take longer than a normal run or build, as all of the application dependencies may have to be built for the new target platform before your application can be compiled.

Distributing Your Application

To see this in action, we can open a Linux Terminal and set up the environment for each build. When compiling for the current platform, we don't need to specify the `CGO_ENABLED` or `CC` variables as these have correct defaults. After each build, we have a single application binary for the desired platform that we will put to one side and use in the next step (for instance, packaging):

Compiling with CGo for Linux, macOS, and Windows

Once the binary files have been compiled, we could distribute the application – this would be the normal process for command line utilities or web applications. However, with GUI-based applications, a user will expect visual elements, such as icons and integration with application launchers for their platform. That information is added in the packaging phase and varies for each platform and toolkit.

Packaging

To finish creating the release files for a graphical application, we have to add extra imagery and metadata alongside the binary that was just compiled. These need to be in specific formats, which are different for each operating system.

Linux

The format for an application package on Linux varies between distributions (.rpm, .deb, and .tar.gz are common formats for distribution), but they all require the same assets, which we will build now. As well as the compiled application, we need an icon file and a desktop entry file (a standard defined by FreeDesktop.org: standards.freedesktop.org/desktop-entry-spec/desktop-entry-spec-latest.html). The icon file is a simple image file in one of the supported formats: PNG, XPM, and SVG. PNG is recommended for a bitmap icon and SVG is the format to use if your icon is vector-based.

Create metadata files

The .desktop file is a simple text file in a standard key-value format with grouping. There are certain keys that are required as well as many optional ones (which we will not cover here). A basic desktop entry file may look like this:

```
[Desktop Entry]
Type=Application
Name=My Application
Exec=myapp %f
Icon=myapp.png
Categories=Utility
```

Save the content to a suitably named file, such as myapp.desktop, next to your compiled binary file. This file sets out the basic application information—the type of executable it describes (Application) and the name that will be used for display (you can add additional information with Comment if required). The name can be localized (displayed in different languages) as well—for this, use the Name[fr]=French Name format. We then specify the executable (this can be just the filename, in which case the location will be looked up, or an absolute path to the installed binary). The %f parameter indicates that the executable can accept a single file parameter and is useful for things such as dragging and dropping files onto your application icon (omit this if you do not support command arguments). We need to specify the icon parameter to tell the system the how to find the icon for this application (in this case, it will look for myapp.png in the theme icon paths). Optionally, we can specify categories that this application should appear within—excluding this element may mean the icon does not appear in system menus. A full list of supported categories is available online at specifications.freedesktop.org/menu-spec/latest/apa.html#main-category-registry.

Distributing Your Application

> **TIP**
> To make it easier for users to find your software once it's installed, be sure to choose a clear name and set the right category for your application. You can use the `Comment` property to provide more information, but that may not always be shown.
> On some systems, the category is more than a menu grouping. For example, items in the *Settings* category may be placed into a control panel rather than the main application list.

Packaging release

Linux packages are distributed in one of two ways: as source code or as a binary (compiled) package. When shipped as source code, a makefile, or similar, would be included to instruct the compiler on how to create the executable. With Go, this is different due to the standard structure and build tools, so we don't need to include a make file. As developers, we simply invoke `go install` for the current project or `go get` for one that is not yet downloaded. Anyone familiar with Go will know this process and so there is no required build information in this case.

However, we are packaging for distribution to regular users, not developers. For this to work , we could use distribution-specific packaging (which we will look at later in this chapter) or build a package that could work for any Linux system. To do the latter, we can prepare a structured package that can simply be expanded onto a user's system. The standard installation location for non-system packages is `/usr/local`, so we start at that location for our files (we mirror this structure in the current directory). The expected tree of files should look like the following (*hicolor* is the name of the fallback theme for looking up icons):

File path	Description
`usr/local/share/applications/myapp.desktop`	`Desktop Entry` metadata
`usr/local/share/icons/hicolor/512x512/apps/myapp.png`	Application icon (for a 512 x 512 px bitmap image)
`usr/local/share/icons/hicolor/scalable/apps/myapp.svg`	Application icon (for a vector image)
`usr/local/bin/myapp`	Executable file (from go build)

With all of these files in the right folder we can build an application package using the `tar` utility. The full command to create a new file with this content is `tar -cf myapp.tar.gz usr`, as shown in the following screenshot:

```
chapter14/release> find usr/
usr/
usr/local
usr/local/share
usr/local/share/icons
usr/local/share/icons/hicolor
usr/local/share/icons/hicolor/512x512
usr/local/share/icons/hicolor/512x512/apps
usr/local/share/icons/hicolor/512x512/apps/chapter14.png
usr/local/share/applications
usr/local/share/applications/chapter14.desktop
usr/local/bin
usr/local/bin/chapter14
chapter14/release> tar -cf chapter14.tar.gz usr
chapter14/release> file chapter14.tar.gz
chapter14.tar.gz: POSIX tar archive (GNU)
chapter14/release>
```

Packaging the contents of our usr/local directory structure

The resulting package can be shared for installation, and the recipient should use `sudo tar -xf myapp.tar.gz` from the root of their filesystem. In this example, we pass the additional `-C /` to avoid having to change directory, as indicated in the following screenshot:

```
chapter14/release> sudo tar -C / -xf chapter14.tar.gz
chapter14/release> chapter14
chapter14/release>
```

After installing the packaged application we can run it from $PATH

This package format will work for all Linux distributions, but packaging for package managers is additional work. We will look at distribution tools later in this chapter.

macOS

Applications to be distributed for macOS also require a particular directory structure and associated metadata. These files will not be installed like the previously shown Linux example, but instead run from the directory we are creating. This format is called an **application bundle** and requires certain metadata files that we must create to describe the application.

Creating metadata files

The main metadata file for macOS applications is called `Info.plist` and, like the desktop entry for Linux, it is a structured text file. For a Go project, it is best to edit the text directly rather than using the installed Xcode tools. This file contains a list of key-value pairs that describe the application we've built. It's important that you do not change the values for `CFBundlePackageType` or `CFBundleInfoDictionaryVersion` as these identify the file to macOS as an application.

The main keys for customization are `CFBundleExecutable`, which sets the name of the executable file; `CFBundleName`, for the human-visible name of the application; and `CFBundleIconFile`, to specify the icon filename. It's important to set sensible values for `CFBundleIdentifier` as this uniquely identifies this application, and `CFBundleShortVersionString`, which specifies what version of the application is included. Putting all of these values into the `plist` format, you should have a file similar to the following:

```
<!DOCTYPE plist PUBLIC \"-//Apple Computer//DTD PLIST 1.0//EN\"
    \"http://www.apple.com/DTDs/PropertyList-1.0.dtd\">
<plist version=\"1.0\">
    <dict>
        <key>CFBundleExecutable</key>
        <string>myapp</string>
        <key>CFBundleIdentifier</key>
        <string>com.example.myapp</string>
        <key>CFBundleName</key>
        <string>MyApp</string>
        <key>CFBundleIconFile</key>
        <string>myapp.icns</string>
        <key>CFBundleShortVersionString</key>
        <string>1.0</string>
        <key>CFBundleInfoDictionaryVersion</key>
        <string>6.0</string>
        <key>CFBundlePackageType</key>
```

```
        <string>APPL</string>
    </dict>
</plist>
```

> **TIP:** Be sure to set a globally unique `CFBundleIdentifier` value – typically by using the reverse domain name format illustrated previously. This configuration is used to associate file types with your application, and the App Store will not accept applications where this is not set correctly.

One additional step when creating a macOS package is that the icon must be in the `ICNS` format. `ICNS` files contain many different sized icons so that macOS can display a clear graphic at various resolutions. There are many graphical tools to manipulate these files (search `create icns file` online), but the XCode command-line tools include `iconutil`, a simple utility that can create these files from a set of icons.

When invoking `iconutil`, we specify that it should convert to `icns` with the `-c icns` parameter, and provide the output file name using `-o <filename>`. The last parameter is the `iconset` input—a directory of appropriately named files that will be included. For our 1024 x 1024 pixels icon, we call it `icon_512x512@2x.png`, but it is recommended to provide multiple different resolutions. Running the command will create the `.icns` file we need for our application icon, as follows:

```
iconutil -c icns -o Chapter14.app/Contents/Resources/chapter14.icns
chapter14.iconset/
```

Packaging release

Now that the metadata has been created, we can create the directory structure required for a macOS application bundle. The location of the files is important, and is set out as follows:

File `pathDescription`

`myapp.app/Contents/Info.plist`	The application metadata outlined in the preceding
`myapp.app/Contents/Resources/myapp.icns`	The application icon in ICNS format
`myapp.app/Contents/MacOS/myapp`	The application executable

Distributing Your Application

After creating these directories and moving files to the correct location, you have a complete application bundle. This can be executed by double-clicking the icon and it can be distributed in this state. Installation consists of dragging this icon into the `Applications` folder of the computer, as follows:

```
[chapter14/release> ls chapter14.iconset/
icon_512x512@2x.png
[chapter14/release> iconutil -c icns -o Chapter14.app/Contents/Resources/chapter1
4.icns chapter14.iconset/
[chapter14/release>
[chapter14/release> find Chapter14.app/
Chapter14.app/
Chapter14.app//Contents
Chapter14.app//Contents/Info.plist
Chapter14.app//Contents/MacOS
Chapter14.app//Contents/MacOS/chapter14
Chapter14.app//Contents/Resources
Chapter14.app//Contents/Resources/chapter14.icns
chapter14/release>
```

Creating the .app directory structure and adding metadata creates a macOS application

Looking at the result in Finder, we see the new directory as an application, its `.app` extension is hidden, and the icon is the same we set up before. You can launch, install, or remove this app like any other:

Our .app directory shows as the application it describes

Windows

Metadata for applications in Windows is embedded into the executable file rather than in additional files. To do this, we create metadata files and then use a resource tool to include them in the final executable.

Creating metadata files

To include application metadata, we create an application manifest file like those used in Chapter 3, *Go to the Rescue!*, and Chapter 4, *Walk – Building Graphical Windows Applications*, when we were building applications using the Common Controls widget set (via Walk and andlabs UI). The contents of the `assemblyIdentity` instance is used to determine the metadata about the executable. For a platform-independent GUI, the file should look like the following:

```
<?xml version="1.0" encoding="UTF-8" standalone="yes"?>
<assembly xmlns="urn:schemas-microsoft-com:asm.v1" manifestVersion="1.0"
xmlns:asmv3="urn:schemas-microsoft-com:asm.v3">
    <assemblyIdentity version="1.0.0.0" processorArchitecture="*"
name="Chapter14" type="win32"/>
</assembly>
```

Don't, however, remove the `<dependency>` section if you are using Walk, andlabs UI, or another toolkit that needs to have a dependency listed in its manifest file.

> **TIP**
> To add more metadata that may be useful to users (for example, product name and version) you will need to manually set extra values. The goversioninfo tool from `github.com/josephspurrier/goversioninfo/` is the easiest way to add these values. Be aware that you can only write to the `.syso` file once, as running these tools again will overwrite the previous content.

To prepare our icon for Windows, it must be converted into a `.ico` file (the Microsoft icon format). While there are no icon conversion tools pre-installed with Windows, there are many paid-for applications available that will work. If you prefer a free solution, there are websites that offer image conversion services for no cost. If your development platform is Linux or macOS, you could install `icotool`, which supports the `.ico` format.

Packaging release

To package the data for release, we will embed this metadata into the application binary. Doing so requires creating a binary resource file (ending in `.syso`) that will encapsulate the manifest and icon files. The easiest way to do this is with the `rsrc` tool that was used in Chapter 4, *Walk – Building Graphical Windows Applications*. If you have not yet installed `rsrc`, you can do so with `go get github.com/akavel/rsrc`. We tell the tool where to find the manifest and icon files and it will output an `rsrc.syso` file in the current directory, as follows:

```
rsrc -manifest myapp.exe.manifest -ico myapp.ico
```

Distributing Your Application

If you are compiling for a 64 bit target, you will need to specify an additional `-arch amd64` parameter. It is important that the resource file generated is for the same architecture (either i386 or amd64) as the application you are compiling.

Now that the metadata has been bundled into a resource file, we have to re-build our project. Make sure that, this time, you add the `-ldflags="-H windowsgui"` parameter, otherwise the resulting application will display a Terminal window when starting:

```
go build -ldflags="-H windowsgui"
```

Once the build is complete, we will have created a Windows executable with the icon and metadata included. You can now launch this from the command line or by double-clicking the icon:

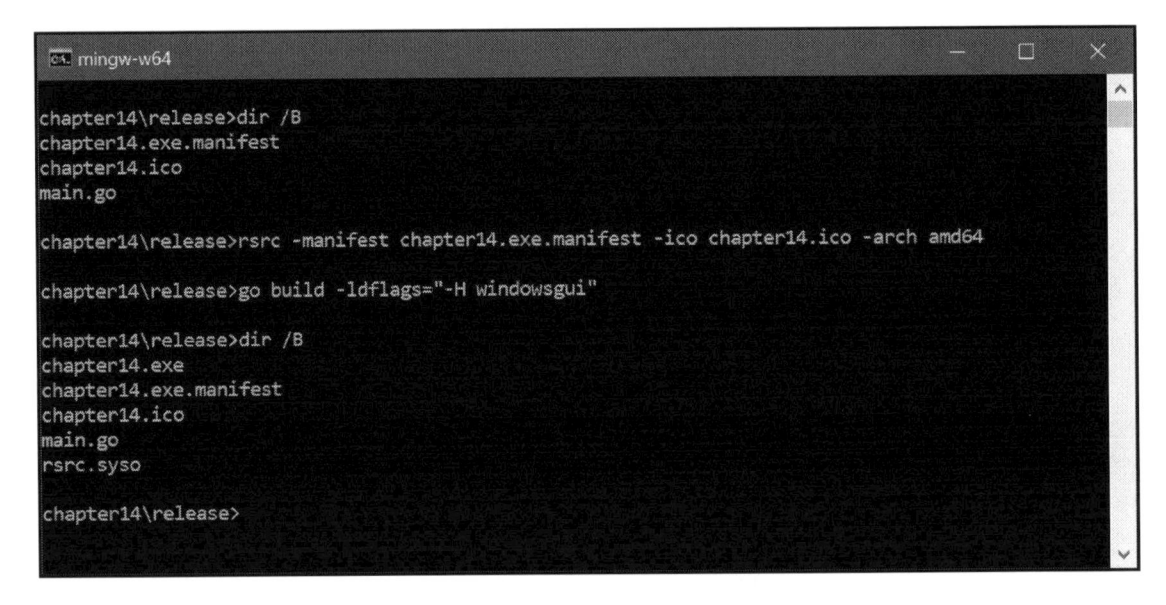

Building the application after generating a resource bundle will automatically include the data

Here, we see the same directory in Windows Explorer. The application is on the left in the screenshot that follows, displayed using the icon we included:

[386]

Chapter 14

Our Windows application with the icon embedded

These processes are slow and can be prone to errors. To avoid doing this process manually, we will explore tools that could automate this.

Cross-platform packaging tools

As you can see, each operating system requires very different packaging. Additionally, the tools that would normally make the process simple are typically platform-specific, making it more difficult to build from a single system. The distribution of GUI applications is an area in which Go tools are also lacking. The Go language is great for rapidly creating cross-platform software, but it is not designed to handle the complication of graphical application packaging.

In `Section 2`, *Toolkits Using Existing Widgets*, we explored toolkits that are very mature, but as they are either not written for Go, or are not designed to be cross-platform, they do not provide the tools we could use. `Section 3`, *Modern Graphical Toolkits*, looked at toolkits that are more focused on providing graphical capabilities rather than application life cycle, and so do not provide suitable tools either.

fyne package

One exception is the Fyne project as it aims to provide APIs for full application life cycle, and so the tools support distributing complete desktop apps across multiple platforms. While the project is still early it does have a tool that can help with application packaging (even if you've not used Fyne in your code). The `fyne package` command is designed to generate and package all the required metadata for an application to distribute on macOS, Linux, or Windows. Invoking with the `-os <platform>` parameter (using one of "darwin", "linux", or "windows") will create a fully packaged application in the current directory. Before executing this command the application should already be compiled for release.

For example, we can create a macOS application bundle from a Linux computer using `fyne package -os linux`. There are many additional parameters that can change the contents of the application, and the most useful will be the `-icon <filename>` parameter (which is required). If you were not already using Fyne, then the command should be installed using `go get fyne.io/fyne/cmd/fyne`, as follows:

```
chapter14/release> ls
chapter14.png  main.go
chapter14/release> go get fyne.io/fyne/cmd/fyne
chapter14/release>
chapter14/release>
chapter14/release> export GOOS=darwin
chapter14/release> export CGO_ENABLED=1
chapter14/release> export CC=o32-clang
chapter14/release> go build
chapter14/release> fyne package -os darwin -icon chapter14.png
chapter14/release>
chapter14/release> find chapter14.app/
chapter14.app/
chapter14.app/Contents
chapter14.app/Contents/MacOS
chapter14.app/Contents/MacOS/chapter14
chapter14.app/Contents/Info.plist
chapter14.app/Contents/Resources
chapter14.app/Contents/Resources/icon.icns
chapter14/release>
```

Building a macOS application bundle on Linux with "fyne package"

As you can see in the preceding screenshot, the tool generated an `.app` directory structure (which defines a macOS application) from a Linux Terminal. We used the same platform name for the `GOOS` environment and the `-os` parameter to `fyne package`. It's recommended to build for one platform and then package it before changing the target operating system to avoid potential errors in the output package.

The applications we have built in this section could be distributed right away. Uploading to a website or sharing the files in some other manner would work, but we want to make the process completely seamless for users. Let's wrap up this chapter by looking at the various distribution channels that exist for desktop application delivery directly to end users.

Distributing to platform marketplaces

Most operating systems now have a central location for discovering and installing applications. Apple created the Mac App Store, Windows has the Microsoft Store, and each Linux distribution has its preferred package manager. Having an application listed in (and hosted by) a platform marketplace significantly increases the number of users you can expect and also reduces associated hosting costs. When paired with carefully prepared metadata (as described at the beginning of this chapter), a marketplace can easily become your largest distribution channel. How to get applications included in these directories is specific to each platform, so we will look at the process for each in turn.

Mac App Store

The Mac App Store is the desktop version of Apple's famous iOS App Store. It provides many thousands of applications available to buy and download, or gift to others. There is also curated content, which includes listings of the most popular apps in various categories, as well as staff picks and recommended software. Apple provides education discounts as well as free copies to family members if one person makes a purchase. You can also redeem gift cards towards making purchases of apps or subscriptions. Unfortunately, the Mac App Store cannot be browsed online as it requires the App Store software, which is pre-installed on compatible Mac computers.

As well as having the development tools installed, you will also need to sign up to the Apple Developer Program. If you are not already a member you can sign up on their website here: `developer.apple.com/programs/enroll/`. The development resources are free to access, but there is an annual subscription charge for access to the code signing tools, which are required to publish software to any of their App Stores.

Packaging

Packaging applications for submission are managed by the XCode tools (which you should already have installed). The process is optimized for submitting apps that have been built with XCode and, as it does not support Go, we have some manual steps to complete.

Distributing Your Application

The application package that we created earlier (for macOS distribution) will have to be signed before we can upload to the App Store. Code signing is a complicated process to set up, so for the purpose of this description, it is assumed that you already have a distribution certificate installed. You need to note the name of the certificate (use Keychain Access to find your developer certificates) and then use that name in the following command:

```
codesign -s "CertificateName" /path/to/MyApp.app
```

The resulting app package is ready to be uploaded to the App Store Connect website for validation.

Uploading

App Store applications are managed through the App Store Connect website (at appstoreconnect.apple.com/). Log in using your Apple developer account and create a new application (if you have not already done so). This is where you add the metadata that will be displayed in the store—be sure to check the information carefully as some data cannot be changed after release. Well-chosen descriptions and screenshots will help your application to be more easily discovered. Within this app definition, you need to start preparing a new release, with an appropriate version number and supporting information. You will probably notice that you are not yet able to select a build—to enable this, we first need to upload the compiled package.

The application loader tool is the easiest way to upload a new build: open the app and log in with your Apple ID. Once logged in, you will be asked to choose the application to upload; select the matching application and progress to the upload. Once complete, the build will appear in the App Store Connect website (you may need to refresh the page). If you prefer command-line tools for managing the progress, you can use xcrun altool, which provides the same capability. Once you've chosen this new build, you can press the **Submit for Review** button to start the review process.

Reviewing

As soon as an app is submitted for review, it goes through an automated set of code checks. This process verifies that the application does not contain obvious errors in metadata or code signing and performs code analysis to ensure you are not using APIs that are private to Apple or otherwise restricted. Assuming that these automated checks pass, then the application will be sent for final acceptance by a member of the App Store review team.

The review team checks your application for quality, reliability, compliance with the **Human Interface Guidelines** (**HIG** – `developer.apple.com/app-store/review/`), and that it meets other criteria for inclusion on the store. This process typically takes a day or two, but can be longer for the first release of a new application. Once the process is complete your software will be available to purchase or download on the App Store. In your first week of distribution, it may even be included in the *New and Noteworthy* section.

Microsoft Store

The Microsoft Store is the official location for finding and installing software, apps, and games for all of the current Windows, Windows Phone, and Xbox devices. As well as offering hosting and search facilities it handles payments for non-free software and supports discounts and vouchers as well. You can browse the contents of the Microsoft Store online (at `www.microsoft.com/store/apps`) or by using the store apps on each of the systems it supports.

To submit an application to the Microsoft Store, you will require a Microsoft account (which you may already have if you signed in to Windows, Xbox, or Office 365). You will also have to start an annual subscription to access the relevant portions of the developer portal. You can log in and sign up at `appdev.microsoft.com/StorePortals`.

Packaging

The tools required to create an application package for uploading to the Microsoft Store are included as part of the Windows Software Development Kit. If you have not already installed this you can download it from `developer.microsoft.com/en-us/windows/downloads`, either as part of Visual Studio, or as a separate package.

To upload an application to the store we must create a `.appx` file (an application package). This requires an additional manifest file, named `AppxManifest.xml`, which contains the metadata about the application being packaged. Its contents are documented on the Microsoft website at `docs.microsoft.com/en-us/uwp/schemas/appxpackage/how-to-create-a-basic-package-manifest`. The resulting manifest file should have at least one `Application` element within the `Applications` section.

To create the package from our source files, we use a `MakeAppx.exe` command, as indicated in the following code snippet. By using the `/d` parameter, we can specify a directory of files to package – if you want to use a subset of the files, you can create a mapping file and specify that with the `/f` parameter instead:

```
MakeAppx.exe bundle /d sourcedir /p myapp.appx
```

Once the `.appx` file has been created, it must be signed. The `SignTool.exe` command can be used to sign an application package. Setting up the certification to support application signing is outside the scope of this chapter, but the documentation on the Microsoft developer portal will take you through the process. Ensure that the publisher listed in the manifest file matches the certificate that you create to sign the package.

Uploading

The completed package should be uploaded to the developer portal within the `Packages` page. When preparing for upload, make sure that all of your application metadata has been added to the correct locations so that people will find your software easily.

Once the package is uploaded, it will be checked for various errors that could stop it from being released. Should you encounter any warnings, you will need to remove the uploaded build from the portal and fix the issue. Once resolved, you will need to fully re-package, re-sign, and upload the new package for re-testing.

Reviewing

Once your package is uploaded and has passed the initial validation it will be added to a queue to be reviewed. The Microsoft staff will review your application for correctness and suitability, and validate that it is of high enough quality for inclusion in the store. Assuming that these checks all pass, they will publish it for distribution across the devices that you specified during the submission process.

Linux package manager

For many years, Linux distributions have had a reputation for handling package distribution well. A desktop system will likely have a graphical package management application that provides easily searchable indexes containing thousands of packages. More recently, various applications have been created to help with software discovery (to make finding new packages easier).

Applications such as *Discover* (more information on this can be found at `userbase.kde.org/Discover`) can be used on most systems by working with many different package managers. Others, such as *Ubuntu Software Center*, aim to make it easier to find applications for specific systems based on categories, ratings, and other enhanced metadata.

Despite there being hundreds of different Linux distributions only a handful of packaging formats are needed to support them. In this section we look at the three most popular formats: *Debian*, *Red Hat*, and *Tarball*. Once packages have been created for a system the application developer can submit it to a package list. As Linux is an open source system, however, you may find that an existing package maintainer may be happy to do that for you!

Debian (.deb)

Distribution for Debian is very similar to the `.tar.gz` distribution we created earlier, with the addition of specific metadata that allow the Debian tools to search and correctly install the software. Packaging for Debian is described in detail on their website (`wiki.debian.org/HowToPackageForDebian`), but the basic process is to add the metadata (*Debianization*), build the package to conform to their filesystem layout, and then (optionally) sign the package so that users know they can trust the content.

Packaging

The `dh_make` command is provided to automate the creation of required metadata files, and running it inside the existing Linux packaging directory structure will add the necessary files. Once run, you should check all the files in the `debian/` directory to update information as appropriate. The `debuild` command will create a Debian package for our software once the metadata has been added. After it's creation, you should use the `lintian` command to check the package for a number of common errors.

Although not required, you could then sign the package using the `debsigs` tool. This creates a signed package, which provides cryptographic proof that the package contains what the developers intended. As mentioned earlier, setting up certificates and signing is complex and not covered by this book.

Distribution

Once your package is prepared you can distribute the file directly to other Debian users. However, the aim was to include it in the package listing. To do so requires a process that starts by filing **Intent to Package** in their bug tracker (bugs.debian.org/cgi-bin/pkgreport.cgi?pkg=wnpp;dist=unstable). To complete the process, you will need to find a sponsor for your package or become a Debian developer. Either of which will require you to contact the development community to learn more; full details can be found at wiki.debian.org/DebianMentorsFaq.

Red Hat (.rpm)

RPM files are very similar to Debian packages but with a different set of metadata. Once again, there are standard tools that can help with the creation of these files and to create the final package. To start with, you should install the rpm or rpm-build package in your Linux distribution, which should include the necessary commands.

Packaging

First, we must create a .spec file to describe the package. The rpmdev-newspec command can provide one from the templates option to get you started. Update the contents according to your application information. This file will contain all the metadata about your software (including its source location, the license, and authors). The spec file also provides the build information required to assemble the package, as well as instructions for installation scripts, and more.

Once the metadata is complete, the package can be built using the rpmbuild command. It is normal that this will not succeed on the first attempt. Read the output and update the .spec file accordingly, then re-run the build command. The finished output will be your completed .rpm file ready for testing. At this time, you can test the file by installing it manually (on a compatible Linux computer) and verifying that the software works as expected.

Distribution

Now that the package is prepared, it can be distributed using your website – an RPM file can be downloaded and installed relatively easily. Inclusion in Linux distributions is a complicated process and the details are different for each variant. CentOS, Fedora, and Red Hat Enterprise Linux all use the RPM package format, as do many others, but the process of submission is not well-documented. The Fedora project has comprehensive documentation, which you can refer to at fedoraproject.org/wiki/Package_Review_Process. For most package inquiries, the best approach is to contact the current distribution maintainers.

Tarball (.tar.gz)

The tarball is a generic packaging for binary (and source-based) distribution of applications. The .tar.gz package that we built earlier in this chapter is an example of a possible tarball distribution. With Linux, most applications are open source, meaning that packaging is typically done from the source code rather than from the compiled output. It is possible to use a binary release, as we have built, but bear in mind that some distributions may push back on including such a package based on their own policies.

Arch Linux

The Arch Linux package manager, pacman, relies on PKGBUILD files to understand how to locate and install software packages. The PKGBUILD file is a specific format of shell script (executable text file for the command line) that describes the package metadata, any dependencies that it must install first, and the installation process for a package. Full details of the PKGBUILD file can be found at wiki.archlinux.org/index.php/PKGBUILD. A valid file must contain at least pkgname, pkgver, pkgrel, and arch variables.

To create a package once the PKGBUILD file is created, you run the makepkg command. This will execute the steps defined in the script file and prepare the resulting package. It is recommended to check the finished package file using the namcap command which validates that certain common mistakes have not been made.

Newly created packages can be submitted to the *Arch User Repository* where other Arch Linux users will be able to install it. Notable packages can be promoted from this location to the official repository over time. Details for submitting your package can be found at wiki.archlinux.org/index.php/Arch_User_Repository#Submitting_packages.

Gentoo Linux

Gentoo Linux is (not uniquely) a source-based distribution. This means that the package system contains just instruction files that describe how to download and install software. This file is called an `ebuild` file and, like the `PKGBUILD` file previously, contains information about metadata, dependencies, and build instructions. Unlike Arch Linux, this descriptor file is the complete distribution – packagers do not build a binary distribution package using the metadata file.

The process for submitting a new package to Gentoo Linux (once you have created the `ebuild` file) is described on their community documentation https://wiki.gentoo.org/wiki/Submitting_ebuilds. As with other distributions, you will need to become part of the development community to add the package yourself, but you may convince an existing developer to maintain the package for you.

Others

Many other Linux distributions use similar packaging systems, but to mention them all would be too lengthy for this chapter. Each of their websites will provide information about how to complete a package and submit to their application listings.

Containers

An increasingly popular approach to application distribution is that of **application containerization**. This approach means that each application is packaged into a *container*, similar to how Docker and other tools are doing for server-based software. An application container is a single file that simulates a filesystem, into which an application is installed. Applications can be downloaded from a website or through a package manager and do not need to be installed to run. The same container file will run on any Linux distribution; there are even some container formats that aim to support multiple operating systems as well. AppImage, Snap, and Zero Install are some popular formats, each with particular benefits or target audiences. If you want to distribute a single Linux package for your application and are not so concerned about including it in the platform software lists, this approach may be right for you.

Summary

In this final chapter, we looked at how to package and distribute Go-based graphical applications. Unlike the distribution of command-line or system utilities, the process of delivering a GUI application requires additional metadata and packaging. Users of graphical apps expect to find and install software in a particular manner that varies based on their operating system. We started by looking at the importance of good metadata and how to select an icon and description that will attract potential users to try out our new software. We then learned how to package assets into our Go-based applications. As the language is designed for single binary distribution, we had to incorporate all supporting files into the executable before distributing.

Packaging for different platforms can be complicated, so we walked through the steps required to build native-looking graphical packages for macOS, Windows, and Linux. Each package has its own metadata format and package structure but we were able to package our simple application for each of the specific formats. The packages that resulted from this step could be distributed through a website or other file sharing mechanism. However, we wanted to deliver the app where our users would expect to find it—in the system app store. And so we worked through the process of preparing and distributing the packages for each platform's marketplace. The Windows and macOS stores provide an opportunity for applications to earn revenue following release and the Linux software listings will help to increase visibility of our software package.

Having learned the various approaches to building GUIs with Go and exploring the toolkits available, we've made it all of the way to a complete and published graphical application. Hopefully, you've learned a lot along the way and have managed to create the app that you had been aiming to build—using only Go to support a performant, maintainable, and beautiful user interface.

Installation Details

In preparation for running the code examples in this book, you will need to have both the Go compiler and a C compiler installed (to support Cgo). If either of these are not set up, this appendix will guide you through the installation.

Installing Go

As a relatively new programming language, Go doesn't come pre-installed on many operating systems. This section steps through setting it up for any readers who haven't already done so.

Microsoft Windows

Configuring a development environment for Windows can be complicated as there aren't many tools installed by default. Due to this, there are many options for setting up using external tools and packages (such as MSYS, MinGW, and Ubuntu Subsystem) but exploring these is out of the scope of this book. Thankfully, it's possible to start developing Go applications without the need for many additional development tools.

Git

Firstly, if you haven't already done so, you need to download and install Git. The download is available at `https://git-scm.com/download/win`, and it should start automatically when you visit that page. Run the file that's downloaded, and the setup will start (if a notice says this isn't verified then tap the **Install Anyway** button). The default options should work for most users—make sure that **Use Git from the Windows Command Prompt** is selected to avoid more work later on.

Installation Details

Once this is completed, open a Command Prompt window (search for `cmd` from the **Start** menu if you don't have a shortcut) and type `git --version`—you should see something like the following output:

```
C:\>git --version
git version 2.16.2.windows.1

C:\>
```

Testing Git is installed by checking the version

Go

Next, you should install Go—that can be found at `https://golang.org/dl/`. On this page, choose the featured Microsoft Windows download (the name will end in `.msi`). As with the Git installation, you'll need to run the downloaded file and possibly confirm that you would like to continue installing an unverified program. Once again, the default values should be suitable—if you change any of the configuration, make sure to update the following lines appropriately.

Once that installer has finished, return to your Command Prompt and type `go version`, which should output the version number and quit:

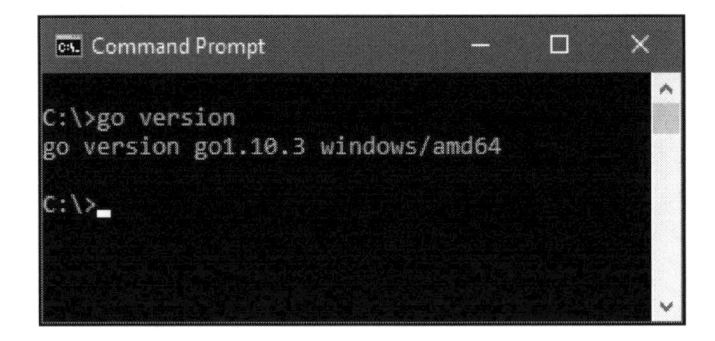

```
C:\>go version
go version go1.10.3 windows/amd64

C:\>
```

Testing Go is installed by checking the version

Environment

If the preceding installations succeeded, then your environment should be correctly configured. If you made some changes during the installation, you may need to make some adjustments to your environment configuration:

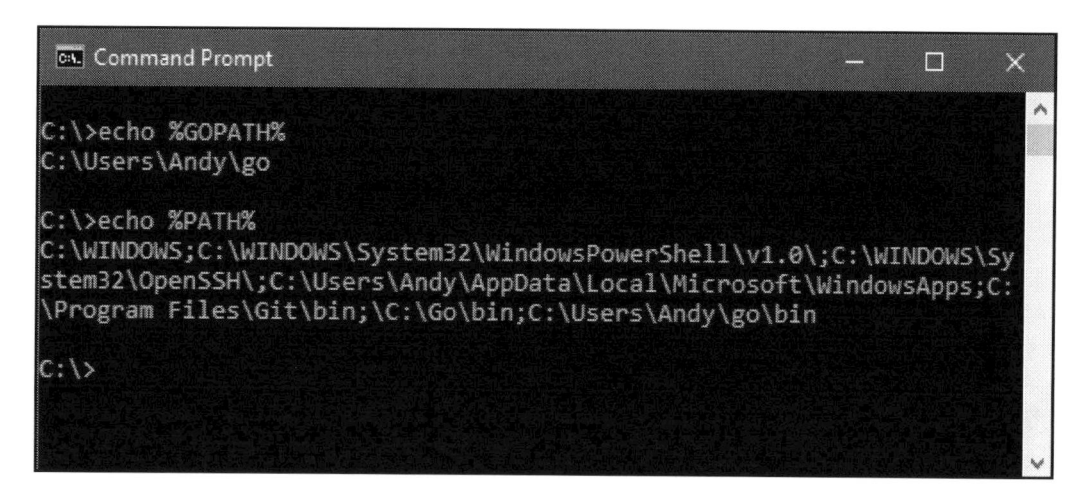

```
C:\>echo %GOPATH%
C:\Users\Andy\go

C:\>echo %PATH%
C:\WINDOWS;C:\WINDOWS\System32\WindowsPowerShell\v1.0\;C:\WINDOWS\System32\OpenSSH\;C:\Users\Andy\AppData\Local\Microsoft\WindowsApps;C:\Program Files\Git\bin;\C:\Go\bin;C:\Users\Andy\go\bin

C:\>
```

Checking that our %GOPATH%/bin appears in %PATH%

In the preceding output, you can see that `Git\bin`, `Go\bin`, and `%GOPATH%` are included in your `%PATH%` environment for finding executable files. If this isn't the case, you may need to log out or reboot for the settings to take effect.

Apple macOS

Many developer tools (including Git) are installed as part of the `XCode` package. If you haven't already installed Xcode for other development work, you can download it for free from the Mac App Store. Once installed, you should also set up the command-line tools—to do this go to the Xcode menu and select **Preferences**, then **Downloads** and **Install Command Line Tools**.

[401]

Installation Details

If you're unsure about whether or not you've installed these already, then open the Terminal application and execute `xcode-select`—if installed, that will execute normally, and if not, you'll be prompted to run the installation:

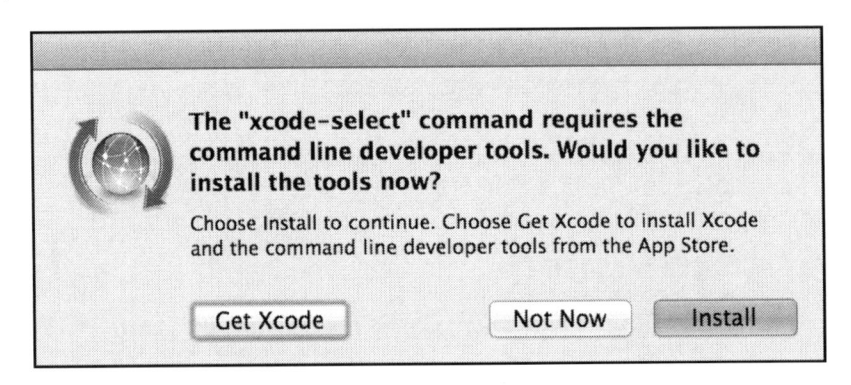

The installation dialog window if developer tools are not installed

In addition to these tools, you'll need to install Go. You can get the download package from `https://golang.org/dl/`—tap the featured download link for Apple macOS and run the installer package that downloads. You may need to close any open Terminal windows to update your environment variables.

Linux

Setting up the prerequisite software on Linux should only require installing the correct packages for your distribution. The `git` package will provide the source control tools and the Go language should be in the `go` or `golang` package. Installing these will provide the necessary commands to run the examples in this book. You may need to add `~/go/bin` to your `PATH` environment variable to be able to run tools that Go installs later.

Setting up Cgo

To use most of the libraries and functionality explored in this book, you'll also need to use Cgo (the built-in Go to C language bridge). Cgo requires the availability of a C compiler and some related tools depending on the operating system. This section outlines how to set them up.

Microsoft Windows

For Cgo to function on Windows, you'll need to have the `gcc` (or compatible) compiler installed. If Visual Studio is already installed, then you may have a C compiler. For those who don't, this section steps through configuring a build environment on the command line. The easiest way to get up and running (in my experience) is to download and install MSYS2 (a software distribution) and build a platform for Windows. Using MSYS2, we can install the `mingw-w64` packages, which provide an updated distribution of the *gcc for Windows* project named **mingw**.

Download the installer from `www.msys2.org/`—choose either the 32 bit (i686) or 64 bit (x86_64) versions, depending on your computer architecture. Once downloaded, run this installer, which will download the basic packages to your computer, including the package manager (pacman). Once complete, it'll launch the MSYS Command Prompt, which will be used for any projects requiring Cgo. You'll need to update the `PATH` environment variable to use the existing Go and Git installations:

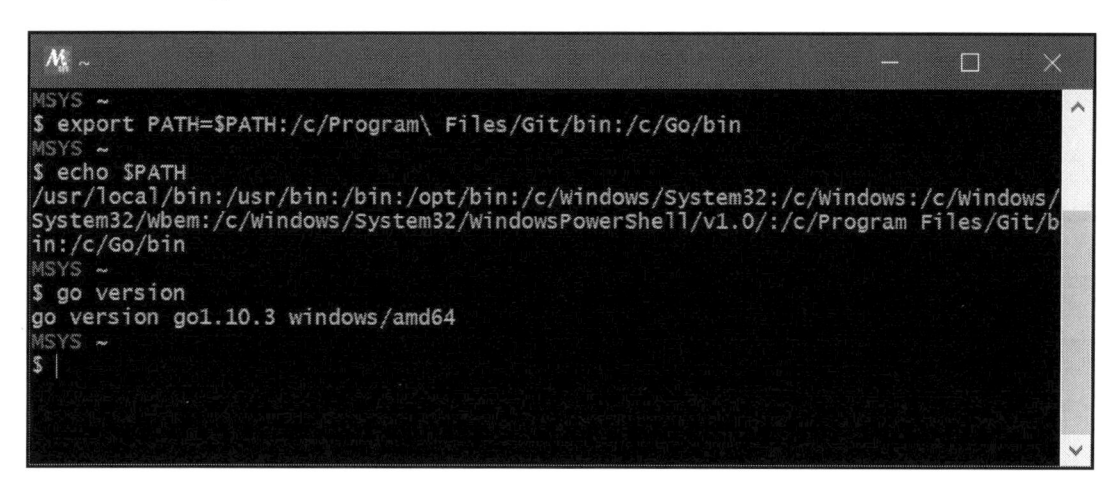

An MSYS console provides access to many additional packages

Once you have the command line set up, the package manager is used to install a C compiler and toolchain as well as `pkg-config` (which is used by Cgo to find packages):

```
pacman -S mingw-w64-x86_64-toolchain mingw-w64-x86_64-pkg-config
```

Installation Details

Once complete, you'll be able to execute `gcc` and `pkg-config` from the MSYS command line—these tools are essential for a working Cgo setup. The following output may display an error, but it shows that the tools are found:

```
MSYS ~
$ export PATH=$PATH:/c/msys64/mingw64/bin
MSYS ~
$ gcc
gcc.exe: fatal error: no input files
compilation terminated.
MSYS ~
$ pkg-config
Must specify package names on the command line
MSYS ~
$
```

Pacman on MSYS provides the packages we need

Apple macOS

To enable Cgo support on macOS, you'll need the development tools included with the Xcode distribution. If you've done development work on your Macintosh computer before, or if you followed the previous instructions for installing Git tools, you'll already have this installed. If you've installed Xcode but not used the command-line tools before, then you can install these from a Terminal window with the following command:

```
xcode-select --install
```

Linux

Cgo on Linux requires the presence of `gcc`, which is often installed by other packages in a Linux environment. If executing `gcc` from a Terminal yields an error such as `gcc: command not found`, then you'll need to install the `gcc` package from your system's package manager.

Cross Compiler Setup

When building applications that need access to native APIs, we can use CGo. Although not much harder for regular development, this does make cross compiling much more complicated. For every target platform you want to build for, there must be a C compiler that knows how to create native binary files. This appendix outlines the steps required to set up cross compilation targets for each combination referenced earlier in this book.

> Most Go applications don't require this setup for cross compiling as the Go compiler is designed to build for all supported platforms. Additional steps, such as those following, will be required if the resulting applications (or the toolkits they use) are linking to operating system libraries through CGo.

Cross compiling for macOS with CGo

When cross compiling for macOS, it's necessary to install the SDK (Software Development Kit) from Apple as well as a suitable compiler. The instructions for Windows (using MSYS2—described in the previous `Appendix`, *Installation Details*) and Linux are almost identical; the main work is to install the macOS SDK.

To macOS from Linux or Windows

To prepare for cross compilation to Darwin, we must install the macOS SDK and a build toolchain that can use it. The easiest way to do this is with the *osxcross* project. This example shows how to download and install the SDK and tools to build for macOS without using a Macintosh computer. This illustration uses Linux but the process is the same for Windows developers using MSYS2 or Cygwin Command Prompts.

We'll be using `clang` rather than `gcc` as it's more portable by design. For this process to work, you'll need to have `clang`, `cmake`, and `libxml2-dev` installed using your package manager:

- On Linux use: `pacman -S clang cmake libxml2-dev` (or `apt-get` or `yum`, depending on your distribution)
- On Windows use: `pacman -S mingw-w64-x86_64-clang mingw-w64-x86_64-cmake mingw-w64-x86_64-libxml2`

Next, we need to download the macOS SDK, which is bundled with Xcode. If you don't already have an Apple developer account, you'll need to sign up and agree to their terms and conditions. Using this account, log in to the download site at https://developer.apple.com/download/more/?name=Xcode%207.3 and download `XCode.dmg` (7.3.1 is recommended for osxcross).

Then, we can install the osxcross tool—start by downloading it with `git clone https://github.com/tpoechtrager/osxcross.git` and then change into the downloaded directory. Using these tools, we extract the macOS SDK from the downloaded `Xcode.dmg` file using the package tool provided, `./tools/gen_sdk_package_darling_dmg.sh <path to Xcode.dmg>`. The resulting `MacOSX10.11.sdk.tar.xz` file should be copied into the `tarballs/` directory.

Lastly, we build the osxcross compiler extension by executing `./build.sh`. Following this, there should be a new directory named `target/bin/`, which you should add to your `PATH` environment variable. The compiler can now be used in CGo builds by setting the environment variable, `CC=o32-clang`. More details about this process and how to adapt it for other platforms are available on the osxcross project website at https://github.com/tpoechtrager/osxcross.

Cross compiling for Windows with CGo

Building for Windows from another platform requires an installation of the `mingw` toolchain (similar to that which we installed on Windows to support CGo). This should be available in your package manager with a name similar to `mingw-w64-clang` or `w64-mingw`, but if not, you can install directly using the instructions at https://github.com/tpoechtrager/wclang.

To Windows from macOS

To install the packages on macOS, it's recommended to use the Homebrew package manager. You probably already have this installed from earlier chapters in this book (for example, when setting up the GTK+ library), but if not, you can download it from `https://brew.sh`. Once Homebrew is set up, the compiler package is installed using `brew install mingw-w64`.

Once installed, the compiler can be used with CGo by setting `CC=x86_64-w64-mingw32-gcc` (for the C toolchain) and `CXX=x86_64-w64-mingw32-g++` (for C++ requirements).

To Windows from Linux

Installing on Linux should just require finding the correct package in your distribution's listing. For example, for Debian or Ubuntu, you would execute `sudo apt-get install gcc-mingw-w64`.

Once installed, the compiler can be used with CGo by setting `CC=x86_64-w64-mingw32-gcc` (for the C toolchain) and `CXX=x86_64-w64-mingw32-g++` (for C++ requirements).

Cross compiling for Linux with CGo

To cross compile for Linux, we'll need a GCC or compatible compiler that can build Linux binary files. On macOS, the easiest platform to use is musl-cross (musl has many other advantages that you can read more about at `www.etalabs.net/compare_libcs.html`). On Windows, the `linux-gcc` package will be suitable. Let's work through the steps for each of these.

To Linux from macOS

To install the dependencies for cross compiling for Linux, we'll use the Homebrew package manager again—see the previous sections or https://brew.sh/ for installation instructions. Using Homebrew, we'll install the appropriate packages by opening a Terminal and executing the following commands
(the HOMEBREW_BUILD_FROM_SOURCE variable works around an issue with musl-cross depending on potentially old versions of libraries):

- export HOMEBREW_BUILD_FROM_SOURCE=1
- brew install FiloSottile/musl-cross/musl-cross

Once the installation is complete (this may take some time as it's building a complete compiler toolchain from source), you should be able to build for Linux. To do so, you'll need to set the environment variables, CC=x86_64-linux-musl-gcc and CXX=x86_64-linux-musl-g++.

To Linux from Windows

Using MSYS2 as earlier, we can install the gcc package to provide cross compilation for Linux:

```
pacman -S gcc
```

After the installation has completed, we can tell our Go compiler to use gcc by setting the environment variable CC=gcc. Compilation should now succeed following the instructions in your current example, such as the following:

```
GOOS=linux CGO_ENABLED=1 CC=gcc go build
```

It's possible, at this point, that you may see additional errors due to missing headers. To fix this, you'll need to search for, and install, the required libraries. If, for example, your error stated that SDL couldn't be found then you would use pacman -Ss sdl to search for the right package to install. If you can't find an appropriate package, you may need to install Cygwin www.cygwin.com/ (as it has a larger package library) or Windows subsystem for Linux docs.microsoft.com/en-us/windows/wsl/ (as that brings a full Linux distribution to your Windows desktop).

Comparison of GUI Toolkits

In this book, we explored seven popular GUI toolkits for the Go language. It's recommended to read each chapter and understand the benefits and potential drawbacks of each toolkit before making a decision on which to use in a project. For a quick reference, the following table should help to short-list options based on a number of important factors:

Name	License	Multiple Platforms	Active	Themes	Native widgets	Idiomatic	Cross compiling	Richness
Walk	BSD	✔	✔	✘	✔	✔	✘	↑
andlabs UI	MIT	✔	✔	✘	✔	![1]	✔	-
Go-GTK	LGPL[2]	✔	✔	✔	![3]	✘	![4]	↑
qt	LGPL	✔	✔	✔	![3]	✘	✔[5]	↑
Shiny	BSD	✔	✘	![6]	✘	✔	✔	↓
nk	MIT	✔	✔	![6]	✘	✘	✔	-
Fyne	BSD	✔	✔	![6]	✘	✔	✔	↓

[1] The top, declarative, layer of the andlabs UI is designed for Go development; however, it exposes C idioms from the lower-level library.
[2] The `go-GTK` library is available in multiple licenses, but the inclusion of the GTK+ widgets requires LGPL.
[3] Using theming capabilities, a native-looking user interface can be obtained.
[4] Cross compiling should be possible, but it requires many libraries to be compiled for each target system.

[5] The supported way to cross compile is through the use of containers rather than directly on the development computer.
[6] Themes can be set from code but there's no collection of user installable themes.

The preceding table should help with the choice of which GUI technology to use. There's no single best option and selection should be made based on your most important criteria. Clarification of each heading is as follows:

License: Every toolkit is available under an open source license that allows for open or closed source and commercial usage. However, as a statically compiled language, there are complications when using the LGPL. If statically linking with an LGPL project, your code should either be distributed under the same license or you'll need to provide an alternative compiled output without the library statically linked. The easiest option in this case may be to leave the toolkit as a dynamically compiled library that the user would have to install before your application can function. Some of the toolkits are available under a separate commercial license that can be paid for to avoid licensing complications.

Multiple Platforms: A tick mark represents the toolkit supporting at least Linux, macOS, and Windows. Some of the options provide support for many more platforms.

Active: Is the project actively maintained? An active project doesn't guarantee the availability of commercial support.

Themes: A tick mark represents user installable themes that can customize application appearance. Some toolkits support setting a theme using code that allows application developers to change the look and feel.

Native Widgets: Does the framework use native system widgets? A tick means that applications will utilize the system widgets. Some toolkits make it possible to look like the system widgets by installing a special theme.

Idiomatic: Is the toolkit built to fit with the Go language idioms? This may not be important to every project, but it can improve the speed of development and ease of maintenance. It can also be easier to debug applications that use an idiomatic toolkit.

Cross compiling: Cross compilation is usually important for Go applications. Not all toolkits support this completely due to the complexity of working with low level graphics libraries.

Richness: This is a measure of how complete the selection of widgets is. An up arrow indicates that you could build a complete application using the provided features. A bar (neither up nor down) shows that most applications should be possible but that it may be necessary to construct complex widgets using the available components. A down arrow shows a minimal widget set—simple or medium complexity applications are possible but many widgets would need to be built from the basic components provided.

Connecting GoMail to a Real Email Server

In many chapters of this book, we've explored ways of building a Go-based email application called **GoMail**. All of these examples have used a dummy email server—some code in the `client` package, which allows us to build the GUI portions of a mail client without needing to manage server communication. In this final appendix, we step through adding code to connect to a real email server.

Building on the exploration in `Chapter 12`, *Concurrency, Networking, and Cloud Services* (particularly the authentication—*OAuth 2.0* example), we'll use the Gmail public API and the built-in capabilities of the Go language to bring this together.

Download Gmail credentials

In `Chapter 12`, *Concurrency, Networking, and Cloud Services*, we wrote the OAuth2 handlers and Gmail integration using only the standard library. For this final code exploration, we'll use the helpful library that Google has created for interacting with Gmail servers. To use this library, we need the client credentials in a different format (`credentials.json`). To access this, log in to your Google account and go to the Go quickstart page at https://developers.google.com/gmail/api/quickstart/go. Once here, you'll need to click on **ENABLE THE GMAIL API** and then **DOWNLOAD CLIENT CONFIGURATION**. This will download the `credentials.json` file that we'll need to initialize the library in the next section, *Creating server provider*.

Once you've downloaded the credentials file, you'll need to install the two required libraries using `go get -u google.golang.org/api/gmail/v1` and `go get -u golang.org/x/oauth2/google`. You're then ready to add the code to connect to Gmail and access your emails.

Creating a server provider

The following code outlines the contents of the `gmail.go` file that's available in the `client` package of the repository for this book. If you want to jump straight to trying out this functionality, then simply copy your `credentials.json` file to the current directory and skip to the next section, *Update an example to use Gmail*.

We start by adding the necessary OAuth2 setup and token storage by copying the `getClient()`, `getTokenFromWeb()`, `tokenFromFile()`, and `saveToken()` functions from Google's Gmail quickstart Go file at `github.com/gsuitedevs/go-samples/blob/master/gmail/quickstart/quickstart.go`. These are very similar to the OAuth2 code that was created before but works better with the Google libraries.

Downloading inbox messages

Next, we need to set up the client from the credentials file that has been saved (in the current directory). We add a new function to parse the data, set up the authentication, and configure `*gmail.Service` using the following code:

```go
func setupService() *gmail.Service {
    b, err := ioutil.ReadFile("credentials.json")
    if err != nil {
        log.Fatalf("Unable to read client secret file: %v", err)
    }

    config, err := google.ConfigFromJSON(b, gmail.GmailReadonlyScope,
        gmail.GmailComposeScope)
    if err != nil {
        log.Fatalf("Unable to parse client secret file to config: %v", err)
    }
    client := getClient(config)

    srv, err := gmail.New(client)
    if err != nil {
        log.Fatalf("Unable to retrieve Gmail client: %v", err)
    }

    return srv
}
```

The service returned from this function will be used for each subsequent call to the Gmail API as it contains the authentication configuration and credentials. Next, we need to prepare the email list by downloading all of the messages in the user's inbox. The `INBOX` LabelID is used to filter messages that haven't been archived. This function requests the message list and iterates through the metadata to initiate the full download of each message. For a full implementation, we would need to add paging support (the response contains `nextPageToken`, which indicates when more data is available), but this example will handle up to 100 messages:

```
func downloadMessages(srv *gmail.Service) {
    req := srv.Users.Messages.List(user)
    req.LabelIds("INBOX")
    resp, err := req.Do()
    if err != nil {
        log.Fatalf("Unable to retrieve Inbox items: %v", err)
    }

    var emails []*EmailMessage
    for _, message := range resp.Messages {
        email := downloadMessage(srv, message)
        emails = append(emails, email)
    }
}
```

To download each individual message, we need to implement the `downloadMessage()` function referenced previously. For the specified message, we download the full content using the Gmail Go API. From the resulting data, we extract the information we need from the message headers. As well as parsing the `Date` header, we need to decode the message body, which is in a serialized, Base64 encoded format:

```
func downloadMessage(srv *gmail.Service, message *gmail.Message)
*EmailMessage {
    mail, err := srv.Users.Messages.Get(user, message.Id).Do()
    if err != nil {
        log.Fatalf("Unable to retrieve message payload: %v", err)
    }

    var subject string
    var to, from Email
    var date time.Time

    content := decodeBody(mail.Payload)
    for _, header := range mail.Payload.Headers {
        switch header.Name {
        case "Subject":
            subject = header.Value
```

```
            case "To":
                to = Email(header.Value)
            case "From":
                from = Email(header.Value)
            case "Date":
                value := strings.Replace(header.Value, "(UTC)", "", -1)
                date, err = time.Parse("Mon, _2 Jan 2006 15:04:05 -0700",
                    strings.TrimSpace(value))
                if err != nil {
                    log.Println("Error: Could not parse date", value)
                    date = time.Now()
                } else {
                    log.Println("date", header.Value)
                }
            }
        }
    }

    return NewMessage(subject, content, to, from, date)
}
```

The `decodeBody()` function is as shown in the following. For plain text emails, the content is in the `Body.Data` field. For multi-part messages (where the body is empty), we access the first of the multiple parts and decode that instead. Decoding the Base64 content is handled by the standard library decoder:

```
func decodeBody(payload *gmail.MessagePart) string {
    data := payload.Body.Data
    if data == "" {
        data = payload.Parts[0].Body.Data
    }
    content, err := base64.StdEncoding.DecodeString(data)
    if err != nil {
        fmt.Println("Failed to decode body", err)
    }

    return string(content)
}
```

The final step in preparing this code is to complete the `EmailServer` interface methods. The `ListMessages()` function will return the result of `downloadMessages()`, and we can set up `CurrentMessage()` to return the email at the top of the list. Full implementation is in this book's code repository.

Sending messages

To send a message, we have to package up the data in a raw format to send through the API. We'll re-use the `ToGMailEncoding()` function from the `Post` example in `Chapter 12`, *Concurrency, Networking, and Cloud Services*. Before encoding the email, we set an appropriate "From" email address (be sure to use the email address of the account you are signed in with or a registered alias) and the current date for the time of sending. After encoding, we set the data to the `Raw` field of a `gmail.Message` type and pass it to the Gmail `Send()` function:

```
func (g *gMailServer) Send(email *EmailMessage) {
    email.From = "YOUR EMAIL ADDRESS"
    email.Date = time.Now()

    data := email.ToGMailEncoding()
    msg := &gmail.Message{Raw:data}

    srv.Users.Messages.Send(user, msg).Do()
}
```

This minimal code will be enough to implement sending a message. All of the hard work has been done by the earlier setup code—which provided the `srv` object.

Listening for new messages

Although Google provides the ability to use push messaging, the setup is very complicated—so instead, we'll poll for new messages. Every 10 seconds, we should download any new messages that have arrived. To do this, we can use the history API, which returns any messages that appeared after a specific point in history (set using `StartHistoryId()`). `HistoryId` is a chronological number that marks the order that messages arrived in. Before we can use the history API, we need to have a valid `HistoryId`—we can do this by adding the following line to the `downloadMessage()` function:

```
g.history = uint64(math.Max(float64(g.history), float64(mail.HistoryId)))
```

Once we have a point in history to query from, we need a new function that can download any messages since this point in time. The following code is similar to `downloadMessages()` in the preceding code but will only download new messages:

```
func (g *gMailServer) downloadNewMessages(srv *gmail.Service)
[]*EmailMessage{
    req := srv.Users.History.List(g.user)
```

Connecting GoMail to a Real Email Server

```
        req.StartHistoryId(g.history)
        req.LabelId("INBOX")
        resp, err := req.Do()
        if err != nil {
            log.Fatalf("Unable to retrieve Inbox items: %v", err)
        }

        var emails []*EmailMessage
        for _, history := range resp.History {
            for _, message := range history.Messages {
                email := downloadMessage(srv, message)
                emails = append(emails, email)
            }
        }

        return emails
    }
```

To complete the functionality, we update our `Incoming()` method so that it sets up the channel and starts a thread to poll for new messages. Every `10` seconds, we'll download any new messages that have appeared and pass each to the `in` channel that was created:

```
    func (g *gMailServer) Incoming() chan *EmailMessage {
        in := make(chan *EmailMessage)

        go func() {
            for {
                time.Sleep(10 * time.Second)

                for _, email := range downloadNewMessages(srv) {
                    g.emails = append([]*EmailMessage{email}, g.emails...)
                    in <- email
                }
            }
        }()

        return in
    }
```

The complete code can be found in the `client` package of this book's code repository. Let's look at how to use this new email server in our previous examples.

Updating an example to use Gmail

In any one of the GoMail example apps, you'll need to edit the main server setup in `main.go`. Replace the server initiation by changing `client.NewTestServer()` to `client.NewGMailServer()`. With the `credentials.json` file in place, running this new code will obtain a connection to your Gmail account for reading and sending emails. Note that, for this example, you'll need to run from the command line and follow the OAuth2 setup steps. To make a better user experience, you can provide a more sophisticated implementation of the `getTokenFromWeb()` function.

Other Books You May Enjoy

If you enjoyed this book, you may be interested in these other books by Packt:

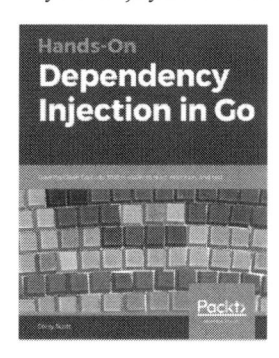

Hands-On Dependency Injection in Go
Corey Scott

ISBN: 9781789132762

- Understand the benefits of DI
- Explore SOLID design principles and how they relate to Go
- Analyze various dependency injection patterns available in Go
- Leverage DI to produce high-quality, loosely coupled Go code
- Refactor existing Go code to adopt DI
- Discover tools to improve your code's testability and test coverage
- Generate and interpret Go dependency graphs

Hands-On Software Architecture with Golang
Jyotiswarup Raiturkar

ISBN: 9781788622592

- Understand architectural paradigms and deep dive into Microservices
- Design parallelism/concurrency patterns and learn object-oriented design patterns in Go
- Explore API-driven systems architecture with introduction to REST and GraphQL standards
- Build event-driven architectures and make your architectures anti-fragile
- Engineer scalability and learn how to migrate to Go from other languages
- Get to grips with deployment considerations with CICD pipeline, cloud deployments, and so on
- Build an end-to-end e-commerce (travel) application backend in Go

Leave a review - let other readers know what you think

Please share your thoughts on this book with others by leaving a review on the site that you bought it from. If you purchased the book from Amazon, please leave us an honest review on this book's Amazon page. This is vital so that other potential readers can see and use your unbiased opinion to make purchasing decisions, we can understand what our customers think about our products, and our authors can see your feedback on the title that they have worked with Packt to create. It will only take a few minutes of your time, but is valuable to other potential customers, our authors, and Packt. Thank you!

Index

A

activity notifications
  spinner 350
  status panel 350
andlabs UI
  background 99
  building 105
  code, writing 103
  command line, executing 106
  generic API, for multiple platforms 106
  history 99
  library (workaround), rebuilding 102
  prerequisites 101
  setup 102
  starting with 100
App Store Connect website
  reference 390
App Store Optimization (ASO) 370
app theme
  customizing 23, 24, 25, 27
Apple macOS
  Cgo, setting up 404
  Go, installing 402
application bundle 382
application containerization approach 396
application layout
  adaptive design 303, 304
  custom 305
  device form factors 303
  planning 300
  responsive design 303, 304
  standard 300, 301, 302
application
  describing 371
  menu 310
  menus 309
  multiple windows 312
  navigating 306
  progressive disclosure 307, 308
  toolbars 309
architecture, Shiny
  about 186
  higher layer 188
  lower layer 187
assets
  bundling 371
  fyne bundle 374
  go-bindata tool 371
  packr tool 372
  rsrc 374
Asynchronous JavaScript and XML (AJAX) 40
authentication
  about 342
  OAuth 2.0, using 342
  request 342, 344
  tokens, storing 344, 346

B

background progress 317
Balsamiq
  reference 204
benefits, native graphical applications
  integrated user experience 19
  maintainability 20
  offline functionality 19
  performance 18
  reliability 19
  testing 20
built-in types, widgets
  Flex 198
  Flow 198
  image 198
  label 198

padder 198
sheet 198
sizer 198
space 198
text 198
uniform 198

C

caching 333
Cascading Style Sheets (CSS) 33, 141
Cgo
  about 52
  installing, on Apple macOS 404
  setting up 402
  setting up, on Microsoft Windows 403
challenges, cloud integration
  communications 39
  data parsing 40
  standard components 40
challenges, concurrency
  complexity, avoiding 37
  threads, switching 36, 37
challenges, multiple native GUIs
  about 130
  consistent style 130
  cross-compilation 133
  testing 133
channels
  about 55, 57, 61
  used, for communication 328, 330
cloud integration 38
cloud services
  connecting to 338
  data, posting 347, 348
  encoding 338
  encoding, in JSON format 339, 340
  encoding, in XML format 340, 341
  GUI integration 349
color tool
  reference 197
concurrency 36, 323
concurrency, language design
  about 55
  channels 57, 61
  goroutines 56, 57

sync package 62, 64
considerations, for consistent user experience
  actions, queuing 352
  internet connections, dealing with 353, 354
  responses, caching 351
consistent style
  about 130
  brand styles 130
  user experience 131
continuous integration, for GUIs
  external dependencies, avoiding 362
  GUI test automation, approaches 361
control interface
  box 107
  containers 108
  menu 110
  widgets 109
controls 107
cross compilation, for Linux
  CGo, using 407
  to Linux from macOS 408
  to Linux from Windows 408
cross compilation, for macOS
  CGo, using 405
  to macOS from Linux or Window 405
cross compilation, for Windows
  CGo, using 406
  to Windows from macOS 407
  to Windows, from Linux 407
cross-compilation
  enabling, for Linux on macOS 135
  enabling, for Linux on Windows 135, 136
  enabling, for macOS on Linux 137
  enabling, for Windows on Linux 136
  enabling, for Windows on macOS 136
  solutions 137
cross-compiling 53
cross-platform application
  for application 53
  Walk, using 95, 96
cross-platform approach
  about 51, 53
  cross-compiling 53
  standard library 55
  using, for application 51

Cygwin
　reference 408

D

Debian (.deb)
　about 393
　distribution 394
　packaging 393
declarative API
　APIs, using for flexibility 78, 79
　benefits 76
　comparing, with native API 76, 78
distribution 44
dots per inch (DPI) 263
drawing API, Nuklear
　command queue 242
　draw function 242
drivers
　gl 189
　win 189
　x11 189

E

ebuilds
　reference 396
encoding 338
Enlightenment Foundation Libraries (EFL)
　reference 258
event handling 171
Extensible Markup Language (XML) 40

F

Fyne
　application, running 262
　background 257
　building 262
　canvas (drawing) 267
　cross-compiling 262
　drivers 265
　example 260
　Hello World application, writing 261
　image viewer, building 282
　layouts 267, 268
　prerequisites 258
　rendering 263
　setup 259
　starting with 258
　supported platforms 266
　themes 270
　user interface, building 272
　vector graphics 263
　vision 257
　widgets 267, 269

G

generic API
　area 111
　controls 107
　drawing primitives 111
　for multiple platforms 107
Gmail
　credentials, downloading 413
　using, by updating example 419
GNU Image Manipulation Program (GIMP) 140
Go, installing on Microsoft Windows
　about 399
　environment 401
　Git, download link 399
　Go, installation link 400
go-bindata tool
　reference 371
Go-GTK library
　about 141
　installing 142
　prerequisites 141
　test application, building 143, 144
　test application, running 144
Go
　about 48, 50
　installing 399
　installing, on Apple macOS 401
　installing, on Linux 402
　installing, on Microsoft Windows 399
　quickstart page, reference 413
　reference 186
GoMail application
　about 173
　compose layout 176
　cross compilation 180
　layout 173, 176

[427]

signaling 178
thread handling 179
goroutines
  about 55, 56, 57
  graphical updates 330, 332
goversioninfo tool
  reference 385
graphical application
  apps 17
  customer retention 17
  desktop, migrating to internet 15, 16
  history 12, 13
  personal computers 13, 15
  smart phones 17
Graphical User Interface (GUIs)
  about 11
  accessory windows 30, 32
  and visual hierarchy 28
  continuous integration 361
  mobile standards 34
  multiple documents 28, 30
  visual hierarchy 32
Graphics Device Interface (GDI) 189
GTK+ library
  about 140, 141
  data, passing 146, 147
  installing 142
  installing, on Linux 142
  installing, on macOS 142
  installing, on Windows 142
  namespaces 145, 147
  signals 145
GTK+-based applications
  about 148
  compose layout 152, 153
  cross compilation 156
  layout 149, 151, 152
  signaling 154, 155
  theming 156, 161
  thread, handling 155
GUI integration
  about 349
  activity notifications 349
  incoming messages 349
GUI updates 323

GUI, Walk API
  detail vie 91
  detail view 92
  list view 92, 93
  view model 90

H

headless mode 361
Homebrew
  reference 135, 376
Human Interface Guidelines (HIG)
  reference 391

I

icons
  about 370
  application icon 370
image viewer
  background processing 293, 295
  building 282
  communicating, with GUI 289, 293
  file listing 286
  layout, completing 287
  layout, creating 282, 284
  navigation 285
integrated development environments (IDEs) 28
integrated user experience 19

J

JavaScript Object Notation (JSON) 40

L

layout, andlabs UI
  email compose dialog 119
  main email window 117, 119
layout, Fyne
  compose dialog 275
  main email window 272, 275
layout, Nuklear
  about 240
  email compose dialog 248, 249
  main email window 246
  NkLayoutRow 240
  NkLayoutRowTemplate 241

NkLayoutSpace 241
Linux package manager
  about 392
  containers 396
  Debian (.deb), reference 393
  Red Hat (.rpm) 394
  Tarball (.tar.gz) 395
Linux
  Cgo, setting up 404
  Go, installing 402
  GTK+ library, installing 142
  recipe/qt, installing 167
long-running processes
  completion, checking 326, 328
  managing 324
  shutdown, signaling 324, 325
lower layer, Shiny
  buffer 187
  texture 187
  Windows 187

M

Mac App Store
  about 389
  packaging 389
  reviewing 390
  uploading 390
macOS
  cross compiling, with CGo 405
  GTK+ library, installing 142
  recipe/qt, installing 166
maintainability 20
metadata 370
Microsoft Store
  packaging 391
  reference 391
  reviewing 392
  uploading 392
Microsoft Windows
  Cgo, setting up 403
  Go, installing 399
mingw 403
minor alerts 316
msys2 installer
  reference 403

Multi Document Interface (MDI) 72
multiple native GUIs
  challenges 130
multiple platforms development
  about 41
  cross-platform APIs 41
  design 42
  icons 42
  testing 43
multiple windows
  managing 312
multithreading 36

N

native API
  comparing, with declarative API 76, 78
Native Development Kit (NDK) 230
native performance 18
notifications 316
Nuklear
  application, creating 233, 236
  background 225
  cross-compiling 237
  design 225
  drawing API 242
  example 232
  hello.go, building 236
  hello.go, running 236
  layout 238, 240
  platform support 227
  prerequisites 228
  reference 226, 244
  rendering 227
  rendering modules 227
  setup 231
  skinning 238, 243
  starting with 228
  supported platforms 228
  user interface, building 244
  widgets 238

O

offline functionality 19
operating system
  customizing 67

P

package structure
  reference 357
package, preparing for cross-platform packaging tools
  about 387
  fyne package 387
package, preparing for Linux
  about 379
  metadata files, creating 379
  packaging release 380, 381
package, preparing for macOS
  metadata files, creating 382
  packaging release 383
package, preparing for Windows
  about 384
  metadata files, creating 385
  packaging release 385
packaging 44
packr tool
  reference 372
Palo Alto Research Center (Xerox PARC) 12
personal computer (PC) 14
PKGBUILD file
  reference 395
platform marketplaces
  distributing 389
  Linux package manager 392
  Mac App Store 389
  Microsoft Store 391
platform specifics
  managing 364, 366
platform-specific considerations
  about 318
  application instances 319, 321
  features 321
  window grouping 319
prerequisites, andlabs UI
  about 101
  Linux 101
  macOS 101
prerequisites, Fyne
  about 258
  Linux 258
  macOS 259
prerequisites, Nuklear
  about 228
  Android 230
  Linux 229
  macOS 229
  Windows 229
prerequisites, therecipe/qt
  about 166
  CGo, preparing 166
  qt (the bindings), installing 168
  Qt, installing 166
progressive disclosure
  about 307
  Microsoft Edge example 307
  skyscanner flight search example 308

Q

Qt applications
  theming capabilities 180
qt apps
  reference 180
Qt design
  reference 172
Qt object model
  about 171
  inheritance 171
  memory management 171
  signals 172
  slots 172
Qt theme 180
Qt Windows Extras
  reference 321
Qt
  background 164
  installing, on Linux 167
  installing, on macOS 166
  installing, on Windows 167
  License / Qt account 167
  reference 166

R

Red Hat (.rpm)
  distribution 395
  packaging 394

release
  building 375, 377
  compiler installation 376
  packaging 378
  preparing 376
reliability 19
remote resources
  accessing, on local network 333
  images 333, 335
  JSON 335, 336
  loading 333
resource data
  caching 336, 337
RPC (remote procedure call) 320

S

Scalable Vector Graphics 263
Search Engine Optimization (SEO) 370
separation of concerns
  about 356
  application structure 356
server provider
  creating 414
  inbox messages, downloading 414, 416
  messages, sending 417
  new message, listening 417
SHared Memory (SHM) 189
Shiny
  hello world window, writing 199
  about 189, 199
  architecture 186
  background 186
  building 202
  code, supporting 200
  cross-compiling 192
  cross-compiling, for macOS 193
  design 186, 194, 196
  example 190
  hello.go file, running 202
  icons 196
  included drivers 189
  material design 194
  setup 190
  supported platforms 186, 188
  themes 197

user interface, building 203
  vision 186
  widgets 194, 198
skinning 243
Software Development Kit (SDK)
  about 133
  reference 230
standard dialogs
  toolkits 313
standard library 55
stretchy parameter 108
sync package
  about 62, 64
  reference 64

T

Tarball (.tar.gz)
  about 395
  Gentoo Linux 396
task status 316
test-driving UI development
  about 358
  designed to be testable scenario 358
  example application test 359
testing
  about 20
  reference 357
themes, Fyne
  about 270
  packaged themes 271
theming capabilities
  of Qt applications 180
therecipe/qt
  building 169
  executing 170
  prerequisites 166
  starting with 165
threads 323
two dimensional (2D) 242

U

user experience
  consistency, maintaining 351
user interface, andlabs UI
  background processing 129

[431]

background threads example 129
building 114
communicating with 127
GUI, communicating with 124
menu 122
styling 114
toolbar 122
user interface, building
  about 272
  toolbar 277
user interface, designing
  reference 80
user interface, Fyne
  background processing 281
  communicating, with GUI 279
  email, sending 280, 281
  emails, loading 279
  layout, creating 272
  menu 278
user interface, Nuklear
  background processing 255
  building 244
  communicating, with GUI 252, 254
  layout 245
  menu 250
  toolbar 250
user interface, Shiny
  about 203
  background processing 219, 222
  communicating, with GUI 215, 217
  design 204
  file list 209, 211
  Image view 212, 214
  layout 205, 207
  navigation 208
user interface, Walk API
  background processing 93, 95

building 80, 81
communicating, with GUI 89
layouts 82, 84, 85
menu, adding with declarative API 86
style 81
toolbar, adding with declarative API 86, 88, 89
user interface
  about 116
  layout 116

W

Walk project
  aims 72
  background 71
  building 74, 75
  code 73, 74
  running 75
  setup 72
  starting with 72
  used, in cross-platform application 95, 96
web services
  about 66
  and cloud integration 38
  included, as standard 64
Window hints
  about 314, 315
  sizes 315
Window types
  modal window 314
  standard dialogs 313
Windows API (WinAPI) 71
Windows Application Library Kit 71
Windows, Icons, Menus and Pointer (WIMP) 11
Windows
  GTK+ library, installing 142
  recipe/qt, installing 167
  types 312

Made in the USA
Middletown, DE
22 November 2020